Proceedings in
Information and Communications Technology 1

Y. Suzuki   M. Hagiya
H. Umeo   A. Adamatzky (Eds.)

Natural Computing

2nd International Workshop on Natural Computing
Nagoya, Japan, December 2007
Proceedings

 Springer

Editor

Yasuhiro Suzuki
Nagoya University, Japan
E-mail: ysuzuki@is.nagoya-u.ac.jp

Masami Hagiya
The University of Tokyo, Japan
E-mail: hagiya@is.s.u-tokyo.ac.jp

Hiroshi Umeo
Osaka Electro-Communication University, Japan
E-mail: umeo@cyt.osakac.jp

Andrew Adamatzky
University of West England, Bristol, UK
E-mail: andrew.adamatzky@uwe.ac.uk

Library of Congress Control Number: 2008938541
CR Subject Classification(1998): F.1.1, J.2, J.3, C.1.3

ISSN   1867-2914
ISBN-10   4-431-88980-9 Springer Tokyo Berlin Heidelberg New York
ISBN-13   978-4-431-88980-9 Springer Tokyo Berlin Heidelberg New York

Springer is a part of Springer Sciene+Business Media
springer.com

©Springer 2009

Typesetting: by authors and data conversion by Scientific Publishing Services, Chennai

Printed on acid-free paper   SPIN: 12439072   5 4 3 2 1 0

Preface

Most natural and artificial systems transform information in a predictable or programmable way; such transformation can be interpreted as computation. Recently we have witnessed a burst of research in unconventional computing, resulting in the development of experimental prototypes of natural computers – plasmodium computers, reaction-diffusion processors, amorphous computers, DNA computers – as well as theoretical paradigms of natural computation such as cellular automata, artificial chemistry, P-systems, evolutionary computing, and neural networks.

The International Workshop on Natural Computing (IWNC) aims to bring together computer scientists, biologists, mathematicians, electronic engineers, physicists, and humanitarians, to critically assess present findings in the field, and to outline future developments in nature-inspired computing.

The presented papers initially were submitted to the 2nd International Workshop on Natural Computing (IWNC2), Nagoya, Japan, December 10–13, 2007. The workshop, organized by Nagoya University, was one in a series of conferences inaugurated in 2006 in Bristol, United Kingdom.

IWNC is focused on theoretical and experimental studies of nature-inspired principles of information processing, novel and emerging paradigms of computation and computing architectures, and case studies of implementation of simulated or real-world computing devices in biological, social, chemical, engineering, and physical systems. These include:

- Cellular automata: structure formation, self-reproduction, evolutionary games, image processing, cryptography, random number generation, computational universality, traffic dynamics, alternative discrete-physics models, tiling, population dynamics, etc.
- Computation with pattern formation: reaction-diffusion computations, slime mold computing, amorphous computations, computing with the Belousov-Zhabotinsky reaction, computing devices inspired by biochemical reactions, etc.
- DNA and molecular computation: biomolecular information processing, biomolecular computers, theoretical models and analysis, implementation in vitro and in vivo, self-assembled systems, etc.
- Molecular communication: communication among biological nanomachines, networks of nanoscale structures, computation with liposomes, etc.
- Understanding nature as computation: (computational) systems biology, complex networks, artificial life, ecosystems, traffic dynamics (in a cell), etc.
- Theoretical framework: Ultradiscretization, computing with few bodies, dynamical system theory for discrete systems, crystallization, etc.
- Understanding human and social activities as computations: social networks, computational cognitive science, multisensory design, computational humanity research, etc.

The 2nd IWNC brought together more than 80 distinguished computer scientists, physicists, chemists, mathematicians, biologists, and other researchers working in the field of the theory of natural computing and its applications. Special attention was devoted to the general concepts, theories, methods, and techniques associated with modeling, analysis, and implementation in various systems including biological, physical, ecological, and social systems.

This volume contains 20 refereed papers addressing several important topics in natural computing, covering theoretical results and highlighting potential applications. At the workshop, a total of 30 papers were presented as regular talks, and there were two special sessions: Self-organization and Computation (Chair: K. Yoshikawa, Kyoto University) and Non-linear Science (Chair: Y. Sugiyama, Nagoya University). Additionally, there were 16 poster presentations. In order to highlight the multidisciplinary aspect of natural computing, the 3rd International Symposium on Multi-Sensory Design (ISMD) was organized as a satellite symposium within the scope of the 2nd IWNC. ISMD included technical talks, invited lectures, and a body workshop, focused on the sense of touch, by the Haptica project. Each paper was reviewed by at least two members of the program committees. We are extremely grateful to the reviewers, who undertook the difficult task of selecting the best papers. Their expertise and efficiency ensured the high quality of the conference. We would like to take this opportunity to express our sincere thanks to Hideyuki Nakashima from Future University, Hakodate, Japan, for accepting our invitation to deliver a plenary lecture at the workshop, and to Masahiro Ohka from Nagoya University, Japan. We also thank Yukio Pegio Gunji from Kobe Unversity, Japan, and Kohichiro Hajiri, who kindly accepted our invitation to give plenary lectures in the satellite symposium.

We are grateful to the authors who showed an interest in the 2nd IWNC by submitting their papers for consideration. A special word of thanks goes to Fuminori Akiba and Kiyofumi Motoyama for their assistance to ISMD. It is also a pleasure to express our sincere gratitude to our colleagues in the organizing committees and the program committee. The organization of the 2nd IWNC was made possible thanks to the financial and technical support of the Mitsubishi Foundation, the Graduate School of Information Science of Nagoya University, the Special Interest Group on Natural Computing (SIGNAC), the Japanese Society for Artificial Intelligence, the Special Interest Group of Mathematical Modeling and Problem Solving, and the Information Processing Society of Japan. Finally, we would like to express our gratitude for the kind support of the Nagoya Convention and Visitors Bureau.

August 2008

Yasuhiro Suzuki
Masami Hagiya
Hiroshi Umeo
Andrew Adamatzky

Organization

2nd IWNC Organization

Conference Chairs

Yasuhiro Suzuki (Chair)	Nagoya University (Japan)
Masami Hagiya (Co-chair)	University of Tokyo (Japan)
Hiroshi Umeo (Co-chair)	Osaka Electro-Communication University (Japan)
Andrew Adamatzky (Co-chair)	University of the West England (UK)

Organizing Committee

Giancarlo Mauri	Universita degli Studi di Milano, Bicocca (Italy)
Vincenzo Manca	University of Verona (Italy)
Kenichi Morita	Hiroshima University (Japan)
Hidetoshi Miike	Yamaguchi University (Japan)
Yasumasa Nishiura	Hokkaido University (Japan)
George Paun	Romanian Academy (Romania)
Tomohiko Yamaguchi	National Institute of Advanced Industrial Science and Technology (Japan)
Kenichi Yoshikawa	Kyoto University (Japan)

Program Committee

Y. Akama (Japan)
T. Arita (Japan)
M. Arita (Japan)
T. Asai (Japan)
D. Besozzi (Italy)
P. Dittrich (Germany)
G. Franco (Italy)
Y. Gunji (Japan)
K. Imai (Japan)
O. Katai (Japan)
S. Kobayashi (Japan)
E. Kita (Japan)
T. Nakagaki (Japan)
S. M. Nomura (Japan)

K. Nishinari (Japan)
M. Oswald (Austria)
T. Sakurai (Japan)
H. Sayama (USA)
T. Suda (USA)
Y. Sugiyama (Japan)
J. Takabayashi (Japan)
K. Tokita (Japan)
K. Tominaga (Japan)
K. Ueda (Japan)
M. Yamamura (Japan)
M. Yamashita (Japan)
C. Zandron (Italy)
K. P. Zauner (UK)

Referees

A. Adamatzky (UK)
Y. Akama (Japan)
M. Arita (Japan)
T. Arita (Japan)
D. Besozzi (Italy)
F. Peper (Japan)
G. Franco (Italy)
M. Hagiya (Japan)
K. Imai (Japan)
S. Kobayashi (Japan)
K. Morita (Japan)
T. Nakagaki (Japan)

S. Nomura (Japan)
M. Oswald (Austria)
T. Sakurai (Japan)
H. Sayama (USA)
Y. Sugiyama (Japan)
Y. Suzuki (Japan)
K. Tominaga (Japan)
K. Tokita (Japan)
H. Umeo (Japan)
M. Yamamura (Japan)
K. Yoshikawa (Japan)

Sponsoring Institutions

The Mitsubishi Foundation
Special Interest Group on Natural Computing (SIGNAC),
Japanese Society for Artificial Intelligence
Graduate School of Information Science, Nagoya University
Nagoya Convention and Visitors Bureau
Special Interest Group of Mathematical Modeling and Problem Solving,
Information Processing Society Japan

Table of Contents

Natural Computing

Combinatorial Optimization by Amoeba-Based Neurocomputer with Chaotic Dynamics

Masashi Aono[1], Yoshito Hirata[2], Masahiko Hara[1], and Kazuyuki Aihara[2]

[1] Flucto-Order Functions Asian Collaboration Team, RIKEN (The Institute of Physical and Chemical Research), Wako, Saitama 351-0198, Japan
[2] Institute of Industrial Science, The University of Tokyo, Meguro-ku, Tokyo 153-8505, Japan, and ERATO Aihara Complexity Modelling Project, JST, Shibuya-ku, Tokyo 151-0064, Japan
masashi.aono@riken.jp,
yoshito@sat.t.u-tokyo.ac.jp

Abstract. We demonstrate a computing system based on an amoeba of a true slime mold *Physarum* capable of producing rich spatiotemporal oscillatory behavior. Our system operates as a neurocomputer because an optical feedback control in accordance with a recurrent neural network algorithm leads the amoeba's photosensitive branches to search for a stable configuration concurrently. We show our system's capability of solving the traveling salesman problem. Furthermore, we apply various types of nonlinear time series analysis to the amoeba's oscillatory behavior in the problem-solving process. The results suggest that an individual amoeba might be characterized as a set of coupled chaotic oscillators.

1 Introduction

A plasmodium of the true slime mold *Physarum polycephalum* (Fig. 1A), a unicellular amoeboid organism, is an attractive model organism for studying cellular information processing. The amoeba can be considered as a kind of oscillatory media. Indeed, in the amoeba's gel layer (a sort of cellular membrane), collectively interacting microscopic actomyosin systems (fibrous proteins in muscles) generate rhythmic contraction-relaxation cycle to induce vertical oscillation of the body thickness at a period of 1 to 2 min. The vertical thickness oscillation produces various spatiotemporal patterns and induces horizontal shuttle-streaming of intracellular sol to change the macroscopic shape [1]. Because the amoeba exhibits sophisticated computational capacities in its shape changing, many researchers have been studying the amoeba for the understanding of biological information processing and the development of biologically inspired computers.

As a demonstration of the computational capacity, Nakagaki and coauthors showed that the amoeba can solve a maze by connecting the shortest route between food sources at terminals of the maze to optimize the nutrient absorption efficiency [2,3]. Takamatsu and coauthors investigated the amoeba's spatiotemporal oscillation patterns within simple boundary conditions by considering an individual amoeba as a coupled oscillator system [4] and showed the amoeba's capability

Y. Suzuki et al. (Eds.): IWNC 2007, PICT 1, pp. 1–15, 2009.
© Springer 2009

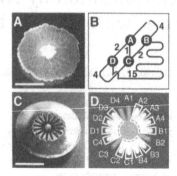

Fig. 1. (A) An individual unicellular amoeba (scale bar = 7 mm). (B) The map of four cities used to solve the traveling salesman problem. The edge lengths do not precisely reflect the distances. (C) Au-coated plastic barrier structure on an agar plate without nutrients (scale bar = 7 mm). The amoeba acts only inside the structure where agar is exposed, because of its aversion to the metal surface. (D) The amoeba's configuration representing the circular trip route $A \rightarrow B \rightarrow C \rightarrow D \rightarrow A$. White rectangles indicate illuminated regions.

of spontaneous transition among multiple quasi-stable oscillation patterns [5,6]. Aono and Gunji proposed a computing system employing the amoeba as a computing medium to execute a non-classical computation by concurrent operations of the amoeba's photosensitive branches induced by real-time optical feedback [7]. Based on this proposal, the authors constructed the amoeba-based computing systems with the optical feedback to implement recurrent neural network algorithms and demonstrated that the systems work as associative memory [8], constraint satisfaction problem solver [9,10,11], combinatorial optimization problem solver and autonomous meta-problem solver [12]. So far, employing the amoeba, some other researchers presented some computing devices/systems including logic operators [13], robot controller [14], and unconventional problem solvers [15,16].

In this paper, first we implement neurocomputing to exploit the amoeba's searching behavior guided by the optical feedback incorporating a recurrent neural network algorithm, and examine our system's capability of solving the traveling salesman problem. Second, we verify our hypothesis that an individual amoeba is characterized as a set of coupled chaotic oscillators by applying various types of surrogate data analysis to oscillatory movements of the amoeba's branches in the problem-solving process. From the viewpoints of both science and engineering, to examine whether the amoeba's behavior is merely random or not would be an interesting subject and help to explore how biological systems process information.

2   Methods

2.1   Traveling Salesman Problem

The traveling salesman problem (TSP), known as a particularly hard problem among typical combinatorial optimization problems [17], is stated as follows:

Given a map of N cities defining the travel distances from any city to any other city, search for the shortest circular trip route for visiting each city exactly once and returning to the starting city. In the map shown in Fig. 1B with four cities A, B, C, and D, each circular route takes the total distance 12, 20, or 24, where the circular route $A \rightarrow B \rightarrow C \rightarrow D \rightarrow A$ is one of the shortest (optimal) solutions. For a map of N cities, the number of all possible circular routes $N!$ runs into astronomical numbers when the number of cities N becomes larger. Often this makes it practically impossible to search for the exactly optimal solution. Therefore, various approximation algorithms for quickly obtaining good solutions have been proposed so far [18,19].

2.2   Implementation of Neurocomputing

Representation of Neuron State. According to the algorithm proposed by Hopfield and Tank [20] as an approximation algorithm, the N-city TSP can be solved with $N \times N$ neurons. To implement the four-city TSP solution, we fabricated a barrier structure with 16 radial lanes (grooves) (Fig. 1C), where each lane is called a "neuron" to be distinguished from the amoeba's "branch" expanding in the lane. We place the amoeba inside the barrier structure put on an agar plate containing no nutrient. The amoeba changes its horizontal shape by concurrently expanding or shrinking its multiple branches.

As shown in Fig. 1D, each neuron is labeled with $i \in \{Pn \mid P \in \{A, B, C, D\}, n \in \{1, 2, 3, 4\}\}$ to indicate the city name P and its visiting order n. When the amoeba expands its branch in the neuron Pn, it represents that P was selected as the nth visiting city. For example, the configuration in Fig. 1D represents the shortest circular route $A \rightarrow B \rightarrow C \rightarrow D \rightarrow A$.

For each neuron i at time t, we define the state $x_i(t) \in [0.0, 1.0]$ as the fraction of the area occupied by the amoeba's branch inside the corresponding neuron (lane), where the state is measured by means of digital image processing of a transmitted light image. Because the amoeba's branch inherently expands and tends to occupy the entire neuron, the state x_i increases in principle when the neuron is not illuminated.

Neural Network Dynamics for Optical Feedback. The amoeba's branch exhibits a photoavoidance response. It is said that a branch is shrunk by light stimulation because the light-induced contraction enhancement of the gel layer intensifies the sol efflux (extrusion) from the stimulated part [21]. Accordingly, when the neuron i is illuminated, the increase of the state x_i can be inhibited and its decrease can be promoted. When light illumination for neuron i is turned on, we represent this as $y_i(t) = 1$, otherwise $y_i(t) = 0$ (turned off). The illumination is applied with image pattern projection by a projector connected to PC for image processing in our optical feedback system (see Ref. [10] for more details in experimental setups).

The optical feedback system automatically updates each neuron's illumination status $y_i \in \{0, 1\}$ at every 6 sec in accordance with the following neural network dynamics that we newly designed to fit our experimental setups by slightly modifying the original dynamics of Hopfield and Tank [20]:

$$y_i(t+1) = 1 - f(\Sigma_j \ w_{ij} \ \sigma(x_j(t); a, b, c)), \tag{1}$$

$$\sigma(x; a, b, c) = a/(1 + Exp\{-b(x-c)\}), \tag{2}$$

$$f(X) = \begin{cases} 0 \ (\text{ if } X < \theta \ ) \\ 1 \ (\text{ otherwise }), \end{cases} \tag{3}$$

$$w_{ij} = \begin{cases} -\alpha & (\text{ if } i = Pn, \ j = Pm, \text{ and } n \neq m \ ) \\ -\beta & (\text{ if } i = Pn, \ j = Qn, \text{ and } P \neq Q \ ) \\ -\gamma \ dst(P, Q) & (\text{ if } i = Pn, \ j = Qm, P \neq Q \text{ and} |n - m| = 1) \\ 0 & (\text{ otherwise }). \end{cases} \tag{4}$$

We newly introduced the sigmoid function σ to enhance the adjustability of the system's sensitivity, where its parameters are set as $a = 1, b = 35$, and $c = 0.25$ in the experiment. The step function f is defined with a negative threshold $\theta = -0.5$.

Representation of TSP Solution. As shown in Eq. 4, each neuron i is connected to every neuron j with the non-positive and symmetric coupling weight w_{ij} (i.e., $w_{ij} = w_{ji} \leq 0$). The inhibitory coupling defined by the negative weight $w_{ij} (= w_{ji} < 0)$ creates a conflicted situation between the neurons i and j in which the increase of x_j results in the decrease of x_i, and vice versa. Namely, when the amoeba's branch in neuron j expands to take a certain threshold value $x_j(t)$, it becomes a trigger for illuminating neuron i as $y_i(t+1) = 1$.

The inhibitory coupling weights are introduced to establish the following three conditions for obtaining a solution of TSP, where the parameters are set as $\alpha = 0.5, \beta = 0.5$, and $\gamma = 0.025$ in the experiment.

1. Prohibition of revisiting a once-visited city: If city P is visited the nth, P cannot be visited the $m(\neq n)$th, either before or after that. This condition is represented by the inhibitory coupling weight $w_{ij} = -\alpha$ between the neuron $i = Pn$ and $j = Pm$. For example, when the state of the neuron $A1$ increases beyond a certain threshold value, the conflicting neurons $A2, A3$, and $A4$ are inhibited by the illuminations.

2. Prohibition of simultaneous visits to more than one city: If city P is visited the nth, no other city $Q(\neq P)$ can be visited at the same time n. The inhibitory coupling $w_{ij} = -\beta$ between neurons $i = Pn$ and $j = Qn$ represents this condition. For example, when neuron $A1$ exceeds the threshold, the conflicting neurons $B1, C1$, and $D1$ are inhibited.

   Any configuration representing a circular route by satisfying both conditions 1 and 2 gives a "valid" solution of TSP. When selecting a valid combination of edges in the map, the amoeba can fully expand up to four branches without being illuminated. In other words, the illumination pattern no longer forces the amoeba to reshape, and the amoeba fully completes the inherent expanding movements of branches inside all non-illuminated neurons. Thus, we expected that all valid solutions would be more stable than other transient configurations.

3. Reflection of travel distance between cities: If city P is visited the nth, and right before or right after that city $Q(\neq P)$ is visited the $m(=n\pm1)$th, the cost of traveling this route proportionally reflects the distance between P and Q written as $dst(P,Q)$. This rule is reflected in the inhibitory coupling $w_{ij} = -\gamma\ dst(P,Q)$ between neurons $i = Pn$ and $j = Qm$, where if $n = 4$ then $m = n+1 =: 1$, and if $n = 1$ then $m = n-1 =: 4$.

Under this setting, as long as the amoeba selects a valid combination of edges, the amoeba cannot recognize the distances of the selecting edges because the amoeba cannot be illuminated. To compare the distances of shorter and longer edges, therefore, the amoeba needs to select some "invalid" combination of edges by expanding some mutually conflicting branches. The expanding movements of the conflicting branches evoke some illuminations in such a way that some branches for longer edges are more frequently inhibited by the illuminations. This makes a longer solution less stable than a shorter solution. Thus, we expected that the shortest solution would be the most stable among all solutions.

In summary, the neural network algorithm evolves the amoeba's configuration in such a way that the state transition approaches a more favorable configuration representing a circular route with a shorter total distance. When the system reaches a configuration in which all neurons become unchanged, we regard the stable configuration as an output result of the computing.

3 Results

3.1 Problem-Solving Process

In the experiment, the map shown in Fig. 1B was given as a problem to be solved. Figure 2 shows an example of the problem-solving process. As shown in Fig. 2A, to start the time evolution from the initial configuration in which all neurons are set to $x_i(0) = 0$, we put a spherically shaped amoeba $(1 \pm 0.25$ mg$)$ at the center of the barrier structure. In the early stage, the spherical amoeba flattened into a disc-like shape and expanded its thin periphery horizontally with the circular symmetry.

Figure 2B shows the state transition in a period of oscillation at the time when the amoeba came to have some expanding branches that were about to reach their own threshold values for triggering the illuminations. At this stage, the illuminations blinked continually at short intervals. This is because the state $x_i(t)$ changes in a non-monotonous manner as the amoeba's branch alternates between small-scale expansion and shrinkage in a fluctuating manner at each period of the oscillation. This evoked a wide variety of illumination patterns necessary for exploring broader search space within a short time. By examining diverse illumination patterns with the fluctuating oscillatory movements, the

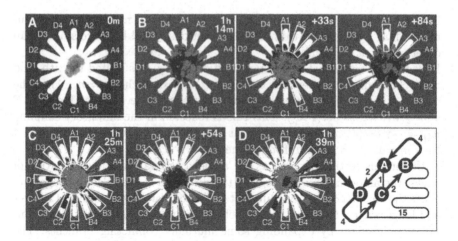

Fig. 2. Experimentally observed problem-solving process of four-city TSP. (A) Initial configuration recorded as a transmitted light image before digital image processing. (B) Early stage of searching process. Three panels show successive time evolution within a period of oscillation. By means of digital image processing, the phase of vertical thickness oscillation (a period $\simeq$ 1 to 2 min) is binarized into the relaxing (thickness increasing) and contracting (decreasing) states, represented by the black and gray pixels, respectively. (C) Final stage of searching process. Two panels show time evolution within a half period of oscillation. (D) The shortest solution $D \to C \to B \to A \to D$ with the total distance 12.

amoeba preceded its shape changing in search of an infrequently illuminated configuration; that is, a more stable solution with a shorter total distance.

Figure 2C shows the state transition in a half period of the oscillation at the time when the amoeba entered the final stage of the problem-solving process. Although the amoeba was about to reach a valid solution, the illuminations still blinked. The expanding branches $D1, C2, B3,$ and $A4$ were the least frequently illuminated ones, whereas others were in the middle of their shrinking.

Figure 2D shows that the amoeba reached an optimal solution $D \to C \to B \to A \to D$ with the shortest total distance 12. A successful solution can be recognized as the stabilization of the illumination pattern. The solution was stably maintained for about 5 h.

3.2   Statistical Results

We carried out 13 experimental trials with the parameter setup almost identical to the above one. The amoeba reached a valid solution in every trial. We certified that a solution had been reached only when two conditions were met; i) the illumination pattern was stabilized without any change for more than 30 min, and ii) the configuration calculated by inverting the illumination pattern (i.e., $1 - y_i$ for all i) represented a circular route.

Fig. 3. Frequency distributions of solutions reached. In 10 of 13 trials, the amoeba reached the shortest solution.

Figure 3 shows the frequencies of reaching the shortest, the second-shortest, and the longest solutions. In 10 of 13 trials, the amoeba reached the shortest solution, whereas the longest solution was never reached. Namely, our system scored more than 75% success rate of reaching the optimal solution.

In some cases, multiple solutions were searched in a trial. After the long maintenance of a solution, sometimes the amoeba's branches spontaneously invaded the illuminated regions contrary to its photoavoidance and evoked the illuminations for some branches selecting the solution. This behavior destabilized the once-reached solution and restarted the problem-solving process to search for other solutions. Our report on this spontaneous destabilization will be presented elsewhere [12].

4 Analysis

In the problem-solving process, we saw that the amoeba's fluctuating oscillatory movements (i.e., non-monotonous changes in neuron states mentioned in section 3.1) are responsible for evoking diverse illumination patterns to explore broader search space and might be essential for enhancing our system's optimization capability. In this section, we verify our hypothesis that the fluctuating oscillatory movements are characterized as behavior generated by a set of coupled chaotic oscillators. We applied various types of surrogate data to the oscillatory movements of branches in the problem-solving process and tested several properties of their time series data. For verifying our hypothesis, it is necessary to show the following four properties: Each branch's oscillation is *chaotic* [22], which means its time series has (1) *serial dependence*, (2) *nonlinearity*, and (3) *long-term correlations*; and multiple branches are coupled together as they exhibit (4) *synchronization*. For the four properties, we analyzed the time series of the volume $v_i(t)$ for each branch i, where $v_i(t)$ is calculated from a transmitted light image at each time t by accumulating the darkness levels of all pixels in each neuron i in assuming that the darkness reflects the vertical thickness. We prepared a different type of surrogates for each property. We start this section by explaining the details of surrogate data analysis.

4.1   Surrogate Data Analysis

Surrogate data analysis [23,24,25,26], which is similar to Monte Carlo tests in statistics, is hypothesis testing mainly used in nonlinear time series analysis. For testing a hypothesis, first we set a null-hypothesis for a given dataset. Then we generate a certain number of random datasets, called *surrogate data* or *surrogates*, that follow the null-hypothesis. For each random dataset, we calculate a test statistic. Because we have a set of the random datasets, we can approximate the distribution of the test statistic and hence its confidence interval. If the test statistic obtained from the given dataset is out of this confidence interval, then the null-hypothesis is rejected. Otherwise, we cannot reject the null-hypothesis.

Our datasets are nonstationary and have long-term trends. Namely, the base line of each time series $v_i(t)$ varies at a time scale much larger than that of the oscillation period because each branch gradually expands or shrinks by oscillating continually. Therefore, we needed to carefully select appropriate types of surrogate data. We used four different types of surrogate data for testing hypotheses. The first three are related to the chaotic dynamics of each individual branch, whereas the fourth one is applied to show the synchronization among multiple branches coupled.

Small Shuffle Surrogates. The first type of surrogates, *Small Shuffle (SS) surrogates* [23], test *serial dependence* in small fluctuations of short-term variability. If a time series has serial dependence, its future depends on its past somehow. Therefore, the serial dependence is a necessary condition for deterministic dynamics including deterministic chaos. One can generate SS surrogates by adding Gaussian noise to time indexes and ordering points in the time series according to the noise-contaminated time indexes. Because we destroy the serial dependence in generating SS surrogates, we can test the serial dependence by comparing them with the original data. To test the absence of the serial dependence, we separated our dataset into that of each branch and used it as a scalar time series. For each scalar time series, we generated 199 surrogates for making the significance level for an individual test 1%.

As a test statistic, we use mutual information. To obtain the mutual information, we need to divide the phase space. Our datasets, however, have trends and therefore the partition may not be able to be decided straightforward. Thus, here we applied the idea of *permutation entropy* [27] for calculating the mutual information.

Permutations represent orderings of successive numbers. For example, when we have a series $3, 7, 4$, its permutation is $(0, 2, 1)$ because $3 < 4 < 7$, i.e., 3, 4, and 7 are the 0th, second, and first values from the smallest, respectively. If there exist two or more same numbers, then we define its permutation so that the number appearing earlier has a smaller order. In this example, the length of the permutation is 3. Accordingly, we can define a permutation from a series with an arbitrary length uniquely. Let $p_i(t)$ be the permutation with length 3 for branch i at time t defined from $v_i(t-2), v_i(t-1)$ and $v_i(t)$. Denote by $P(o)$ the probability for permutation o. We also use O for the set of all permutations. Then, the permutation entropy is defined as follows:

$$-\sum_{o \in O} P(o) \log P(o). \tag{5}$$

Let $P(o, p, \kappa)$ be the probability that one observes o at time t and p at time $t + \kappa$, simultaneously. Then, similarly, the mutual information using the permutation entropy is defined as

$$\sum_{o,p \in O} P(o, p) \log \frac{P(o, p, \kappa)}{P(o)P(p)}. \tag{6}$$

This quantity shows a large value if we can guess p from o with a high chance. In this paper, we used 3 for the length of permutation and 20 for the maximal delay.

Each delay κ corresponds to an individual test and shows a rejection or non-rejection. We combine these individual tests and make a combined test by counting the number of rejections in the individual tests. Because the significance level of each individual test was set to 1%, if we assume the number n of rejections follows the binomial distribution, the z-score is calculated as

$$z = \frac{n - 0.01 * 20}{\sqrt{0.01 * (1 - 0.01) * 20}}. \tag{7}$$

We can obtain the p-value by using the cumulative distribution of normal distribution with the mean 0 and the standard deviation 1.

Symmetrized Truncated Fourier Transform Surrogates. The second type of surrogates, *Symmetrized Truncated Fourier Transform (STFT) surrogates* [24], test nonlinearity within datasets with trends. Nonlinearity is necessary for chaos: If a system is linear, it cannot behave in a complex manner. The basic idea for these surrogates is to keep the amplitudes of the Fourier transform and the phases of the lowest 5% frequencies as they are, and randomize the 95% of phases for the high frequencies. Because the amplitudes of the Fourier transform are kept unchanged, the autocorrelations, and hence linear correlations, are preserved. By keeping the phases of low frequencies as they are, the trends are preserved. However, by randomizing the phases of high frequencies, nonlinear correlations that may exist are destroyed. Therefore, using STFT surrogates, we can test nonlinearity.

For STFT surrogates, we treated a time series for each branch individually and generated 199 surrogates for each branch. We used the mutual information for the test statistic. The test is the same as that for SS surrogates.

Pseudo-Periodic Surrogates. The third type of surrogates, *Pseudo-Periodic (PP) surrogates* [25], test *long-term correlations* beyond pseudo-periodicity within a given dataset. If the dynamics of given system is dominated by dynamical noise, which is intrinsic to the system, the long-term correlations are destroyed and thus the dynamics cannot be deterministic chaos. Thus, long-term correlations beyond pseudo-periodicity are a prerequisite for deterministic chaos. Before generating PP surrogates, we removed the trends of time series for each branch by the following procedure: (1) taking the Fourier transform, (2) setting the phases of 95% frequencies from the highest to 0, (3) taking the inverse Fourier transform, and (4) subtracting the inverse Fourier transform from the original data. Then we generated PP surrogates for each branch.

In this paper, we used the method introduced in Ref. [25] for generating PP surrogates. The main idea of the method is that "a linear combination of any two segments of the same periodic orbit will generate another periodic orbit." Thus, if the original data is not periodic, different components are mixed up, and non-periodic correlations are destroyed. The PP surrogates, therefore, enable us to test whether the given dataset is a noisy periodic orbit or not. In this method, we simply take a sum $\alpha v_i(t) + \sqrt{1 - \alpha^2} v_i(t + \tau)$ with delay τ for $t = 1, 2, \cdots, N - 51 - 39 + 1$. We randomly drew α each time from $[0.6, 0.8]$ uniformly, set the minimum τ to 51, and incremented τ by 1 to generate 39 surrogates for the time series of each branch. We only generated 39 surrogates, because generating more surrogates leads the time series to become too short. Since the number of surrogates is 39, the significance level of the individual test is 5%. For PP surrogates, we used the mutual information as a test statistic as well as the previous tests.

Twin Surrogates. The fourth type of surrogates, *Twin surrogates* [26], generate datasets that preserve the dynamics of given dataset but start from different initial conditions. Twin surrogates can be used for testing *phase synchronization* among multiple time series. To generate twin surrogates, first, we build a recurrence plot of a given time series: $R_{s,t} = \Theta(\epsilon - \|(v_i(s), v_i(s + 3), v_i(s + 6)) - (v_i(t), v_i(t + 3), v_i(t + 6))\|)$ for $s, t = 1, 2, \cdots, N - 6$, where Θ is the Heaviside function, and ϵ is a pre-defined threshold. Second, we find *twins* defined as columns in the recurrence plot sharing the same neighbors, i.e., s and t such that $R_{s,u} = R_{t,u}$ for each $u = 1, 2, \cdots, N - 6$. Then, we start the generation of a surrogate by arbitrarily choosing a starting point from the given time series. Now we have the starting point with a certain current time index. We repeat the following procedure for generating the surrogate until its length becomes identical to that of the given time series. If the current point has no *twin*, the next point, which is appended at the end of the surrogate, is defined by a point following the current one in the given time series. On the other hand, if the current point has a *twin*, we choose a point between the current point and its *twin*, find the next point of the chosen point from the given time series, and append it at the end of the surrogate.

For testing phase synchronization among branches, we first removed the trends of the given datasets in a similar way as those of PP surrogates. We generated 199 Twin surrogates for each branch individually and made 199 sets of Twin surrogates by choosing a surrogate from those of each branch. For each set of surrogates and the given dataset, we first took the Hilbert transform and obtained the phases $\theta_j(t)$ for each branch j at time t ($t = 1, 2, \cdots, N$). Then we calculated the following quantity:

$$\frac{1}{N}\sum_{t=1}^{N}\left|\frac{1}{16}\sum_{j=1}^{16}exp[i\theta_j(t)]\right|. \tag{8}$$

We call this quantity as *synchronization index*. When the phases of some branches are synchronized, the complex number $\frac{1}{16}\sum_{j=1}^{16}exp[i\theta_j(t)]$ will deviate from 0 for a certain direction, and thus Eq. (8) takes a positive value. In a set of Twin surrogates, each branch starts from a different initial condition and thus their phases are likely to be different. If the synchronization is significant, therefore, Eq. (8) for a set of Twin surrogates is expected to be smaller than that of the original dataset. That is why Twin surrogates with the above test statistic can test phase synchronization.

4.2 Results

Time Window of Datasets Used. From each dataset, to analyze the amoeba's dynamics in the problem-solving process, we extracted the time window from the early stage of the problem-solving process to the time when the amoeba was about to reach a solution. The lengths of the extracted time windows were distributed within 20 to 45 min.

Serial Dependence. We tested serial dependence using SS surrogates. The total number of branches that showed rejections was 55 with 5% significance level as shown in Table reftable:surrogates. This number is significantly large (*p*-value: 1.68×10^{-122}). Thus, it is safe to assume that a certain portion of time series for branches have serial dependence.

Nonlinearity. We tested nonlinearity using STFT surrogates. The total number of branches that showed rejections was 33 (Table reftable:surrogates). Out of 55 branches that passed the test of serial dependence, there were 25 branches that passed the test of nonlinearity as well. This number 25 is significantly greater than that we can expect using the significance level of 5% (*p*-value: 2.05×10^{-43}). Therefore, it is likely that at least the dynamics of some branches are nonlinear.

Long-Term Correlations. The total number of branches that passed the test of long-term correlations using PP surrogates was 14 (Table reftable:surrogates). Out of 25 branches that passed the above two tests, there were 5 branches that also passed the test of long-term correlations. Because 5 out of 25 is significantly greater than that we can expect from the 5% significance level (*p*-value: 2.90×10^{-4}), it is likely that at least some branches have long-term correlations beyond pseudo-periodicity in their dynamics. We focused on the branch whose number of rejected delays was the largest. The rejected delays were $42, 48, 54, 90$, and 120 sec. In case of another branch whose number of rejected delays was the second longest, the rejected delays were $66, 72, 90$, and 96 sec. We further increased the maximum delay up to 240 sec for these two branches, but the number of rejected delays did not increase. Therefore, it is estimated that the long-term

Table 1. Numbers of rejections out of 16 branches for each dataset in each surrogate test that treated the component for each branch as a scalar time series. SS, STFT, and PP correspond to Small Shuffle, Symmetrized Truncated Fourier Transform, and Pseudo-Periodic surrogates, respectively and these surrogates tested serial dependence, nonlinearity, and long-term correlations of the given datasets, respectively. We used 5% for the significance level for each test. For references, we also list the number of branches for which the mean of $v_i(t)$ for the first 120 sec can be significantly smaller than for that for the window of 120 sec in the following part. Namely, these numbers of branches were extended significantly in some part of the test periods.

surrogates \ data	1	2	3	4	5	6
SS (serial dependence)	4	12	9	10	8	12
STFT (nonlinearity)	7	6	4	1	5	10
PP (long-term correlations)	1	4	4	2	2	1
number of extended branches	16	16	16	14	14	16

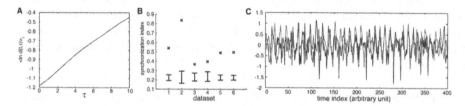

Fig. 4. Characteristics of time series. (A) Neighboring orbits diverge exponentially. We applied the method of Ref. [28] in TISEAN package [29]. In this method, one looks at how exponentially fast the distance $d(t, \tau)$ of point t to its nearest neighbor diverges along the time τ. We used 1 for the delay and 12 for the embedding dimension. (B) Synchronization indexes for original datasets ($\times$) and Twin surrogates (error bars). In all the datasets, the indexes for the original dataset is out of the 99% confidence interval, meaning that phase synchronization is likely to exist among branches. (C) Detrended time series of neighboring branches. They looked completely synchronized sometimes after the time index passed 200 since the two time series sometimes overlapped each other.

correlations in the branch's dynamics would remain up to around 120 sec, which is comparable to an oscillation period of 1 to 2 min.

The results altogether show that at least some of the amoeba's branches surely exhibit non-random oscillation characterized as chaotic. Indeed, by applying the method introduced in Ref. [28] to one of branches, we observed that small differences of initial conditions diverge exponentially as shown in Fig. 4A.

Phase Synchronization. Our next interest is how the dynamics of each branch is organized as a population. We used Twin surrogates and tested phase synchronization. The results are shown in Fig. 4B. It strongly supports phase synchronization among branches, where the phase synchronization found was in in-phase. Actually, when we plotted detrended time series of neighboring branches, they looked completely synchronized sometimes as shown in Fig. 4C.

4.3   Summary

In summary, our analysis revealed the fact that at least some of the amoeba's branches surely exhibit chaotic oscillation, and the majority of branches strongly synchronize. Thus, an individual amoeba might be characterized as a set of coupled chaotic oscillators. This implies that the amoeba searches for a solution by exploiting synchronization of chaotic oscillation.

5   Discussion and Conclusion

In theoretical models of coupled chaotic neurons, it has already been shown that chaotic dynamics is highly efficient for solving combinatorial optimization problems [30,31]. In this paper, we showed i) experimental results that our amoeba-based neurocomputer is capable of solving four-city TSP and ii) analytical results that the amoeba might be characterized as a set of coupled chaotic oscillators. These results altogether suggest a possibility that the amoeba actually exploits synchronization of chaotic oscillation for efficient optimization.

In our experiment, the optimal solution of TSP might be the most "comfortable" condition for the amoeba. This is because, when selecting the optimal solution under the setting of our optical feedback, the amoeba can minimize the probability of being illuminated by aversive light stimuli. Indeed, we have confirmed that the optimal solution is maintained longer than other (valid) solutions. Therefore, our results may mean that the synchronization of chaotic oscillation is essential for the amoeba's survival because it enables to search for conditions that are more comfortable in harsh environments filled with aversive stimuli. Further investigations of the amoeba's oscillatory dynamics will contribute to the understanding of biological information processing.

There may be a view that the optical feedback system, an extrinsic factor that gives the amoeba hints to select the optimal route, is a major contributor to the optimization, but the amoeba's intrinsic behavior is not. However, we have already confirmed that the optimization performance dramatically decreases if the optical feedback system is reconfigured to be incapable of sensing the small-scale oscillatory movements of the amoeba's branches in the searching process (i.e., non-monotonous changes in neuron states mentioned in section 3.1). The amoeba's fluctuating oscillatory behavior, therefore, is essential for enhancing our system's optimization capability. We will report this result elsewhere.

At present, we do not intend to replace conventional silicon-based devices with the amoeba because its processing speed is quite slow. However, it may be possible to implement our scheme with other faster oscillatory medium, if we could identify a key factor in the dynamics of the amoeba's oscillatory behavior for the efficient search.

References

1. Nakagaki, T., Yamada, H., Ueda, T.: Interaction between cell shape and contraction pattern. Biophys. Chem. 84, 195–204 (2000)
2. Nakagaki, T., Yamada, H., Toth, A.: Maze-Solving by an Amoeboid Organism. Nature 407, 470 (2000)
3. Nakagaki, T., Yamada, H., Hara, M.: Smart network solutions in an amoeboid organism. Biophys. Chem. 107, 1–5 (2004)
4. Takamatsu, A., Fujii, T., Endo, I.: Time delay effect in a living coupled oscillator system with the plasmodium of *Physarum polycephalum*. Phys. Rev. Lett. 85, 2026–2029 (2000)
5. Takamatsu, A., Tanaka, R., Yamada, H., Nakagaki, T., Fujii, T., Endo, I.: Spatiotemporal symmetry in rings of coupled biological oscillators of *Physarum* plasmodial slime mold. Phys. Rev. Lett. 87, 078102 (2001)
6. Takamatsu, A.: Spontaneous switching among multiple spatio-temporal patterns in three-oscillator systems constructed with oscillatory cells of true slime mold. Physica D 223, 180–188 (2006)
7. Aono, M., Gunji, Y.-P.: Beyond input-output computings: Error-driven emergence with parallel non-distributed slime mold computer. BioSystems 71, 257–287 (2003)
8. Aono, M., Hara, M.: Dynamic Transition among Memories on Neurocomputer Composed of Amoeboid Cell with Optical Feedback. In: Proceedings of The 2006 International Symposium on Nonlinear Theory and its Applications, pp. 763–766 (2006)
9. Aono, M., Hara, M.: Amoeba-based Nonequilibrium Neurocomputer Utilizing Fluctuations and Instability. In: Akl, S.G., Calude, C.S., Dinneen, M.J., Rozenberg, G., Wareham, H.T. (eds.) UC 2007. LNCS, vol. 4618, pp. 41–54. Springer, Heidelberg (2007)
10. Aono, M., Hara, M.: Spontaneous deadlock breaking on amoeba-based neurocomputer. BioSystems 91, 83–93 (2008)
11. Aono, M., Hara, M., Aihara, K.: Amoeba-based Neurocomputing with Chaotic Dynamics. Commun. ACM 50(9), 69–72 (2007)
12. Aono, M., Hara, M., Aihara, K., Munakata, T.: Amoeba-Based Emergent Computing: Combinatorial Optimization and Autonomous Meta-Problem Solving. International Journal of Unconventional Computing (in press)
13. Tsuda, S., Aono, M., Gunji, Y.-P.: Robust and emergent *Physarum* logical-computing. BioSystem 73, 45–55 (2004)
14. Tsuda, S., Zauner, K.P., Gunji, Y.-P.: Robot Control with Biological Cells. In: Proceedings of Sixth International Workshop on Information Processing in Cells and Tissues, pp. 202–216 (2005)
15. Tero, A., Kobayashi, R., Nakagaki, T.: *Physarum* solver: A biologically inspired method of road-network navigation. Physica A 363, 115–119 (2006)
16. Adamatzky, A.: Physarum machine: implementation of a Kolmogorov-Uspensky machine on a biological substrate. Parallel Processing Letters (in press)
17. Garey, M.R., Johnson, D.S.: Computers and Intractability: A Guide to the Theory of NP-Completeness. W. H. Freeman and co., New York (1979)
18. Arbib, M.A. (ed.): The Handbook of Brain Theory and Neural Networks. MIT Press, Cambridge (2003)
19. Holland, J.H.: Adaptation in Natural and Artificial Systems, 2nd edn. University of Michigan Press, Ann Arbor (1975); (2nd edn.: MIT Press, 1992)

20. Hopfield, J.J., Tank, D.W.: Computing with Neural Circuits: A model. Science 233, 625–633 (1986)
21. Ueda, T., Mori, Y., Nakagaki, T., Kobatake, Y.: Action spectra for superoxide generation and UV and visible light photoavoidance in plasmodia of *Physarum polycephalum*. Photochem. Photobiol. 48, 705–709 (1988)
22. Ott, E.: Chaos in Dynamical Systems, 2nd edn. Cambridge University Press, Cambridge (2002)
23. Nakamura, T., Small, M.: Small-shuffle Surrogate Data: Testing for Dynamics in Fluctuating Data with Trends. Phys. Rev. E 72, 056216 (2005)
24. Nakamura, T., Small, M., Hirata, Y.: Testing for Nonlinearity in Irregular Fluctuations with Long-term Trends. Phys. Rev. E 74, 026205 (2006)
25. Luo, X., Nakamura, T., Small, M.: Surrogate Test to Distinguish between Chaotic and Pseudoperiodic Time Series. Phys. Rev. E 71, 026230 (2005)
26. Thiel, M., Romano, M.C., Kurths, J., Rolfs, M., Kliegl, R.: Twin Surrogates to Test for Complex Synchronisation. Europhys. Lett. 75, 535–541 (2006)
27. Bandt, C., Pompe, B.: Permutation Entropy: A Natural Complexity Measure for Time Series. Phys. Rev. Lett. 88, 174102 (2002)
28. Rosetnstein, M.T., Collins, J.J., De Luca, C.J.: A Practical Method for Calculating Largest Lyapunov Exponents from Small Data Sets. Physica D 65, 117–134 (1993)
29. Hegger, R., Kantz, H., Schreiber, T.: Practical Implementation of Nonlinear Time Series Methods: The TISEAN Package. Chaos 9, 413–435 (1999)
30. Aihara, K., Takabe, T., Toyoda, M.: Chaotic Neural Networks. Phys. Lett. A 144, 333–340 (1990)
31. Hasegawa, M., Ikeguchi, T., Aihara, K.: Combination of Chaotic Neurodynamics with the 2-opt Algorithm to Solve Traveling Salesman Problems. Phys. Rev. Lett. 79, 2344–2347 (1997)

Factorizing RSA Keys
(An Improved Analogue Solution)

Ed Blakey

Oxford University Computing Laboratory, Wolfson Building,
Parks Road, Oxford, OX1 3QD, United Kingdom
edward.blakey@queens.ox.ac.uk

Abstract. Factorization is notoriously difficult. Though the problem is not known to be **NP**-hard, neither efficient, *algorithmic* solution nor technologically practicable, *quantum-computer* solution has been found. This apparent complexity, which renders infeasible the factorization of sufficiently large values, makes secure the RSA cryptographic system.

Given the lack of a practicable factorization system from algorithmic or quantum-computing models, we ask whether efficient solution exists elsewhere; this motivates the *analogue* system presented here. The system's complexity is prohibitive of its factorizing arbitrary, natural numbers, though the problem is mitigated when factorizing $n = pq$ for primes p and q of similar size, and hence when factorizing *RSA keys*.

Ultimately, though, we argue that the system's polynomial time and space complexities are testament not to its power, but to the inadequacy of traditional, Turing-machine-based complexity theory; we propose *precision complexity* (defined in [3]) as a more relevant measure.

Keywords: Factorization, analogue, complexity, cryptography.

1 Introduction

1.1 What Is Computation?

We discuss factorization in the context of non-standard (that is, non-Turing-machine) computation. Given the prevalence of the digital computer—an implementation of the standard computational model—, it may be beneficial for the reader to consider the preliminary question: *what is computation?*

It is convenient to think of *computation* as 'that which is performed by a computer', though there is a crucial caveat: we must interpret 'computer' to be more general than its common usage (namely, shorthand for 'digital computer') suggests. Specifically, we may view as a computer any system to which input values can be supplied and (possibly after processing by the system) from which output values can be drawn; then the *computation* is the relation—often a function—mapping input values to output values.

Whereas, in the digital case, input and output may take the form of the user's typing in values and reading values from a screen, our more general view of

Y. Suzuki et al. (Eds.): IWNC 2007, PICT 1, pp. 16–27, 2009.

computation sees the user *manipulating parameters* of the system (so as to effect input) and *measuring parameters* (to obtain output); e.g., a chemical computer may require input values and offer output values encoded in the concentrations of solutions—the user supplies a solution the concentration of which is suitably chosen to reflect (i.e., *encode*) his desired input value, and is (after the reactions, etc. of the system) presented with a solution the concentration of which reflects (encodes) the corresponding output value.

This extended view of computation—which accommodates not only standard, algorithmic (e.g., digital) computers, but also more natural, physical systems: quantum, DNA, analogue and optical computers amongst others—allows us to approach traditionally difficult problems in new ways.[1] Specifically, we consider here an *analogue-computer* solution to the problem of factorization.

1.2   Motivation

Though the factorization problem is easily posed—given $n \in \mathbb{N}$, what natural numbers exactly divide n?—, it seems inherently difficult to solve.

In [7], we see that the run-time of the best, known, *algorithmic* factorization methods grows exponentially with the size (i.e., number of digits) of the value factorized; this exponential time complexity renders infeasible the factorization of numbers beyond a certain size. So, whilst the equivalent decision problem[2] is not known to be **NP**-hard, neither do we expect an imminent, efficient algorithm.

The best, known, *quantum-computing* methods are technologically hard to implement; notably, Shor's algorithm ([10]), despite having run-time polynomial in the input value's size, has yet to factorize in practice a value greater than 15.

This apparent difficulty of factorizing via algorithmic or quantum means, along with the comments of Sect. 1.1, lead us to ask whether other computation models offer efficient solution. This question motivates the analogue system of [2] and the improved system below.

1.3   Original Analogue System

We recall the analogue factorizing system of [2]. Though a full description is deferred ([2] offers details of the system; [4] is the associated pending patent), we now outline some salient points.

Factorizing n is exactly the task of finding integer solutions x, y to $y = \frac{n}{x}$; i.e., finding points (x, y) in the integer grid $\mathbb{Z} \times \mathbb{Z}$ and on the curve $y = \frac{n}{x}$ (which curve is a hyperbola and, a fortiori, a conic section). Factorization, then, is the search for points in the intersection of a planar grid and a cone.

---

[1] As we shall see, however, part of the cost of this is the need for innovative forms of complexity analysis.

[2] The *decision* factorization problem asks, given $n \in \mathbb{N}$ and $l \leq n$, whether n has a factor a with $1 < a < l$. Ability efficiently to decide this implies ability efficiently to factorize: only logarithmically many decisions are needed to identify a factor.

Radiation can be reflected such that its interference pattern has a regular structure, of which the points of maximal wave activity may model $\mathbb{Z} \times \mathbb{Z}$.[3]

A second source of radiation, together with a part-circular sensor, can be used to model the cone: the source is the vertex, and the sensor's circle a cross section, of the cone. Diminishment of second-source radiation as it passes through an integer (i.e., maximally active) point in the first-source interference pattern is detected at the sensor; the coordinates of points of such detection can, Turing-computationally trivially, be converted into the coordinates of the sought integer points on the cone. These coordinates are factors of n. (We reiterate that full details of this system are available in [2].)

Of interest here is that the system's time and space complexities are *constant* in the size of n: the factorization of n requires neither more physical space nor more time as n increases. This is in contrast with known factorization algorithms, of which the required time is *exponential* in the size of n (see [7]).

This apparent efficiency is not, however, testament to the system's power, but rather exemplifies the inadequacy of traditional complexity theory for capturing the true complexity of non-Turing (e.g., analogue) computers. The system *does* require increasing—*exponentially* increasing—resource as n increases: for larger n, the user is required to position the apparatus and measure the position of points on the sensor with increasing *precision*. Intuitively, then, the system has non-constant *precision complexity*; this intuition is formalized in [3], in which precision complexity is motivated, defined and investigated.

1.4   Improving the Analogue System

We wish to improve this system in light of the impediment to its performance due to its precision complexity. A drawback of the system's design is the 'artificial' implementation of the cone[4]—essentially manual positioning of the vertex and a cross-sectional arc. Direct implementation of the cone by some physical phenomenon would, one expects, improve the precision of the apparatus. We seek, therefore, a naturally occurring, precisely shaped cone.

Consider a burst at time 0 of radiation from a point source in a plane P, and suppose that the radiation propagates at constant velocity v, regardless of direction or distance from source. The points reached by the radiation at time $t \geq 0$ describe a circle of radius vt (see Fig. 1(a)). Regarding this increasing circle in the space with two spatial axes (those of P) and one temporal axis, we have a perfectly constructed cone (see Fig. 1(b)).

The cone's original implementation, which we seek to replace with this radiation burst, exists in three spatial dimensions; relative to this, the proposed

---

[3] In fact, subset $\left\{ (x,y) \in \mathbb{Z} \times \mathbb{Z} \mid 0 \leq x \leq y \leq n \wedge \frac{x+y}{2} \in \mathbb{Z} \right\}$ is modelled. This suffices as (a) factors of n need be sought only in $\{1, \ldots, n\}$; (b) having found factor pair $(p, n/p)$, finding $(n/p, p)$ is unnecessary; and (c) we assume that n is odd (see [2]).

[4] The drawback is crucial: a small imprecision in the shape/position of the cone leads only to a small imprecision in the resultant conic section, but this leads to the system's reporting wildly incorrect 'factors', in part because a small perturbation in n can cause a large perturbation in the *factors of n*.

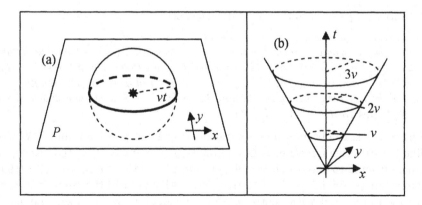

Fig. 1. (a) The circle of radiation in P at time t. (b) The circle plotted against t.

replacement is effectively rotated so as to span two spatial dimensions and one temporal. We now rotate the grid—in the intersection of which with the cone we are interested—similarly. The plane Q of the grid must lie parallel to and positively distant from the cone's axis, so that the resultant conic section is the required hyperbola; accordingly, in the radiation-burst implementation, Q is modelled as a permanent line in P, positively distant from the point source (Q thus spans one spatial and one temporal dimension). Within Q, the grid itself consists of points equally spaced along both axes: existing instantaneously at regular time intervals, and at regularly spaced points along the spatial axis.

The principle, then, is as with the original analogue system—we seek points of intersection of a cone and a planar grid—, though the implementation is different: before, the cone and grid existed in three-space; now, they exist in the plane, the cone as a steadily increasing circle, the grid as a flashing row of points. Further, since we seek intersection points with the grid, we need consider only those instants when the grid points are 'on', at which instants (together) the cone is modelled as a family of concentric circles with arithmetically progressional radii; *we seek the intersection of a row of points and a nest of concentric circles.*

The improved, analogue factorization system, of which the design is motivated by the informal comments of Sect. 1.4, is now formally described.

2   Analogue Factorization System

2.1   Apparatus

We describe the apparatus as lying in a plane; a physical realization would see the relevant features (X, Y, a and b) extended into the third dimension, though with readings being taken, etc. within the plane.

Definition 1 (provisional; see Definition 2)

- *Let n be the positive, natural number to be factorized.*[5]
- *Let X be an opaque screen occupying the line $(\mathbb{R} \setminus \{0, 2\sqrt{n}\}) \times \{0\}$. The breaks at $(0,0)$ and $(2\sqrt{n}, 0)$ are slits in the screen; call these a and b respectively.*
- *Let S be a source at $(\sqrt{n}, -\sqrt{n})$ of (say, e.m.) radiation of wavelength 1.*
- *Let Y be a screen occupying the line $\{0\} \times \mathbb{R}^+$.[6] The negligible width of slit a in X lies to the $x > 0$ side of Y.*

The intention is to observe radiation incident on Y from S via a and b. Where we find constructive interference at a point E on Y, we have that the respective distances from E to a and to b are integer multiples of the wavelength of S (that is, the distances are integers).[7] E is therefore both on one of the family of circles of integer radius and with centre b, and coincident with an integer point on the y-axis. This implementation, then, allows identification of the sought points described informally in Sect. 1.4 (we seek, recall, the intersection of a row of points and a nest of concentric circles).

Note that the layout of the apparatus (specifically the distance separating a and b, and the position of S) depends on n. In order to use the same apparatus to factorize different values, then, we scale each axis in the plane by a factor of $\frac{1}{2\sqrt{n}}$; accordingly, we replace the previous definition by the following.

Definition 2 (to replace Definition 1)

- *Let n be the positive, natural number to be factorized.*
- *Let X be an opaque screen occupying the line $(\mathbb{R} \setminus \{0, 1\}) \times \{0\}$. The breaks at $(0,0)$ and $(1,0)$ are slits in the screen; call these a and b respectively.*
- *Let S be a source at $(\frac{1}{2}, -\frac{1}{2})$ of (say, e.m.) radiation of wavelength $\frac{1}{2\sqrt{n}}$.*
- *Let Y be a screen occupying the line $\{0\} \times \mathbb{R}^+$. The negligible width of slit a in X lies to the $x > 0$ side of Y.*

See Fig. 2.

In so replacing Definition 1, we may reuse the apparatus to factorize any n, having to change only the wavelength of S rather than the system's layout.

2.2   Input to the System

As alluded to above, n is supplied to the system by altering to $\frac{1}{2\sqrt{n}}$ the wavelength of the radiation from S.

Note that the operations used in calculating this wavelength can be performed by a Turing machine in time polynomial in the size of n: there is no 'sleight of hand' whereby costly calculation is tacitly assumed to come for free.

---

[5] In [2], we assume for convenience that n is odd; we make no such assumption here.

[6] Note that $0 \in \mathbb{R}^+ := [0, \infty)$.

[7] In fact, we have that the distances' *difference* is a multiple of the wavelength. We henceforth assume, however, that we have instantiated along Y a standing wave or similar with maximally active points at wavelength spacing; we consider points at which constructive interference combines with this maximal standing-wave activity. This does not affect the complexity of the system, which we discuss later.

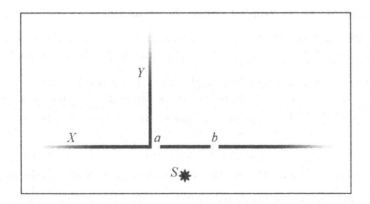

Fig. 2. The apparatus described in Definition 2

2.3   Output from the System

Having set up the apparatus as in Definition 2 (including provision to the system of n, encoded in the wavelength of S), an interference pattern is produced on Y (since, on the $y > 0$ side of X, a and b act as separate, mutually coherent sources,[8] of which the respective waves interfere).

Since effective sources a and b are in phase, a point E on Y exhibits full, constructive interference (and so maximal brightness) if and only if the respective distances from E to a and to b are integer multiples of the wavelength $\frac{1}{2\sqrt{n}}$.

Proposition 1. *This maximal brightness is attained.*

Proof. The respective distances from $E := \left(0, \frac{n-1}{2\sqrt{n}}\right)$ to a and to b are $\frac{n-1}{2\sqrt{n}}$ and $\sqrt{\left(\frac{n-1}{2\sqrt{n}}\right)^2 + 1^2} = \frac{n+1}{2\sqrt{n}}$, each an integer multiple of $\frac{1}{2\sqrt{n}}$. Hence, E exhibits full, constructive interference. $\qquad\square$

The process whereby output is read from the system consists of: identifying a maximally bright point E on Y, measuring the y-coordinate h of E, and calculating the values $p := \sqrt{n}\left(\sqrt{h^2+1} + h\right)$ and $\frac{n}{p}$.

As is proven below, the values p and $\frac{n}{p}$[9] so corresponding to any point of maximal brightness are factors of n. Further, each factor of n occurs as such p or $\frac{n}{p}$ for some maximally bright point. Thus, by processing all such points as described here, all factors of n are found.

As during input, there is no tacit presumption of a computationally complex operation: the process of finding p and $\frac{n}{p}$ given h is algorithmically efficient.

---

[8] This coherence is because S lies on the perpendicular bisector of ab.
[9] Since $h \geq 0$, we have that $\frac{n}{p} \leq \sqrt{n} \leq p$.

2.4   Proof of the System's Correct Functioning

Proposition 2. *A point on Y is maximally bright if and only if the corresponding value p is a factor of n no less than $\sqrt{n}$ (and so $\frac{n}{p}$ a factor at most $\sqrt{n}$).*

Proof. If $E := (0, h)$ is maximally bright, then the respective distances—h and $\sqrt{h^2 + 1}$—from E to a and to b are integer multiples of $\frac{1}{2\sqrt{n}}$; that is, $\alpha := 2\sqrt{n}h$ and $\beta := 2\sqrt{n}\sqrt{h^2 + 1}$ are integers (as, hence, are α^2 and β^2). Now

$$\beta^2 - \alpha^2 = 4n\left(h^2 + 1\right) - 4nh^2 = 4n, \tag{1}$$

which is even; so α^2 and β^2 have the same parity, as do α and β. Hence, $\beta \pm \alpha$ are even, and $\frac{\beta \pm \alpha}{2}$ are integers, with product $\frac{\beta + \alpha}{2} \cdot \frac{\beta - \alpha}{2} = \frac{\beta^2 - \alpha^2}{4} \overset{(1)}{=} n$; that is, $\frac{\beta \pm \alpha}{2}$ are factors of n. Now $p := \sqrt{n}\left(\sqrt{h^2 + 1} + h\right)$ is exactly $\frac{\beta + \alpha}{2}$, a factor of n. Further, where $q = \sqrt{n}\left(\sqrt{h^2 + 1} - h\right)$, pq is $n\left(\sqrt{h^2 + 1} + h\right)\left(\sqrt{h^2 + 1} - h\right) = n\left(h^2 + 1 - h^2\right) = n$, and $p \geq q$, so $p \geq \sqrt{n}$, as required.

Conversely, suppose that $E := (0, h)$ is such that $p := \sqrt{n}\left(\sqrt{h^2 + 1} + h\right)$ is a factor of n ($p \geq \sqrt{n}$ since $h \geq 0$). Let $q = \sqrt{n}\left(\sqrt{h^2 + 1} - h\right)$; $pq = n$, and so (since $p|n$) $q \in \mathbb{Z}$. p and q are integers, as are $p \pm q$, and $p + q = 2\sqrt{n}\sqrt{h^2 + 1}$ and $p - q = 2\sqrt{n}h$; i.e., $\sqrt{h^2 + 1}$ and h—the respective distances from E to b and to a—are integer multiples of $\frac{1}{2\sqrt{n}}$. Thus, E is maximally bright, as required. $\square$

Having set up the system as in Definition 2, including having input n (encoded as a wavelength), the factors of n are found by measuring the y-coordinates of maximally bright points on Y and converting these into values p and $\frac{n}{p}$; Proposition 2 guarantees that the values so produced from all maximally bright points on Y are the factors of n and only the factors of n.

2.5   Practical Considerations

The description given of the system is an abstraction of any physical realization: aspects of the description require modification before the system can be practically implemented. We note above that the confinement of the apparatus to a plane is one such aspect; the screens X and Y, and slits a and b, should actually have positive, z-axis height, while S should remain as much as is practicable a point source, in the plane of which measurements on Y are taken.

Further, we cannot physically realize the infinitely long screen X. However, since we require of X and S only that, on the $y > 0$ side of X, a and b act as mutually coherent sources, we may replace X with a finite box

$$\left(\{(x, 0) \mid -1 \leq x \leq 2\} \setminus \{(0,0), (1,0)\}\right) \cup \left\{(x, x - 2) \mid \tfrac{1}{2} \leq x \leq 2\right\}$$
$$\cup \left\{(x, -x - 1) \mid -1 \leq x \leq \tfrac{1}{2}\right\},$$

sealed but for a and b, and containing S (which retains its position); we assume the interior to be non-reflective, absorbing radiation from S that does not directly reach a or b. (Of course, the box has positive height in light of the preceding paragraph.) Fig. 3 shows the apparatus after this and the next modification.

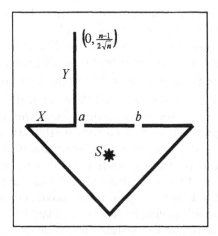

Fig. 3. The apparatus as modified in Sect. 2.5

Similarly, we cannot realize the infinitely long screen Y. It suffices, though, for Y to occupy the y-axis from 0 to $\frac{n-1}{2\sqrt{n}}$, since factors p of n (where, recall, $p \geq \frac{n}{p}$), which are in $\{\lceil\sqrt{n}\rceil, \ldots, n\}$, correspond (as in the output process of Sect. 2.3) to maximally bright points with y-coordinates in $\left[0, \frac{n-1}{2\sqrt{n}}\right]$.[10]

(A practical consideration not made in this theoretical context concerns the production of radiation of sufficiently short wavelength; as n increases, the required wavelength of S corresponds to an increasingly impractical energy.)

3 Complexity of the System; RSA Factorization

3.1 Time and Space Complexity

Consider first the system's time complexity. Use of the system consists of (a) provision to the system of the value n to be factorized, by way of adjustment of the wavelength of source S; (b) 'processing' by the system of n, by forming an interference pattern on Y; (c) measurement of the y-coordinates of maximally bright points on Y; and (d) conversion of these coordinates into factors of n. Of these, only (a) and (d) take longer as n increases (because of the Turing-machine-realm processing of n to find the corresponding wavelength and of y-coordinates to find factors), and even these take only polynomially long in the size $\log(n)$ of n; thus, the processing, physical-computing stages have *constant* time complexity, and their algorithmic

---

[10] In making this observation, we remove the problem of Y being infinite, but reintroduce the undesirable property of the system's layout depending on n. This renders the system unsuitable for factorizing arbitrary, natural numbers, but is not a problem when factorizing numbers satisfying certain criteria; it is common, furthermore, for public keys used in the RSA cryptographic system to satisfy these criteria.

'harness', which prepares input and interprets output, has *polynomial* time complexity (as does the system as a whole, therefore).[11]

Consider now the system's space complexity. The apparatus has negligible, constant height (along the z-axis), a constant width (along the x-axis) of three (due to the box that replaces X), and a depth (along the y-axis) of $\frac{n+3\sqrt{n}-1}{2\sqrt{n}} \in \mathcal{O}(\sqrt{n})$ (due to the box that replaces X and the shortened screen Y); the volume of the apparatus lies in $\mathcal{O}(\sqrt{n})$, and is, hence, *exponential* in the size of n.

Let us put this in perspective. To factorize an arbitrary, 100-digit number (a relatively unambitious aim in the context of factorizing RSA keys, for example), we expect an apparatus depth of a 50-digit number of units and a width of three. The apparatus must be of the order of 10^{50} times as deep as it is wide; it is necessarily either too deep to be practicably accommodated, too narrow for slits with sufficiently small spacing feasibly to be manufactured, or both.

These considerations render the system unsuitable as a practical solution to the general problem of factorization. We now consider a subproblem, restriction to which greatly mitigates the problems discussed here.

3.2   RSA Factorization

From maximally bright point $(0, h)$ on Y, we find factors $p := \sqrt{n}\left(\sqrt{h^2+1} + h\right)$ and $\frac{n}{p}$ of n; but there is no a priori, n-independent upper bound for h: factors of n are found from values of h as large as $\frac{n-1}{2\sqrt{n}}$, which tends to ∞ as n does.

However, as h increases, the corresponding factors p and $\frac{n}{p}$ grow apart. When n is a square, there is a maximally bright point at $(0, 0)$, corresponding to the factorization $n = \sqrt{n}\sqrt{n}$; small h give close factor pairs. At the other extreme, for any positive, natural n, there is by Proposition 1 a maximally bright point at $\left(0, \frac{n-1}{2\sqrt{n}}\right)$, corresponding to the factorization $n = 1n$; large h give greatly differing pairs of factors. In fact, we have the following.

Proposition 3. *The factors $p := \sqrt{n}\left(\sqrt{h^2+1} + h\right)$ and $q := \frac{n}{p}$ corresponding to maximally bright point $(0, h)$ on Y differ by $2\sqrt{n}h$.*

Proof. $q = \sqrt{n}\left(\sqrt{h^2+1} - h\right)$, for then (as in the proof of Proposition 2) $pq = n$. So $p - q = \sqrt{n}\left(\sqrt{h^2+1} + h\right) - \sqrt{n}\left(\sqrt{h^2+1} - h\right) = 2\sqrt{n}h$, as required.   □

Suppose now that we modify the system so that the size of Y is bounded; specifically, suppose that Y occupies the line segment $\{0\} \times [0, l]$ for some fixed (and, hence, n-independent), positive, real l. From Sect. 3.1, then, the system has constant space complexity.[12]

---

[11] Note that, under certain implementations, the sensor that identifies maximally bright points on Y is required to 'scan' Y in time linear in the length of Y. This length is in $\mathcal{O}(\sqrt{n})$, rendering the system's time complexity exponential in the size $\log(n)$ of n. In Sect. 3.2, however, we modify the system so that this is no longer a concern.

[12] Its time complexity, further, is polynomial under all models of the sensor on Y.

For sufficiently large n (i.e., those with $\frac{n-1}{2\sqrt{n}} > l$), Y is no longer large enough to accommodate all maximally bright points corresponding to factors of n: those factor pairs corresponding to maximally bright points $(0, h)$ with $h > l$ are overlooked. However, we have the following.

Proposition 4. *If a pair (p, q) of factors of n (with $pq = n$ and $p \geq q$) satisfies $p \leq mq$, where $m = 2l + 1$, then these factors are not overlooked.*

Proof. Required is that the y-coordinate h of the maximally bright point corresponding to the factor pair (p, q) does not exceed l, for then this point falls on the modified (i.e., shortened) screen Y.

Since, by hypothesis, $p \leq mq$, $p - q \leq (m - 1) q$; since, again by hypothesis, $pq = n$ and $p \geq q$, $q \leq \frac{n}{q}$, whence $q \leq \sqrt{n}$. Together, these give that

$$p - q \leq (m - 1) \sqrt{n} \ . \tag{2}$$

Since, by definition, $m = 2l + 1$,

$$l = \frac{m - 1}{2} \ . \tag{3}$$

Hence, $h \overset{\text{Prop. } 3}{=} \frac{p-q}{2\sqrt{n}} \overset{(2)}{\leq} \frac{(m-1)\sqrt{n}}{2\sqrt{n}} = \frac{m-1}{2} \overset{(3)}{=} l$; $h \leq l$, as required. $\qquad\square$

Corollary 1. *If $l \geq \frac{1}{2}$, then all factor pairs (p, q) $(pq = n, p \geq q)$ with $p \leq 2q$ are found by the modified system.*

Proof. If $l \geq \frac{1}{2}$, then $m := 2l + 1 \geq 2$; so $p \leq 2q$ implies that $p \leq mq$, whence Proposition 4 can be invoked. $\qquad\square$

In modifying the system so that Y occupies $\{0\} \times \left[0, \frac{1}{2}\right]$, we lose the ability to factorize arbitrary, natural numbers; by Corollary 1, however, we can still factorize those values n of which each factor p no less than $\sqrt{n}$ (but strictly less than n^{13}) satisfies $p \leq \frac{2n}{p}$. Further, we note that, for a public key $n = pq$ (with p and q prime) of the RSA system, the situation in which $q \leq p \leq 2q$ is common.[14]

Having noted an impracticality of the system when factorizing arbitrary, natural numbers (namely that, as n grows, the required ratio of the system's depth to its breadth grows exponentially), we have nonetheless found a subproblem—factorizing RSA keys—that this impracticality does not hinder.[15]

---

[13] We excuse the system for omitting to demonstrate that $n = 1n$.

[14] Were we even to weaken this condition to $q \leq p \leq 10q$, say—a conservative requirement of RSA keys—, then we can, by Proposition 4, still factorize n provided that Y spans $\{0\} \times \left[0, \frac{9}{2}\right]$. This proviso causes no difficulty in implementation.

[15] Further, in a sense, the subproblem captures the 'hardest' instances of (general) factorization: traditional, general-factorization algorithms typically take longest on input of the form pq, where p and q are primes of the same approximate size.

3.3 Precision Complexity

Having restricted factorization to RSA keys, we have a system with constant space and polynomial time complexity. The system, though, suffers from its *precision* complexity (see [3] for a formal account of precision): if the system rounds n to an integer, then the 'allowed', corrigible input error is $\pm\frac{1}{2}$; hence, the wavelength of S must be set in the interval $\left(\frac{1}{2\sqrt{n+\frac{1}{2}}}, \frac{1}{2\sqrt{n-\frac{1}{2}}}\right]$, which shrinks exponentially in the size of n. Containing the error to this extent requires precision (whilst setting the wavelength of S) *exponential* in the size of n.

Rather than an efficient system, we have yet further motivation[16] for extension of complexity theory beyond the essentially algorithmic. By introducing notions of complexity that, for certain physical computers, cater better than those of the traditional theory, [3] represents the beginnings of such extension.

(We suggest that the lack of such extension before [3] is because nearly all actual computation conforms to an algorithmic model (real-world computers are typically digital, running programs that implement algorithms), and also because of an overestimation of the ambit of Church's Thesis[17] (which ambit, we suggest, falls under computability rather than complexity); consequently, resource is typically taken to be a property—run-time, space, or another measure satisfying Blum's axioms[18]—of an algorithm, Turing machine, or equivalent.)

4 Conclusion

4.1 Summary

In Sect. 1, we note the apparent difficulty of algorithmic/quantum-computing factorization, and ask whether other computation models offer efficient solution. We recall an analogue system ([2]), but note its prohibitive complexity and seek to improve the system, motivated by a consideration of naturally occurring cones.

In Sect. 2, we define an improved analogue factorization system, detailing its apparatus and input/output processes. We discuss and resolve some, though not all, of the practical difficulties with the system's implementation.

In Sect. 3, we note the system's favourable time complexity, but that its space complexity impedes implementation. We resolve this by restricting the apparatus, though this restricts accordingly the problem solved by the system: while an implementable system for factorizing arbitrary, natural numbers seems out of reach, we present a system for factorizing a certain type of natural number—which type includes RSA keys—that is not subject to some of these concerns.

---

[16] We add this example to the soap bubble method ([9]) for finding minimum-length spanning networks connecting given vertices, the DNA computing technique ([1]) for tackling the directed Hamiltonian path problem, etc.

[17] Church's Thesis is introduced in [8] and discussed in [6], [11] and many others.

[18] Blum's axioms (see [5]) ensure that (a) a measure of resource is defined exactly at inputs at which the measured computation is defined, and (b) it is decidable whether a given value is indeed the measure of resource corresponding to a given input.

However, we note that the system's impressive time and space complexities are testament not to the system's efficiency, but to the inability of traditional, Turing-machine complexity theory to accommodate certain physical computers; we suggest that the notions of [3] better formalize the system's complexity.

Acknowledgements. We thank Bob Coecke and Joël Ouaknine (at Oxford) for their support and supervision, the IWNC reviewers for their detailed comments, and Rebecca Palmer (at Leeds) for noticing the omission rectified in footnote 7.

References

1. Adleman, L.M.: Molecular Computation of Solutions to Combinatorial Problems. Science 266, 1021–1024 (1994)
2. Blakey, E.: An Analogue Solution to the Problem of Factorization. Oxford University Computing Science Research Report CS-RR-07-04 (2007),
   ftp://ftp.comlab.ox.ac.uk/pub/Documents/techreports/RR-07-04.pdf
3. Blakey, E.: On the Computational Complexity of Physical Computing Systems. Unconventional Computing proceedings, pp. 95–115 (2007),
   http://users.ox.ac.uk/~quee1871/uc07_paper.pdf
4. Blakey, E.: System and Method for Finding Integer Solutions. United States patent application 20070165313 (2007)
5. Blum, M.: A Machine-Independent Theory of the Complexity of Recursive Functions. J. of the Assoc. for Computing Machinery 14(2), 322–336 (1967)
6. Bovet, D.P., Crescenzi, P.: Introduction to the Theory of Complexity. Prentice Hall, Englewood Cliffs (1994)
7. Brent, R.P.: Recent Progress and Prospects for Integer Factorisation Algorithms. In: Du, D.-Z., Eades, P., Sharma, A.K., Lin, X., Estivill-Castro, V. (eds.) COCOON 2000. LNCS, vol. 1858, pp. 3–20. Springer, Heidelberg (2000)
8. Church, A.: An Unsolvable Problem of Elementary Number Theory. American J. of Math. 58, 345–363 (1936)
9. Miehle, W.: Link-Length Minimization in Networks. Operations Research 6(2), 232–243 (1958)
10. Shor, P.W.: Polynomial Time Algorithms for Prime Factorization and Discrete Logarithms on a Quantum Computer. SIAM J. Computing 26, 1484–1509 (1997)
11. Sipser, M.: Introduction to the Theory of Computation. PWS (1997)

Toward a Representation of Hybrid Functional Petri Nets by MP Systems

Alberto Castellini, Giuditta Franco*, and Vincenzo Manca

Verona University, Computer Science Dept.,
Strada Le Grazie 15, 37134 Verona, Italy
{alberto.castellini,giuditta.franco,vincenzo.manca}@univr.it

Abstract. In this work we analyse and compare Hybrid Functional Petri Nets [10], an extension of Petri Nets [12] for biopathways simulation, and Metabolic P Systems [8,9]. An introduction to both of them is given, together with highlights about respective similarities and differences for biopathways modelling. The case study of glycolytic pathway with the *lac* operon gene regulatory mechanism was modeled by traditional Petri Nets in [6] and recently by Hybrid Functional Petri Nets in [10,4]. This model is here mapped into an MP system having the same dynamics.

Keywords: Metabolic P systems, Petri Nets, biological dynamics.

1 Introduction

Biological processes can be seen as networks of selective and non-linear interactions among biochemical elements or complexes, having different functions and producing coherent behaviours. Some interesting models alternative to traditional Ordinary Differential Equations (ODE) are based on rewriting systems, coming from the context of formal language theory, where biochemical elements correspond to symbols and chemical reactions to rewriting rules defined on commutative strings (also called multisets). Namely, P systems provide multisets of objects and sets of rewriting rules within a hierarchical membrane structure [11].

A class of P systems which proved to be significant and successful to model dynamics of biological phenomena related to metabolism in biological systems has been given by *Metabolic P systems*, also called MP systems [8]. Their evolution is computed by a deterministic algorithm called *metabolic algorithm* [1], based on the *mass partition principle* which defines the transformation rate of object populations (rather than single objects), according to a suitable generalization of chemical laws. The dynamics of some well known biological systems have already been investigated by mapping their classical ODE models to the ODE-equivalent MP systems [5]. A few significant processes modeled by MP systems so far include the Belousov-Zhabotinsky reaction (in the Brusselator formulation), the Lotka-Volterra dynamics, the circadian rhythms and the mitotic cycles in early amphibian embryos [1,9].

---

* Corresponding author.

Y. Suzuki et al. (Eds.): IWNC 2007, PICT 1, pp. 28–37, 2009.

In this context, it seems natural to wonder which is the relationship between discrete models of biological phenomena and computational models. In particular, "what is computation, if we restrict ourself to a framework of modeling?". This is in fact a different perspective than that of natural computing, where the work of biological systems is exploited to perform a computation (e.g., by means of DNA or bacteria). Here we rather ask if the biological dynamics of our models can be called "computation".

MP systems represent a class of dynamical systems, as well as grammars, cellular automata, Lindenmayer systems, and Kauffman networks do. Indeed, any computational system can be seen as a dynamical system, where the states correspond to the system configurations and the dynamics is given by the computation (driven by the transitions). Dynamical systems instead, are more general than computational systems, namely because the global system dynamics can be known even if the step by step transition rules are unknown. Another difference is that the dynamics of a system modeling a biological process works differently than how a traditional computation does. Indeed, the effect of a dynamics is mainly to consume resources in order to keep the system alive, while a computation has the goal to produce an output corresponding to a given input. A computation is characterized by the three phases of uploading an input, running of the computation, and downloading the output, while a dynamics differently "exploits" input and output information to produce a behaviour, that is to guarantee some properties and regularities to the systems. In other words, the main point of a computation is in its termination (the result), whereas a dynamics is interesting as long as it is non-terminating (i.e., *how* it allows the system to survive).

Petri Nets [12] (introduced as logic circuits to describe concurrency in artificial systems, such as operative systems or event-driven systems) have recently been employed to model biological pathways [3,4,6] and in particular metabolic processes. The recent development of MP systems theory, based on fluxes [7] shows deep similarities with a novel Petri Nets extension, named *Hybrid Functional Petri Nets* (HFPN) [10], introduced to overcome the drawbacks of its traditional model for the biopathways simulation. This work starts a thorough comparison between the formalisms of MP systems and HFPN, in order to highlight similarities, differences, and feasibilities to model biochemical systems.

Some basic principles of MP systems are introduced in the next Section 2, while in Section 3 a formal description of the HFPN (graphical) model is proposed. In this paper we briefly report an MP system equivalent to the HFPN given in [10,4] to model the glycolytic pathway with the *lac* operon gene regulatory mechanism. It is presented in Section 4 together with the mapping we implemented and a comparison of the respective simulations.

2   MP Systems

MP systems are deterministic P systems developed to model dynamics of biological phenomena related to metabolism. The notion of MP system we consider here is essentially based on [8,9].

Definition 1 (MP system). *An MP system is a construct [7]:*

$$M = (X, V, R, \tau, Q, q_0, \Phi, \nu, \sigma)$$

where:

1. *X is a finite set of **substances** (the types of molecules). Sometimes, when the context avoids any possible confusion, a symbol x for a substance represents also the quantity associated to x in the current state;*
2. *V is a finite set of **parameters**, equipped with a set of functions $H = \{h_1, h_2, \ldots, h_{|V|}\}$ regulating their respective time evolution.*
3. *R is a finite set of **reactions**, i.e., pairs of strings over X (represented, as usual, in the arrow notation);*
4. *τ is the **temporal interval** between two consecutive states;*
5. *Q is the set of **states**, that is, the functions $q : X \cup V \to \mathbb{R}$ from substances and parameters to real numbers. If we assume some implicit orderings among the elements of X, V and an observation instant i ranging in the set of natural numbers, the state q at the instant i can be identified as a vector $q_i = (x_1[i], x_2[i], \ldots, v_1[i], v_2[i], \ldots)$ of real numbers, constituted by the values which are assigned, by the state q, to the elements of these sets;*
6. *$q_0 \in Q$ is the **initial state**, that is, $(X[0], V[0]) = q_0$;*
7. *Φ is a set of **regulation functions** ϕ_r one-to-one associated to each rule $r \in R$. These functions define the evolution of the substances according to the following autonomous first-order difference equation (called metabolic algorithm), where $X[i]$ and $V[i]$ are respectively the vectors of substances quantities and parameters at step i, A_R is the stoichiometric matrix entirely deduced by the reactions of R, and U is the vector of **fluxes** $U[i] = (\varphi_r(X[i], V[i])|r \in R)$:*

$$X[i+1] = A_R \times U[i] + X[i] \tag{1}$$

8. *ν is a natural number which specifies the number of molecules of a (conventional) mole of M, as **population unit** of M;*
9. *σ is a function which assigns to each $x \in X$, the **mass** $\sigma(x)$ of a mole of x (with respect to some measure unit).*

MP graphs, introduced in [9], are a natural representation of MP systems modelling biochemical reactions, as bipartite graphs with two levels, in which the first level describes the *stoichiometry* of reactions, while the second level expresses the *regulation* which tunes the flux of every reaction (i.e. the quantity of chemicals transformed at each step) depending on the state of the system (see for example Figure 3).

3 Formalization of Hybrid Functional Petri Nets

HFPN inherit the graph model representation from the discrete Petri Nets, which is a mathematical representation of discrete distributed systems. They add the continuous *places* and *transitions* (from the Hybrid Petri Nets [3]), which proved to be useful to model, respectively, concentrations and reactions of biological systems. A software[1] has also been developed to compute biological simulation by HFPN [4].

---

[1] Cell Illustrator Project web site: http://www.genomicobject.net

In the following we briefly report the intuitive (graphical) definition of HFPN models just as given in [10], and then we propose a formalization of them. In general, a (discrete or continuous) *place* P_γ contains a certain (natural or real) number m_γ of *tokens*, while (discrete or continuous) *transitions* (e.g., T in Figure 1) define *firing rules*, that move tokens from input places to output places. Finally, three kinds of *arcs* connect places and transitions by pointing out the firing direction and the quantity of tokens (*speeds*) moved by the transitions. Only *normal* arcs are able to move the tokens, and their labels represent strict lower bound conditions for the transition firing. *Inhibitory* and *test* arc labels respectively represent upper bound and lower bound conditions that must be satisfied to activate the transition firing.

In Figure 1 the functioning of an HFPN (continuous) transition T_c is displayed. The **input arcs** a_1, a_2, a_3, a_4 are directed from a place to the transition. The **output arcs** b_1 and b_2 are directed from the continuous transition to a continuous place and they can be only of *normal* type. No activation labels are expected for these arcs.

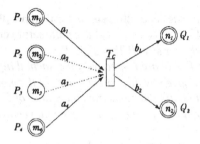

Fig. 1. An HFPN continuous transition [10]. T_C is a continuous transition, P_1, P_2, P_4, Q_1, Q_2 are continuous places, P_3 is a discrete place; m_1, m_2, m_3, m_4, n_1 and n_2 represent the content of the corresponding places. Labels a_2, a_3 denote test arcs, the other are normal arcs.

In general [10], a (continuous or discrete) transition T specifies three functions: *i)* the **firing condition** given by a predicate $c(m_1(i), \dots, m_p(i))$ (if T is continuous, as long as this condition is true T fires continuously; if T is discrete, whenever the condition is true T gets ready to fire), *ii)* a nonnegative function $f_j(m_1(i), \dots, m_p(i))$ for each input arc a_j, called **firing speed** of **consumption** of the (real, integer) number of tokens removed by firing from P_j through arc a_j, and *iii)* a nonnegative (continuous, or integer) function $g_j(m_1(i), \dots, m_p(i))$ called **production speed** for each output arc b_j, that specifies the number of tokens added by firing to Q_j through arc b_j. If a_j is a test or an inhibitory input arc, then we assume $f_j \equiv 0$ and no amount of tokens is removed from P_j through the input arc a_j. If $[b_j](i)$ denotes the amount of tokens added to Q_j at time i through the output arc b_j of a continuous transition, then $g_j(m_1(i), \dots, m_p(i))$ represents the fluctuation of $b_j(i)$ in one step.

Moreover, for discrete transitions, the **delay function** is given by a nonnegative integer valued function $d(m_1(i), \dots, m_p(i))$. If the firing condition gets satisfied at time i, the corresponding transition fires after a number of steps equal to its delay $d(m_1(t), \dots, m_p(t))$. If the firing condition has changed during the delay time, the transition T looses the chance of firing.

A time unit is assumed, called **Petri time**, in terms of which the firing speeds and the discrete transition *delays* (waiting time before firing) are given. In the case that simulation granularity must be increased, a fraction of Petri time named **sampling interval** is considered.

An interesting difference between discrete and continuous transitions is the firing policy. A discrete transition moves the expected amount of tokens (equal to the firing speed value) in only one step of the sampling interval, while the continuous transition moves it in one Petri time unit, though step by step with respect to the sampling interval. Therefore, in one Petri time, both kinds of transition have moved the same amount of tokens but in a different way.

More formally, HFPN can be defined as in the following.

Definition 2 (HFPN). *An HFPN is a construct:*

$$N = (P, T_1, T_2, I, E, S, m_0, Pt, SI, D, C, F, G)$$

where:

1. $P = \{p_1, \ldots p_n\}$ *is a finite set of* **discrete** *or* **continuous places;**
2. $T_1 = \{t_1, \ldots t_k\}$ *and* $T_2 = \{t_{k+1}, \ldots t_z\}$ *are finite sets of* **continuous** *and* **discrete transitions** *respectively; let us call* $T = T_1 \cup T_2$;
3. $I \subseteq P \times T$ *and* $E \subseteq T \times P$ *are respectively the* **normal input arcs** *and the* **output arcs** *of the transitions, given by the stoichiometry of the modeled system;*
4. S *is the set of* **states**, *that are functions from the places of* P *to real numbers, where the state* m *at the time* i *can be identified as the real vector* $P[i] = (m_1(i), m_2(i), \ldots, m_n(i))$;
5. $m_0 \in S$ *is the* **initial state**, *that is,* $m_0 = P[0]$;
6. Pt *is the time unit of the model (related to that one of the modeled real system), called* **petri time**, *whereas* SI *is the* **sampling interval**, *which represents the number of petri times between two computational steps;*
7. $D = \{d_{k+1}, \ldots, d_z\}$ *is a finite set of* **delays**, *given by nonnegative functions* $d_j : S \to \mathbb{R}$ *which specify the time that the transition* t_j *must wait before firing;*
8. $C = \{c_1, \ldots c_z\}$ *is a set of* **firing conditions**, *given by boolean functions on the states* $c_j : S \to \{0, 1\}$ *which control the activation of the corresponding transition* t_j;
9. $F = \{f_1, \ldots, f_{|I|}\}$ *is a set of* **consumption firing speeds**, *given by non-negative functions* $f_x : S \to \mathbb{R}$, *where* $x = (p_\gamma, t_j)$, *that specify the quantity that the transition* t_j *can remove from the places* p_γ *in the state* $P[i]$. *For all* $x = (p_\gamma, t_j)$ *in which* p_γ *is a discrete place, we have* $f_x : S \to \mathbb{N}$;
10. $G = \{g_1, \ldots, g_{|E|}\}$ *is a set of* **production firing speeds**, *given by non-negative functions on the states* $g_y : S \to \mathbb{R}$, *where* $y = (t_j, p_\gamma)$, *that specify the quantity that the transition* t_j *can add to the places* p_γ *in the state* $P[i]$. *For all the* $y = (t_j, p_\gamma)$ *in which* p_γ *is a discrete place we have* $g_y : S \to \mathbb{N}$.

The following algorithm computes the dynamics of an HFPN, providing the sequence of states up to $P[h + 1]$, for $h \in \mathbb{N}$, of any system $N = (P, T_1, T_2, I, E, S, m_0, Pt, SI, D, C, F, G)$. First, the algorithm initializes the functions l_j for all the discrete transitions t_j (instrs 2 and 3). These functions are defined by the algorithm itself in order to control the delay waiting for the discrete transitions.

HFPN Dynamics to compute the first $h + 1$ consecutive states of N

HFPN-Evolution(N,h+1)

1. **begin**
2. **for** $j = k + 1, \ldots, z$ **do**   // $t_j \in T_2$
3.   **if** $d_j(m_0) = 0$ **then** $l_j(0) = 1$ **else** $l_j(0) = 0$;

4. **for** $i = 0, \ldots, h + 1$ **do**

5. **for** $\gamma = 1, \ldots, n$ **do** $m_\gamma(i + 1) := m_\gamma(i)$;
6. **for** $j = 1, \ldots, k$ **do**   // $t_j \in T_1$
7.   **if** $c_j(P[i]) = 1$ **then**
8.   **for** $\gamma = 1, \ldots, n$ **do**
9. $x := (p_\gamma, t_j)$;
10. $y := (t_j, p_\gamma)$;
11.   **if** $x \in I$ **then** $m_\gamma(i + 1) := m_\gamma(i + 1) - f_x(P[i]) \cdot SI$;
12.   **if** $y \in E$ **then** $m_\gamma(i + 1) := m_\gamma(i + 1) + g_y(P[i]) \cdot SI$;

13. **for** $j = k + 1, \ldots, z$ **do**   // $t_j \in T_2$
14.   **if** $l_j(i) = 0$ **then**
15.   **if** $c_j(P[i]) = 1$ **then** $l_j(i + \frac{d_j(P[i])}{SI} - 1) := 1$;
16.   **for** $k = 1, \ldots, \frac{d_j(P[i])}{SI} - 2$ **do**
17. $l_j(i + k) := 2$;
18.   **else** $l_j(i + 1) := 0$;
19.   **if** $l_j(i) = 1$ **then**   // t_j is ready to fire
20.   **if** $c_j(P[i]) = 1$ **then**   //firing
21.   **for** $\gamma = 1, \ldots, n$ **do**
22. $x := (p_\gamma, t_j)$;
23. $y := (t_j, p_\gamma)$;
24.   **if** $x \in I$ **then** $m_\gamma(i + 1) := m_\gamma(i + 1) - f_x(P[i])$;
25.   **if** $y \in E$ **then** $m_\gamma(i + 1) := m_\gamma(i + 1) + g_y(P[i])$;
26.   **if** $d_j(P[i]) > 0$ **then** $l_j(i + 1) := 0$;
27.   **else** $l_j(i + 1) := 1$;
28. **write** $(m_1(i + 1), m_2(i + 1), \ldots, m_n(i + 1))$
29. **end**

In order to compute the state of a given HFPN system, the algorithm checks the discrete transitions in the previous state. In fact, each of them can be either waiting for its condition to be true or for the delay to pass in order to fire, otherwise it can be ready to fire. This information is kept by the function l_j for each discrete transition t_j, then all the values $l_j(1), l_j(2), \ldots, l_j(h)$ and consequently all the states $P[1], P[2], \ldots, P[h]$ need to be computed. For each of the instants $1, \ldots, h$, the state $P[i + 1]$ is initialized by the current state $P[i]$ (instr 5), and then processed by the firings as in the following.

There are two main for cycles (instrs 6 and 13): the first one controls the application of the continuous transitions (from T_1) and the second one controls the application of the discrete transitions (from T_2) which are equipped with delay functions. By the first of these for cycles (instr 6), each continuous transition with true condition fires, and the contents of the involved places are consequently modified (instrs 11 and 12). In each place connected to the transition, by an arc of I, the content decreases of $f_x(P[i]) \cdot SI$ (instr 11), and in each place to which the transition is connected, by an arc of E, the content increases of $g_y(P[i]) \cdot SI$ (instr 12).

In the last for cycle (instr 13), the firing of discrete transitions t_j is ruled firstly by the value of a corresponding function l_j (instrs 14 and 19) and secondarily by the boolean value of the corresponding condition c_j (instrs 15 and 20). If a transition t_j has a null delay, its function l_j is identically equal to 1 (instr 27).

In the case of delay $d_j(P[i])$ greater than zero, if l_j at the time i has value 0 (instr 14), it means that the transition has already fired or the condition c_j has never been true yet. As soon as the condition is true, the function l_j is set to 2 for each time of the next d_j steps, and it is set to 1 at the time the transition will be ready to fire (after the delay). Then, the transition fires only if the condition is true (instr 20). At this point the function l_j is set to 0 (denoting that the transition is waiting for the condition to be true).

HFPN is an intrinsically parallel model which assumes the simultaneous firing of all the transitions in every computational step. The algorithm presented below, however, is a sequential pseudo-code that obtains an equivalent evolution of the system, at the step i, if the quantity of tokens contained in each place p_γ is greater or equal to the sum of the quantities actually taken from the same place. This is an assumption considered more or less explicitly in all the HFPN literature.

We note the structure complexity of this algorithm with respect to the simplicity of the finite difference equation which computes the MP dynamics (Eq. 1). This aspect is not only a matter of elegance, but allows us to develop mathematical theories [7] for investigating dynamical features of biological systems.

4   The *lac* Operon Gene Regulatory Mechanism and Glycolytic Pathway

Glycolytic pathway is the network by which some organisms obtain carbon from glucose. The E. coli bacterium synthesizes carbon both from glucose and lactose but it uses lactose only in the case of glucose lack. If the bacterium grows in an environment with both glucose and lactose, then it consumes only the glucose, but if the environment contains only lactose, then E. coli starts to synthesize special enzymes that metabolize lactose by transforming it in glucose for the glycolytic pathway [4].

A specific regulation mechanism placed on the *lac* operon allows the expression of the suitable genes for this particular situation. Figure 2 shows the dual control of *lac* operon (represented by the horizontal line) along which i) the I gene produces a *repressor* protein at a constant rate, ii) the *promoter* region allows the RNA polymerase to trigger for the operon transcription, iii) the *operator* region matches with the repressor protein to inhibit the transcription, and iv) the Z, Y and A genes produce the enzymes for the synthesis of glucose from lactose inside the cell.

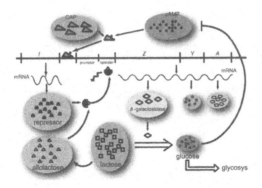

Fig. 2. The regulatory mechanism of glycolytic pathway in E. coli [10]

The pathway described above was first modeled by the traditional Petri nets [6] and recently an HFPN model has been developed in [10,4]. Namely, every substance has been modeled by a place, every chemical reaction by a transition, and the related reactivities and thresholds have been mapped to the firing speeds and conditions. It was assumed that

$$f_{(p_\gamma, t_j)}(s_i) = \bar{f}_j(s_i) \cdot w_{\gamma,j} \quad \text{and} \quad g_{(t_j, p_\gamma)}(s_i) = \bar{f}(s_i)_j \cdot w_{\gamma,j} \qquad (2)$$

where $w_{\gamma,j} \in \mathbb{N}$, $\gamma = 1, \ldots, |P|$, $j = 1, \ldots, |T|$. In (2), $\bar{f}_j$ denotes a common function among all the consumption and production firing speeds of the transition t_j, while $w_{\gamma,j}$ represents the weight of the arc (p_γ, t_j) or (t_j, p_γ).

We mapped the HFPN model to the MP system represented in Figure 3, having the same temporal evolution, by applying the following mapping procedure. Intuitively, every place p_γ has been replaced by a substance x_γ having the same initial value, every transition t_j has been mapped to a rule r_j, and a parameter v_j with an initial value $\frac{d_j(m_0)}{SI} - 1$ has been generated for every discrete transition. The firing speeds have been mapped, together with their firing conditions c_j, to both the corresponding regulation functions φ_j and the stoichiometric matrix elements $a_{\gamma,j}$. Finally, for every discrete transition t_j we defined a function h_j which controls the evolution of the respective delay parameter v_j.

More formally, given any Hybrid Functional Petri Net $N = (P, T_1, T_2, I, E, S, m_0, Pt, SI, D, C, F, G)$, an MP system $M = (X, V, R, \Phi, H, Q, q_0, \nu, \sigma, \tau)$ having the same dynamics can be obtained by the following mapping.

- $X := P$. Places p_j of N are mapped into substances x_j of M, for $j = 1, \ldots, n$;
- $V := \{v_1, \ldots v_{z-k}\}$. Elements of T_2 (discrete transitions t_j) are mapped into parameters (v_{j-k}), having initial values related to the corresponding delays from D $(\frac{d_j(m_0)}{SI} - 1$, with $j = k+1, \ldots, z)$, and evolving according to the functions in H (see below);
- $R := T$. The transitions of N are mapped into the rules of M, and the stoichiometric A is obtained by the graphical structure of the HFPN;
- The time interval τ has to be the HFPN time between two computational steps, that is $\tau := SI \cdot Pt$.

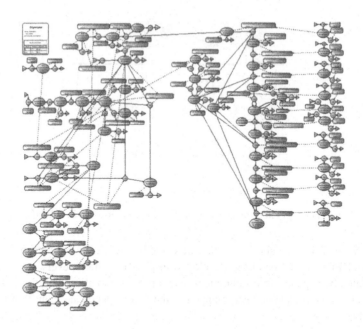

Fig. 3. An MP system model of the *lac* operon gene regulatory mechanism and the glycolytic pathway obtained by the mapping of the HFPN network in [4]

- $Q = \{q \mid q : X \cup V \to \mathbb{R}, q_{|X} \in S\}$. Every state of M assigns real values to both the n substances (corresponding to the places of N) and the $z - k$ parameters (which keep track of delays);
- $q_0 := (m_0, V[0])$, where m_0 is the initial state of M and $V[0] = (v_1(0), \dots, v_{z-k}(0)) = (\frac{d_{k+1}}{SI} - 1, \dots, \frac{d_z}{SI} - 1)$, with $d_{k+1}, \dots, d_z \in D$.
- $\Phi = \{\varphi_1, \dots, \varphi_k, \varphi_{k+1}, \dots, \varphi_z\}$. Regulation functions are deduced from T which has k continuous transitions and $z - k$ discrete transitions. They are defined as $\varphi_j(q) = c_j(q) \cdot \bar{f}_j(q) \cdot SI$ for $j \in \{1, \dots, k\}$ and as $\varphi_j(q) = (c_j(q) \wedge q(v_{j-k}) \le 0) \cdot \bar{f}_j(q)$ for $j \in \{k+1, \dots, z\}$, where $q \in Q$, and $\bar{f}_j$ is deduced according to Equation (2).
- $H = \{h_1, \dots, h_{z-k}\}$. Each function $h_j(q)$ rules the evolution of the parameter v_j as a "counter of waiting", set by the delay $d_{j+k}(q) \in D$, which supports the "simulation" of the discrete transition t_{j+k}. H functions can be defined as:

$$h_j(q) = (q(v_j) \le 0)(d_j(q)/SI - 1) + \\ + ((c_j(q) \wedge q(v_j) = d_j(q)/SI - 1) \vee \\ \vee (0 < q(v_j) < d_j(q)/SI - 1))(q(v_j) - 1).$$

- The value ν and the mass function σ of M are arbitrarily chosen with respect to the modeled system, indeed they do not have any correspondence in N. They work as biological data measurements, thus they do not effect the system dynamics.

A formalization of this mapping (together with a mapping form MP systems to HFPN models) besides its proof of correctness will be eventually described in an extended version of this paper.

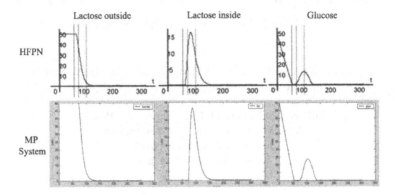

Fig. 4. Simulation result of the *lac* operon gene regulatory mechanism and glycolytic pathway modeled by the HFPN in [4] (top) and by the MP system

The MP system of Figure 3 has been designed using the simulator *MPsim*, a Java-based software tool developed in [1,2], that provided the concentration evolutions in the bottom of Figure 4. By the comparison between the HFPN evolution of lactose and glucose (top) and the corresponding MP system evolution (bottom) we observe a perfect equivalence of the two models. Other equivalence results have been obtained by the simulation of some mutants of the *lac* operon corresponding to pathological conditions.

References

1. Bianco, L., Fontana, F., Franco, G., Manca, V.: P Systems for Biological Dynamics. In: Ciobanu, G., et al. (eds.) Applications of Membrane Computing. Springer, Heidelberg (2006)
2. Bianco, L., Manca, V., Marchetti, L., Petterlini, M.: Psim: a Simulator for Biomolecular Dynamics Based on P Systems. In: IEEE Congress on Evolutionary Computation, September 25-28 (2007)
3. David, R., Alla, H.: On Hybrid Petri Nets. Discrete Event Dynamic Systems 11(1-2), 9–40 (2001)
4. Doi, A., Fujita, S., Matsuno, H., Nagasaki, M., Miyano, S.: Constructing Biological Pathway Models with Hybrid Functional Petri Nets. In Silico Biology 4, 23 (2004)
5. Fontana, F., Manca, V.: Discrete Solution of Differential Equations by Metabolic P Systems. Theoretical Computer Science 372, 165–182 (2007)
6. Hofestädt, R.: A Petri Net Application of Metabolic Processes. Journal of System Analysis, Modeling and Simulation 16, 113–122 (1994)
7. Manca, V.: Discrete Simulations of Biochemical Dynamics. In: Garzon, M., Yan, H. (eds.) Preliminary Proceedings of the 13th International Meeting on DNA Computing, Memphis, TN, June 4-8, University of Memphis (2007)
8. Manca, V.: The Metabolic Algorithm for P Systems: Principles and Applications. TCS 404(1-2), 142–155 (2008)
9. Manca, V., Bianco, L.: Biological Networks in Metabolic P Systems. BioSystems 91(3), 489–498 (2008)
10. Matsuno, H., Tanaka, Y., Aoshima, H., Doi, A., Matsui, M., Miyano, S.: Biopathways Representation and Simulation on Hybrid Functional Petri Net. In Silico Biology 3, 32 (2003)
11. Păun, G.: Membrane Computing. An Introduction. Springer, Berlin (2002)
12. Reisig, W.: Petri Nets: An Introduction. EATCS, Monographs on Theoretical Computer Science (1985)

Computing with Feedforward Networks of Artificial Biochemical Neurons

Huub M.M. ten Eikelder, Sjoerd P.M. Crijns, Marvin N. Steijaert,
Anthony M.L. Liekens, and Peter A.J. Hilbers

Eindhoven University of Technology, P.O. Box 513,
5600 MB Eindhoven, The Netherlands
h.m.m.t.eikelder@tue.nl
http://bmi.bmt.tue.nl/

Abstract. Phosphorylation cycles are a common motif in biological intracellular signaling networks. A phosphorylaton cycle can be modeled as an *artificial biochemical neuron*, which can be considered as a variant of the artificial neurons used in neural networks. In this way the artificial neural network metaphor can be used to model and study intracellular signaling networks. The question what types of computations can occur in biological intracellular signaling networks leads to the study of the computational power of networks of artificial biochemical neurons. Here we consider the computational properties of artificial biochemical neurons, based on mass-action kinetics. We also study the computational power of feedforward networks of such neurons. As a result, we give an algebraic characterization of the functions computable by these networks.

Keywords: Cell signaling networks, phosphorylation cycle, artificial neurons.

1 Introduction

Biochemical signal transduction networks are responsible for the intracellular communication, amplification and interpretation of real-time stimuli [1]. As an illustration of a signaling network, *E. coli* controls its motor proteins in order to move to high nutrient concentrations, based on sensory information from the environment [2,3]. For the implementation of its biochemical circuitry, the cell makes use of a network of phosphorylation cycles. The phosphorylation reaction (i.e., the addition of a phosphate group to a substrate protein) is mediated by a kinase enzyme, whereas the inverse reaction (dephosphorylation) is catalyzed by a phosphatase enzyme. The substrate protein itself, either phosphorylated or dephosphorylated, may also act as a kinase or phosphatase in other phosphorylation cycles, thus leading to a chain or network of phosphorylation cycles, see Figure 1. In higher organisms, these networks may be composed of 80 or more interacting kinases and phosphatases, allowing for increased computational complexity within a single cell [4]. Understanding of these complex biochemical networks has important pharmaceutical applications and may yield new computational applications [5,6].

Y. Suzuki et al. (Eds.): IWNC 2007, PICT 1, pp. 38–47, 2009.

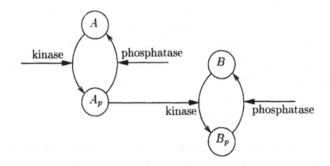

Fig. 1. Two coupled phosphorylation cycles, A_p acts as kinase for the $B - B_p$ cycle

The use of the Artificial Neural Networks metaphor for understanding signaling networks has been mentioned by Arkin and Ross[7], Bray[8] and Bhalla [9]. Hjelmfelt et al. [10] describe a chemical neuron and use it to perform logic operations. In this paper we focus on the possibilities of chemical neurons for computing real-valued functions. We introduce a simple artificial chemical neuron, as a model for a phosphorylation cycle. Concentrations of kinases and phosphatases serve as the excitatory and inhibitory inputs of such a neuron. The enzymatic rate constants at which the substrate is phosphorylated and dephosphorylated serve as the weights on connections between the biochemical neurons. By assuming mass-action reaction kinetics (i.e., assuming that the reaction rate equals the product of the concentrations of the reactants and the rate constant of the reaction) and omitting the influence of intermediate complexes, we can easily compute the transfer function of an artificial biochemical neuron, which is further on referred to as *mass-action neuron*. Biological signaling networks consisting of coupled phosphorylation cycles can now be modeled as networks of mass-action neurons. To investigate the type of computations that can be performed by biological signaling networks we study the computational power of networks of mass-action neurons. Here we restrict ourselves to layered feedforward networks. It turns out that, in contrast to networks of classical artificial neurons, a simple algebraic description of the functions computable by such a network can be given.

2   Phosphorylation Cycles

Consider a phosphorylation cycle where an enzyme X facilitates the phosphorylation of a species A into the phosphorylated form A_p. The phosphorylated form A_p can again decay to the dephosphorylated form A. Assuming an excess of phosphate donors, these two reactions can be written as

$$A + X \xrightarrow{w} A_p + X$$
$$A_p \xrightarrow{v} A,$$

where w and v are the rate constants of the two reactions. Let a and a_p be the concentrations of A and A_p respectively and let x be the enzyme concentration. Clearly the sum of the concentrations of A and A_p is constant, i.e., $a + a_p = c$, where the constant c depends on the initial condition. Using mass-action kinetics the dynamics of the phosphorylation cycle is described by

$$\frac{da_p}{dt} = w(c - a_p)x - va_p.$$

Since all rates and concentrations are positive, the solution of this linear differential equation tends exponentially fast to the equilibrium concentration $\widehat{a}_p$ given by

$$\widehat{a}_p = c\frac{wx}{v + wx}.$$

Hence the "output concentration" $\widehat{a}_p$ depends hyperbolically on the input concentration x.

The generalization to multiple inputs is trivial. Suppose that the phosphorylation of A into the phosphorylated form A_p can be facilitated by a number of kinase enzymes, say $X_1, \ldots, X_n$, with corresponding rates $w_1, \ldots, w_n$. The corresponding chemical reactions are

$$A + X_1 \xrightarrow{w_1} A_p + X_1$$

$$\vdots$$

$$A + X_n \xrightarrow{w_n} A_p + X_n$$

$$A_p \xrightarrow{v} A.$$

Again $a + a_p = c$, i.e., the sum of the A and A_p concentrations is constant. The differential equation for this system is

$$\frac{da_p}{dt} = \sum_{i=1}^{n}[w_i x_i(c - a_p)] - va_p.$$

The solution of this differential equation goes exponentially fast to the equilibrium concentration given by

$$\widehat{a}_p = c\frac{\sum_{i=1}^{n} w_i x_i}{v + \sum_{i=1}^{n} w_i x_i}.$$

Hence the output concentration $\widehat{a}_p$ is now a hyperbolic function of a weighted combination of the inputs $x_1, \ldots, x_n$. Note that, since v and all w_i are positive reaction rate constants, $\widehat{a}_p$ is always an increasing function of each input x_i.

To obtain decreasing functions we consider the dephosphorylation of A_p into A. So far this dephosphorylation has a fixed rate constant v. Suppose that this dephosphorylation is also facilitated by phosphatase enzymes $Y_1, \ldots, Y_m$ with rate constants $v_1, \ldots, v_m$. The chemical reactions are now

$$A + X_1 \xrightarrow{w_1} A_p + X_1$$

$$\vdots$$

$$A + X_n \xrightarrow{w_n} A_p + X_n$$

$$A_p + Y_1 \xrightarrow{v_1} A + Y_1$$

$$\vdots$$

$$A_p + Y_m \xrightarrow{v_m} A + Y_m.$$

This system is described by the differential equation

$$\frac{da_p}{dt} = \sum_{i=1}^{n} w_i x_i (c - a_p) - \sum_{j=1}^{m} v_j y_j a_p,$$

with equilibrium concentration

$$\widehat{a_p} = c \frac{\sum_{i=1}^{n} w_i x_i}{\sum_{j=1}^{m} v_j y_j + \sum_{i=1}^{n} w_i x_i}.$$

Clearly $\widehat{a_p}$ is increasing as function of the x_i and decreasing as function of the y_i.

3 The Mass-Action Neuron

The last system above is the basic form of the artificial mass-action neuron. However, we shall not make a distinction between kinases and phosphatases. Hence both phosphorylation and dephosphorylation are facilitated by enzymes $X_1, \ldots, X_n$, with rate constants $w_1, \ldots, w_n$ for the phosphorylation and $v_1, \ldots, v_n$ for the dephosphorylation. This allows for an easier mathematical description. A biologically more realistic model with the same functionality can also be constructed, but it leads to a more complex network. Furthermore, we assume that there is also phosphorylation by an enzyme with a constant concentration and dephosphorylation by an enzyme with a constant concentration. In biological terms this means that these enzymes are not regulated by the network. Since we can absorb the constant concentration of these two enzymes in the corresponding rate constants, this means there is a reaction $A_p \xrightarrow{v_0} A$ with rate constant v_0 and a reaction in the opposite direction with rate constant w_0. The total set of chemical reactions is thus given by

$$A \xrightarrow{w_0} A_p$$

$$A + X_1 \xrightarrow{w_1} A_p + X_1$$

$$\vdots$$

$$A + X_n \xrightarrow{w_n} A_p + X_n$$

$$A_p \xrightarrow{v_0} A$$

$$A_p + X_1 \xrightarrow{v_1} A + X_1$$

$$\vdots$$

$$A_p + X_n \xrightarrow{v_n} A + X_n.$$

The corresponding equilibrium concentration of a_p is given by

$$\hat{a}_p = c\frac{w_0 + \sum_{i=1}^n w_i x_i}{v_0 + \sum_{i=1}^n v_i x_i + w_0 + \sum_{i=1}^n w_i x_i}.$$

The enzyme concentrations $x_1, \ldots, x_n$ are the inputs to the mass-action neuron, and its output y is defined as the equilibrium concentration $\hat{a}_p$. Note that, since input and output of a mass-action neuron represent concentrations, they cannot be negative. The various rate constants $w_0, \ldots, w_n$ and $v_0, \ldots, v_n$ and the total concentration c are parameters, that describe the behavior of the neuron. If we

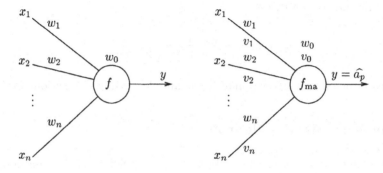

Fig. 2. Schematic description of a standard artificial neuron (left) and a mass-action neuron (right)

compare the mass-action neuron with the standard artificial neuron, as depicted in Figure 2, we see that for each input x_i there are now two parameters, viz., the parameter w_i that describes the contribution of x_i to the phosphorylation process, and the parameter v_i, that describes the contribution of x_i to the dephosphorylation process. Moreover, in contrast to the standard artificial neuron the mass-action neuron has two bias parameters, viz., w_0 and v_0. In principle, the total concentration c is also a parameter of the artificial neuron. However, we shall see that in most cases we can assume $c = 1$.

To stress the similarity with the classical artificial neuron, we rewrite the output y of the mass-action neuron as

$$y = f_{\text{ma}}(p/q), \quad \text{with} \quad f_{\text{ma}}(z) = c\frac{z}{z+1}, \tag{1}$$

where

$$p = w_0 + \sum_{i=1}^n w_i x_i \quad \text{and} \quad q = v_0 + \sum_{j=1}^n v_j x_j.$$

If we consider f_{ma} as the transfer function of the neuron, then the difference with the classical artificial neuron is that the input of f_{ma} is not a linear combination of the inputs, but a quotient of two such linear combinations, both with positive coefficients.

Mass-action neurons can be combined in various network types. In this paper we only consider layered feedforward networks, i.e., networks consisting of a number of layers, where the neurons in layer r have the outputs of the neurons in layer $r-1$ as their inputs. The inputs for the neurons in the first layer are the actual network inputs, the outputs of the neurons in the last layer are the actual network outputs. Each neuron has its own unique phosphorylation cycle, and a species that is phosphorylated in one neuron, and thus is the output of that neuron, can act as an enzyme in a neuron in the next layer.

4 Computational Power of Feedforward Networks of Mass-Action Neurons

We now discuss the computational power of feedforward networks of mass-action neurons. We consider the case of a network with only one input. It is clear from (1) that a mass-action neuron with one input can compute any function of the form

$$y = c \frac{w_0 + w_1 x}{v_0 + w_0 + (v_1 + w_1)x}. \tag{2}$$

Since c is the total concentration of the species A and its phosphorylated form A_p, it must be a positive number. Furthermore, the parameters w_0, w_1, v_0 and v_1 are rate constants, which means that they are nonnegative. To simplify the analysis of the computational power, we assume that all rate constants are strictly positive. It is easily seen that with this assumption the mass-action neuron can compute every function of the form

$$y = C \frac{x + a}{x + b},$$

where C, a and b are positive constants.

Next we consider a feedforward network with one hidden layer with n mass-action neurons and one mass-action output neuron, see Figure 3. We assume that the parameters of the neurons in the first layer are selected such that the output of neuron i in the hidden layer is given by $(x+a_i)/(x+b_i)$, where a_i and b_i are positive constants.

The output y of the whole network is then given by

$$y = c \frac{w_0 + \sum_{i=1}^n w_i(x + a_i)/(x + b_i)}{v_0 + w_0 + \sum_{i=1}^n (v_i + w_i)(x + a_i)/(x + b_i)}.$$

Multiplying numerator and denominator by $\prod_{i=1}^n (x + b_i)$ yields

$$y = c \frac{w_0 \prod_{i=1}^n (x + b_i) + \sum_{i=1}^n w_i(x + a_i) \prod_{j=1, j \neq i}^n (x + b_j)}{u_0 \prod_{i=1}^n (x + b_i) + \sum_{i=1}^n u_i(x + a_i) \prod_{j=1, j \neq i}^n (x + b_j)}, \tag{3}$$

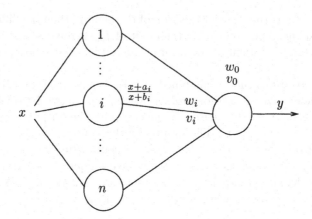

Fig. 3. Feedforward network with mass-action neurons

where $u_i = v_i + w_i$. Hence the output y of the network is a function that is the quotient of two n-th degree polynomials. Clearly, each of these polynomials has positive coefficients.

We now study the class of functions that can be computed by the network in more detail. Clearly, both numerator and denominator of (3) are linear combinations of the $n + 1$ polynomials $p_0, p_1, \ldots, p_n$ given by

$$p_0(x) = \prod_{j=1}^{n}(x + b_j)$$

$$p_i(x) = (x + a_i) \prod_{j=1, j \neq i}^{n}(x + b_j) \quad \text{for} \quad i = 1, \ldots, n.$$

So we study linear combinations of the form

$$f(x) = \sum_{i=0}^{n} \lambda_i p_i(x). \tag{4}$$

We say that the coefficients a_i and b_i satisfy property P if $b_i \neq b_j$ for all $i, j = 1, \ldots, n$ with $i \neq j$, and if $a_i \neq b_i$ for all $i = 1, \ldots, n$.

Lemma 1. *Suppose the constants a_i and b_i satisfy property P. Then every n-th degree polynomial $f(x)$ with real coefficients can be written in the form (4).*

Proof. Let f be an n-th degree polynomial. Define the coefficients λ_i by

$$\lambda_i = \frac{f(-b_i)}{p_i(-b_i)} = \frac{f(-b_i)}{(a_i - b_i)\prod_{j=1, j \neq i}^{n}(b_j - b_i)}.$$

Let the polynomial g be given by $g(x) = f(x) - \sum_{i=1}^{n} \lambda_i p_i(x)$. Clearly g is again a polynomial with degree at most n. It is easily verified that $g(-b_i) = 0$ for $i = 1, \ldots, n$. Since all b_i are mutually different, this means that $g(x) = \lambda_0 \prod_{j=1}^{n}(x + b_j)$. Hence we have shown that $f(x)$ can be written as (4).

This lemma does not imply that, for positive a_i and b_i that satisfy property P, the network can compute every quotient of two n-th degree polynomials. The reason is that in (3) all coefficients w_i and u_i must be positive. However, for arbitrary polynomials f, the coefficients λ_i found in the proof of Lemma 1 are not necessarily positive. This raises the question which n-th degree polynomials can actually occur in the numerator and denominator of (3). Trivially, if the a_i and b_i are positive, all such polynomials must have positive coefficients themselves. However, not all polynomials with positive coefficients can be generated, as can be concluded from the following theorem. In the sequel we shall use the nomenclature of control theory, where a polynomial that has only roots with negative real parts is called a *stable* polynomial.

Theorem 1. *Suppose the constants a_i and b_i are positive. Then every n-th degree polynomial $f(x)$ of the form (4) with coefficients $\lambda_i \geq 0$ is stable.*

Proof. Since all constants a_i and b_i are positive, the polynomials $p_0, \ldots, p_n$ are stable by construction. Unfortunately, a linear combination of stable polynomials with positive coefficients is not necessarily stable. In [11] it is shown that every linear combination of the form (4), with all $\lambda_i \geq 0$, is stable if each possible combination $\lambda p_i(x) + (1 - \lambda)p_j(x)$ is stable for $0 \leq \lambda \leq 1$. This condition is easily checked. First we consider combinations with $i = 0$. It is easily seen that

$$\lambda p_0(x) + (1 - \lambda)p_j(x) = (x + \lambda b_j + (1 - \lambda)a_j) \prod_{k=1, k \neq j}^{n} (x + b_k).$$

Clearly, for all λ with $0 \leq \lambda \leq 1$ this polynomial is stable. Next consider combinations with $i, j > 0$. Then

$$\lambda p_i(x) + (1 - \lambda)p_j(x) = q(x) \prod_{k=1, k \neq i, k \neq j}^{n} (x + b_k),$$

where

$$q(x) = \lambda(x + a_i)(x + b_j) + (1 - \lambda)(x + a_j)(x + b_i).$$

It suffices to check the roots of $q(x)$. Elementary algebra shows that $q(x) = x^2 + Ax + B$ with A and B positive. This implies that the roots of $q(x)$ have negative real parts.

Application of this theorem to numerator and denominator of (3) (where we assumed that $a_i > 0$, $b_i > 0$, $w_i \geq 0$ and $v_i \geq 0$) implies that both terms must be stable polynomials. Hence the feedforward network shown in Figure 3 computes quotients of stable n-th degree polynomials. Since the stable polynomials are a proper subset of the polynomials with positive coefficients, this also implies that numerator and denominator of (3) cannot be arbitrary polynomials with positive coefficients.

Finally, we remark that not every pair of stable polynomials can occur as numerator and denominator of (3). That can easily be seen as follows. Suppose

$f(x)$ and $g(x)$ are two stable polynomials of degree n. Assume that they can occur as numerator and denominator of (3). That means both $f(x)$ and $g(x)$ are a linear combination of $p_0(x), p_1(x), \ldots, p_n(x)$, both with positive coefficients. Hence the polynomial $f(x) + g(x)$ is also a linear combination of $p_0(x), p_1(x), \ldots, p_n(x)$ with positive coefficients. Theorem 1 implies that $f(x) + g(x)$ is again a stable polynomial. However, there exist examples of stable polynomials for which their sum is not a stable polynomial, see for instance [11]. Consequently, not every pair of stable polynomials $f(x)$ and $g(x)$ can occur as numerator and denominator of (3).

5   Discussion and Future Work

We have shown that a feedforward network with one hidden layer that contains n mass-action neurons can compute quotients of n-th degree polynomials. Moreover, both polynomials, i.e., in numerator and denominator, have only roots with negative real parts. This result shows that feedforward networks with mass-action neurons can compute very complicated functions, indicating that even relatively simple biological networks, without any feedback mechanism, can already perform complicated computations.

An obvious generalization is the case of layered feedforward networks with more than one hidden layer. Suppose such a network has r hidden layers, with n_i mass-action neurons in the i-th hidden layer. For the situation with one input x it is easily shown that each output neuron can compute a function $P(x)/Q(x)$ where $P(x)$ and $Q(x)$ are both polynomials with degree N given by

$$N = \prod_{i=1}^{r} n_i.$$

Moreover, if all reaction rates are positive, then the coefficients of P and Q are again positive. In case of one hidden layer the polynomials P and Q are stable, i.e., they have only roots with negative real parts. A straightforward generalization of this last result to the multiple hidden layer case seems not possible. Training of feedforward networks with mass-action neurons can be done by a variant of the well-known error backpropagation algorithm. In this way it is in principle possible to find parameters such that the behavior of a feedforward network of mass-action neurons corresponds to actual biological measurements.

The transfer function of a mass-action neuron with one input is given by (2). The input x is used as kinase, with coefficient w_1, and as phosphatase, with coefficient v_1. From a biochemical point of view it is somewhat strange that one enzyme catalyzes both the phosphorylation reaction and the dephosphorylation reaction. This type of enzymes can be avoided by introducing additional chemical neurons, that compute copies of intermediate values. Then the output of one chemical neuron can be used as a kinase, while the equivalent output of its copy can be used as a phosphatase. In fact, a similar situation occurs when using feedforward networks of classical artificial neurons. There it is not uncommon that the output of one neuron is connected to neurons in the next layer with positive as well as negative weights. However, actual biological neurons are either excitatory, which means they excite all their target neurons, or inhibitory, which means they inhibit all their target neurons.

Our description of a phosphorylation cycle with the law of mass-action does not take into account the formation of intermediate complexes. A more precise approach, which also models the substrate-enzyme complex, leads to the Michaelis-Menten kinetics [12]. Using the description of the equilibrium of a phosphorylation cycle given by Goldbeter and Koshland [13], it is possible to define a *Michaelis-Menten neuron*, which can be seen as a biologically more realistic model. Biological networks of phosphorylation cycles will often have a more complicated structure than layered feedforward networks. The neural networks metaphor relates these biological networks to recurrent neural networks, consisting of chemical neurons. We plan to report on these various aspects in a forthcoming paper.

Acknowledgement. This work is supported by the European Commission through the Evolving Cell Signaling Networks in Silico (ESIGNET) project of the Sixth Framework Programme.

References

1. Cohen, P.: The Regulation of Protein Function by Multisite Phosphorylation, a 25 Year Update. Trends Biochem. Sci. 25(12), 596–601 (2000)
2. Bray, D.: Bacterial Chemotaxis and the Question of Gain. Proc. Nat. Acad. Sci. 99(1), 123–127 (2002)
3. Rao, C., Arkin, A.: Control Motifs for Intracellular Regulatory Networks. Annu. Rev. Biomed. Eng. 3, 391–419 (2001)
4. Gomperts, B.D., Kramer, I.M., Tatham, P.E.R.: Signal Transduction. Academic Press, London (2002)
5. Kitano, H.: Systems Biology, A Brief Overview. Science 295(5560), 1662–1664 (2002)
6. Ball, P.: Chemistry Meets Computing. Nature 406, 118–120 (2000)
7. Arkin, A., Ross, J.: Computational Functions in Biochemical Reaction Networks. Biophys. J. 67(2), 560–578 (1994)
8. Bray, D.: Protein Molecules as Computational Elements in Living Cells. Nature 376(6538), 307–312 (1995)
9. Bhalla, U.: Understanding complex signaling networks through models and metaphors. Progr. Biophys. Mol. Biol. 81, 45–65 (2003)
10. Hjelmfelt, A., Weinberger, E., Ross, J.: Chemical Implementation of Neural Networks and Turing Machines. Proc. Nat. Acad. Sci. 88(24), 10983–10987 (1991)
11. Bartlett, A., Hollot, C., Lin, H.: Root Locations of an Entire Polytope of Polynomials: It Suffces to Check the Edges. Math. Control Signals Systems 1, 61–71 (1988)
12. Dixon, M., Webb, E.C.: Enzymes. Longman (1979)
13. Goldbeter, A., Koshland, D.: An amplified sensitivity arising from covalent modification in biological systems. Proc. Nat. Acad. Sci. 78(11), 6840–6844 (1981)

Information Processing with Structured Chemical Excitable Medium

J. Gorecki[1,2], J.N. Gorecka[3], Y. Igarashi[1], and K. Yoshikawa[4]

[1] Institute of Physical Chemistry, Polish Academy of Science,
Kasprzaka 44/52, 01-224 Warsaw, Poland
[2] Faculty of Mathematics and Natural Sciences,
Cardinal Stefan Wyszynski University,
ul. Dewajtis 5, 01-815 Warsaw, Poland
[3] Institute of Physics, Polish Academy of Sciences,
Al. Lotnikow 36/42, 02-668 Warsaw, Poland
[4] Department of Physics, Graduate School of Science,
Kyoto University, Kyoto 606-8502, Japan

Abstract. It is well known that an excitable medium can be used for information processing with pulses of excitation. In such medium messages can be coded or in the number of pulses or in the sequences of times separating subsequent excitations. Information is processed as the result of two major effects: interactions between pulses and interactions between a pulse and the environment. The properties of excitable medium provide us with a number of features remaining those characterizing biological information processing. For example, pulses of excitation appear as the result of an external stimulus and they can propagate in a homogeneous medium with a constant velocity and a stationary shape dissipating medium energy.

In the paper we focus our attention on a quite specific type of nonhomogeneous medium that has intentionally introduced geometrical structure of regions characterized by different excitability levels. Considering numerical simulations based on simple reaction-diffusion models and experiments with Bielousov-Zhabotinsky reaction we show that in information processing applications the geometry plays equally important role as the dynamics of the medium. A chemical realization of simple information processing devices like logical gates or memory cells are presented. Combining these devices as building blocks we can perform complex signal processing operations like, for example, excitation counting. We also demonstrate that a structured excitable medium can perform sensing functions because it is able to determine a distance separating observer from the source or sense the rate of changes in excitability level. Talking about the perspectives we present ideas for programming information processing medium with excitation pulses.

Keywords: Information processing, excitability, BZ-reaaction, Oregonator.

Y. Suzuki et al. (Eds.): IWNC 2007, PICT 1, pp. 48–69, 2009.
© Springer 2009

1   Introduction

Unconventional methods of information processing attract increasing scientific attention nowadays. Motivation for research in this field comes from the common believe that, with respect to a number of problems, unconventional computing offers an interesting alternative to the classical von Neumann computer architecture [1], based on the clock controlled sequence of executed instructions and data flow. In some cases there are strong arguments supporting the statement that unconventional algorithms should be able to work faster and more efficiently than the classical ones. Most of unconventional algorithms are based on the optimum use of the physical properties of medium in which information is processed (computing medium). As an example let us recall quantum computing [2] or DNA-computing [2][3]. The advantage of these information processing techniques is related to high parallelism of operations performed by the medium.

Among many branches of unconventional computation one can recognize the field called reaction-diffusion computing [4]. The name comes after the mathematical description of time evolution of computing medium. In the most standard case a spatially distributed chemical reactor works as the medium. The state of reactor is defined by local concentrations of reagents involved at all points. The interactions between reactions proceeding in different places occur via diffusion of molecules, so the evolution equations include both reaction and diffusion terms. It has been found that the medium with Bielousov-Zhabotynsky (BZ) reaction [5] is one of interesting candidates for investigation, because its state is characterized by color and so it can be easily observed and described.

First successful applications of BZ-reaction for information processing were related with the use of homogeneous medium and nonhomogeneous initial conditions. For example, a membrane filled with reagents of an oscillatory photosensitive BZ-reaction was applied for direct image processing [6]. The processed picture was introduced as space dependent phase of chemical oscillations, fixed by the initial illumination level generated by the projected image. The effects of image processing can be easily observed as periodic changes in local color of the solution. The fact that in BZ reaction rapid changes of color are separated by long periods when colors slowly evolve is especially useful for image processing. Oscillatory BZ-reaction can perform such operations as darkness inversion, contour enhancement or detail removing as illustrated in Fig. 1. Of course, the medium processes an image in a highly parallel way, transforming all points at the same real time [7].

Any spatially distributed chemical medium that has more than one steady state can be easily used as a classifier over the set of all possible initial conditions. It is natural to say that two initial conditions belong to the same class if in both cases the system converges to the same steady state as the result of time evolution. Alternatively, one can say that the set of initial conditions is naturally divided into basins of attraction of system dynamics. A spectacular example of chemical medium that can be used for such classification has been described in [9,10], where the authors defined chemical dynamics and identified initial conditions for which a region characterized by a high concentration of a selected reagent converged to the shape similar to a particular symbol from Latin [9] or Hebrew [10] alphabets.

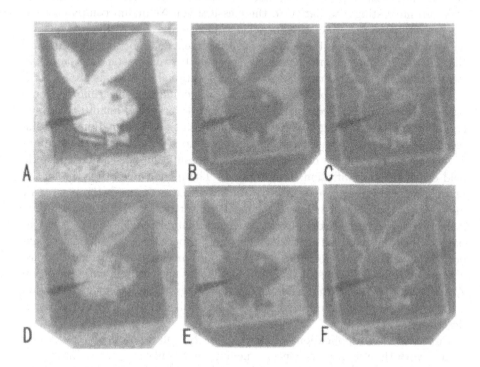

Fig. 1. Image transformations during the time evolution of oscillating medium with Ru-catalyzed BZ reaction. (A) - initially projected image, (B-F) a sequence of snapshots showing image processing during a typical time evolution [8].

Excitability is a wide spread type of nonequilibrium behavior [5,11] observed in numerous chemical systems including BZ reaction [12], CO oxidation on Pt [13], or combustion of gases [14]. The excitable systems share common properties. They have a stable stationary state (the rest state) they remain in if they are not perturbed. The rest state is stable with respect to small perturbations, so when the system is excited with a moderate kick the perturbation from the steady state uniformly decays in time. However, if an excitation is sufficiently large then system response is strongly nonlinear and it is accompanied by large changes in concentrations of species involved observed as pronounced extremum of concentration. If an excitable medium is spatially distributed then excitations can propagate in space. Unlike mechanical waves that dissipate the initial energy and finally decay, traveling excitation pulses use the energy of medium to propagate and dissipate it. In a typical homogeneous spatially distributed excitable medium an excitation pulse generated by a local perturbation converges to its stationary shape independent of the initial condition. Usually the maximum of activator is followed by the maximum of inhibitor, an agent that slows down reaction rates. As the result of high inhibitor concentration the system is refractory after excitation, which means that it takes a certain recovery time before it can be excited again. For propagating pulses it means that the region behind a pulse is in the refractory regime characterized by a large amplitude of inhibitor and it cannot be re-excited. One of the consequences of a long refractory period is annihilation of colliding counterpropagating pulses.

The excitable medium with homogeneous properties can be used to solve geometrically oriented problems. For example, by initiating excitation pulses from a set of points and observing where pulses coming from different sources collide we can compute the corresponding Voronoi diagram [4]. Similarly, studying collision of pulses initiated at a contour we can calculate its skeleton [4]. And yet again, both computing the Voronoi diagram and the skeleton is performed by the system in parallel, with the use of excitations spreading thought the whole computing medium.

In the following we focus our attention on a quite specific type of nonhomogeneous excitable medium that has an intentionally introduced geometrical structure of regions characterized by different excitability levels. Historically, one of the first applications of structured chemical medium for information processing was the solution of the problem of finding the shortest path in a labyrinth [15]. In order to do it the labyrinth should be constructed of excitable channels, where pulse propagation is stable separated by non-excitable regions where, due to different reaction regime, excitations are rapidly dumped. Such structure does not allow for interactions between pulses propagating in different channels. An excitable medium solves the labyrinth problem using the most efficient, highly parallel prairie fire algorithm. If we excite a labyrinth at point A and observe that an excitation arrives at point B after time t then we know that the path linking the points is shorter than vt, where v is the speed of propagating pulse. During the time evolution after initial excitation pulses can collide and annihilate, but the one that propagates along the shortest path has always unexcited medium in front so its speed can be regarded as constant if the labyrinth is large enough and if the influence of corners can be neglected when compared with the time of propagation in the straight channels. It is quite remarkable that the complexity of labyrinth structure has no influence on the time required for an excitation to travel between A and B, but it depends only on the distance between the considered points.

The information processing with a homogeneous, unstructured medium looks attractive; the medium is so smart that it can solve a problem after the initial condition is set. This fire and forget approach can be applied to the number of problems listed above, but in a general case a homogeneous computing medium may need an intelligent observer who controls the progress of information processing and provides necessary feedback if the things go wrong. It seems that structured excitable computing media allow for simpler realization of a larger number of computational tasks than unstructured ones. Excitable channels direct pulses to the required regions without external feedbacks. Rings that allow for stable rotation of excitation pulses can be used as memory cells. Annihilation of counterpropagating pulses in a channel can be applied to control information flow and provides a feedback necessary for self-learning. If we assign logic values to the presence of pulses then chemical phenomena related to interaction of pulses can be interpreted as logical operations. Within such framework chemical reactors that perform non-trivial information processing functions can be constructed.

In the following we present a few examples illustrating that in information processing applications the medium geometry plays equally important role as its dynamics. As the result devices that perform complex signal processing operations can be build with structured medium characterized by relatively simple kinetics of reactions involved. We discuss chemical realizations of basic information processing systems like logical gates or memory cells and we show that by combining these devices as building blocks the medium can perform complex signal processing operations like for example counting of excitations arriving to a selected point.

2   Basic Information Processing Operations with Structured Excitable Medium

In the introduction we discussed a few applications of chemical medium for information processing. In each application listed (image processing, labyrinth solving, classification of initial states, geometrical constructions) the translation of chemical phenomena into information was different. In the following we focus our attention on quite unified approach that relates information with traveling pulses. A propagating pulse is interpreted as a bit of information moving in space. A train of pulses forms a signal. In some cases we use even more restricted approach interpreting the excitation as the logical TRUE state and the rest state as the logical FALSE [16].

Excitable chemical systems offer a number of generic properties that seem to be useful for processing information coded in excitation pulses. Information can be transformed via interaction of pulses with the medium or via pulse-to-pulse interactions. The results presented below are mainly based on numerical simulations of time evolution of pulses in computing medium. Numerical simulations play an important role, because the models are relatively simple and easy to compute, but still accurate enough to give a correct qualitative agreement with experimental results. Many results discussed below have been confirmed in experiments with Ru-catalized Bielousov-Zhabotynsky reaction. For this reaction simulations can be done with different variants of the Oregonator model [17], [18], [19], [20]. For example, for three variable model, the evolution equations are:

$$\varepsilon_1 \frac{\partial u}{\partial t} = u(1 - u) - w(u - q) + D_u \nabla^2 u$$

$$\frac{\partial v}{\partial t} = u - v$$

$$\varepsilon_2 \frac{\partial w}{\partial t} = \phi + fv - w(u + q) + D_w \nabla^2 w$$

Here u, v and w denote dimensionless concentrations of the following reagents: $HBrO_2$, $Ru(4,4'\text{-dm-bpy})_3^{3+}$ and Br^-, respectively. In the considered system of equations u is an activator and v is an inhibitor. The units of space and time in equations given above are dimensionless and they have been chosen to scale the reaction rates to a simple, rate constant free form. The diffusion of ruthenium catalytic complex is neglected because it is much smaller than those of the other reagents. Reaction dynamics is described by a set of parameters: f, q, ε_1, ε_2 and ϕ. Among them ϕ represents the rate of bromide production caused by illumination and it is proportional to the applied light intensity. Illumination is an inhibiting factor of photosensitive BZ reactions so, by adjusting the proper ϕ as a function of space variables, we can easily define regions with the required excitability level, like for example excitable stripes surrounded by non-excitable neighborhood. The mobile reagents can freely diffuse between areas of both types, so a pulse propagating in the excitable region can penetrate into a non-excitable part and disappears after some distance.

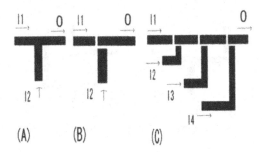

Fig. 2. Logical OR gate constructed with a chemical computing medium. The black regions are excitable, the white space is non-excitable. (A) - simple junction, (B) - a junction in which interactions between inputs are excluded, (C) - the logical OR operation over multiple arguments.

Angle dependent penetration of non-excitable barriers is one of the effects useful in information processing. Let us consider an excitable medium divided by a non-excitable stripe. It can be easily shown that the maximum width of non-excitable stripe for which a pulse propagating on one side of a stripe generates an excitation on the other side depends on the angle between the wave vector of the pulse and the normal to the stripe. A pulse with wave vector perpendicular to the stripe can excite a medium separated by a wider stripe than a pulse that propagates along the stripe [21]. Thus the width of a gap separating excitable regions can be adjusted such that it is transparent to perpendicular pulses, but not to those propagating along the gap. This property is frequently used in chemical realizations of information processing devices. For example, such gaps can be applied to construct a junction of two excitable input channels that automatically stops interactions of pulses arriving from one input channel on the other one. If we just join to input channels I1 and I2 into one output O (see Fig. 2A) then a pulse arriving form one of input channels would separate at the junction and resulting excitations enter both the output channel and the other input channel perturbing arriving signals. However, if we consider input channels separated by non-excitable gaps with carefully selected widths as illustrated in Fig. 2B then the propagation of pulses from the inputs to the output is not perturbed, but there is no interference between inputs because a signal arriving from one input channel always propagate parallel to the gap separating it from the other input channel. Of course the structure from Fig. 2B works as the logical OR gate if logical values are assigned to pulses. By copying this structure (see Fig. 2C) we obtain a device that returns the logical alternative of multiple input signals. Here different lengths of input channels fix the right timing of arriving input signals. They have to be adjusted such that a single input state does not produce multiple output pulses.

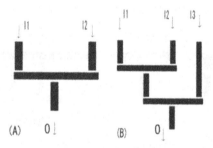

Fig. 3. (A) - the logical AND gate. The black regions are excitable, the white space is non-excitable. (B) - the geometry of a gate calculating logical AND operation over 3 arguments.

Another interesting and useful property of structured excitable medium is related to its answer to combined excitations. Activations introduced by multiple excitations generate a stronger perturbation than this resulting from a single pulse. Let us consider two parallel channels separated by a non-excitable gap that is non-penetrable for a pulse propagating in one of channels. It can be shown [22]

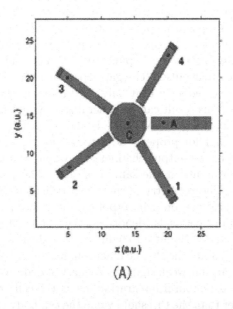

(A)

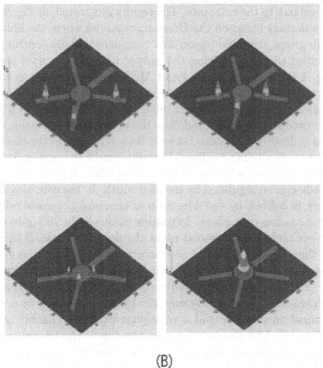

(B)

Fig. 4. Artificial chemical neuron constructed with structured excitable medium. (A) - the geometry of excitable (dark) and non-excitable areas (white); (B) - the excitation of neuron body by 3 arriving stimuli.

that the width of such gap can be selected to allow for cross excitation of one channel by two counterpropagating pulses in the other one. This feature of structured excitable medium allows for easy realization of the AND gate as illustrated in Fig 3A. Here the gaps separating inputs from the horizontal channel can be penetrated by perpendicular pulses. The gap separating the output channel and the horizontal one is selected such that only excitation generated by annihilating pulses can cross it. This result can be generalized to multiple inputs and the geometry of channels in 3-input AND gate is shown on Fig. 3B. Moreover, it can be demonstrated that for properly adjusted geometry of excitable regions one can get excitation of the output channel only when the required number of excitations arrive from inputs at the same time [23]. Thus, such device works as an artificial neuron. The geometry of chemical artificial neuron is inspired by the structure of biological neuron [24]. Topologically in both structures we find a number of narrow input channels (dendrites) that transmit excitations to the larger cell body connected with output channels. One of the studied realizations is illustrated on Fig. 4 [23]. In the chemical neuron, like in real neurons, dendrites (input channels 1-4) transmit weak signals which are added together through the processes of spatial and temporal integration inside the cell body. If the aggregate excitation is larger than the threshold value the cell body gets excited, if not the cell body relaxes to the rest state. The results illustrated on Fig. 5 come from numerical simulations based on the Oregonator model where the illumination of the surrounding non-excitable region was considered as the control parameter. It can be verified that by applying the proper illumination level the structure shown in Fig. 4 can work as a four input McCulloch-Pitts neuron with any required integral threshold [23]. Illumination of the non-excitable regions can be used as a control parameter because it influences the amplitude of a pulse propagating in an excitable channel (and thus the strength of excitation). Activator concentration is fixed by a balance between its production in the channel and its diffusion to the surrounding medium. Illumination of the non-excitable regions fixes the concentration of activator so it controls diffusion rate. Alternatively the pulse amplitude can be regulated by channel width. In the case of wide channels this amplitude is defined by the dynamics of chemical processes only and it is close to that for pulses on a plane. In narrow channels the diffusion of activator towards non-excitable neighborhood plays the dominant role. If the channel is very narrow then the amplitude of activator may drop below the critical value and a propagating pulse dies. This feature can be used to construct a chemical signal diode [25]. The asymmetry required for unidirectional signal transmission can be introduced by a non-symmetrical junction formed by a rectangular excitable channel on one side and a triangular excitable channel on the other (see D1 on Fig. 11). The distance between the top of the triangle and the side of the rectangle is selected such that a pulse of excitation propagating in the rectangular channel and terminating at its end gives sufficiently strong perturbation to excite the triangle tip and thus the excitation is transmitted. For the same distance the excitation of rectangular channel by a pulse moving towards the top of triangular channel is too small to excite it, because the amplitude of the pulse moving in the triangular part decreases as the result of diffusion to the neighboring non-excitable areas. Therefore, the propagation of a pulse moving from the triangular channel to the rectangular one is terminated.

An interesting example of behavior resulting from refractory region behind a pulse can be observed in a cross-shaped structure build of excitable channels, separated by gaps penetrable for perpendicular pulses [26],[27] shown in Fig. 6. The answer of cross-shaped junction to a pair of pulses arriving from two perpendicular directions was studied as a function of the time difference between pulses. Of course, if the time difference is large pulses propagate independently. If the time difference is small then the cross-junction acts like the AND gate and the output excitation appears in one of the corner areas. However, for a certain time difference the first arriving pulse is able to redirect the second and force it to follow (Fig. 6). The effect is related with uncompleted relaxation of the central area of the junction at the moment when the second pulse arrives. It appears if the size of central area is not larger than the distance traveled by a pulse within the refractory time. Such relation shows a nice match between geometry and properties of dynamics. The pulse redirection seems interesting for programming with excitation pulses, but in practice it requites a high precision in selecting the right time difference.

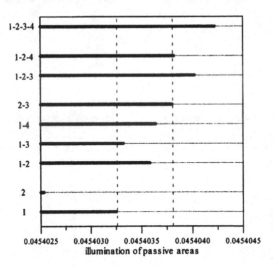

Fig. 5. The response of the neuron to different types of combined excitations as the function of illumination of non-excitable regions. The numbers given on the left list the excited channels. The illuminations for which the neuron body gets excited are marked by a thick line.

Non-excitable barriers in structured medium can play more complex role in information processing then that described above. The problem of barrier crossing by a periodic train of pulses can be seen as an excitation via a periodic

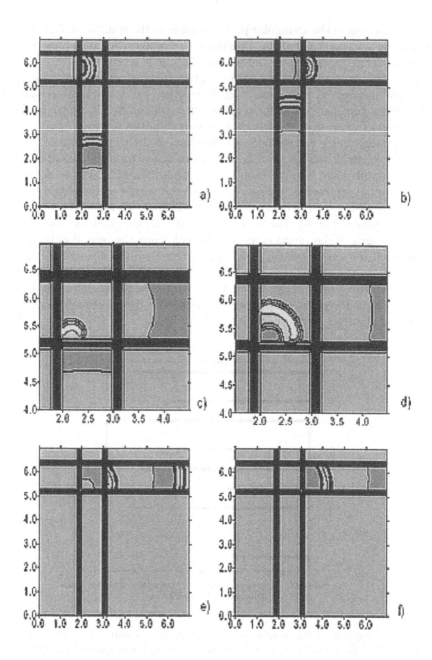

Fig. 6. The distribution of excitable and non-excitable regions in a cross-shaped junction. Here the excitable regions are gray and the non-excitable black. Consecutive figures illustrate an interesting type of time evolution caused by interaction of pulses. Two central figures are enlarged in order to show how uncompleted relaxation influences the shape of the second arriving pulse and changes the direction of its propagation [26].

perturbation of the medium [28]. The answer of the medium is quite characteristic. The firing number as a function of perturbation strength has a devil-staircase-like form. In the case of barrier crossing the strength of excitation behind a barrier generated by an arriving pulse depends on the character of non-excitable medium, on barrier width and on the frequency of the incoming signal (usually, due to uncompleted relaxation of the medium the amplitude of spikes decreases with frequency). A typical, complex frequency transformation after barrier crossing is illustrated in Fig. 7. Many experimental and numerical studies on firing number of a transmitted signal have been published [29], [30], [31], [32]. It is interesting that the shape of regions characterized by the same firing number in the space of two parameters: barrier width and signal frequency is not generic and depends on the type of excitable medium. For example in the case of FitzHugh - Nagumo dynamics trains of pulses with small periods can cross wider barriers than trains characterized by low frequency, for the Rovinsky - Zhabotinsky model the dependence is reversed.

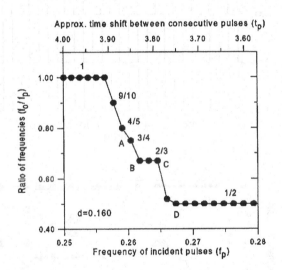

Fig. 7. A typical dependence of firing number as a function of frequency of arriving pulses. The firing number is defined as the ratio between frequency of output signal (f_o) after crossing a non-excitable gap separating excitable channel and the input one (f_p). Results obtained for the FitzHugh - Nagumo model [30].

High sensitivity of transmitted signal frequency with respect to the character of input perturbation can be used to construct a sensor estimating the distance separating the source of periodic excitations from the observer. The idea is illustrated in Fig. 8 [33]. The sensor is build with a number of similar excitable signal channels (in Fig.8A they are numbered 1-4) that are wide enough to ensure a stable propagation of pulses. These sensor channels are separated one from another

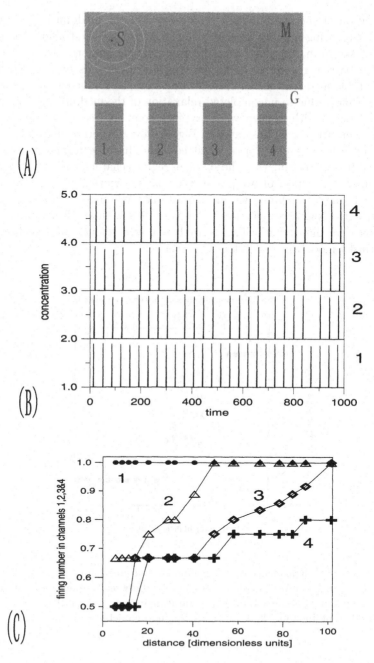

Fig. 8. Schematic illustration of a device sensing the distance separating it from a source of periodic excitations S. (A) - the geometry of excitable (dark) and non-excitable (light) regions. (B) - the signals in sensor channels for the source close to the sensor. (C) - the firing numbers as function of distance separating sensor and the source [33].

by parallel non-excitable gaps that do not allow for the interference between pulses propagating in the neighboring channels. They are also separated from the active medium M by a non excitable sensor gap G. The width of this gap is crucial for sensor sensitivity. If the gap is too wide then no excitation of the medium M can generate a pulse in the sensor channels. If the gap is narrow then any excitation in front of a sensor channel can pass G and create a pulse in the channel so signals in every sensor channel are identical. The width of the gap should be selected such that the firing number (defined as the ratio between the number of pulses that crossed the gap G to the number of pulses of excitation that were created in the medium M) depends on the wave vector characterizing a pulse at the gap in front of channel. If the source of periodic excitations S is close to the array of sensor channels then the wave vectors characterizing excitations in front of various channels are different. Thus, different frequencies of excitations in various channels are expected. On the other hand, if the source of excitations is far away from the gap G then the wave vectors in front of different channels should be almost identical and so the frequencies of excitations in sensor channels would not differ. Therefore, the system shown in Fig. 8A can sense the distance separating it from the source of excitations. If this distance is small the firing numbers in neighboring sensor channels are different and these differences decrease when the source of excitations moves away. The results of simulations (Figs. 8B,C) and experiments [33] confirm it.

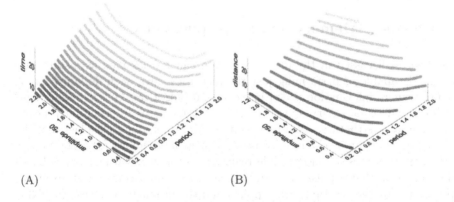

(A)   (B)

Fig. 9. The survival of a pulse propagating in a stripe of medium with time dependent excitability. (A) - the time when the amplitude of propagating pulse decreases below an arbitrarily selected value 0.1, (B) - the distance traveled by the pulse up to this moment.

It has been recently observed [34] that pulse propagation in an excitable medium is sensitive to the rate of temporal changes in excitability level. That survival of a propagating excitation pulse in a medium with increasing illumination depends on the rate of change and, as it may be expected, a pulse dies if the changes are too rapid. Fig. 9 illustrates the phenomenon. We considered a wide stripe of excitable medium with dynamics described by Oregonator model ($f = 3$, $q = 0.002$, $\varepsilon_1 = 0.004$, $\varepsilon_2 = 1$). At the beginning the illumination level is ϕ_0. The pulse of excitation is initiated and we allow it to propagate until it reaches the stationary form. Next illumination level is linearly increased to the value $\phi_1 = 0.1$ slightly above the excitability limit, so the propagating pulse should vanish. Finally if the value of ϕ reaches 0.1 it remains unchanged. Precisely speaking the considered time dependent illumination is:

$\phi(t) = \phi_0$ if $t < T$,
$\phi(t) = \phi_0 + 2 * A * \frac{t}{T}$ if $t \in [0, T]$,
and
$\phi(t) = 0.1$ if $t > T$

where the amplitude of changes is defined as $A = (0.1 - \phi_0)/2$. Figs. 9 A,B illustrate the time after which the maximum value of u in the propagating pulse decreases below an arbitrarily selected value 0.1 and the distance traveled by the pulse up to the moment it happens (u exceeds 0.6 in a stable pulse). Both values are plotted as a function of the period T and amplitude A. It can be seen that for any initial ϕ_0 the time of pulse propagation as well as the distance traveled increase with T. Therefore, a simple observation of the distance traveled by a pulse in a channel which properties change in time brings information on the rate of temporal changes.

3   Chemical Memory and Its Applications

The devices discussed in the previous section can be classified as instant machines [7] capable of performing just the task they have been designed for. A memory where information coded in excitation pulses can be written-in, kept, read-out and, if necessary, erased significantly increases information processing potential of structured excitable medium. Moreover, due to the fact that the state of memory can be changed by a spike, the memory allows for programming with excitation pulses. One possible realization of a chemical memory is based on observation that a pulse of excitation can rotate on a ring-shaped excitable area as long as the reactants are supplied and the products removed [35,36,37]. Therefore, a ring with a number of spikes rotating on it can be regarded as a loaded memory cell. Such memory can be erased by counterpropagating pulses. The idea of memory with loading pulses rotating in one direction and erasing pulses in another has been discussed in [38]. Our later studies [39] were oriented on increase of reliability of ring shaped memory. A large ring can be used to memorize a large amount of information because it has many states corresponding to different numbers of rotating pulses. However, in such case loading the memory with subsequent pulses may fail because the input can be blocked by the refractory tail left by one of already rotating pulses. Therefore, a memory

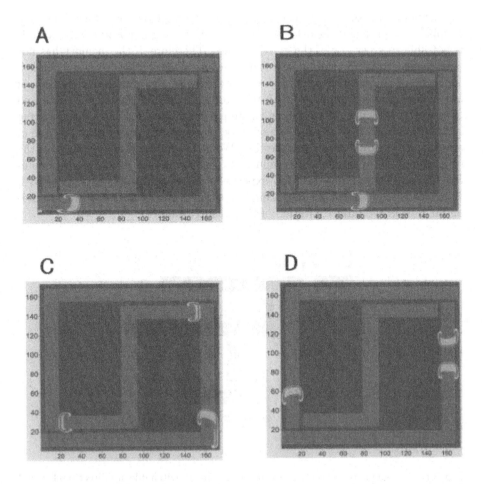

Fig. 10. Four snapshots illustrating simulations of memory erasing by an excitation coming from erasing channel. The memory ring is formed by two L-shaped excitable channels, the Z-shaped erasing channel is inside the ring.

capable of storing just a single bit seems to be more reliable. Such memory has two states: loaded when there is a rotating pulse on the ring and erased when the ring is in the rest state. An example of ring memory is shown in Fig. 10. The red areas define the memory ring composed of two L-shaped excitable areas and Z-shaped erasing channel in the mid of the ring. The blue regions are non-excitable. The excitable areas are separated by gaps penetrable only for pulses propagating perpendicularly. Such choice breaks the symmetry and only excitations rotating counterclockwise are stable. The rotating pulse does not affect the erasing channel because it always propagates parallel to it. The erasing excitation is generated in the center of Z-shaped area and it splits into two erasing pulses (Fig. 10B). These pulses can cross the gaps separating the erasing channel from the memory ring and create a pair of pulses rotating clockwise (Figs. 10 C/D). A spike that propagates clockwise on the memory ring is not stable because it is not able to cross any of the gaps and dies. Therefore, if the memory has not been loaded then an erasing excitation does not load it. On the other hand, if the memory is loaded then pulses rotating clockwise resulting from excitation of the erasing channel annihilate with the loading pulse and the memory is erased (Fig. 10D). The idea of two places where erasing pulses can enter memory ring is used to ensure that at least one of those places is fully relaxed and so one of erasing pulses can always enter the ring. We have confirmed reliable work of the ring memory in a number of computer experiments with random positions of rotating and erasing pulses. A few experiments gave qualitative agreement with simulations: the loaded memory ring preserved information for a few minutes and it was erased after excitation of the erasing channel.

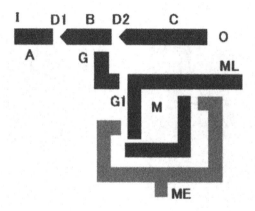

Fig. 11. The geometry of active areas (black) in a switchable unidirectional signal channel. The channel is formed by A, B and C segments. The transmission through the segment B is controlled by the state of memory M.

Using memory described above we can construct more complex devices controlled by excitation pulses. Fig. 11 shows the idea of switchable signal channel. Three segments of active medium A, B and C linked by the signal diodes D1 and D2 form a channel transparent to pulses traveling from the input I to the output O if the memory M is not loaded. The pulses propagating in the channel A-B-C do not interfere with the memory because their wave vectors are parallel to the gap G. When the memory M is activated it periodically sends pulses to the segment B. These pulses enter the segment B through the gap G and after entering they propagate along the passive area in the diode D2. Therefore, they do not excite the segment C. They propagate towards the diode D1 and die at it. If there is a signal coming from the input I then it is annihilated within the section B by these pulses. As the result the system presented in Fig. 11 is a unidirectional signal channel that can be open or closed depending on the state of the memory M, thus it is programmable by pulses coming from the memory load (ML) and the memory erase (ME) channels.

Using structured excitable medium and simple circuits described above one can construct devices, that perform more complex signal processing operations. As an example we present a simple chemical realization of excitation counter. The system returns the number of arriving excitations in any chosen positional representation [22]. Such counter can be assembled from single digit counters. The construction of a single digit counter depends on the representation used. Here we consider the positional representation with the base 3. The geometry of a single digit counter is schematically shown in Fig. 12. Its main elements are two memory cells M_1 and M_2 and two coincidence detectors C_1 and C_2. At the beginning let us assume that none of the memory cells is loaded. When the first pulse arrives through the input channel I_0, it splits at all junctions and excitations enter segments B_0, B_1 and B_2. The pulse that has propagated through B_0 loads the memory cell M_1. The pulses that have propagated through B_1 and B_2 die at the bottom diodes of segments C_1 and C_2 respectively. Thus, the first input pulse loads the memory M_1 and does not change the state of M_2. When M_1 is loaded then pulses of excitation are periodically sent to segments B_0 and C_1 via the bottom channel. Now let us consider what happen when the second pulse arrives. It does not pass through B_0 because it annihilates with the pulses arriving from the memory M_1. The excitations generated by the second pulse can enter B_1 and B_2. The excitation that propagated through B_2 dies at the bottom diode of the segment C_2. The pulse that has propagated through B_1 enters C_1, annihilates with a pulse from memory M_1 and activates the coincidence detector. The output pulse from the coincidence detector loads the memory M_2. Therefore, after the second input pulse both memories M_1 and

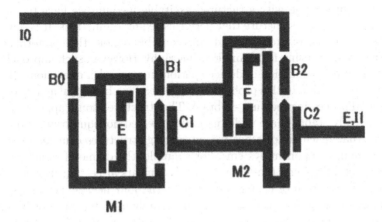

Fig. 12. The counter of excitation pulses that arrive at the input I0. Figure shows the geometry of excitable channels (black) in a single digit counter for the positional representation with the base 3.

M_2 are loaded. If the third pulse arrives the segments B_0 and B_1 are blocked by spikes sent from the memory rings. The generated excitation can enter channel B_2 and its collision with a pulse coming from the memory cell M_2 activates the output channel of C_2. The output signal is directed to the counter of responsible for the digit at next position (I1) and it is also used to erase all memory cells. Thus after the third pulse both memory cells M1 and M2 are erased. The counter shown in Fig. 11 returns a digit in a representation with the base 3 : here 0 is represented by the $(M_1, M_2) = (0, 0)$, 1 by $(1, 0)$, 2 by $(1, 1)$ and the next pulse changes the state of memory cell into $(M_1, M_2) = (0, 0)$. Of course, using $n - 1$ memory cells in a single digit counters we can represent digits of the system with base n. A cascade of single digit counters gives a positional representation of the number of arriving pulses.

4   Discussion

We hope that a number of examples discussed in the paper convince the reader that structured excitable medium can be successfully used for processing information coded in excitation pulses. All the considered systems transform information in an unconventional (non-von Neumann) way, i.e. without an external clock or synchronizing signal that controls the sequence of operations. On the other hand, in many cases the right timing of performed operations is hidden in the geometrical distribution and sizes of excitable regions. What is also important all presented systems perform their functions without any external feedback or control. The described devices can be used as building blocks for more complex systems that process signals formed of excitation pulses. Some of them like the memory cell or pulse counter can be controlled with spikes. Therefore, there is a room for programming and learning. However, for the further development of information processing with structured excitable medium we have to solve the problem of creating a structure that performs required functions. It is quite easy to guess a structure of excitable and non-excitable regions that performs simple tasks and create it using for example lithography. However, such approach looks hard in practical realization of devices performing complex operations. It seems that a better solution to this problem is suggested by a biological analog of structured signal processing medium - a brain. The structure should appear as a thermodynamically stable phase under carefully selected nonequilibrium conditions. We know that much simpler but yet interesting structures come as metastable phases in multicomponent systems. For example, the diamond structure in oil-water-surfactant system, that spontaneously appears at certain thermodynamic conditions has a form of centers linked with the four nearest neighbors. If the reactants corresponding for excitability are soluble in water, but not in oil then the water rich phase forms the structure of excitable channels and processing elements just as the result of thermodynamic conditions. Within a certain range of parameters, such structure is thermodynamically stable. This means that the network has auto-repair ability and robustness against unexpected destruction. Moreover, the structure is three dimensional, what allows for higher density of processing elements than that obtained with classical two-dimensional techniques like for example lithography. In practice we should select the conditions that create the maximum number of connections between processing elements. As the next step their number should be reduced in the process of learning with the use of switchable signal channels for example. Realization of such project is a fascinating subject for our future study.

References

1. Feynman, R.P., Allen, R.W., Heywould, T.: Feynman Lectures on Computation. Perseus Books, New York (2000)
2. Calude, C.S., Paun, G.: Computing with cells and atoms. Taylor and Francis, London (2002)
3. Adleman, L.M.: Molecular computation of solutions to combinatorial problems. Science 266, 1021–1024 (1994)
4. Adamatzky, A., De Lacy Costello, B., Asai, T.: Reaction-Diffusion Computers. Elsevier Science, UK (2005)
5. Kapral, R., Showalter, K.: Chemical Waves and Patterns. Kluwer Academic, Dordrecht (1995)
6. Kuhnert, L., Agladze, K.I., Krinsky, V.I.: Image processing using light-sensitive chemical waves. Nature 337, 244–247 (1989)
7. Rambidi, N.G., Maximychev, A.V.: Towards a Biomolecular Computer. Information Processing Capabilities of Biomolecular Nonlinear Dynamic Media. BioSystems 41, 195–211 (1997)
8. Szymanski, J.: Private information (2008)
9. Kawczynski, A.L., Legawiec, B.: Two-dimensional model of a reaction-diffusion system as a typewriter. Phys. Rev. E 64, 056202(1-4) (2001)
10. Kawczynski, A.L., Legawiec, B.: A two-dimensional model of reaction-diffusion system as a generator of Old Hebrew letters. Pol. J. Chem. 78, 733–739 (2004)
11. Kuramoto, Y.: Chemical Oscillations, Waves, and Turbulence. Springer, Berlin (1984)
12. Mikhailov, A.S., Showalter, K.: Control of waves, patterns and turbulence in chemical systems. Phys. Rep. 425, 79–194 (2006)
13. Krischer, K., Eiswirth, M., Ertl, G.J.: Oscillatory CO oxidation on Pt(110): modelling of temporal self-organization. J.Chem. Phys. 96, 9161–9172 (1992)
14. Gorecki, J., Kawczynski, A.L.: Molecular dynamics simulations of a thermochemical system in bistable and excitable regimes. J. Phys. Chem. 100, 19371–19379 (1996)
15. Steinbock, O., Toth, A., Showalter, K.: Navigating complex labyrinths - optimal paths from chemical waves. Science 267, 868–871 (1995)
16. Toth, A., Showalter, K.: Logic gates in excitable media. J. Chem. Phys. 103, 2058–2066 (1995)
17. Field, R.J., Noyes, R.M.: Oscillations in chemical systems. IV. Limit cycle behavior in a model of a real chemical reaction. J. Chem. Phys. 60, 1877–1884 (1974)
18. Gaspar, V., Bazsa, G., Beck, M.T.: The influence of visible light on the Belousov–Zhabotinskii oscillating reactions applying different catalysts. Z. Phys. Chem(Leipzig) 264, 43–48 (1983)

19. Krug, H.J., Pohlmann, L., Kuhnert, L.: Analysis of the modified complete Oregonator accounting for oxygen sensitivity and photosensitivity of Belousov–Zhabotinskii systems. J. Phys. Chem. 94, 4862–4866 (1990)
20. Amemiya, T., Ohmori, T., Yamaguchi, T.: An Oregonator-class model for photoinduced Behavior in the $Ru(bpy)_3^{2+}$-Catalyzed Belousov–Zhabotinsky reaction. J. Phys. Chem. A. 104, 336–344 (2000)
21. Motoike, I., Yoshikawa, K.: Information Operations with an Excitable Field. Phys. Rev. E 59, 5354–5360 (1999)
22. Gorecki, J., Yoshikawa, K., Igarashi, Y.: On chemical reactors that can count. J. Phys. Chem. A 107, 1664–1669 (2003)
23. Gorecka, J., Gorecki, J.: Multiargument logical operations performed with excitable chemical medium. J. Chem. Phys. 124, 084101 (2006)
24. Haken, H.: Brain Dynamics. Springer Series in Synergetics. Springer, Berlin (2002)
25. Agladze, K., Aliev, R.R., Yamaguchi, T., Yoshikawa, K.: Chemical diode. J. Phys. Chem. 100, 13895–13897 (1996)
26. Sielewiesiuk, J., Gorecki, J.: Chemical impulses in the perpendicular junction of two channels. Acta Phys. Pol. B 32, 1589–1603 (2001)
27. Sielewiesiuk, J., Gorecki, J.: Logical functions of a cross junction of excitable chemical media. J. Phys. Chem. A 105, 8189–8195 (2001)
28. Dolnik, M., Finkeova, I., Schreiber, I., Marek, M.: Dynamics of forced excitable and oscillatory chemical-reaction systems. J. Phys. Chem. 93, 2764–2774 (1989); Finkeova, I., Dolnik, M., Hrudka, B., Marek, M.: Excitable chemical reaction systems in a continuous stirred tank reactor. J. Phys. Chem. 94, 4110–4115 (1990); Dolnik, M., Marek, M.: Phase excitation curves in the model of forced excitable reaction system. J. Phys. Chem. 95, 7267–7272 (1991); Dolnik, M., Marek, M., Epstein, I.R.: Resonances in periodically forced excitable systems. J. Phys. Chem. 96, 3218–3224 (1992)
29. Suzuki, K., Yoshinobu, T., Iwasaki, H.: Unidirectional propagation of chemical waves through microgaps between zones with different excitability. J. Phys. Chem. A 104, 6602–6608 (2000)
30. Sielewiesiuk, J., Gorecki, J.: On complex transformations of chemical signals passing through a passive barrier. Phys. Rev. E 66, 016212 (2002); Sielewiesiuk, J., Gorecki, J.: Passive barrier as a transformer of chemical signal frequency. J. Phys. Chem. A 106, 4068–4076 (2002)
31. Taylor, A.F., Armstrong, G.R., Goodchild, N., Scott, S.K.: Propagation of chemical waves across inexcitable gaps. Phys. Chem. Chem. Phys. 5, 3928–3932 (2003)
32. Armstrong, G.R., Taylor, A.F., Scott, S.K., Gaspar, V.: Modelling wave propagation across a series of gaps. Phys. Chem. Chem. Phys. 6, 4677–4681 (2004)
33. Gorecki, J., Gorecka, J.N., Yoshikawa, K., Igarashi, Y., Nagahara, H.: Sensing the distance to a source of periodic oscillations in a nonlinear chemical medium with the output information coded in frequency of excitation pulses. Phys. Rev. E 72, 046201 (2005)
34. Tanaka, M., Nagahara, H., Kitahata, H., Krinsky, V., Agladze, K., Yoshikawa, K.: Survival versus collapse: Abrupt drop of excitability kills the traveling pulse, while gradual change results in adaptation. Phys. Rev. E 76, 016205 (2007)
35. Lázár, A., Noszticzius, Z., Försterling, H.-D., Nagy-Ungvárai, Z.: Chemical pulses in modified membranes I. Developing the technique. Physica D 84, 112–119 (1995); Volford, A., Simon, P.L., Farkas, H., Noszticzius, Z.: Rotating chemical waves: theory and experiments. Physica A 274, 30–49 (1999)
36. Nagai, Y., Gonzalez, H., Shrier, A., Glass, L.: Paroxysmal Starting and Stopping of Circulatong Pulses in Excitable Media. Phys. Rev. Lett. 84, 4248–4251 (2000)

37. Noszticzuis, Z., Horsthemke, W., McCormick, W.D., Swinney, H.L., Tam, W.Y.: Sustained chemical pulses in an annular gel reactor: a chemical pinwheel. Nature 329, 619–620 (1987)

38. Motoike, I.N., Yoshikawa, K., Iguchi, Y., Nakata, S.: Real–Time Memory on an Excitable Field. Phys. Rev. E 63, 036220 (2001)

39. Gorecki, J., Gorecka, J.N.: On mathematical description of information processing in chemical systems. In: Mathematical Approach to Nonlinear Phenomena; Modeling, Analysis and Simulations, GAKUTO International Series, Mathematical Sciences and Applications, vol. 23, pp. 73–90 (2005) ISBN 4762504327

Wholeness and Information Processing in Biological Networks: An Algebraic Study of Network Motifs

Taichi Haruna* and Yukio-Pegio Gunji

Department of Earth and Planetary Sciences, Faculty of Science, Kobe University
1-1, Rokkodaicho, Nada, Kobe, 657-8501, Japan
cheetha@kcc.zaq.ne.jp

Abstract. In this paper we address network motifs found in information processing biological networks. Network motifs are local structures in a whole network on one hand, they are materializations of a kind of wholeness to have biological functions on the other hand. We formalize the wholeness by the notion of sheaf. We also formalize a feature of information processing by considering an internal structure of nodes in terms of their information processing ability. We show that two network motifs called bi-fan (BF) and feed-forward loop (FFL) can be obtained by purely algebraic considerations.

Keywords: Network motifs, wholeness, information processing, sheaves.

1 Introduction

Network motifs are local structures found in various biological networks more frequently than random graphs with the same number of nodes and degrees [5,6]. They are considered to be units of biological functions [2]. Their significance in biological networks such as gene transcription regulations, protein-protein interactions and neural networks are widely discussed (e.g. [2] and references therein). In general, what kinds of network motifs are found depends on the nature of each biological network. However, some common motifs are found in different kinds of biological networks. In particular, motifs called feed-forward loop (FFL) and bi-fan (BF) are common in both gene transcription regulation networks and neural networks [5]. It is pointed out that both networks are information processing networks [5]. There is already an explanation by natural selection about what kinds of motifs arise [9], however, the relationship between motifs and information processing is not yet clear.

In this paper, we investigate the relationship between motifs and information processing by abstract algebra such as theories of sheaves, categories and topoi [7,8]. It is crucial to represent motifs and information processing by suitable ways. Our formalism is based on two simple ideas. The first idea is that although motifs

---

* Corresponding author.

Y. Suzuki et al. (Eds.): IWNC 2007, PICT 1, pp. 70–80, 2009.

are local structures in a whole network, motifs themselves are coherent wholes to have biological functions. This fact is formalized as a condition related to sheaves, in which coherent parts are glued uniquely as a whole. The second idea is that in information processing networks each node has two roles, receiver and sender of information. Information is processed between reception and sending. Therefore nodes in information processing networks can be considered to have an internal structure in terms of information processing ability. We assume a simple internal structure and formalize it by so-called Grothendieck construction.

This paper is organized as follows. In section 2, the idea that motifs as coherent wholes are formalized by sheaves. However, we will see that no interesting consequence on the emergence of network motifs can be derived by only this idea. In section 3, we assume that each node of an information processing network has information processing ability and their hypothetical simple internal structure is presented. Integrating this idea and the idea described in section 2, we will derive network motifs FFL and BF as conditional statements. Finally in section 4, we give conclusions.

2   Motifs as Coherent Wholes

The basic structure of networks is just a correspondence between a set of nodes and a set of arrows. Finding motifs in a given network implies introduction of a kind of wholeness. Nodes and arrows in a motif make a coherent whole. In this section we describe this wholeness mathematically.

All networks in this paper are assumed to be directed graphs. A directed graph G consists of a quadruplet $(A, O, \partial_0, \partial_1)$. A is a set of arrows and O is a set of nodes. ∂_0, ∂_1 are maps from A to O. ∂_0 is a source map that sends each arrow to its source node. ∂_1 is a target map that sends each arrow to its target node. A network motif is given by a directed graph $M = (M_A, M_O, \partial_0^M, \partial_1^M)$. We assume that for any node $x \in M_O$ there exists an incoming arrow to x or an outgoing arrow from x (that is, there is no isolated node in M). The category of directed graph $\mathcal{G}rph$ is defined as follows. Objects are directed graphs and morphisms are homomorphisms of directed graphs.

Let G be a directed graph that represents a real network. Given a motif M, we would like to find all local structures found in G that are the same pattern as M. How they can be described mathematically? First let us consider nodes and arrows as local structures of directed graphs. The set of nodes in G can be identified with the set of homomorphisms of directed graphs from the trivial directed graph consisting of a single node without arrows $\{*\}$ to G

$$\text{Hom}(\{*\}, G).$$

As the same way, the set of arrows in G can be identified with the set of homomorphisms of directed graphs from the directed graph with two distinct nodes and a single arrow between them $\{n_0 \to n_1\}$ to G

$$\text{Hom}(\{n_0 \to n_1\}, G).$$

By the analogy with the above identifications, we define the set of all local structures in G that are the same pattern as M by the set of homomorphisms of directed graphs from M to G

$$\text{Hom}(M, G).$$

The above three Hom's can be treated at the same time by the technique called Grothendieck construction. We describe this in the next subsection.

2.1   Grothendieck Construction

Let M be a motif. We define a finite category $\mathcal{C}_M$ as follows. We have three objects $0, 1, 2$. The set of morphisms is generated by identities, two morphisms m_0, m_1 from 0 to 1 and morphisms u_f from 1 to 2 for each $f \in M_A$ with relations $u_f m_i = u_g m_j (i, j \in \{0, 1\})$ when $\partial_i^M f = \partial_j^M g$.

$$0 \underset{m_1}{\overset{m_0}{\rightrightarrows}} 1 \overset{u_f}{\rightarrow} 2$$

We define a functor E from $\mathcal{C}_M$ to $\mathcal{G}rph$. The correspondence of objects is defined by

$$E(0) = \{*\}, \quad E(1) = \{n_0 \rightarrow n_1\}, \quad E(2) = M.$$

The correspondence of morphisms is determined by

$$E(m_0)_O(*) = n_0, \quad E(m_1)_O(*) = n_1, \quad E(u_f)_A(\rightarrow) = f \text{ for } f \in M_A.$$

Here we denote a homomorphism of directed graphs D by a pair of maps $D = (D_A, D_O)$, where D_A is a map between the set of morphisms and D_O is a map between the set of nodes.

The functor E defines a functor R_E from $\mathcal{G}rph$ to the category $\mathcal{S}ets^{\mathcal{C}_M^{op}}$ of presheaves on $\mathcal{C}_M$, where $\mathcal{S}ets$ is the category of sets. Given a directed graph G we define

$$R_E(G) = \text{Hom}(E(-), G).$$

Grothendieck construction [8] says that a tensor product functor is defined as a left adjoint functor to R_E. Here we do not go into general theory but just give a concrete representation of the left adjoint L_E. Let F be a presheaf on $\mathcal{C}_M$. Omitting the calculation, we obtain L_E by

$$L_E(F) = F \otimes_{\mathcal{C}_M} E \cong F(1) \underset{F(m_1)}{\overset{F(m_0)}{\rightrightarrows}} F(0).$$

From this one can see that the composition $L_E R_E$ is isomorphic to the identity functor on $\mathcal{G}rph$. In general, the reverse composition $R_E L_E$ is not isomorphic to the identity functor on $\mathcal{S}ets^{\mathcal{C}_M^{op}}$. However, if we define a suitable Grothendieck topology J_M on $\mathcal{C}_M$ and consider the category of all J_M-sheaves $\mathcal{S}h(\mathcal{C}_M, J_M)$ then the composition $R_E L_E$ can become isomorphic to the identity on $\mathcal{S}h(\mathcal{C}_M, J_M)$. Thus we can obtain an equivalence of categories $\mathcal{S}h(\mathcal{C}_M, J_M) \simeq \mathcal{G}rph$. We describe the topology J_M in the next subsection.

2.2   Grothendieck Topologies

By defining a Grothendieck topology J on a small category $\mathcal{C}$, we can obtain a system of covering in $\mathcal{C}$ and consequently address relationships between parts and whole [8]. J sends each object C in $\mathcal{C}$ to a collection $J(C)$ of sieves on C. A set of morphisms S is called *sieve* on C if any $f \in S$ satisfies $\mathrm{cod}(f) = C$ and the condition $f \in S \Rightarrow fg \in S$ holds. Let S be a sieve on C and $h : D \to C$ be any morphism to C. Then $h^*(S) = \{g | \mathrm{cod}(g) = D, \; hg \in S\}$ is a sieve on D. If $R = \{f_i\}_{i \in I}$ is a family of morphisms with $\mathrm{cod}(f_i) = C$ for any $i \in I$ then $(R) = \{fg | \mathrm{dom}(f) = \mathrm{cod}(g), \; f \in R\}$ is a sieve on C.

Definition 1. *A Grothendieck topology on a small category $\mathcal{C}$ is a function that sends each object C to a collection $J(C)$ of sieves on C such that the following three conditions are satisfied.*

  (i) **maximality** $t_C \in J(C)$ *for any maximal sieve* $t_C = \{f | \mathrm{cod}(f) = C\}$.
 (ii) **stability** *If* $S \in J(C)$ *then* $h^*(S) \in J(D)$ *for any morphism* $h : D \to C$.
(iii) **transitivity** *For any* $S \in J(C)$, *if* R *is any sieve on* C *and* $h^*(R) \in J(D)$ *for all* $h : D \to C \in S$ *then* $R \in J(C)$.

We call a sieve S that is an element of $J(C)$ a *cover* of C.
    Let M be a motif and $\mathcal{C}_M$ be the category defined by the previous subsection. We define a Grothendieck topology J_M on $\mathcal{C}_M$ by

$$J_M(0) = \{t_0\}, \; J_M(1) = \{t_1\}, \; J_M(2) = \{t_2, S_M = (\{u_f\}_{f \in M_A})\}.$$

Indeed, J_M satisfies the above three axioms. First maximality is obvious. Second, stability is satisfied since $v^*(t_i) = t_j$ for any arrow $v : j \to i$ and $v^*(S_M) = t_j$ for any $v : j \to 2$. Finally, for transitivity, suppose that for any sieve R on i and $v : j \to i \in t_i$, $v^*(R) \in J_M(i)$ holds for each $t_i \in J_M(i)$. By putting $v = \mathrm{id}_i$ we obtain $R \in J_M(i)$. For $S_M \in J_M(2)$, suppose that $v^*(R) \in J_M(j)$ holds for any sieve R on 2 and any $v : j \to 2 \in S_M$. By putting $v = u_f$, we obtain

$$u_f^*(R) = \{v | u_f v \in R\} \in J_M(1).$$

Hence $\{v | u_f v \in R\} = t_1$. This implies that $u_f = u_f \mathrm{id}_1 \in R$. Since this holds for any $f \in M_A$, we have $S_M = (\{u_f\}_{f \in M_A}) \subseteq R$, which means $R = S_M$ or $R = t_2$. In both cases $R \in J_M(2)$.

2.3   Sheaves

Roughly speaking, sheaves are mechanism that glue coherent parts into a unique whole [8].

Definition 2. *Let $\mathcal{C}$ be a small category and J be a Grothendieck topology on $\mathcal{C}$. Let F be a presheaf on $\mathcal{C}$ and $S \in J(C)$ be a cover of an object C. A matching family of F with respect to S is a function that sends each element $f : D \to C$ of S to an element $x_f \in F(D)$ such that*

$$F(g)x_f = x_{fg}$$

holds for all $g : D' \to D$. An amalgamation for such a matching family is an element $x \in F(C)$ such that

$$F(f)x = x_f$$

for all $f \in S$. A presheaf F on $\mathcal{C}$ is called sheaf with respect to J (in short, J-sheaf) if any matching family with respect to any cover $S \in J(C)$ for any object C has a unique amalgamation.

A sieve S on an object C can be identified with a subfunctor of Yoneda embedding $\text{Hom}(-, C)$. Hence a matching family of a presheaf F with respect to S is a natural transformation $S \to F$. We denote the collection of matching family of F with respect to S by $\text{Match}(S, F)$.

The condition of sheaf can be restated as follows. Given a Grothendieck topology J on a small category $\mathcal{C}$, a presheaf F on $\mathcal{C}$ is J-sheaf if and only if the map

$$\kappa_S : F(C) \to \text{Match}(S, F) : x \mapsto F(-)x$$

is bijective for any object C and any cover $S \in J(C)$.

2.4   The Category of Directed Graphs as a Grothendieck Topos

Now we derive a condition in which a presheaf on $\mathcal{C}_M$ becomes J_M-sheaf. Yoneda's lemma says that $F(i) \cong \text{Match}(t_i, F)$ holds by κ_{t_i} for any presheaf F on $\mathcal{C}_M$. Hence we just consider whether

$$F(2) \cong \text{Match}(S_M, F)$$

holds by κ_{S_M} for $S_M \in J_M(2)$. We have the following proposition.

Proposition 3. $\text{Match}(S_M, F) \cong \text{Hom}(M, L_E(F))$.

Proof. Let a natural transformation $\mu : S_M \to F$ be given. Components of μ are

$$\mu_2 = \emptyset : S_M(2) = \emptyset \to F(2),$$
$$\mu_1 : S_M(1) = \{u_f | f \in M_A\} \to F(1),$$
$$\mu_0 : S_M(0) = \{u_f m_i | f \in M_A, \ i \in \{0, 1\}\} \to F(0).$$

We define a homomorphism of directed graphs $d : M \to L_E(F)$ by

$$d_A : M_A \to F(1) : f \mapsto \mu_1(u_f),$$
$$d_O : M_O \to F(0) : n \mapsto \mu_0(u_f m_i) \text{ for } n = \partial_i^M f.$$

d_O is a well-defined map by the definition of $\mathcal{C}_M$.

Conversely, suppose a homomorphism of directed graphs $d : M \to L_E(F)$ is given. A matching family $\mu : S_M \to F$ is defined by

$$\mu_1 : S_M(1) \to F(1) : u_f \mapsto d_A(f),$$
$$\mu_0 : S_M(0) \to F(0) : u_f m_i \mapsto d_O(\partial_i^M f).$$

It is clear that these constructions are the inverse of each other.   □

By the proposition, a necessary and sufficient condition that a presheaf F on $\mathcal{C}_M$ is a J_M-sheaf is that the map

$$\tau : F(2) \to \mathrm{Hom}(M, L_E(F)) : \alpha \mapsto d^\alpha$$

is a bijection. d^α is a homomorphism of directed graphs defined by

$$d^\alpha_A : M_A \to F(1) : f \mapsto F(u_f)\alpha,$$
$$d^\alpha_O : M_O \to F(0) : n \mapsto F(u_f m_i)\alpha \text{ for } n = \partial^M_i f.$$

In other words, a presheaf F on $\mathcal{C}_M$ is J_M-sheaf if and only if

$$R_E L_E(F) \cong F$$

holds. Since $L_E R_E$ is isomorphic to the identity functor on $\mathcal{G}rph$, $R_E(G)$ is always J_M-sheaf for any directed graph G. If we denote the category of J_M-sheaves on $\mathcal{C}_M$ by $\mathcal{S}h(\mathcal{C}_M, J_M)$ then we obtain an equivalence of categories

$$\mathcal{S}h(\mathcal{C}_M, J_M) \simeq \mathcal{G}rph.$$

2.5 Sheafification

Given a presheaf F on $\mathcal{C}_M$, what is the best sheaf which "approximates" the presheaf F? The technique which answers this question is called *sheafification* [8]. In this subsection we calculate the sheafification of presheaves on $\mathcal{C}_M$ by a procedure so-called Grothendieck's '+'-construction.

Let F be a presheaf on a small category $\mathcal{C}$ and J a Grothendieck topology on $\mathcal{C}$. A new presheaf F^+ is defined by

$$F^+(C) = \mathrm{colim}_{S \in J(C)}\mathrm{Match}(S, F).$$

The colimit is taken by the reverse inclusion order defined on $J(C)$. This colimit can be described as follows. Elements of the set $F^+(C)$ are equivalence classes of matching families $\mu \in \mathrm{Match}(S, F)$. Two matching families $\mu \in \mathrm{Match}(S, F)$ and $\nu \in \mathrm{Match}(T, F)$ are equivalent if and only if there exists a covering sieve $R \in J(C)$ such that $R \subseteq S \cap T$ such that $\mu|_R = \nu|_R$.

In general, F^+ is not a J-sheaf but it is known that $(F^+)^+$ is a J-sheaf. However, we shall prove that F^+ is already a J_M-sheaf for a presheaf F on $\mathcal{C}_M$ in what follows.

By Yoneda's lemma, we have

$$F^+(i) = \mathrm{colim}_{S \in J_M(i)}\mathrm{Match}(S, F) \cong \mathrm{Match}(t_i, F) \cong F(i)$$

for $i = 0, 1$. For $F^+(2)$, since $\mu|_{S_M} \in \mathrm{Match}(S_M, F)$ for any $\mu \in \mathrm{Match}(S_M, F)$, μ is equivalent to $\mu|_{S_M}$. Besides, because two different elements in $\mathrm{Match}(S_M, F)$ belong to different equivalence classes,

$$F^+(2) = \mathrm{colim}_{S \in J_M(2)}\mathrm{Match}(S, F) \cong \mathrm{Match}(S_M, F) \cong \mathrm{Hom}(M, L_E(F)).$$

This implies that $F^+ \cong R_E(L_E(F))$ which means F^+ is a J_M-sheaf. Since sheafification of a presheaf is unique up to isomorphisms, we can calculate a sheafification of presheaves on $\mathcal{C}_M$ with respect to the topology J_M by applying $R_E L_E$ to them.

3 Information Processing Networks

Let us recall the points in the previous section. Network motifs are coherent wholes. By defining a suitable category and a topology on it, we can address the relationships between parts and whole by sheaves.

In section 2, an object in $\mathcal{G}rph$ is considered to represent a real network. On the other hand, an object in $Sets^{\mathcal{C}_M^{op}}$ is constructed artificially in relation to finding a motif from the outside of the network. The construction would describe the wholeness of motifs in a mathematically favorable way as an equivalence of categories, however, it does not provide any suggestion what kinds of motifs arise in real networks.

In this section we focus on information processing biological networks such as gene transcription regulation networks or neural networks. We extract a common property of information processing networks in terms of information processing ability and integrate the property into the setting in section 2.

3.1 Information Processing Pattern

In information processing networks, each node in a network can be both a receiver and a sender of information. It processes information between reception and sending. Hence it should be considered to have an internal structure in terms of its information processing ability. One of the simplest candidates for the internal structure is a directed graph consisting of two different nodes and a single arrow between them. The arrow corresponds to information processing, the source of the arrow corresponds to reception of information and the target of the arrow corresponds to sending of information. Suppose two nodes in an information processing network are connected by an arrow. How can we describe this situation with the proposed internal structure of nodes? If we identify the sending of information at the source node with the reception of information at the target node then we could describe the situation by simply identifying the target of the arrow corresponding to the source node with the source of the arrow corresponding to the target node. The situation is depicted in Fig. 1.

Now we integrate the above idea into Grothendieck construction in section 2. We make use of the fact that the category of directed graphs is isomorphic to a presheaf category defined by the following diagram.

$$\bullet \overset{s}{\underset{t}{\rightrightarrows}} \bullet$$

We define a pattern M by a directed graph

$$\bullet \overset{e_0}{\rightarrow} \bullet \overset{e_1}{\rightarrow} \bullet.$$

Fig. 1. Broken ellipses denote two nodes at the network level. They have an internal structure that represents information processing ability. A broken curved arrow denotes an arrow connecting them in the network.

This pattern is not a motif in the sense in section 2 but is defined in terms of the internal information processing ability of nodes. It represents a specific information processing pattern associated with an arrow in a network. We call the pattern M *information processing pattern*. The motifs in section 2 are defined by an external observer who describes the local structure of networks. On the other hand, the information processing pattern M is defined in terms of an internal perspective on information processing and is relevant to how the specific local structures of information processing networks (BF and FFL) appear as we explain bellow.

Let $\mathcal{C}_M^*$ be a finite category with two objects $1, 2$. We have just two morphisms corresponding to e_0, e_1 from 1 to 2 other than identities. The two morphisms are also denoted by e_0, e_1 since there would be no confusion. $\mathcal{C}_M^*$ is a subcategory of $\mathcal{C}_M$. We denote the restriction of the functor $E : \mathcal{C}_M \to \mathcal{G}rph$ to $\mathcal{C}_M^*$ by the same symbol E. Note that a presheaf on $\mathcal{C}_M^*$ can be seen as a directed graph $F = (F(2), F(1), F(e_0), F(e_1))$. A functor R_E from $\mathcal{G}rph$ to $\mathcal{S}ets^{\mathcal{C}_M^{*op}} \cong \mathcal{G}rph$ can be defined by the same way as in section 2. By Grothendieck construction, R_E has a left adjoint L_E. We again just give a concrete description of the left adjoint omitting the calculation.

Let F be a presheaf on $\mathcal{C}_M^*$. We have

$$L_E(F) = F \otimes_{\mathcal{C}_M^*} E \cong F(1) \overset{\partial_0^F}{\underset{\partial_1^F}{\rightrightarrows}} F(1) \times \{0,1\}/\sim,$$

where $\sim$ is an equivalence relation on $F(1) \times \{0,1\}$ generated by the following relation R on $F(1) \times \{0,1\}$. For $(a,1), (b,0) \in F(1) \times \{0,1\}$

$$(a,1)R(b,0) \Leftrightarrow \exists \alpha \in F(2) \text{ s.t. } a = F(e_0)\alpha, b = F(e_1)\alpha,$$

that is, $(a,1)R(b,0)$ if and only if there is an arrow from a to b. We define $\partial_i^F(a) = [(a,i)]$ $(i = 0,1)$ for $a \in F(1)$, where $[(a,i)]$ is an equivalence class that includes (a,i). The adjunction obtained here is the same one derived heuristically in [3].

3.2   A Derivation of Network Motifs

The wholeness of network motifs is represented by sheaves in section 2. However, it is not useful to consider sheaves in the setting in this section since the category $\mathcal{C}_M^*$ loses information how arrows are connected in M. Instead, we adopt the

(a)   (b)

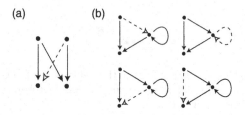

Fig. 2. If real arrows exist then dotted arrows must exist. (a)bi-fan (BF). (b)feed-forward loop (FFL) with a loop.

condition $R_E L_E(F) \cong F$ for a representation of the wholeness. This is equivalent to the condition of sheaf in the setting of section 2. Recall that a presheaf F on $\mathcal{C}_M^*$ can be seen as a directed graph $F = (F(2), F(1), F(e_0), F(e_1))$. We now consider that presheaves on $\mathcal{C}_M^*$ correspond to real networks. Objects in $\mathcal{G}rph$ are supposed to have only auxiliary roles. Roles of the presheaf category and $\mathcal{G}rph$ are reversed from those in section 2.

A necessary and sufficient condition that a binary directed graph F satisfies $R_E L_E(F) \cong F$ is already obtained in [3]. If we write $a \rightarrow b$ when there exists an arrow from a to b in F then the condition can be stated as follows.

$$\text{If } a \rightarrow b \leftarrow c \rightarrow d \text{ then } a \rightarrow d.$$

The necessary part is explained in the next paragraph. This implies that if three arrows in F make a sub-pattern of bi-fan (BF) then they are indeed included in a BF (Fig. 2 (a)). If one of four arrows in a BF is a loop then the BF becomes a feed-forward loop (FFL) with a loop (Fig. 2 (b)). Such type of FFL with a loop at the relay point is often observed in real biological networks [1]. Thus we can derive both BF and FFL as conditional statements from algebraic descriptions of wholeness and information processing.

We can interpret the emergence of bi-fan as the stabilization of information processing pattern M. Let F be a directed graph. For nodes $x, y \in F$, $(x, 1)R(y, 0)$ means that there exists an arrow from x to y, $x \rightarrow y$. Suppose $a \rightarrow b \leftarrow c \rightarrow d$ in F. This implies that

$$(a, 1)R(b, 0), \ (c, 1)R(b, 0) \text{ and } (c, 1)R(d, 0).$$

By the construction of the equivalence relation from R,

$$(a, 1)R(b, 0) = (b, 0)R^{-1}(c, 1) = (c, 1)R(d, 0)$$

implies $(a, 1)R(d, 0)$, which means $a \rightarrow d$. We here use the reflexive law twice, the symmetric law once and the transitive law twice. The reflexive law guarantees the identity of symbol (x, i). (x, i) represents a role (e_0 or e_1) in information processing pattern M. The symmetric law here could be seen as a kind of feedback if we interpret an arrow in a network as a transduction of information, since the symmetric law reverses the relation $(c, 1)R(b, 0)$ which means $c \rightarrow b$

in the network. Finally, the transitive law provides the compositions of relations R and R^{-1}, which are interpreted as propagation of information transduction and feedback. Thus by the construction of the equivalence relation from R, roles $(a,1), (b,0), (c,1)$ and $(d,0)$ in M are integrated as a whole and stabilized. Hence we would like to say that information processing pattern M is stable in F if $R_E L_E(F) \cong F$ holds.

3.3   Another Derivation of the Fixed Point Condition

The condition $R_E L_E(F) \cong F$ says that F is a fixed point of $R_E L_E$ up to an isomorphism of directed graphs. We have just obtained the fixed point condition in relation to the sheaf condition, however, we can derive the fixed condition independent of the sheaf condition. In this subsection we outline the derivation briefly. The details will be presented elsewhere.

Recall that the information processing pattern M represents how two nodes are connected by an arrow at the network level. Hence each connection between two nodes by an arrow at the network level can be seen as an image of M by R_E. This condition can be generalized to any directed graph F:

$$F \cong R_E(G) \text{ for some directed graph } G.$$

We can prove that this condition is equivalent to the fixed point condition $R_E L_E(F) \cong F$. Note that '$\cong$' in '$F \cong R_E(G)$' refers to a directed graph isomorphism in general, however, '$\cong$' in '$R_E L_E(F) \cong F$' stands for that a specific directed graph homomorphism which is a component of the unit of the adjunction $\eta_F : F \to R_E L_E(F)$ is an isomorphism.

The proof proceeds roughly as follows. Suppose $R_E L_E(F) \cong F$ holds. Then we obtain $F \cong R_E(G)$ by putting $G = L_E(F)$. Conversely, suppose $F \cong R_E(G)$ for some directed graph G. If $R_E \cong R_E L_E R_E$ holds then we have $F \cong R_E(G) \cong R_E L_E R_E(G) = R_E L_E(R_E(G)) \cong R_E L_E(F)$. Hence it is sufficient to prove $R_E \cong R_E L_E R_E$. However, one can show that $\eta_{R_E(G)} R_E(\epsilon_G) = \mathrm{id}_{R_E L_E R_E(G)}$ for any directed graph G where η and ϵ are the unit and the counit of the adjunction, respectively. We also have $R_E(\epsilon_G)\eta_{R_E(G)} = \mathrm{id}_{R_E(G)}$, which is just one of the two triangular identities for the adjunction. To be precise, we also need $L_E \cong L_E R_E L_E$ by the natural transformations appeared in the other triangular identity, which can be also checked in our adjunction, for the complete proof.

4   Conclusions

In this paper we derive network motifs found in information processing biological networks from purely algebraic considerations on wholeness and information processing. We first consider the wholeness of network motifs as sheaves on a finite Grothendieck site. This is an external description of the wholeness of network motifs that is not useful to consider the emergence network motifs. Hence we need a kind of internal perspective. We introduce an information processing pattern defined in relation to internal information processing ability of nodes.

We show that the wholeness of the information processing pattern is materialized as network motifs such as BF and FFL.

We can generalize the idea of information processing pattern described in this paper. The generalization is presented in [4]. Another example of information processing pattern which seems to be relevant to real networks will be found in [4]. Note that information processing patterns defined in this paper are called *intrinsic motifs* in [4].

The notion of natural computation would be closely related to the idea of information processing pattern introduced in this paper. In this respect, an information processing pattern might be seen as a formal representation of a computation performed by nature *per se*. We believe that algebraic methods including category and topos theory are useful to grasp the formal aspects of natural computation.

Acknowledgments. T. Haruna was supported by JSPS Research Fellowships for Young Scientists.

References

1. Alon, U.: Introduction to Systems Biology: Design Principles of Biological Circuits. CRC Press, Boca Raton (2006)
2. Alon, U.: Network motifs: theory and experimental approaches. Nature Rev. Genet. 8, 450–461 (2007)
3. Haruna, T., Gunji, Y.-P.: Duality Between Decomposition and Gluing: A Theoretical Biology via Adjoint Functors. Biosystems 90, 716–727 (2007)
4. Haruna, T.: Algebraic Theory of Biological Organization. Doctral Dissartation, Kobe University (2008)
5. Milo, R., et al.: Metwork Motifs: Simple Building Blocks of Complex Networks. Science 298, 824–827 (2002)
6. Milo, R., et al.: Superfamilies of Evolved and Designed Networks. Science 303, 1538–1542 (2004)
7. MacLane, S.: Categories for the Working Mathematician, 2nd edn. Springer, New York (1998)
8. MacLane, S., Moerdijk, I.: Sheaves in Geometry and Logic: A First Introduction to Topos Theory. Springer, New York (1992)
9. Sporns, O., Kotter, R.: Motifs in Brain Networks. PLos Biol. 2, 369 (2004)

Regulation Effects by Programmed Molecules for Transcription-Based Diagnostic Automata towards Therapeutic Use

Miki Hirabayashi[1], Hirotada Ohashi[1], and Tai Kubo[2]

[1] Department of Quantum Engineering and Systems Science, The University of Tokyo, 7-3-1 Hongo, Bunkyo-ku, Tokyo 113-8656, Japan
[2] Neuroscience Research Institute, National Institute of Advanced Industrial Science and Technology (AIST), AIST Tsukuba Central 6, 1-1-1 Higashi, Tsukuba, Ibaraki 305-8566, Japan
miki@crimson.q.t.u-tokyo.ac.jp, ohashi@q.t.u-tokyo.ac.jp,
tai.kubo@aist.go.jp

Abstract. We have presented experimental analysis on the controllability of our transcription-based diagnostic biomolecular automata by programmed molecules. Focusing on the noninvasive transcriptome diagnosis by salivary mRNAs, we already proposed the novel concept of diagnostic device using DNA computation. This system consists of the main computational element which has a stem shaped promoter region and a pseudo-loop shaped read-only memory region for transcription regulation through the conformation change caused by the recognition of disease-related biomarkers. We utilize the transcription of malachite green aptamer sequence triggered by the target recognition for observation of detection. This algorithm makes it possible to release RNA-aptamer drugs multiply, different from the digestion-based systems by the restriction enzyme which was proposed previously, for the in-vivo use, however, the controllability of aptamer release is not enough at the previous stage. In this paper, we verified the regulation effect on aptamer transcription by programmed molecules in basic conditions towards the developm! ent of therapeutic automata. These results would bring us one step closer to the realization of new intelligent diagnostic and therapeutic automata based on molecular circuits.

Keywords: Biomolecular computing, nucleic acid detection systems, DNA computing, molecular programming, autonomous diagnostic devices, molecular circuits.

1 Introduction

Biomolecular computing using the artificial nucleic acid technology is expected to bring new solutions to various health problems. Several studies on potential approaches to the rational construction of intelligent sensors or circuits have been done to detect the specific input sequences [1]. We have been focusing on

Y. Suzuki et al. (Eds.): IWNC 2007, PICT 1, pp. 81–89, 2009.

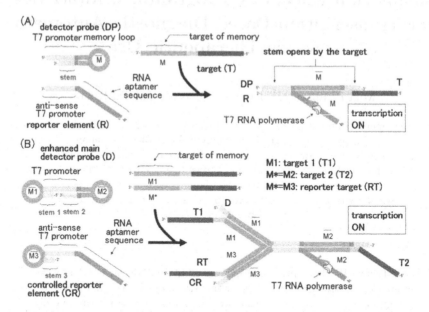

Fig. 1. Basic concept of target detection [3]. (A) The previous system. (B) The present system.

noninvasive transcriptome diagnosis by salivary mRNAs using DNA computation and presented the novel concept of diagnostic biomolecular automata. Here we demonstrated that we can regulate the detection and reporting process by well-designed programmed molecules.

Salivary transcriptome diagnostics is expected as a novel clinical approach for early disease detection. Recently, it was reported that the combination of several disease-related salivary mRNA biomarkers yielded sensitivity (91%) and specificity (91%) in distinguishing oral squamous cell carcinoma (OSCC) from the controls [2]. There are several problems in existing detection methods for the expression of these biomarkers. The method using SYBR Green intercalating dyes has the advantage in the cost performance, however, intercalatig dyes label all double-stranded (ds)DNA including undesirable PCR products. The method using sequence-specific fluorescent reporter probes is accurate and reliable, but expensive. In order to present a practical diagnostic tool, we already proposed the novel concept for salivary transcriptome diagnosis using DNA computation [3]. This can realize the cost-effective and sequence-specific intelligent system by the transcription-based algorithm using a functional aptamer to report the detection results based on structural regulation. Basically our system consists of the detector probe and the reporter element (Fig. 1A). The detector probe has one stem for transcriptional regulation using the sense T7 promoter sequence and one read-only memory loop for target recognition. The reporter element has an anti-sense promoter domain and a malachite green (MG) aptamer sequence domain. The MG aptamer is an RNA molecule that has affinity to MG, an organic dye. This aptamer increases the fluorescence of MG when bound [4,5].

The stem opens through the binding of a target oligonucleotide complementary to the memory sequence and then the promoter region forms a double strand with the reporter element. This triggers the transcription of the MG aptamer sequence and the fluorescence is observed by the addition of MG. This fluorescence enables us to recognize the existence of the target. Stojanovic's group proposed molecular automata combined the standard oligonucleotide recognition element, a stem-loop molecular beacon with the MG aptamer itself as a part of computational elements for deoxyribozyme-based logic gates [6]. On the other hand, we utilize the transcription process of MG aptamer to detect the targets. The advantage of this transcription-based circuit is to be able to release aptamer drugs [7] instead of the MG aptamer for the therapeutic use in future. However, in the previous work [3], we could not reduce the transcription leak enough, which is the transcription without targets. Although this is not a serious problem for the *in-vitro* diagnostic use when the aptamer is used as a reporter molecule, it is not desirable to release unnecessary aptamer drugs for the *in-vivo* therapeutic use.

In this paper, we introduce the stem-loop structure to both promoter regions of the detector probe and the reporter element in order to regulate the transcription leak towards the *in-vivo* therapeutic use and verified the effects of it. To reduce the background noise, this structure consists of a pseudo-loop shaped target recognition domain and a stem, which does not open without its own target (Fig. 1B). This structural programming was applied on the one end of the detector probe only in the previous system [3], however, we introduce it to the other end of the detector probe and the one end of the reporter element in this work. We confirmed the significant controllability of new programmed molecules in the basic conditions. These results will provide promising applications of autonomous intelligent diagnostic and therapeutic devices using molecular-scale computation.

2   Materials and Methods

2.1   Preparation of Oligonucleotides

DNA sequences of the oligonucleotide used for the construction of the two molecular computer components and two inputs are shown in Tables 1–3. The diagnostic system consists of the two components: detector probes and reporter elements. Oligonucleotides were custom-made and DNase/RNase free HPLC purified by (Operon Biotechnologies, Tokyo, JAPAN) or (Hokkaido System Science, Sapporo, JAPAN) and used as received. Each sequence was folded using mFold server v 3.2 (URL: http://www.bioinfo.rpi.edu/applications/mfold) and visually examined to find sequences of low undesirable secondary structure.

Computational Elements

(1) **enhanced detector probe:** The detector probe is a detector for the target sequence. It had a stem shaped sense T7 promoter region for the transcription

Table 1. Single-stranded DNA models for computational elements

Name	DNA sequences (5'3')	Length
Substitute detector probe (SD)	5'-AGCTTAATACGACTCACTATA GGA-3'	24
Reporter element (R)	5'-GGATCCATTCGTTACCTGGCT CTCGCCAGTCGGGATCCTATAG TGAGTCGTATTAAGCT-3'	59
Enhanced main detector probe (D)	5'-TTAAGCTAGTACCAGGCCTGT AACGATGAAGCTTAATACGACT CACTATAGGAAGCAAGTACTCC TTGTCGATCTTCCTATAG-3'	83
Controlled reporter element (CR)	5'-GGATCCATTCGTTACCTGGCT CTCGCCAGTCGGGATCCTATAG TGAGTCGTATTAAGCTCAGCTT GGAAGTCATGTTTACAAGCTGA G-3'	88

Table 2. Profiling of computational elements

Name	T_m (calculated)	GC %
H3F3A detector domain	64.4 °C	50.0
SAT detector domain	60.8 °C	45.5
IL8 control domain	61.4 °C	40.9
T7 promoter domain	57.0 °C	37.5

Table 3. Single-stranded DNA models for input molecules

Name	DNA sequences (5'3')	Length
H3F3A	5'-TCATCGTTACAGGCCTGGTACTGTGGCGCTC CGTGAAATTAGACGTT-3'	47
SAT	5'-CAGTGAAGAGGGTTGGAGACTGTTCAAGATC GACAAGGAGTACTTGCT-3'	48
IL8	5'-CACCGGAAGGAACCATCTCCATCCCATCTCA CTGTGTGTAAACATGACTTCCAAGCTG-3'	47

regulation of reporter molecules and a pseudo-loop shaped read-only memory region for the target detection previously [3]. The enhanced detector probe has two stems for both transcription leak control and diagnosis (Table 1). The detector probe could receive information from target inputs at the memory domain and transfer signals to the promoter domain through the conformation change by opening the stem.

(2) **controlled reporter element:** The reporter element is an output-producing element. It has an anti-sense T7 promoter domain and an MG RNA aptamer sequence domain [3]. An MG aptamer increases the fluorescence of MG when bound [4,5], allowing us to know that the transcription

occurs. The hybridization of a target at the memory region in the detector probe triggers the stem open and then the promoter region form a double strand with the reporter element. Consequently, the transcription of the MG aptamer sequence is active and fluorescence is observed by the addition of MG. These successive reactions will enable us to recognize the existence of targets. We introduce a pseudo-loop shaped memory region to this new controlled reporter element in order to make a diagnosis based on the combination of biomarkers and regulate the transcription leak (Table 1). When the target recognition domain of this element does not bind to target inputs, the anti-sense promoter region has less accessibility to the promoter module in the main detector probe and this function regulates the transcription of the MG aptamer sequence in the case of no target. Consequently, it is expected that the element can reduce the transcription leak caused by unstable hybridization conditions and increase the quantitative stability.

Input Molecules

We used single-stranded (ss)DNAs to represent disease-related mRNA based on precedents in Ref. [1]. Two concentrations to represent mRNA levels: 0 μM for low level and 2 μM for high level at the detection stage. As disease-related biomarker models, *H3F3A*, *SAT*, and *IL8* mRNAs were selected based on reported cancer association [2]. These are salivary mRNA biomarkers for OSCC. DNA sequences used for the construction of the input models are shown in Table 3. These input ssDNA models include two recognition modules: one for detector probes and the other for additional control elements for the future use.

2.2   Diagnostic Computations

Diagnostic computations consist of three steps: 1) mixing the detector probes for input disease-related biomarker models and other computational elements, and equilibrating them. 2) processing of a string of transcription reactions for diagnosis by T7 RNA polymerase supplementation. 3) quantifying of the fluorescence by MG supplementation.

Step 1. Control of DNA Hybridization

Detector probes, input molecules and reporter elements were mixed in that order and diluted in annealing buffer (50 mM NaCl, 100 mM HEPES pH 7.4) to 3 μM concentration each. The reaction mixtures were incubated for 22 h at 45 °C following denaturation at 94 °C for 2 min in a PCR machine block.

Step 2. Detection of Memory Recall

Hybridization mixture was subjected to transcription reaction using Ambion MEGAscript T7 Kit. The mixtures were incubated at 37 °C for up to 6 hours.

Step 3. Observation of MG Binding

Two μL of the reaction mixtures and MG were mixed in binding buffer (50 mM Tris-HCl, pH = 7.4, 50 mM $MgCl_2$, 1mM NaCl) with the final concentration of 10 μM of MG and the fluorescent spectra were taken on a microplate spectrofluorometer (Japan Molecular Devices, Tokyo, JAPAN, SpectraMax Gemini).

Experiments were performed at the excitation wavelength (λ_{ex}) of 620 nm and emission wavelength (λ_{em}) scan of 650-700 nm. The spectra were exported to Microsoft Excel files.

3   Results

We investigated fundamental noise reduction properties of our new enhanced main detector probe and the controlled reporter element.

3.1   The Control of Transcription Leak

We show that the ability of control of transcription leak by the enhanced main detector probe (D) and the controlled reporter element (CR) compared with the standard reporter element (R) (Fig. 2A). The fluorescence time scans at the transcription stage are shown in Fig. 2B. Each data point represents the average of ten consecutive scans at $\lambda_{em} = 675$ nm. It is confirmed that the system can reduce the transcription leak by using the controlled reporter element. The remains of the leak are attributed to the fact that the reporter probe itself has a function as an opener of the stem-shaped sense promoter region and induces the transcription of reporter molecules. By the reduction of this background noise, our system can be used as the *in-vivo* therapeutic automata which can release aptamer drugs based on the diagnosis.

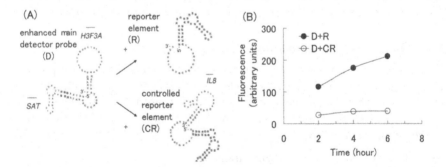

Fig. 2. The reduction effects of transcription leak by new programmed molecules. (A) Transcription-based probes and elements. (B) The effect of controlled reporter elements for reduction of transcription leak. Fluorescence time scans at the transcription stage. Each data point represents the average of ten consecutive scans at $\lambda_{em} = 675$ nm.

3.2   Function of Each Module

In order to realize the stable diagnostic automata, the system must have little leak when the set of biomarkers is incomplete. Here we verified the response ability for the single target of each computational molecule.

We investigated the response of the enhanced detector probe by single detector target (DT): ssDNA for *H3F3A* mRNA (DT1) and ssDNA for *SAT* mRNA

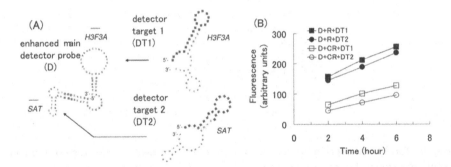

Fig. 3. Comparison transcription leak caused by a single target. (A) Enhanced main detector probe and two kinds of targets. (B) Examination of transcription leak in different conditions. Each data point represents the average of ten consecutive scans at $\lambda_{em} = 675$ nm.

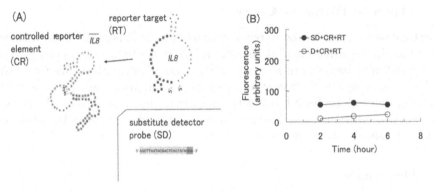

Fig. 4. Target recognition and regulation of the transcription leak by the controlled reporter element. (A) Controlled reporter element and target. (B) Examination of transcription leak in different conditions. Each data point represents the average of ten consecutive scans at $\lambda_{em} = 675$ nm.

(DT2) (Fig. 3A). Figure 3B shows that fluorescence time scans at the transcription stage for the enhanced main detector probe using each detector target. Filled squares and filled circles show that each recognition ability for each target in each memory region is almost same when we use the standard reporter element for detection. This may indicate that a single target can enhance to open the other loop, because we observed that double targets do not double the fluorescence (data not shown). This phenomenon is not desirable for accurate diagnosis, however, open squares and open circles show that the undesirable leak can be reduced by using the controlled reporter element. To have more precise control, it may be effective to allocate a single recognition region for one element.

Then we tested the recognition ability of the controlled reporter element using the reporter target (RT) (Fig. 4A). Figure 4B shows that the target recognition ability is weak when we use the substitute detector probe for detection and

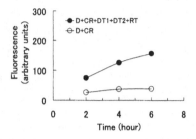

Fig. 5. Total transcription ability. Each data point represents the average of ten consecutive scans at $\lambda_{em} = 675$ nm.

therefore the undesirable leak is little when we use the enhanced detector probe. In order to make a quantitative diagnosis, each characteristic of computational elements must be considered sufficiently.

3.3   Aptamer Releasing Ability

The total performance of the system is shown in Fig. 5. Comprehensively we have succeeded in the reduction of transcription leak at the basic stage (open circles) and significant fluorescence recovery in the biomarker mixture (filled circles). In order to complete diagnostic and therapeutic automata, we must solve the transcription leak problem brought by each target shown in Fig. 3B. We expect that several functions of well-designed error control elements may be useful for this as we showed in the previous work [3].

4   Discussion

We introduced the new computational elements to our transcription-based diagnostic automata and verified the controllability of them in the target mixture for the OSCC prediction set (*H3F3A*, *SAT*, and *IL8*). It was reported that by using the combination of up-regulated salivary mRNAs: *H3F3A* (5.61-fold), *SAT* (2.98-fold), and *IL8* (24.3-fold) for OSCC prediction, the overall sensitivity is 90.6% [2]. In additon to that we already confirmed that our system can realize the cost-effective and sequence-specific real-time detection of a single target in Ref. [3], this paper shows the following potential abilities of our system towards the practical application of biomolecular automata.

(1) Potential ability for flexible programming: We showed that programmed molecule can increase the system controllability in the transcription leak problem.
(2) Potential ability for therapeutic automata: We demonstrated that the system can release the significant amount of aptamers when it recognizes the OSCC biomarker set. Because we adopt the transcription-based diagnostic system instead of the digestion-based system by the restriction enzyme for small cell lung cancer (SCLC) in Ref. [1], the controlled multiple release of RNA aptamer drugs is possible for the therapeutic purpose. To realize the practical application, not only qualitative but also quantitative diagnosis is required.

Well-designed error control elements may solve this problem as we described in the previous work [3].

(3) Potential ability for nonivasive cost-effective and sequence-specific diagnosis: As we mentioned above, our system can perform the cost-effective and sequence-specific real-time detection. The introduction of the MG-RNA-aptamer transcription for the fluorescence detection realizes the cost-effective real-time observation. Moreover the regulated transcripiton by the specific target sequence in the pseudo-loop shaped read-only memory region enables the sequence-specific detection. Our system may bring the important technology to make a diagnosis using saliva at home in the near future. By additional programming, we expect that we wiil be able to complete our approach and provide promising application of intelligent biomolecular automata.

References

1. Benenson, Y., Gil, B.-D.U., Adar, R., Shapiro, E.: An autonomous molecular computer for logical control of gene expression. Nature 429, 423–429 (2004)
2. Li, Y., John, M.A.R.St., Zhou, X., Kim, Y., Sinha, U., Jordan, R.C.K., Eisele, D., Abemayor, E., Elashoff, D., Park, N.-H., Wong, D.T.: Salivary transcriptome diagnostics for oral cancer detection. Clin. Cancer Res. 10, 8442–8450 (2004)
3. Hirabayashi, M., Ohashi, H., Kubo, T.: Experimental validation of the transcpritonbased diagnostic automata with quantitative control by programmed molecules. In: Preliminary Proceedings of the 13th International Meeting on DNA Computing, Memphis, Tennessee, USA, pp. 101–110 (2007)
4. Babendure, J.R., Adams, S.R., Tsien, R.Y.: Aptamers switch on fluorescence of triphenylmethane dyes. J. Am. Chem. Soc. 125, 14716–14717 (2003)
5. Hirabayashi, M., Taira, S., Kobayashi, S., Konishi, K., Katoh, K., Hiratsuka, Y., Kodaka, M., Uyeda, T.Q.P., Yumoto, N., Kubo, T.: Malachite green-conjugated microtubules as mobile bioprobes selective for malachite green aptamers with capturing/ releasing ability. Biotechnol. Bioeng. 94(3), 473–480 (2006)
6. Kolpashchikov, D.M., Stojanovic, M.N.: Boolean control of aptamer binding states. J. Am. Chem. Soc. 127, 11348–11351 (2005)
7. Bunka, D.H.J., Stockley, P.G.: Aptamers come of age - at last. Nat. Rev. Microbiol. 4, 588–596 (2006)

On Detection and Isolation of Defective Cells in Self-Timed Cellular Automata

Teijiro Isokawa[1], Ferdinand Peper[2], Shin'ya Kowada[1],
Naotake Kamiura[1], and Nobuyuki Matsui[1]

[1] Division of Computer Engineering, Graduate School of Engineering, University of
Hyogo, 2167 Shosha, Himeji, Hyogo, 671-2280 Japan
[2] Nano ICT Group, National Institute of Information and Communications
Technology, 588-2 Iwaoka, Iwaoka-cho, Nishi-ku, Kobe, 651-2492 Japan

Abstract. Defect-tolerance, the ability to overcome unreliability of
components in a system, will be essential to realize computers built by
nanotechnology. This paper reviews two approaches to defect-tolerance
for nanocomputers that are based on self-timed cellular automata, a type
of asynchronous cellular automaton, where the cells' defects are assumed
to be of the stuck-at fault type. One approach for detecting and isolating
defective components (cells) is in a so-called off-line manner, i.e., through
isolating defective cells and laying out circuits in the cellular space. In
the other approach, defective cells can be detected and isolated while
computation takes place, i.e., in an on-line manner. We show how to
cope with defects in the cellular space in a self-contained way, while a
computation task is conducted on it.

1 Introduction

The trend towards nanometer-scale logic devices may lead to computers with
high speed and low power consumption, but this will require new techniques and
architectures. Such nanocomputers may require a regular structure, like in cellular arrays [1,2,3], to allow mass manufacturing based on molecular self-assembly.
Another important issue for nanoscale integration densities is the reduction of
power consumption, and, related to it, heat dissipation. Getting rid of the clock,
i.e., using asynchronous timing, has been suggested as a promising way toward
this end, especially when done in the context of cellular automata (CA) [2,3]. CA
have been used for computation by embedding circuits on their cellular space
and simulating the operation of these circuits by state transitions of the cells.
For asynchronous CA this has resulted in embeddings on the cellular space of
circuits that are asynchronous [2,3].

A major obstacle to the realization of nanocomputers is the reduced reliability
of nanodevices as compared to their VLSI counterparts, due to noise, quantum
effects, etc. Discarding chips that have defects, as done in VLSI manufacturing,
is inefficient and, moreover, it cannot deal with defects occurring during computations. So, other approaches need to be explored to achieve defect-tolerance,
self-repair, and/or self-healing.

Y. Suzuki et al. (Eds.): IWNC 2007, PICT 1, pp. 90–100, 2009.
© Springer 2009

In this paper, we introduce asynchronous cellular automata with the capability of detecting and isolating defective cells. We assume that the defect model in our cellular automata is so-called stuck-at fault, i.e., a cell is unable to update the state by the cell itself or from outside of the cell and its state can still be read by neighboring cells. The case of defective cells able to update their states, but only so incorrectly, is not considered.

Two types of approaches for defect tolerance are introduced, i.e., in an off-line and an on-line manner. In the off-line manner, the processes of detection and isolation of defective cells are conducted before computation starts [4]. This is realized by distributing so-called test signals in the cellular space for isolating defective cells from non-defective cells and then by configuring circuits for computation in a non-defective area. In the on-line manner to detect defects, computation is conducted while simultaneously defects are detected and isolated in the cellular space. This is achieved by introducing *random fly* configurations that move around randomly in the cellular space and that check whether each cell is alive[5].

2   Preliminaries

2.1   Self-Timed Cellular Automaton

A self-timed cellular automaton (STCA)[2] is a two-dimensional asynchronous CA of identical cells, each of which has a state that is partitioned into four parts in one-to-one correspondence with its neighboring cells. Each part of a cell has a state. Figure 1 shows a cell in STCA where the states of the partitions are denoted as p_n, p_e, p_s, and p_w. Each cell undergoes transitions in accordance with a transition function f that operates on the four parts of the cell p_n, p_e, p_s, p_w and the nearest part of each of its four neighbors q_n, q_e, q_s, q_w. The transition function f is defined by

$$f(p_n, p_e, p_s, p_w, q_n, q_e, q_s, q_w) \rightarrow (p'_n, p'_e, p'_s, p'_w, q'_n, q'_e, q'_s, q'_w), \qquad (1)$$

where a state symbol to which a prime is attached denotes the new state of a partition after update (see Fig. 2). Function f can be described by a finite set of transition rules on the STCA. Dummy transitions, that are transitions without any changes of the partition states, are not included in a set of the transition rules, so we assume that the left-hand side of Fig. 2 always differs from the right-hand side. Furthermore, we assume that transition rules on an STCA are rotation-symmetric, thus each of the rules has four rotated analogues.

In an STCA, transitions of the cells occur at random times, independent of each other. Furthermore, it is assumed that neighboring cells never undergo transitions simultaneously to prevent a situation in which such cells write different values in shared partitions at the same time.

There are several approaches to perform computation on STCAs, such as simulating synchronous CA on them, or embedding delay-insensitive circuits on them [3,6] which are a kind of asynchronous circuits. We will use the latter

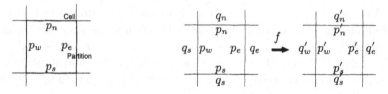

Fig. 1. A cell in Self-Timed Cellular Automaton

Fig. 2. Transition rule in accordance with the function f

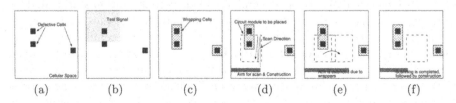

(a)   (b)   (c)   (d)   (e)   (f)

Fig. 3. Schematic diagrams for reconfiguring-based defect tolerance in STCA

approach, because of its lower overhead in terms of the number of required cell states and transition rules. We use two kinds of delay-insensitive circuit elements, {K,E}-elements [7] and the Rotary Element [8]. Each of the element sets have been proven to be computational universal.

3 Defect Tolerance on Self-Timed Cellular Automata (DT-STCAs)

This section shows two types of defect-tolerant STCA models. Detection of defects in an off-line and an on-line manner are described in Sec. 3.1 and 3.2, respectively.

3.1 Reconfiguration-Based Defect Tolerant STCA

The concept of reconfiguration-based defect tolerance is depicted in Fig. 3. We assume a cellular space with defective partitions that are stuck-at faults (Fig. 3(a)). Before performing computation, test signals are injected from the edge of the cellular space (Fig. 3(b)). Each of test signals are represented as special partition states and it is necessary to inject three kinds of signals for detecting the defective partition stuck at any state. As a result of injecting test signals, the cells with defective partitions are isolated by cells in a special state (wrapping cells in Fig. 3(c)). Once wrappings have been made, an arm emerges from the lower left boundary of the working area in the cell space (Fig. 3(d)). This arm is controlled by signals sent to its base, which are generated by a controller in a similar way as in the universal constructor in [9]. Signals move up in the arm until they reach the head, which interprets them as instructions and carries them out. The arm scans the cell space to find an area large enough to place a desired circuit module. Columns are systematically scanned cell by cell (Fig. 3(d)).

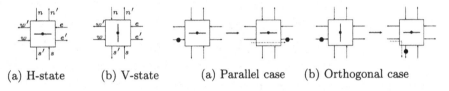

(a) H-state   (b) V-state   (a) Parallel case   (b) Orthogonal case

Fig. 4. A Rotary Element   **Fig. 5.** The operation of an RE on a signal

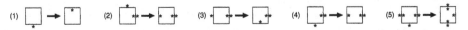

Fig. 6. Transition rules implementing the RE

When the head of the arm detects a wrapper, the arm is extended by a distance equalling the width of the module, after which the process is done once more in a fresh part of cell space (Fig. 3(e)), and so on until an area is found for placing a module (Fig. 3(f)).

Rotary Element(RE) and its Implementation on STCA. A *Rotary Element (RE)* [8] is a logic element with four input lines $\{n, e, s, w\}$, four output lines $\{n', e', s', w'\}$, and two states—the H-state and the V-state—which are displayed as horizontal and vertical rotation bars respectively (Fig. 4). A signal coming from a direction parallel to the rotation bar passes straight through to the opposite output line, without changing the direction of the bar (Fig. 5(a)); a signal coming from a direction orthogonal to the bar turns right and rotates the bar by 90 degrees (Fig. 5(b)).

Embedding an arbitrary RE-circuit on the cellular space of STCA can be achieved by the two states of a partition and the five transition rules shown in Fig. 6 [9]. Rule #1 defines a signal used for ordinary computation. Applying it to the successive shaded cells in Fig. 7 results in a signal proceeding northwards on a straight continuous path of cells, all bits of which are 0. Transmitting a signal towards the east, south, or west is done similarly, because of the rotation-symmetry of transition rules. Rules #2–4 are responsible for routing a signal according to the direction from which the signal comes from. The operation of the rotation bar in an RE is conducted by rule #5.

A rudimentary RE is shown in Fig. 8. The input/output paths at the sides of this RE are bi-directional. Connecting so-called Input/Output Multiplexers to these paths results in a regular RE with four input and four output paths, all uni-directional. Figure 9 illustrates the traces of a signal input to a rudimentary RE from a line (a) parallel with or (b) orthogonal to the rotation bar. Since all the elements of RE-circuits can be realized by stable partition pairs, any circuit on this STCA can be represented by a certain configuration of stable partition-pairs.

Reconfiguration-Based Defect Tolerant STCA. Partitions in this STCA have 8 states, denoted by the set of symbols { , *, #, &, +, @, %, $}.

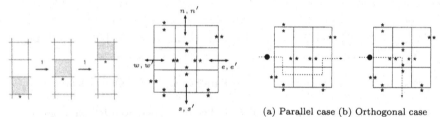

Fig. 7. Signal transmission northwards

Fig. 8. RE realized on STCA

(a) Parallel case (b) Orthogonal case

Fig. 9. Signal passing through RE

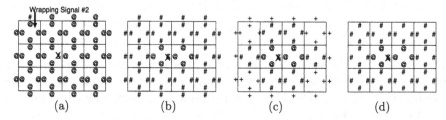

Fig. 10. Detecting and isolating a defective cell. Defective partition is denoted by a cross mark.

First we describe the detection and isolation processes. Defective cells are isolated from the rest of the cell space by setting the cells surrounding them in special states. This process is conducted by injecting so-called *test-signals* in the cell space, which spread and eventually leave rectangular wrappers around defective areas. Defects lying within a distance of a few cells of each other are wrapped in a joint rectangle, whereas defects further away get their own rectangles (Fig. 3). We use three kinds of signals (#1, #2, and #3) with states @, #, and +, respectively. After injecting test signal #1, we inject test signal #2 (Fig. 10(a)), which then spreads over the whole cell space, except for the cells containing or adjacent to the defective partition (Fig. 10(b)). Upon this, the basic skeleton of a wrapper is formed (Fig. 10(c)). After test signal #3 is injected, the concave parts of the skeleton are filled in (Fig. 10(d)).

Scanning non-defective area and constructing the modules of a circuit is conducted by an arm configuration. Figure 11 shows the head configuration at the end of the arm. This head accepts several kinds of signals for controlling the position of the head, checking whether the head runs into wrappers, and putting the stable pairs for constructing modules. An example of the head receiving a signal is shown in Fig. 12. This head advances one cell to the right after receiving one signal encoded by the partition pair '%+'.

It is possible to construct the circuit modules in non-defective area by manipulating the arm, like shown in Fig. 13, where two circuit modules are placed at both sides of a defective area. These modules are connected by signal paths, one of which crosses the defective area. We have equiped signals with the ability to go around defective area so that modules separated by the defective area can communicate with each other. Circuit operation is unaffected by the lengths of

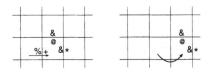

Fig. 11. Head configuration

Fig. 12. The head advances one cell to the right after receiving a signal

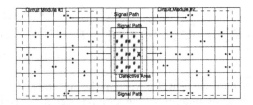

Fig. 13. Isolation is wrapped around defects and circuit modules are placed on the cellular space such that defects are avoided

signal paths and the number of defective areas, because operations and communication between REs are delay-insensitive.

3.2   Defect Tolerant STCA That Can Detect Defects On-Line

This section introduces an STCA that can detect and isolate cells with stuck-at fault defects in an on-line manner, i.e., during computation. Detection and isolation of defects are realized by having configurations of *random flies* move around in the cellular space and attach to faulty cells. Key to distinguishing a faulty from a non-faulty cell is the latter's propensity to eat flies as part of its ability to undergo state changes. All the tasks including computation and detection and isolation of faults are accomplished within the STCA model, i.e., no external or off-line detection mechanisms are required. We first introduce computational elements, called K- and E-elements, used in this STCA.

Computational Elements and Their Implementation on STCA. A K-element has two input ports and one output port and is used for merging two input lines into one line (see Fig. 14). This element accepts a signal coming from either line 1 or line 2 and outputs it on line 3.

An E-element is an element with two input ports (S and T) and three output ports (S', T_u, and T_d), as well as two internal states ('up' or 'down'). Input from port S will be redirected to either of the output ports T_u or T_d, depending on the internal state of the element: when this state is 'up' (resp. 'down'), a signal on the input port T flows to the output port T_u (resp. T_d) as in Figs. 16(a) and 16(b). By accepting a signal on the input port S, an E-element changes its internal state from 'up' to 'down' or from 'down' to 'up', after which it outputs a signal to the output port S', as shown in Fig. 16(c).

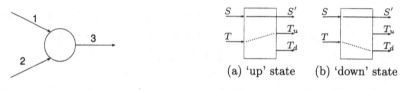

Fig. 14. K-Element

Fig. 15. E-Element in (a) 'up' state and (b) 'down' state

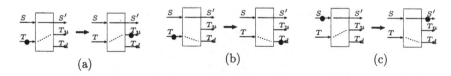

Fig. 16. Operations of an E-element: (a) when in the 'up' state, (b) when in the 'down' state, and (c) changing state upon receiving an input signal on the port S, whereby a blob on a line denotes a signal

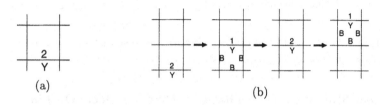

Fig. 17. (a) A signal configuration and (b) its move forward

To embed a network of K-elements and E-elements on an STCA, we first define signals and their paths between elements. A cell is divided in partitions, each of which can be in one of 8 states, denoted by the set of symbols { , 1, 2, 3, X, Y, Z, B}. Figure 17(a) shows a signal toward the north on an STCA, whereby the signal is represented by the partition pair '2Y'. To move the signal forward, this state pair is first changed into '1Y', like in Fig. 17(b). Signal paths are represented by cells of which all the partitions have the state ' '.

An E-element is represented on an STCA by a loop structure (Fig. 18) through which an internal signal is continuously moving, whereby the direction of the signal denotes the state of the element; counterclockwise corresponding to the state 'up' and clockwise to the state 'down'. The internal signal in an E-element, denoted by the partition pair 'X1' or 'X2', moves along the 'XX' loop of the E-element in a similar way as with the propagation of a signal, i.e., two stages are used to move a signal forward by one step. Figures 19(a) and 19(b) show how an internal signal in an E-element in state 'up' and state 'down', respectively, propagates along the loop. An example of E-element operating on a signal is shown in Fig. 20, where the E-element is in the 'down' state. Input signal arrived on the port 'T' is transferred to the output port 'S' by the internal signal in the E-element.

The E-element implemented on an STCA can be used for purposes other than the function of the E-element itself as well. First this element can turn signals

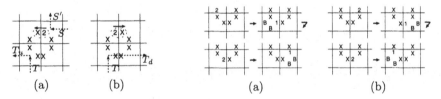

Fig. 18. An E-element config-uration in (a) 'up' state and in (b) 'down' state

Fig. 19. Internal signals circulating in E-elements in (a) 'up' state and (b) 'down' state

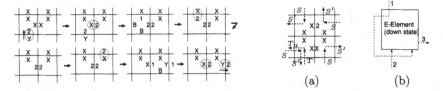

Fig. 20. An E-element in state 'down' op-erating on a signal

Fig. 21. (a) Multiple input ports for S, (b) Construction of a K-element from E-elements

arriving at input port T to the left or the right, depending on whether the state is 'up' or 'down', respectively. Additionally, an input signal on the port S is always turned to the right. Due to the rotational symmetric of the transition rules on the STCA, the input port S can be assumed to be placed at any of the corners of an E-element, as shown in Fig. 21(a). By exploiting this ambiguity of placement of input ports of the E-element when it is embedded in the cellular space, we find that the K-element can actually be constructed from E-elements, whereby the main E-element is configured to conduct the operation of the K-element, and the remaining E-elements are used for turning signals left (see Fig. 21(b)). The implementation of the E-element can thus be used not only for the E-element itself, but also for implementing the K-element. The E-element is thus sufficient to ensure universality.

Random Fly Configurations for Checking Living Configurations. A random fly is a configuration of two cells, as shown in Fig. 22. It will move around in cellular space in random directions as a result of transition rules that are designed to allow more than one way (two ways to be exact) for a random fly to make a step. Which of these two ways is chosen depends on the particular order at which cells are updated, and this is random—due to the asynchronous mode of timing. Figures 23(a) and 23(b) show the two possible ways a random fly can make a step. In either way, the cell undergoing a transition first changes one of its partitions' states to '2', giving two distinct situations that further develop into flies at two different positions. In the end, the fly will have moved either forward to the left, or backward to the right, as can be seen in the rightmost

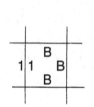

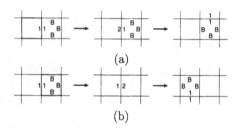

(a)

(b)

Fig. 22. A configuration of a random fly

Fig. 23. Two possible transitions for a random fly

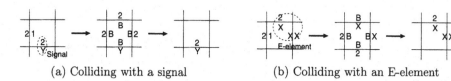

(a) Colliding with a signal   (b) Colliding with an E-element

Fig. 24. A random fly colliding (a) with a signal and (b) with an E-element. In both cases, the fly is annihilated.

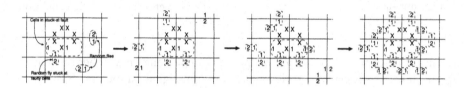

Fig. 25. Isolation of defective E-element by random flies

configurations in Fig. 23. Random flies are generated as a side effect of the operation of an E-element. We do not go into detail how this is done due to lack of space, but merely mention that the density of random flies is relatively high in the neighborhood of E-elements that operate correctly (see [5]). E-elements containing defects will be static, and will thus fail to generate flies.

A collision of a random fly on one hand, with a signal or with a working E-element or with other random flies on the other hand, results in the annihilation of the fly. For such an annihilation to happen, a fly in its standard configuration in Fig. 22 will bump with its '11' head into the obstacle that is to annihilate the fly. Once this head sticks to the obstacle, it has only one way to proceed, and that is to change into configuration '12' according to the sequence of events in Fig. 23(b). The sequence of events in Fig. 23(a) will never be followed in this case, because the cell that would undergo a transition will be unable to do so in the presence of an obstacle. In the cases shown below of a fly colliding with an obstacle, we will thus assume that the fly is in the '12' configuration, because that configuration will eventually occur in any collision.

Figure 24(a) shows a random fly that collides with a signal, after which an intermediate state is reached as the precursor of the final annihilation of the fly. Another example of random fly annihilation occurs when a random fly attaches to the output (or input) port of a working E-element. In this case, it stays at this port until an internal signal circulating in the E-element arrives, after which the fly is annihilated (see Fig. 24(b)). Other situations concerning collisions of random flies with E-elements are treated in similar ways. Random flies are also annihilated when they collide with other random flies. Random flies do not affect the operation of circuit elements in terms of functionality; they may cause some signal delays, though, but these do not affect the computation's outcome, since the underlying circuits are delay-insensitive.

An important aspect of the annihilation mechanism is that random flies stuck to an E-element are only annihilated if the E-element is working properly, i.e., if an internal signal runs around in it. When the internal signal of an E-element stops, for example due to a defect, random flies will no longer be annihilated and will wrap the E-element completely (see Fig. 25). These flies remain in the state '12', so all the partitions pointing outwards of this E-element will assume this state, forming an isolation layer.

4   Conclusions

We have reviewed our previous research on defect-tolerant self-timed cellular automata that can detect and isolate defective cells in this paper. Two approaches are described, i.e., off-line and on-line.

In the off-line manner, defective cells in the cellular space are first checked by injecting test signals and are isolated from non-defective cells by an isolation layer. The modules of a circuit are then placed in the non-defective area. Communications between modules that cross defective areas are realized by signals that can circumvent the defective areas. Each partition of this CA has 8 states, whereas 100 transition rules are needed for all its functions [4].

In the on-line manner, defective cells are detected and isolated while computation takes place. Detection is conducted through random fly configurations moving around in the cellular space. These flies are annihilated when they attach to 'living' components consisting of non-defective cells. Random flies attached to 'dead' configurations remain stuck, and hence their tails form isolation layers. This CA requires 8 states per partition and 63 transition rules [5].

These two CA have complementary functions to each other. The first CA lacks the ability to detect defective cells during computation and the second CA lacks reconfiguration ability. For the realization of defect-tolerance in CA-based nanocomputers, it is thus important to unify these models, a challenge to be addressed in future work.

References

1. Durbeck, L.J.K., Macias, N.J.: The cell matrix: an architecture for nanocomputing. Nanotechnology 12, 217–230 (2001)
2. Peper, F., Lee, J., Adachi, S., Mashiko, S.: Laying out circuits on asynchronous cellular arrays: a step towards feasible nanocomputers? Nanotechnology 14, 469–485 (2003)

3. Peper, F., Lee, J., Abo, F., Isokawa, T., Adachi, S., Matsui, N., Mashiko, S.: Fault-Tolerance in Nanocomputers: A Cellular Array Approach. IEEE Trans. on Nanotechnology 3(1), 187–201 (2004)
4. Isokawa, T., Kowada, S., Takada, Y., Peper, F., Kamiura, N., Matsui, N.: Defect-Tolerance in Cellular Nanocomputers. New Generation Computing (2007)
5. Isokawa, T., Kowada, S., Peper, F., Kamiura, N., Matsui, N.: Online marking of defective cells by random flies. In: El Yacoubi, S., Chopard, B., Bandini, S. (eds.) ACRI 2006. LNCS, vol. 4173, pp. 347–356. Springer, Heidelberg (2006)
6. Lee, J., Peper, F., Adachi, S., Morita, K., Mashiko, S.: Reversible computation in asynchronous cellular automata. In: 3rd Int. Conf. on Unconventional Models of Computation 2002, pp. 220–229. Springer, Heidelberg (2002)
7. Priese, L.: Automata and Concurrency. Theoretical Computer Science 25, 221–265 (1983)
8. Morita, K.: A simple universal logic element and cellular automata for reversible computing. In: Margenstern, M., Rogozhin, Y. (eds.) MCU 2001, vol. 2055, pp. 102–113. Springer, Heidelberg (2001)
9. Takada, Y., Isokawa, T., Peper, F., Matsui, N.: Universal construction and self-reproduction on self-timed cellular automata. Int. J. of Modern Physics C 17(7), 985–1007 (2006)

Towards the Sequence Design Preventing Pseudoknot Formation

Lila Kari and Shinnosuke Seki

Department of Computer Science, University of Western Ontario,
London, Ontario, Canada, N6A 5B7
{lila,sseki}@csd.uwo.ca

Abstract. This paper addresses a pseudoknot-freeness problem of DNA and RNA sequences, motivated by biomolecular computing. Watson-Crick (WK) complementarity forces DNA strands to fold into themselves and form so-called secondary structures, which are usually undesirable for biomolecular computational purposes. This paper studies pseudoknot-bordered words, a mathematical formalization of a common secondary structure, the pseudoknot. We obtain several properties of WK-pseudoknot-bordered and -unbordered words. One of the main results of the paper is that a sufficient condition for a WK-pseudoknot-unbordered word u to result in all words in u^+ being WK-pseudoknot-unbordered is for u not to be a primitive word.

1 Introduction

Adleman's first biomolecular computing experiment [1] has shown that biochemical properties of DNA such as Watson-Crick (WK) complementarity make it possible to solve computational problems, such as NP-complete problems entirely by DNA manipulation in test tubes. In DNA computing, information is encoded into DNA by a coding scheme mapping the original alphabet onto DNA single strands over {Adenine (A), Guanine (G), Cytosine (C), Thymine (T)}. A computation consists of a succession of *bio-operations* [2] based on *base-pairing* and the others. A can chemically bind to T, while C can similarly bind to G. (Note that T is replaced by U in the case of ribonucleic acid (RNA), and that U is complementary to both C and G.) Bases that can thus bind are called *Watson/Crick (WK) complementary*, and two DNA single strands with opposite orientation and with WK complementary bases at each position can bind to each other to form a *DNA double strand*.

Watson-Crick complementarity often makes a single-stranded structure fold into a high-dimensional (partially double-stranded) structure that is optimal in terms of biochemical determinants like Gibbs free-energy [3]. *In vivo* the secondary structures of nucleic acids have a significant role in determining their biochemical functions. On the other hand, *in vitro* biomolecular computing often considers them as disadvantages because it is very likely that the secondary structure formation of a DNA/RNA strand will prevent it from interacting with other DNA/RNA strands in the expected, pre-programmed way. Thence, many

Y. Suzuki et al. (Eds.): IWNC 2007, PICT 1, pp. 101–110, 2009.

studies exist on how to free sequence sets from secondary structures [4], [5], [6], [7], [8], [9], [10].

From the intramolecular point of view, most of these studies investigate the question of how to design sets of DNA/RNA strands that are "free of" the hairpin structure, known as the most common secondary structure. A hairpin structure can be formally modelled by using the notion of an antimorphic involution. An involution is a function f such that f^2 equals the identity, and an antimorphism f over an alphabet Σ is a function such that $f(uv) = f(v)f(u)$ for all words $u, v \in \Sigma^*$. An antimorphic involution is thus the mathematical formalization of the notion of DNA single-strand Watson/Crick complementarity. Indeed, the WK complement of a single DNA strand is the reverse, complement of the original strand. Using this formalization, a hairpin can be described as $z\beta\theta(z)$ as indicated in Fig. 1 (b), and modelled by the notion of a θ-bordered word [9]. In other words, a set of θ-unbordered words is guaranteed to be hairpin-free, and as such, results obtained in [9] on θ-bordered words for antimorphic involution θ are of practical significance.

In this paper, we take a similar approach to modeling and structure-freeness problems that ensures that no pseudoknots structures will be formed. Pseudoknots are a generic term of a cross-dependent structure that are formed primarily by RNA strands. An example of the simplest and most typical pseudoknots is shown in Figure 1, (a). An example of a pseudoknot found in *E.Coli* tmRNA is depicted in Figure 2. This depicts a pseudoknot formed by a strand $u = \rho x \alpha y \gamma \theta(x) \delta \theta(y) \sigma$ where x and $\theta(x)$ respectively y and $\theta(y)$ bind to each other. In this paper we consider the simpler case wherein $\rho = \alpha = \delta = \sigma = \lambda$, *i.e.*, we investigate strands of the form $u = xy\gamma\theta(x)\theta(y)$ where θ is an antimorphic involution function.

We namely generalize the notion of θ-(un)bordered word to that of θ-*pseudoknot-(un)bordered word*. A word is called θ-pseudoknot-bordered if it has a prefix whose image under the composition of the cyclic permutation and θ is its suffix. Formally speaking, a word w is θ-pseudoknot-bordered if $w = xy\alpha = \beta\theta(yx)$ for some words x, y, α, and β. In the case where θ is an antimorphic involution, this indeed is a formal model for simple pseudoknots since $\theta(yx) = \theta(x)\theta(y)$ holds.

This paper is organized as follows: After basic definitions and notations in Sec. 2, we define the notion of θ-pseudoknot-bordered words in Sec. 3 and prove some basic properties. We also show that the notion of θ-pseudoknot-border generalizes the notion of a θ-border. Sec. 4 concludes this paper by providing a counterintuitive result, Corollary 4, which proves that the sufficient condition for a θ-pseudoknot-unbordered word u to satisfy the condition that all words in u^+ have the same property turns out to be that u be not primitive. Proofs of the results in this paper can be found in [11].

2 Preliminaries

This section introduces basic notions of formal language theory and algebra. For details of each notion contained in this section, we refer the reader to [13], [14].

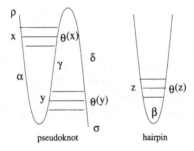

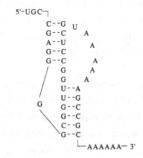

Fig. 1. Examples of a) a pseudoknot and b) a strand with two hairpins

```
5'-UGC┐
       C--G  U
       G--C      A
       A--U    A
       G--C
       G--C    A
      / G     A
     /  G     A
        U--A
        U--G
   G    G--C
    \   G--C
     \  C--G
       G--C
        └AAAAAA─ 3'
```

Fig. 2. A pseudoknot found in E. Coli tmRNA. Here $u = \rho x \alpha y \gamma \theta(x) \delta \theta(y) \sigma$, where $\rho = \text{UGC}$, $x = \text{CGAGG}$, $\alpha = \text{G}$, $y = \text{GCGGUU}$, $\gamma = \text{GG}$, $\delta = \text{UAAAAA}$, $\sigma = \text{AAAAAA}$, and x and $\theta(x)$ respectively y and $\theta(y)$ bind to each other. From [12].

Let Σ^* (resp. Σ^+) be the free monoid (resp. free semigroup) generated by a finite alphabet Σ with the concatenation operation. The identity element of Σ^* is denoted by λ and as such, $\Sigma^+ = \Sigma^* \setminus \{\lambda\}$. An element of Σ^* is called a word. Hereafter words will be denoted by lower-case letters such as x, y, α, β. For a word $w \in \Sigma^*$, $|w|$ denotes the length of w. Let u and w be words over Σ. We say that u is a *prefix* of w if there exists $v \in \Sigma^*$ such that $w = uv$; Similarly, u is a *suffix* of w if $w = vu$ for some $v \in \Sigma^*$. Let $\text{Pref}(w)$ and $\text{Suff}(w)$ be the set of all prefixes and that of all suffixes of w, respectively.

A word $w \in \Sigma^+$ is *primitive* if $w = u^p$ with $u \in \Sigma^+$ implies $p = 1$. It is a well known fact [15], that for any word $w \in \Sigma^*$, there exist a unique primitive word, which is denoted by $\sqrt{w}$ and called the primitive root of w, and a unique positive integer k such that $w = (\sqrt{w})^k$.

Let θ be a mapping on a set S. If $a = \theta(a)$ for all $a \in S$, then θ is called the identity function or simply the identity. An *involution* is a mapping whose square is the identity. In this paper we consider two mappings on Σ^*: a d-morphism and a cyclic permutation. A *d-morphism* on Σ^* is a generic term used to refer to either a morphism or an antimorphism on Σ^*. A mapping θ from Σ^* to itself is defined as a *morphism* (resp. *antimorphism*) on Σ^* if and only if $\theta(xy) = \theta(x)\theta(y)$ (resp. $\theta(xy) = \theta(y)\theta(x)$) for all $x, y \in \Sigma^*$. For a d-morphic involution θ, a word $w \in \Sigma^*$ is called *θ-palindrome* if and only if $w = \theta(w)$. We denote by P_θ the set of all θ-palindromes over Σ^*. For a word $w \in \Sigma^*$ such that $w = xy$ for $x, y \in \Sigma^*$, yx is called a *cyclic permutation* of w. The set of all cyclic permutations of w is denoted by $\mathrm{cp}(w)$; that is, $\mathrm{cp}(w) = \{yx \mid w = xy, x, y \in \Sigma^*\}$.

With applications to the function θ being the Watson-Crick complementarity of DNA sequences in mind, hereafter we shall deal only with non-identity mappings. Thus, this paper excludes singleton alphabet sets, on which there does not exist any non-identity mapping, that is, we assume $|\Sigma| \geq 2$.

3 θ-Pseudoknot-Bordered Words

In this section we introduce the notion of θ-*pseudoknot-bordered word*, for a morphic or antimorphic involution θ. This notion is a formalization of the biological concept of pseudoknot. Indeed, if θ is the Watson-Crick involution, then a θ-pseudoknot-bordered word represents a DNA/RNA strand that forms a pseudoknot as pictured in Fig. 1.

In addition, the notion of θ-pseudoknot-bordered word represents a proper generalization of the classical notion of a bordered word. A non-empty word u is called *bordered* [16] if there exists a non-empty word v that is both a prefix and a suffix of u. An unbordered word is a non-empty word that is not bordered.

The first step towards generalizing the notion of a bordered word was in [9], where the concept of θ-bordered word was first defined, that generalized the identity function by replacing it with a d-morphic involution θ. Here we propose the next step in this direction by employing a cyclic permutation to further extend the notion of a θ-bordered word to that of a θ-*pseudoknot-bordered word*.

Definition 1. *([9]) Let θ be a d-morphic involution, and $v, w \in \Sigma^*$. Then,*

1. *$v \leq_p w$ if and only if $w \in v\Sigma^*$. The word v is a prefix of the word w.*
2. *$v \leq_s^\theta w$ if and only if $w \in \Sigma^*\theta(v)$. The word v is a θ-suffix of the word w.*
3. *$\leq_d^\theta = \leq_p \cap \leq_s^\theta$. If $u, v \in \Sigma^*$ and $v \leq_d^\theta u$ we say that v is a θ-border of u. A word $w \in \Sigma^+$ is said to be θ-bordered if there exists $v \in \Sigma^+$ such that $v <_d^\theta w$, i.e., $w = v\alpha = \beta\theta(v)$ for some $\alpha, \beta \in \Sigma^+$. A non-empty word which is not θ-bordered is called θ-unbordered.*
4. *$v <_p w$ if and only if $w \in v\Sigma^+$. v is a proper prefix of w.*
5. *$v <_s^\theta w$ if and only if $w \in \Sigma^+\theta(v)$. v is a proper θ-suffix of w.*
6. *$<_d^\theta = <_p \cap <_s^\theta$. If $u, v \in \Sigma^*$ and $v <_d^\theta u$ we say that v is a proper θ-border of u.*
7. *For $w \in \Sigma^+$, $L_d^\theta(w) = \{v \mid v \in \Sigma^*, v <_d^\theta w\}$. $L_d^\theta(w)$ denotes the set of all proper θ-borders of a nonempty word w.*
8. *$D_\theta(i) = \{w \mid w \in \Sigma^+, |L_d^\theta(w)| = i\}$. $D_\theta(i)$ denotes the set of all nonempty words that have exactly i θ-borders.*

We now generalize this definition with the goal of defining the notion of the θ-pseudoknot-bordered word. This is accomplished by introducing a cyclic permutation.

Definition 2. *Let θ be a d-morphic involution, and $v, w \in \Sigma^*$. Then,*

1. *$v \leq_{cs}^{\theta} w$ if and only if there exists $v' \in cp(v)$ such that $v' \leq_{s}^{\theta} w$. In other words, $v \leq_{cs}^{\theta} w$ iff $v = xy$, $x, y \in \Sigma^*$, and $w = \beta\theta(yx)$. v is called a θ-pseudoknot-suffix of w.*
2. *$\leq_{cd}^{\theta} = \leq_p \cap \leq_{cs}^{\theta}$. v is said to be a θ-pseudoknot-border of w if $v \leq_{cd}^{\theta} w$, i.e., there exist $x, y \in \Sigma^*$ such that $v = xy$ and $w = xy\alpha = \beta\theta(yx)$ for some $\alpha, \beta \in \Sigma^*$. A non-empty word w is said to be θ-pseudoknot-bordered if w has a non-empty θ-pseudoknot-border. A non-empty word which is not θ-pseudoknot-bordered is called θ-pseudoknot-unbordered.*
3. *$L_{cd}^{\theta}(w) = \{v \mid v \in \Sigma^*, v \leq_{cd}^{\theta} w\}$. $L_{cd}^{\theta}(w)$ denotes the set of all θ-pseudoknot-borders of a nonempty word w.*
4. *$K_{\theta}(i) = \{w \mid |w \in \Sigma^+, L_{cd}^{\theta}(w)| = i\}$. $K_{\theta}(i)$ denotes the set of all nonempty words that have exactly i θ-pseudoknot-borders.*

As in the case of θ-bordered words, the empty word λ is a θ-pseudoknot-border of any word, *i.e.*, $\forall w \in \Sigma^*, \lambda \in L_{cd}^{\theta}(w)$. Indeed, Definition 2 (2) allows the cases $v = xy = \lambda$ and $w = \alpha = \beta$. Thus, a word in $K_{\theta}(1)$ has no θ-pseudoknot-borders other than λ. $K_{\theta}(1)$ is the set of all θ-pseudoknot-unbordered words.

Note also that it is possible that a word w has itself as its θ-pseudoknot-border, as shown by the following example.

Example 1. Let θ be an antimorphic involution on Σ^*, and let $a, b \in \Sigma$ such that $\theta(a) = b$ and $\theta(b) = a$. Consider $u = ababbbaa$, which can be factorized into two θ-palindromes $abab$ and $bbaa$ and thus u is one of its θ-pseudoknot-borders. It is easy to see that the only other θ-pseudoknot-border is λ, and thus $u \in K_{\theta}(2)$. □

Lastly, note that the definitions of $L_d^{\theta}(w)$ and $L_{cd}^{\theta}(w)$ are different in that the former equals the set of all the proper θ-borders while the latter can include also w, if w is a θ-pseudoknot-border of itself. This scenario is different from the classical case of θ as well as the permutation used being the indentity, wherein all words are automatically borders of themselves. We found our proposed definition to be more natural in the case of θ-pseudoknot-borders, since only some words w are θ-pseudoknot-borders of themselves while others are not. This implies however that, while all other proposed notions are strict generalizations of both the θ-border notions and the classical border notion, $L_{cd}^{\theta}(w)$ does not strictly generalize $L_d^{\theta}(w)$ and $L_d(w)$. This was a deliberate choice of definition on our part since a) this definition is more natural and b) all results that we obtained in this paper hold for the other definition choice as well, either unchanged or augmented with a weak additional condition. For example, Proposition 2 holds even if we define L_{cd}^{θ} to be the set of all proper θ-pseudoknot-bordered words, if we require, in addition, that u cannot be factorized into two θ-palindromes, *i.e.*, there exist no $x, y \in P_{\theta}$ such that $u = xy$.

In the sequel, we will employ the expression "xy is a θ-pseudoknot-border of w" to mean "v is a θ-pseudoknot-border of w such that $v = xy$ and $w = xy\alpha = \beta\theta(yx)$ for some $x, y, \alpha, \beta \in \Sigma^*$".

To begin with, we provide some immediate consequences of Definition 2.

Corollary 1. *If θ is a d-morphic involution on Σ^*, the followings hold.*

1. *If a word has some θ-pseudoknot-border of length n, then for every $a \in \Sigma$, the number of letters a in its prefix of length n must be equal to the number of letters $\theta(a)$ in its suffix of length n.*
2. *For all $a \in \Sigma$ such that $a \neq \theta(a)$, $a^+ \subseteq K_\theta(1)$.*
3. *If $xy \leq^\theta_{cd} w^n$ and $|w^{m-1}| < |xy| \leq |w^m|$, then $xy \leq^\theta_{cd} w^k$ for all k with $m \leq k \leq n$.*

Example 2. Let $\Sigma = \{a, b\}$, $w = aababbb$, and θ be the antimorphic involution such that $\theta(a) = b$ and $\theta(b) = a$. Then $L^\theta_{cd}(w) = \{\lambda, a, aa, aaba\}$. In particular, setting $x = aab$ and $y = a$ confirms that $aaba \leq^\theta_{cd} w$. □

Recall that a language L is said to be *dense* if $\forall w \in \Sigma^*, L \cap \Sigma^* w \Sigma^* \neq \emptyset$.

Lemma 1. *Let θ be a d-morphic involution on Σ^*. Then $K_\theta(1)$, the set of all θ-pseudoknot-unbordered words over Σ^*, is a dense set.*

The following lemma and proposition show that if a word is θ-bordered, then it is θ-pseudoknot-bordered.

Lemma 2. *Let θ be a d-morphic involution on Σ^* and $w \in \Sigma^*$. Then $L^\theta_d(w) \subseteq L^\theta_{cd}(w)$ holds.*

Proof. Let $v \in L^\theta_d(w)$. If $v = \lambda$, then by definition, $v \in L^\theta_{cd}(w)$; otherwise $w = v\alpha = \beta\theta(v)$ for some $\alpha, \beta \in \Sigma^*$. This means that we can split v into $x = v$ and $y = \lambda$ so as to satisfy the condition of v being a θ-pseudoknot-border of w, i.e., $w = v\lambda\alpha = \beta\theta(\lambda v)$. This implies that $v \in L^\theta_{cd}(w)$.

Note that there exists a word $w \in \Sigma^*$ and a d-morphic involution θ for which $L^\theta_d(w)$ is strictly included in $L^\theta_{cd}(w)$.

Example 3. Let $\Sigma = \{a, b\}$, $w = aababbb$, and θ be a d-morphic involution satisfying $\theta(a) = b$ and $\theta(b) = a$. Whether θ is morphic or antimorphic involution, $L^\theta_d(w) = \{\lambda, a, aa\}$ but $L^\theta_{cd}(w) = \{\lambda, a, aa, aaba\}$. □

Although, in this example, $L^\theta_{cd}(w)$ for a morphic involution θ and $L^\theta_{cd}(w)$ for an antimorphic involution θ are the same, that is not always the case as indicated in the following examples:

Example 4. Let us consider Σ and θ as in Example 3, a word $w = aabbabaababb$, and its prefix $w_p = aabbab$. When θ is morphic, we can decompose w_p into $x = aa$ and $y = bbab$ such that $\theta(yx)$ becomes the suffix of w. Thus, $aabbab \in L^\theta_{cd}(w)$ for the morphism θ. On the other hand, $aabbab \notin L^\theta_{cd}(w)$ for an antimorphic θ. □

Example 5. Let us consider Σ and θ as in Example 3, a word $w' = aabbabbbabaa$, and its prefix $w'_p = aabbab$. When θ is antimorphic, we can decompose w'_p into $x = aa$ and $y = bbab$ such that $\theta(yx)$ becomes the suffix of w'. Therefore, $aabbab \in L^\theta_{cd}(w')$ for the antimorphism θ. On the other hand, $aabbab \notin L^\theta_{cd}(w')$ for a morphic θ. □

Proposition 1. *Let θ be a d-morphic involution on Σ^*. Then $K_\theta(1) \subseteq D_\theta(1)$.*

For an antimorphic involution θ, note that the inclusion relation of Proposition 1 holds properly, i.e. $K_\theta(1) \subsetneq D_\theta(1)$, as shown in the following example.

Example 6. Let $w = aba$ and θ be an antimorphic involution mapping a to b and vice versa. Suppose $w \notin D_\theta(1)$. Then w should be of the form $a\Sigma^*\theta(a)$ [9]. However, w does not end with $\theta(a)$, and we conclude that $w \in D_\theta(1)$. On the other hand, $w \notin K_\theta(1)$ because $w = xya = a\theta(yx)$ for $x = a$ and $y = b$. $\square$

4 Primitive and θ-Pseudoknot-Unbordered Words

This section addresses the question of whether or not the Kleene closure of a θ-pseudoknot-unbordered word contains only θ-pseudoknot-unbordered words. In other words, if $u \in K_\theta(1)$ we are asking whether or not the inclusion $u^+ \subseteq K_\theta(1)$ holds. This question was solved positively for θ-unbordered words in [9], that is, if $u \in D_\theta(1)$, then $u^+ \subseteq D_\theta(1)$. In contrast, in this section we answer in the negative the question for the case of θ-pseudoknot-unbordered words. Moreover, we provide a sufficient condition for a θ-pseudoknot-unbordered word $u \in K_\theta(1)$ to satisfy $u^+ \subseteq K_\theta(1)$. Unexpectedly, the condition is that u is not primitive (Corollary 4).

To begin with, we provide a necessary and sufficient condition for a word to be θ-pseudoknot-unbordered.

Lemma 3. *Let θ be an antimorphic involution on Σ^*. Then for $u \in \Sigma^+$, u is θ-pseudoknot-unbordered if and only if $\theta(\mathrm{cp}(\mathrm{Pref}(u))) \cap \mathrm{Suff}(u) = \emptyset$.*

The following lemma will be used as a tool to prove that a nonempty word $w \in \Sigma^+$ is θ-pseudoknot-bordered by *reductio ad absurdum*.

Lemma 4. *Let θ be an antimorphic involution, and x and y be θ-palindromes. If a word $u \in \Sigma^+$ has xy as both its prefix and suffix, then u is θ-pseudoknot-bordered, i.e., $u \notin K_\theta(1)$.*

Next, we relate the property of a word w being θ-pseudoknot-unbordered to the fact that u^k is θ-pseudoknot-bordered for some integer $k > 1$. This result relates to the following results obtained for the particular case of the θ-bordered words in [9].

Lemma 5. *([9]) Let θ be an antimorphism on Σ^* and let $u \in \Sigma^+$. Then $\theta(\mathrm{Pref}(u)) \cap \mathrm{Suff}(u) = \emptyset$ if and only if $\theta(\mathrm{Pref}(u^+)) \cap \mathrm{Suff}(u^+) = \emptyset$.*

Corollary 2. *([9]) Let θ be an antimorphic involution on Σ^* and let $u \in \Sigma^+$. Then $u \in D_\theta(1)$ if and only if $u^+ \subseteq D_\theta(1)$.*

In contrast to Corollary 2, it is not always the case that, given a θ-pseudoknot-unbordered word u, the word u^k remains θ-pseudoknot-unbordered for any k, that is, in general we cannot say that $u \in K_\theta(1)$ if and only if $u^+ \subseteq K_\theta(1)$. See the next example.

Example 7. Let θ be an antimorphic involution on Σ^*, and let $a, b \in \Sigma$ such that $\theta(a) = b$ and $\theta(b) = a$. Since θ does not equal the identity, we can always find such letters a and b in Σ.

Let $u = aabbbbaba$. Although $u \in K_\theta(1)$, uu is θ-pseudoknot-bordered for $x = aabbb$ and $y = babaa$. In fact, $uu = xyabbbbaba = aabbbbab\theta(x)\theta(y)$. □

Nevertheless, when θ is an antimorphic involution, we can give a characterization of such counterexamples that takes into account the relative length of the θ-pseudoknot-borders.

Proposition 2. *Let θ be an antimorphic involution on Σ^*. Then for a θ-pseudoknot-unbordered word $u \in K_\theta(1)$, if there exists $k \geq 2$ such that u^k has a nonempty θ-pseudoknot-border w, then $|u| < |w| < \frac{4}{3}|u|$ holds.*

Proof. Suppose for some $k \geq 2$, there were a $w \in L_{cd}^\theta(u^k)$ such that either $|w| \leq |u|$ or $\frac{4}{3}|u| \leq |w|$ hold. If $|w| \leq |u|$, then this w leads us to the contradiction immediately. Next we consider the case $\frac{4}{3}|u| \leq |w| < 2|u|$. Then $w \in L_{cd}^\theta(u^k)$ implies $w \in L_{cd}^\theta(u^2)$. In other words, there exists a decomposition $w = xy$ such that $uu = xy\alpha = \beta\theta(x)\theta(y)$ for some $\alpha, \beta \in \Sigma^+$. Since $|w| \geq \frac{4}{3}|u|$, we have $xy = uu_p$ and $\theta(x)\theta(y) = u_s u$, where $u_p \in \text{Pref}(u)$, and $u_s \in \text{Suff}(u)$. Now we have the following two cases: (1) $|x| \geq |u|$ or $|y| \geq |u|$ holds, or (2) $|x| < |u|$ and $|y| < |u|$ hold.

In the first case, for reasons of symmetry, we only have to consider the case $|x| \geq |u|$. Since $\theta(x)\theta(y) = u_s u$, we can write $\theta(x) = u_s u_p'$ for some $u_p' \in \text{Pref}(u)$. Let $u = u_p' u_s'$, and we can easily check that $u_s' \in \text{Suff}(u_s)$. Therefore, $u_s' u_p' \in \text{Suff}(\theta(x))$, which equals $\theta(u_p')\theta(u_s') \in \text{Pref}(x)$. This means that $\theta(u_p')\theta(u_s') = u$ because u and $\theta(u_p')\theta(u_s')$ are prefixes of x and they have equal lengths. Since $u = u_p' u_s'$, we coclude that both u_p' and u_s' are θ-palindromes. The application of Lemmata 3 and 4 leads now to a contradiction.

Next we consider the second case. This figure shows $xy = uu_p$ and $\theta(x)\theta(y) = u_s u$. Since both x and y are shorter than u, these equations imply that $u = xu_s' = u_p'\theta(y)$, where $u_p' \in \text{Pref}(u)$ and $u_s' \in \text{Suff}(u)$. Comparing this equation with $xy = uu_p$ we derive $y = u_s' u_p$, and hence $u = u_p'\theta(u_p)\theta(u_s')$. This result, together with $u = xu_s'$, implies that u_s' is a θ-palindrome and $x = u_p'\theta(u_p)$. Substituting this x and $u = u_p'\theta(y)$ into $\theta(x)\theta(y) = u_s u$ gives $u_p\theta(u_p')\theta(y) = u_s u_p'\theta(y)$, which means that $u_p = u_s$ and u_p' is a θ-palindrome.

Let us bring now into the picture the original condition $\frac{4}{3}|u| \leq |w| < 2|u|$. Since $|w| = |u| + |u_p|$, $\frac{4}{3}|u| \leq |w|$ means $\frac{1}{3}|u| \leq |u_p|$. Hence, $|xy| = |uu_p| \leq 4|u_p|$. This implies that either $|x| \leq 2|u_p|$ or $|y| \leq 2|u_p|$ holds. We assume the former case holds. Then $\theta(x) = u_s u_p'$ implies $|u_p'| \leq |u_s|$ because $|\theta(x)| = |x| \leq 2|u_p| = 2|u_s|$. Let $u_s = u_1 u_2$ such that $|u_1| = |u_p'|$. Note that $u_s \in \text{Pref}(x)$ because $u_p, x \in \text{Pref}(u)$, $|u_s| < |x|$, and $u_p = u_s$. Comparing $u_s = u_1 u_2$ with $x = \theta(u_1 u_2 u_p')$ based on $u_s \in \text{Pref}(x)$ results in $u_2 = \theta(u_2)$ and $u_1 = \theta(u_p')$, which in turn derives $u_1 = \theta(u_1)$ because $u_p' = \theta(u_p')$. Now Lemmata 3 and 4 lead to a contradiction because u contains the concatenation of two θ-palindromes u_1 and u_2 as its prefix u_p and suffix u_s.

In the case $|w| \geq 2|u|$, either $|x| \geq |u|$ or $|y| \geq |u|$ holds. Thus, we get a contradiction in a similar way as above.   □

Actually, in Example 7, the θ-pseudoknot-border xy of u^2 satisfies $|u| < |xy| < \frac{4}{3}|u|$.

Corollary 3. *Let θ be an antimorphic involution on Σ^*. For a word $u \in K_\theta(1)$, $u^+ \not\subseteq K_\theta(1)$ if and only if $u^2 \notin K_\theta(1)$.*

In what follows, we give a characterization of such a θ-pseudoknot-unbordered word u with the property that u^2 is not included in $K_\theta(1)$.

Lemma 6. *Let θ be an antimorphic involution on Σ^*, and let u be a θ-pseudoknot-unbordered word, i.e., $u \in K_\theta(1)$. Then u^2 has a θ-pseudoknot-border if and only if $u = u_p\alpha\theta(u_p)\beta u_p$ for some $u_p, \alpha, \beta \in \Sigma^+$ such that $u_p\alpha, \beta u_p$ are θ-palindromes.*

Lemma 7. *Let θ be an antimorphic involution on Σ^* and u be a θ-pseudoknot-unbordered word, i.e., $u \in K_\theta(1)$. If u^2 is θ-pseudoknot-bordered, then u is primitive.*

As a contraposition of this lemma, the following corollary holds.

Corollary 4. *If $u \in K_\theta(1)$ and it is not primitive, then u^2 is θ-pseudoknot-unbordered, i.e., $u^2 \in K_\theta(1)$. This further implies that $u^+ \subseteq K_\theta(1)$.*

To complete this discussion, we note that there exists an antimorphic involution θ and a non-primitive word u such that u^k is not θ-pseudoknot-bordered for any $k > 1$.

Example 8. Let $u = abaaabaa$, which is clearly not primitive, and θ be an antimorphic involution such that $\theta(a) = b$ and vice versa. It is easy to see that neither u nor uu are θ-pseudoknot-bordered.   □

Lastly, as the next result shows, given a θ-pseudoknot-unbordered word u, if u^2 is θ-pseudoknot-bordered then u and any θ-pseudoknot-border of u^2 are primitive.

Theorem 1. *Let θ be an antimorphic involution on Σ^*, and $u \in K_\theta(1)$ satisfying $u^+ \not\subseteq K_\theta(1)$. Then any θ-pseudoknot-border of u^2 is primitive.*

The rest of this section will show that for a word $u \in K_\theta(1)$, the factorization of a θ-pseudoknot-border $w \in L_{cd}^\theta(u^2)$ into x and y is unique. In other words, $w = xy = x'y'$ such that $u^2 = xy\alpha = \beta\theta(x)\theta(y)$ and $u^2 = x'y'\alpha' = \beta'\theta(x')\theta(y')$ mean $x = x'$ and $y = y'$. Note that $x \neq y$ because if they were equal, this border xy would not be primitive, which conflicts with Theorem 1.

Lemma 8. *Let θ be an antimorphic involution on Σ^*, and $w \in \Sigma^*$. For $xy \in L_{cd}^\theta(w)$ such that $x \neq y$, $xy = uv = vu$ for some different words $u, v \in \Sigma^+$ if and only if w has a different θ-pseudoknot-border $x'y'$ of the same length as xy, i.e., $x'y' = xy$ but $|x'| \neq |x|$.*

Proposition 3. *Let θ be an antimorphic involution on Σ^*, $w \in \Sigma^*$, and $u \in K_\theta(1)$. If w is a θ-pseudoknot-border of u^2, then the factorization of w into x and y such that $u^2 = xy\alpha = \beta\theta(x)\theta(y)$ for some $\alpha, \beta \in \Sigma^*$ is unique.*

References

1. Adleman, L.: Molecular computation of solutions to combinatorial problems. Science 266, 1021–1024 (1994)
2. Daley, M., Kari, L.: DNA computing: Models and Implementations. Comments on Theoretical Biology 7(3), 177–198 (2002)
3. McCaskill, J.S.: The equilibrium partition function and base pair binding probability for RNA secondary structure. Biopolymers 29, 1105–1119 (1990)
4. Andronescu, M., Dees, D., Slaybaugh, L., Zhao, Y., Condon, A., Cohen, B., Skiena, S.: Algorithms for testing that sets of DNA words concatenate without secondary structure. In: Hagiya, M., Ohuchi, A. (eds.) DNA 2002. LNCS, vol. 2568, pp. 182–195. Springer, Heidelberg (2003)
5. Condon, A.E.: Problems on RNA secondary structure prediction and design. In: ICALP 2003. LNCS, vol. 2719, pp. 22–32. Springer, Heidelberg (2003)
6. Kari, L., Kitto, R., Thierrin, G.: Codes, involutions and DNA encodings. In: Brauer, W., Ehrig, H., Karhumäki, J., Salomaa, A. (eds.) FNC 2002. LNCS, vol. 2300, pp. 376–393. Springer, Heidelberg (2002)
7. Kari, L., Konstantinidis, S., Losseva, E., Wozniak, G.: Sticky-free and overhang-free DNA languages. Acta Informatica 40, 119–157 (2003)
8. Kari, L., Konstantinidis, S., Losseva, E., Sosík, P., Thierrin, G.: Hairpin structures in DNA words. In: Carbone, A., Pierce, N.A. (eds.) DNA 2005. LNCS, vol. 3892, pp. 158–170. Springer, Heidelberg (2006)
9. Kari, L., Mahalingam, K.: Involutively bordered words. International Journal of Foundations of Computer Science (2007)
10. Kobayashi, S.: Testing structure freeness of regular sets of biomolecular sequences (extended abstract). In: Ferretti, C., Mauri, G., Zandron, C. (eds.) DNA 2004. LNCS, vol. 3384, pp. 192–201. Springer, Heidelberg (2005)
11. Kari, L., Seki, S.: On pseudoknot words and their properties (submitted)
12. Jones, S.-G., Moxon, S., Marshall, M., Khanna, A., Eddy, S.R., Bateman, A.: Rfam: annotating non-coding RNAs in complete genomes. Nucleic Acid Research 33, 121–124 (2005)
13. Grätzer, G.: Universal Algebra. Van Nostrand Princeton, NJ (1968)
14. Rozenberg, G., Salomaa, A. (eds.): Handbook of Formal Languages. Springer, Berlin (1997)
15. Lentin, A., Schützenberger, M.P.: A combinatorial problem in the theory of free monoids. In: Proceedings of Combinatorial Mathematics and its Applications, April 10-14, pp. 128–144 (1967)
16. Ehrenfeucht, A., Silberger, D.: Periodicity and unbordered segments of words. Discrete Mathematics 26(2), 101–109 (1979)
17. Jonoska, N., Mahalingam, K., Chen, J.: Involution codes: with application to DNA coded languages. Natural Computing 4(2), 141–162 (2005)

Self-organized Spatio-temporal Oscillation Observed in a Chain of Non-oscillatory Cells

Yue Ma[1,*], Yoshiko Takenaka[2], and Kenichi Yoshikawa[1]

[1] Spatio-Temporal Order Project, ICORP, JST,
Department of Physics, Graduate School of Science,
Kyoto University, Japan
mail@ma-yue.net
[2] Venture Business Laboratory, Kyoto University, Japan

Abstract. Oscillations represent a ubiquitous phenomenon in biology systems. Cells compute their complex genetic network in parallel, and interact each other to generate various patterns, in static or dynamic form. The conventional models of biological periodic oscillations are usually proposed in such a way that cellular signal processing and genetic feedback networks manifest themselves as self-excited oscillators. Thus the collective oscillation is obtained from synchronization of a number of autonomous oscillators. In this paper we propose a hypothesis for the occurrence of collective oscillation on a group of non-oscillatory cell.

1 Introduction

Oscillation is ubiquitous in nature, not only in physics and chemistry but also biology. Biological oscillations can be observed in a wide range of time and length scales, from circadian rhythm about 24 hours [1] to segmentation clock less than 2 hours [2], from whole body oscillatory fevers [3] to periodic gene expression in a single cell [4]. Correspondingly, there are a great number of theoretical models. Despite of the diversity of biological insights, there are common points regarding the models.

Proteins are produced from the transcription and translation process of the specific sequence fraction of DNA. On the other hand, proteins can bind to a transcription promotor on DNA and hence repress or enhance its expression. The negative feedback loop [5,6] and the delay [7,8] in the inner cellular gene-protein network are considered as crucial roles contributed to oscillatory behavior of the expression of DNA and the protein concentration. From the view point of dynamical systems, by choosing appropriate parameter set, such models, with built-in activator-inhibitor or time delay, usually generate limit cycle oscillation due to the existence of Hopf bifurcation. Consequently, in the case of cell group or organism with oscillatory character, such as cardiac tissue and segmentation

---

* Corresponding author.

Y. Suzuki et al. (Eds.): IWNC 2007, PICT 1, pp. 111–121, 2009.

clock in tail of PSM (Presomitic Mesoderm), synchronization of coupled oscillators are often used to explain the collective oscillation [9,10,11].

However, periodic oscillation is only a small part of dynamical behavior for a cell. Oscillation may cease if condition is changed. And in fact, most cells tend to settle down to a stable state. So, we doubt about the indispensability of intrinsic oscillatory cells for a oscillatory organism. In this paper, we propose a novel mechanism for oscillation to take place in a group of cell, in which none of individual cells are intrinsic oscillatory.

The development of a multicellular organism begins with a single cell, which divides and give rise to different type of cells. Different cells are organized according to certain secreted chemicals, called morphogens, or the environment where they arise. Morphogens are made in specific sites and diffuse over the organism to form concentration gradients. On the other hand, environment supply nutrition for organism growth, in such a way that directly contact border get more and far inside cells get less. In either case, we can suppose that there is a certain factor, which we refer to active factor, with high concentration in cells closed to organism border, and decrease inward. In a word, the concerned factor forms a "V" type of concentration gradient.

Above mentioned active factors can affect the fate of cells in a concentration dependent manner [12]. We assume that cells tend to live in a stable state normally, and high concentration of active factor can excite the cell to another stable state. This kind of bistability is very important and has been observed in various biological systems, such as cell signaling and neural process [13,14,15]. Moreover, it was recently suggested that stochastic fluctuation plays an important role on the manner of transition between bistable states [16].

Usually, the bistability takes place from positive genetic regulation loops [17,14]. In this paper, however, we consider the bistability in a broader way. Conventional biochemical theory clarified a key-lock relationship between transcription factor and promoter. In this paper, however, we shed light on a physical regulation of protein production, which has been ignored improperly by biochemists. A DNA molecule that is longer than several micrometers (over 100 000 base pairs) shows the characteristics of a semi-flexible polymer, which exhibits a discrete transition between coiled and compact states; i.e., a first-order phase transition for a single giant DNA molecule (see Fig. 1(a)). The discrete transaction leads to the on/off switching of DNA transcription, and hence the production specific protein, as shown in Fig. 1(b). In this transition, a specific key-lock interaction helps little, and instead the transition is induced by "non-specific" interaction between a DNA molecule and environmental factors within the cell, such as the concentration of polyamine, mRNA, ATP, and so forth [18,19,20]. Moreover, RNA [21], protein [22] and other molecules [23] are also found discrete switch between folding and unfolding or between active and inactive state. Although the details of the mechanism has yet to be clarified, it is believed to play an important role in self-regulation of gene expression in living cells, and might be a more universal law of morphogenesis patten than other biochemical reactions.

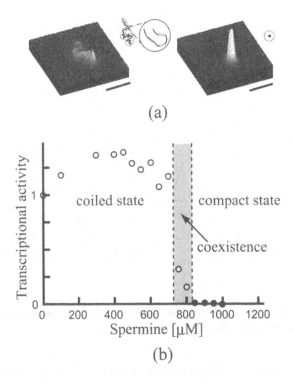

Fig. 1. (a) Structural transition of a giant DNA chain. Brightness distributions of fluorescence microscopy images and schematic representations of a DNA molecule (T4, 166 kbp) in a coiled (left) and a compact (right) state are shown. Due to the blurring effect, the bright molecules appear to be much larger than their actual sizes. Scale bars are 5μm. (Photograph courtesy of Dr. Y. Takenaka [24]) (b) Change in transcriptional activity depending on the structural transition of DNA (BAC, 106 kbp). The transcriptional activities are on and off in the coiled and compact states, respectively. (Originally presented in [20], and reworked with permission).

2   Description of the Model

The on/off switching character of DNA molecular suggests that its free energy F, which is a measure of higher order structure, is a double minimum kinetic. Without losing generality, we assume the kinetic is of quartic, as shown in Fig. 2(a), with respect to specific field parameters η, such as density. Usually, it stays in either OFF or ON corresponding to the intracellular concentration of nonspecific abundant chemical species, such as ATP, polyamines, small ions, etc. Consequently, the state of DNA's higher order structure, either coiled or compact, then effects the processes of transcription. In the scale of molecular, since the effect of inertia can be ignored comparing with viscosity, the change of density is in a ratio of generalized force, so we have $\partial\eta/\partial t \sim -\partial F/\partial\eta$. Clearly, due to the assumption of quartic kinetic of F, $-\partial F/\partial\eta$ turns to be a cubic function. With above considerations, we choose the reaction function of every single cell

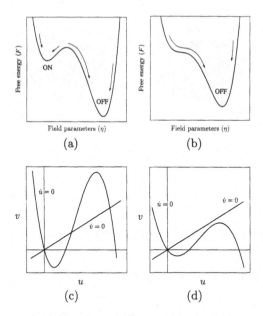

Fig. 2. Free energy (a & b) and nullcline diagrams (c & d) in the situation of bistability (a & c) and mono-stability (b & d), respectively

as the form of FitzHugh-Nagumo (FHN) equations. Moreover, we can determine an active factor as a certain signaling protein, such as ComK in soil bacterium to develop "competence" event [16], or chemicals in intracellular environment, such as mRNA, ATP, etc. We suppose that cells with high concentration of active factor are capable of bistability switching from OFF to ON, as shown in Fig. 2(a), while cells with low concentration of it can only behave OFF state, as shown in Fig. 2(b).

Including an inhibitor, the dynamical reaction function of every single cell can be described as

$$\dot{u} = f(u, v, \Gamma) = \Gamma u(u - \alpha)(1 - u) - v \tag{1}$$

$$\dot{v} = g(u, v) = \epsilon(\beta u - v) \tag{2}$$

where u a variable relating to the activity of DNA, v the inhibitor changing slowly compare to u in the case of $\epsilon \ll 1$. Moreover, Γ in Eq. (1) corresponds to the active factor as described previously. Fig. 2(c)&(d) show the nullclines with bistability and mono-stability when Γ is large and small, respectively. Moreover, cells can produce a signal that acts on adjacent cells and change their fates. We assume this coupling is realized via activator u diffusively. Thus a one-dimensional chain of cell can be described as

$$\dot{u}_i = f(u_i, v_i, \Gamma_i) + D(u_{i-1} + u_{i+1} - 2u_i) \tag{3}$$

$$\dot{v}_i = g(u_i, v_i) \tag{4}$$

where i the index of the cell in the chain, D the diffusion coefficient.

3   Self-sustained Collective Oscillation

3.1   Brief Review

The coupled FHN model is a well studied paradigm for excitable medium, in the context of chemical oscillator, computational neuroscience and so on. Oscillating pattern can be usually obtained by setting parameters beyond a Hopf bifurcation. However for models like Eq. (1, 2), no Hopf bifurcation can be found to make single cell oscillate, instead, only saddle-node bifurcation occurs to produce bistability. To make a bistable system oscillate, people usually give a periodic stimulate [25] or couple with a oscillatory boundary [26]. But for systems completely independent of oscillating elements, little attention has been paid to their emergence of oscillation. A few studies in the context of mathematics and physics have revealed the possibility of collective oscillating pattern.

The first example was proposed by Smale [27], who found two "dead" cells become "alive" via diffusively coupling. Long after that, more literatures [28,29] studied detailed conditions on this behavior. In-phase and anti-phase self-sustained oscillation on excitable membrane via bulk coupling are observed in [30]. The models under consideration are mostly coupled identical excitable cells with mono-stability. On the other hand, in a bistable system, a stationary front can bifurcate to a pair of fronts propagating in opposite directions. It is known as nonequilibrium Ising-Bloch (NIB) bifurcation [31,32]. Perturbation for happening NIB bifurcation can be induced by local spatial inhomogeneity [33]. More global analysis shows that NIB point is only part of story, and conclude that unstable wave front is intrinsic to media that are spatially inhomogeneous [34,35]. An unstable wave front may manifest itself as reflected front, tango wave [36], pacemaker [37] and so on.

Although most studies have been doing on a spatial continuum described by partial differential equations (PDE), continuum models neglect the effects of cellular discreteness [38]. From the viewpoint of biology, size of cells can not be decrease infinitely. This intrinsic property is difficult to be ignored specially in the stage of initial development, when cell size is comparable with tissue's. Moreover, there are mathematical reasons to do the spatial discretization. PDE and ODE (ordinary differential equations) are of different theoretical framework, and produce different results. Several significant features of discreteness, such as wave propagation failure [39], can not happen in a continuum model. Therefore, in this paper, we will use the spatial discrete cell chain described by Eqs. (3-4) as the subject.

3.2   Parameters

As previously described, we assume the active factor, i.e., Γ_i in Eq. (3), is spatially distributed as a "V". Without losing generality, we suppose the gradation is linear. Notating the total of cells as a even number N, the maximum concentration as Γ_m, the minimum around tissue center as Γ_n, we can write the profile of Γ_i as

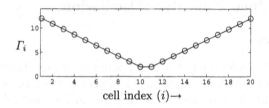

Fig. 3. Profile of Γ_i defined by Eq. 5, when $\Gamma_m = 12, \Gamma_n = 2$

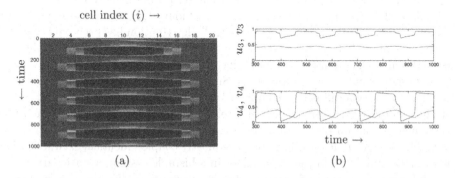

(a)   (b)

Fig. 4. Oscillation observed in a chain of cell when $D = 0.8$. (a) Spatio-temporal plot of the collective oscillation of u_i. Color red and blue indicate $u_i = 1$ and $u_i = 0$, respectively. (b) Part of waveform of u (blue) and v (red) in 3rd and 4th cell.

$$\Gamma_i = \begin{cases} \Gamma_m - \dfrac{\Gamma_m - \Gamma_n}{\frac{N}{2} - 1}(i - 1) & 1 \leqslant i \leqslant \frac{N}{2}, \\[4mm] \Gamma_n + \dfrac{\Gamma_m - \Gamma_n}{\frac{N}{2} - 1}(i - (\frac{N}{2} + 1)) & \frac{N}{2} < i \leqslant N. \end{cases} \tag{5}$$

With the local dynamics described by Eqs. (1,2), cells whose Γ_is are larger than 4.08 can behave bistability. On the other hand, cells with $\Gamma_i < 4.08$ have only one equilibrium. In this paper, we set Γ_m and Γ_n as 12 and 2, respectively. The profile of Γ_i is shown in Fig. 3. Under this condition, only central 4 cells (9th – 12th) are mono-stable, while others with $\Gamma_i > 4$ are bistable. Again, there is no oscillatory cell before coupling. Throughout this paper, following parameters are fixed as

$$\alpha = 0.3, \ \beta = 0.5, \ \epsilon = 0.02, N = 20. \tag{6}$$

We change the coupling strength D and observe the occurrence, variation and disappearance of self-sustained collective oscillation in the cell chain.

3.3   The Occurrence of Self-sustained Oscillation

When diffusion coefficient $D = 0.8$, we can observe a typical oscillation shown in Fig. 4(a). In the figure, horizontal axis is the cell number from left to right, while

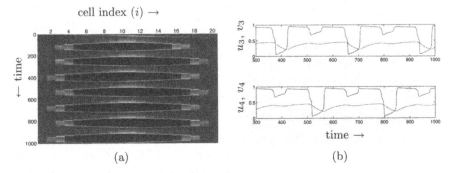

Fig. 5. Oscillation with anti-phase periodic position shift when $D = 1.0$. (a) Spatio-temporal diagram of u_i. Color red and blue indicate $u_i = 1$ and $u_i = 0$, respectively. (b) is waveform diagram of 3rd and 18th cell. Activator u and inhibitor v are colored in blue and red, respectively.

the vertical axis is the time evolution from top down. As the initial condition, we set the 1st cell excited, because of the fact that a stimulate usually inputs from the border. A traveling wave will appear due to the excitation. Then the traveling front sweeps over the cell chain and make all the cells "alive". Although central cells are also turned on by power of diffusion, they can not stay at the excitable state for a long time. Instead, they tend to return to their stable equilibrium soon, and hence generate two counterpropagating wave-backs. These two wave-backs propagate outward until the 3rd and 18th cell and stop suddenly due to the phenomena of *wave propagation failure* [39,40] in spatially discrete media. The 3rd cell can not jump from ON state to OFF state and remain a small amplitude oscillation. The difference between 3rd and 4th cell is shown in Fig. 4(b). At this critical interface, the inhibitor v slowly decreases and the 4th and 17th cells restore excitability after a while. Then central cells can be inspired again by the pair of reflecting wave front. This process repeats and causes the collective oscillation inside the multi-cell tissue without oscillatory cells.

3.4   Period-Doubling Oscillation with In-Phase or Anti-phase Spatial Shift Close to Boundary

If we increase the coupling strength D, property of the oscillation can be changed. In Fig. 5, it is observed that the position of oscillation shift periodically. The 3rd and 18th cells oscillate in a doubled period anti-phase (Fig. 5(b)). Globally, tissue oscillates in two groups with the same cell population but different position: No.3-No.17 (15 cells) and No.4-No.18 (15 cells), respectively.

Interestingly, if we increase the coupling strength D a little more, for example $D = 1.1$, a different type of period-doubling can be observed, as shown in Fig. 6. Comparing with the case of $D = 1.0$, although the critical interface between ON and OFF shifts periodically like Fig. 5, there is no phase difference between cell 3 and cell 18. As shown clearly in Fig. 6(b), these two boundary cells oscillate in-phase, instead of anti-phase (Fig. 5(b)). Therefore in present condition, the

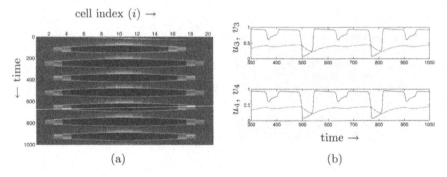

Fig. 6. Oscillation with in-phase periodic population change when $D = 1.1$. (a) Spatio-temporal diagram of u_i. Color red and blue indicate $u_i = 1$ and $u_i = 0$, respectively. (b) is waveform diagram of 3rd and 18th cell. Activator u and inhibitor v are colored in blue and red, respectively.

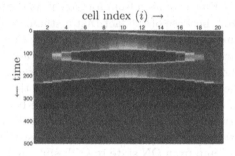

Fig. 7. Spatio-temporal diagram of u_i. Color red and blue indicate $u_i = 1$ and $u_i = 0$, respectively. Oscillation stops after once when $D = 1.4$.

periodic change does not take place on the oscillating position, instead it is the population of oscillating cells. Precisely speaking, tissue oscillate in two groups: No.3-No.18 (16 cells) and No.4-No.17 (14 cells), respectively. Moreover, we have checked that same symmetric collective oscillation can also occur in the case of $D = 1.0$, if we set the initial condition of single cells identically, say all in ON state at $t = 0$. So we consider that these two types of oscillation are caused by same Hopf bifurcation. Because the larger D is, the faster wavefront propagates, a larger coupling strength can reduce the time lag of being inspired between two boundary. If the time lag is smaller than a threshold, two boundary converge to an in-phase oscillation. On the other hand, if the time lag is big, they will behave as anti-phase oscillation.

3.5   Oscillation Death

Increasing coupling strength D to 1.2, we can observe that the periodic position or population change stop. The collective oscillation returns to the normal prototype. Comparing to the case of $D = 0.8$, the total population of oscillating cell increases to 16 (No. 3 to No. 18) from 14 (No. 4 to No. 17).

We observed the sudden death of the oscillation when D is as large as 1.4. From Fig. 7, one can tell clearly that central cells start to oscillate after all cells are excited, but this oscillation is unsustained. In this strong coupling condition, the boundary cells can not recover their excitability so that the propagating wave front from center is unable to stop and reflect to generate successive oscillation.

4 Concluding Remarks

In this paper, we proposed a brand-new scenario for self-organized and self-sustained oscillation in a multi-cellular biological tissue. Distinct from present general idea based on oscillatory genetic network, there is no cell expresses as an oscillator alone. Coupling some cells together, however, we can observe a collective oscillation inside the cell group, i.e., a tissue. Moreover, the oscillation can manifests itself in several ways, corresponding to different coupling strength. Anti-phase and In-phase oscillations occurring on two boundaries lead to the alternative change of oscillating position and oscillating cell population, respectively. The oscillation can be ceased by increasing the coupling strength strong enough.

Our observation have been undergone by numerical simulation. We have not performed mathematical analysis on such phenomenon in the present paper. There have appeared several studies on the self-oscillatory phenomenon in spatially discretized systems in the context of mathematics and physics. This paper, however, introduce these basic idea to the spatio-temporal self-organization in biology system. We are going to design corresponding biological experiments and to find more proofs supporting our hypothesis.

References

1. Schibler, U., Naef, F.: Cellular oscillators: rhythmic gene expression and metabolism. Current Opinion in Cell Biology 17(2), 223–229 (2005)
2. Pourquie, O.: The Segmentation Clock: Converting Embryonic Time into Spatial Pattern. Science 301(5631), 328–330 (2003)
3. Stark, J., Chan, C., George, A.J.T.: Oscillations in the immune system. Immunological Reviews 216(1), 213–231 (2007)
4. Tiana, G., Krishna, S., Pigolotti, S., Jensen, M.H., Sneppen, K.: Oscillations and temporal signalling in cells. Physical Biology 4(2), R1–R17 (2007)
5. Hirata, H., Yoshiura, S., Ohtsuka, T., Bessho, Y., Harada, T., Yoshikawa, K., Kageyama, R.: Oscillatory Expression of the bHLH Factor Hes1 Regulated by a Negative Feedback Loop. Science 298(5594), 840–843 (2002)
6. Hoffmann, A., Levchenko, A., Scott, M.L., Baltimore, D.: The Ikappa B-NF-kappa B Signaling Module: Temporal Control and Selective Gene Activation. Science 298(5596), 1241–1245 (2002)
7. Lewis, J.: Autoinhibition with transcriptional delay: A simple mechanism for the zebrafish somitogenesis oscillator. Current Biology 13(16), 1398–1408 (2003)

8. Chen, L., Aihara, K.: A model of periodic oscillation for genetic regulatory systems. IEEE Transactions on Circuits and Systems I: Fundamental Theory and Applications 49(10), 1429–1436 (2002)
9. Masamizu, Y., Ohtsuka, T., Takashima, Y., Nagahara, H., Takenaka, Y., Yoshikawa, K., Okamura, H., Kageyama, R.: Real-time imaging of the somite segmentation clock: Revelation of unstable oscillators in the individual presomitic mesoderm cells. Proceedings of the National Academy of Sciences 103(5), 1313–1318 (2006)
10. Gonze, D., Goldbeter, A.: Circadian rhythms and molecular noise. Chaos: An Interdisciplinary Journal of Nonlinear Science 16(2), 026110 (2006)
11. Garcia-Ojalvo, J., Elowitz, M., Strogatz, S.: Modeling a synthetic multicellular clock: repressilators coupled by quorum sensing. Proc. Natl. Acad. Sci. USA 101, 10955–10960 (2004)
12. Wolpert, L.: Positional information and the spatial pattern of cellular differentiation. J. Theoret. Biol. 25, 1–47 (1969)
13. Ashwin, P., Timme, M.: Nonlinear dynamics: When instability makes sense. Nature 436(7047), 36–37 (2005)
14. Angeli, D., Ferrell Jr., J.E., Sontag, E.D.: Detection of multistability, bifurcations, and hysteresis in a large class of biological positive-feedback systems. Proceedings of the National Academy of Sciences 101(7), 1822–1827 (2007)
15. Kusters, J.M.A.M., Cortes, J.M., van Meerwijk, W.P.M., Ypey, D.L., Theuvenet, A.P.R., Gielen, C.C.A.M.: Hysteresis and bistability in a realistic cell model for calcium oscillations and action potential firing. Physical Review Letters 98, 098107 (2007)
16. Maamar, H., Raj, A., Dubnau, D.: Noise in gene expression determines cell fate in bacillus subtilis. Science 317, 526–529 (2007)
17. Kim, J.R., Yoon, Y., Cho, K.H.: Coupled feedback loops form dynamic motifs of cellular networks. Biophysical Journal 94, 359–365 (2008)
18. Makita, N., Yoshikawa, K.: Atp/adp switches the higher-order structure of DNA in the presence of spermidine. FEBS Letters 460(2), 333–337 (1999)
19. Tsumoto, K., Yoshikawa, K.: RNA switches the higher-order structure of DNA. Biophysical Chemistry 82(1), 1–8 (1999)
20. Luckel, F., Kubo, K., Tsumoto, K., Yoshikawa, K.: Enhancement and inhibition of DNA transcriptional activity by spermine: A marked difference between linear and circular templates. FEBS Letters 579(23), 5119–5122 (2005)
21. Mamasakhlisov, Y.S., Hayryan, S., Morozov, V.F., Hu, C.K.: RNA folding in the presence of counterions. Physical Review E 75(6), 061907 (2007)
22. Schanda, P., Forge, V., Brutscher, B.: Protein folding and unfolding studied at atomic resolution by fast two-dimensional NMR spectroscopy. PNAS 104(27), 11257–11262 (2007)
23. Etienne-Manneville, S., Hall, A.: RHO gtpases in cell biology. Nature 420(6916), 629–635 (2002)
24. Takenaka, Y., Nagahara, H., Kitahata, H., Yoshikawa, K.: Large-scale on-off switching of genetic activity mediated by the folding-unfolding transition in a giant DNA molecule: An hypothesis. Physical Review E, 031905 (2008)
25. Yanagita, T., Nishiura, Y., Kobayashi, R.: Signal propagation and failure in one-dimensional fitzhugh-nagumo equations with periodic stimuli. Physical Review E (Statistical, Nonlinear, and Soft Matter Physics) 71(3), 036226 (2005)
26. Nekhamkina, O., Sheintuch, M.: Boundary-induced spatiotemporal complex patterns in excitable systems. Physical Review E (Statistical, Nonlinear, and Soft Matter Physics) 73(6), 066224 (2006)

27. Smale, S.: A mathematical model of two cells via turing's equation. In: Marsden, J.E., McCracken, M. (eds.) The Hopf Bifurcation and Its Application. Springer, NY (1974)
28. Pogromsky, A.Y.: Passivity based design of synchronizing systems. Int. J. Bifurcation and Chaos 8(2), 295–319 (1998)
29. Pogromsky, A., Glad, T., Nijmeijer, H.: On diffusion driven oscillations in coupled dynamical systems. International Journal of Bifurcation and Chaos 4, 629–644 (1999)
30. Gomez-Marin, A., Garcia-Ojalvo, J., Sancho, J.M.: Self-sustained spatiotemporal oscillations induced by membrane-bulk coupling. Physical Review Letters 98(16), 168303 (2007)
31. Coullet, P., Lega, J., Houchmanzadeh, B., Lajzerowicz, J.: Breaking chirality in nonequilibrium systems. Physical Review Letters 65, 1352–1355 (1990)
32. Hagberg, A., Meron, E.: Complex patterns in reaction-diffusion systems: A tale of two front instabilities. Chaos 4(3), 477–484 (1994)
33. Bode, M.: Front-bifurcations in reaction diffusion systems with inhomogeneous parameter distributions. Physica D: Nonlinear Phenomena, 270–286 (1997)
34. Prat, A., Li, Y.: Stability of front solutions in inhomogeneous media. Physica D: Nonlinear Phenomena, 50–68 (January 2003)
35. Prat, A., Li, Y., Bressloff, P.: Inhomogeneity-induced bifurcation of stationary and oscillatory pulses. Physica D: Nonlinear Phenomena, 177–199 (January 2005)
36. Li, Y.: Tango waves in a bidomain model of fertilization calcium waves. Physica D: Nonlinear Phenomena, 27–49 (January 2003)
37. Miyazaki, J., Kinoshita, S.: Stopping and initiation of a chemical pulse at the interface of excitable media with different diffusivity. Physical Review E 76, 66201 (2007)
38. Shnerb, N.M., Louzoun, Y., Bettelheim, E., Solomon, S.: The importance of being discrete: Life always wins on the surface. PNAS 97, 10322–10324 (2000)
39. Keener, J.P.: Propagation and its failure in coupled systems of discrete excitable cells. SIAM J. Appl. Math. 47, 556–572 (1987)
40. Comte, J.C., Morfu, S., Marquié, P.: Propagation failure in discrete bistable reaction-diffusion systems: theory and experiments. Phys. Rev. E 64, 027102 (2001)

Exploiting Natural Asynchrony and Local Knowledge within Systemic Computation to Enable Generic Neural Structures

Erwan Le Martelot[1,3], Peter J. Bentley[2], and R. Beau Lotto[3]

[1] Engineering Department, University College London, London, UK
e.le_martelot@ucl.ac.uk
[2] Computer Science Department, University College London, London, UK
[3] Institute of Ophthalmology, University College London, London, UK

Abstract. Bio-inspired processes are involved more and more in today's technologies, yet their modelling and implementation tend to be taken away from their original concept because of the limitations of the classical computation paradigm. To address this, systemic computation (SC), a model of interacting systems with natural characteristics, followed by a modelling platform with a bio-inspired system implementation were introduced. In this paper, we investigate the impact of local knowledge and asynchronous computation: significant natural properties of biological neural networks (NN) and naturally handled by SC. We present here a bio-inspired model of artificial NN, focussing on agent interactions, and show that exploiting these built-in properties, which come for free, enables neural structure flexibility without reducing performance.

1 Introduction

An ant colony is driven by individual agents acting individually, asynchronously and randomly, yet can accomplish complex and precise tasks. It is an example of a non-analytical and natural process performing local computation that leads to a precise and complex global result. Similar to biological systems, artificial bio-inspired approaches suggest some inner natural characteristics. We can state that natural processes are stochastic, asynchronous, parallel, homeostatic, continuous, robust, fault tolerant, autonomous, open-ended, distributed, approximate, embodied, complex, have circular causality and compute locally [1]. Such characteristics are not natively present in current conventional paradigms and models of natural processes that run on conventional computers have to include a simulation of some of these features. This often leads to slower and less straightforward implementations compared to analytical or linear algorithms for which computers are well suited.

Just as the development of Prolog enabled elegant and precise implementations of logical expressions, so the development of a paradigm where processes could be defined in a manner that resembles their true structures would improve our ability to implement bio-inspired processes. To address this, [1] introduced

Y. Suzuki et al. (Eds.): IWNC 2007, PICT 1, pp. 122–133, 2009.

Systemic Computation (SC), a new model of computation and corresponding computer architecture based on a systemics world-view and supplemented by the incorporation of natural characteristics. This work was followed by the introduction of a complete platform for this paradigm [2].

In this paper, we focus on two natural properties of SC: local knowledge and asynchronous computation, applying them to a common bio-inspired paradigm: artificial neural networks (ANN). Local knowledge and asynchrony do not suit conventional computer architectures and classical ANN models often employ global algorithms, constraining the network structure and making them less biologically plausible. Real biological NN imply a more flexible model without the structural limitations imposed by conventional approaches. We thus suggest an ANN implementation using SC. The use of SC requires the use of local knowledge and asynchronous computation. We show that such a model enables the implementation of the same networks as those implemented using conventional global and synchronous approaches, but the SC implementation does not constrain the network structure. We then compare our approach to more classical ones.

2   Motivation and Background

There have been alternative views of computation since its conception: cellular automata have proven themselves to be a valuable approach to emergent, distributed computation; generalisations such as constrained generating procedures and collision-based computing provide new ways to design and analyse emergent computational phenomena; bio-inspired grammars and algorithms introduced notions of homeostasis, fault-tolerance and parallel stochastic learning; bio-inspired paradigms showed good modelling potential for biological systems. New architectures are also popular, like distributed computing (or multiprocessing), computer clustering, grid computing, ubiquitous computing and speckled computing.

To unify notions of biological computation and electronic computation, [1] introduced SC as a suggestion of necessary features for a computer architecture compatible with current processors, yet designed to provide native support for common characteristics of biological processes. Table 1 lists major characteristics that can be found in some computation paradigms. It shows the inner properties (i.e. those that need not be simulated) of natural computation (e.g., ants, neurons, DNA), systemic computation, conventional programming languages (procedural, object-oriented, functional and logical), and bio-inspired paradigms like cellular automata (CA) or membrane computing (P-systems). Table 1 illustrates the proximity between SC and natural computation compared to other common computational paradigms. Previous work [2] showed how simply and naturally a bio-inspired process such as a GA could be created and given more autonomy being made self-adaptive by just adding a single component. Defining systems and interactions only and following the SC rules thus naturally lead to an easily evolvable, stochastic, approximate, continuous and complex process. To provide

Table 1. Features of various computational paradigms. 'Y' indicates the characteristic is built-in and needs no extra implementation; 'N' indicates that extra implementation is needed to simulate the characteristic; 'Y/N' means the method is capable of supporting models that may have or not have the property without extra implementation.

	Nature	S.C.	C. Lang.	C.A.	P-systems
Stochastic (Deterministic)	Y (N)	Y (N)	N (Y)	N (Y)	Y (N)
Asynchronous(Synchronous)	Y (N)	Y (N)	N (Y)	N (Y)	N (Y)
Parallel (Serial)	Y (N)	Y (N)	N (Y)	Y (N)	Y (N)
Continuous (Batch)	Y (N)	Y (N)	Y/N(Y/N)	Y (N)	Y (N)
Distributed (Centralised)	Y (N)	Y (N)	N (Y)	Y (N)	Y (N)
Approximate (Precise)	Y (N)	Y (N)	N (Y)	N (Y)	Y (N)
Embodied (Isolated)	Y (N)	Y (N)	N (Y)	N (Y)	N (Y)
Circular (Linear) causality	Y (N)	Y (N)	N (Y)	N (Y)	Y/N (Y/N)
Local (Global) knowledge	Y (N)	Y (N)	Y/N(Y/N)	Y (N)	Y (N)

evidence that processes can also benefit from built-in asynchronous computation and local knowledge, we focus in this paper on artificial neural networks (ANN).

ANN are suitable to highlight the aforementioned properties as:

- neurons are organised to create a whole (the network) that solves problems,
- neurons are computing locally, yet the result is global,
- neurons are independent (in timing and internal knowledge).

Classical backpropagation (BP) [3] constrains the network to be layered and feed-forward; therefore no change in the neurons' organisation breaking this requirement can be made. Recurrent BP was introduced to overcome one of these constraints and cope with backward connections [3]. Other more biologically plausible techniques, like contrastive Hebbian learning for deterministic networks [5][6], generalised recirculation [8], or spiking neurons networks [7] were introduced and showed successful results. Still, these approaches all define global algorithms, coping with various specific network structures, giving neurons more and more realistic computational abilities, but do not give the neuron entity the ability to be autonomous (i.e. inner data processing) in whatever situation (i.e. disregarding the position in the structure). Such natural flexibility is, from our modelling point of view, what is desirable and missing in approaches using conventional computation. The reason for using SC at all is to move beyond simply attempting to mimic the functional behaviour of natural systems through global algorithmic approximations, and instead (as much as is feasible) duplicate the functional behaviour through mirroring the underlying systems, organisations and local interactions. SC is thus intended to be a truer representation and thus an improved model of natural systems implemented following its paradigm, compared to other approaches.

3   Overview of Systemic Computation

SC [1] is a new model of computation and corresponding computer architecture based on a systemics world-view and supplemented by the incorporation of natural characteristics (previously listed). This approach stresses the importance of structure and interaction, supplementing traditional reductionist analysis with the recognition that circular causality, embodiment in environments and emergence of hierarchical organisations all play vital roles in natural systems. Systemic computation makes the following assertions:

- Everything is a system.
- Systems can be transformed but never destroyed.
- Systems may comprise or share other nested systems.
- Systems interact, and interaction between systems may cause transformation of those systems, where the nature of that transformation is determined by a contextual system.
- All systems can potentially act as context and affect the interactions of other systems, and all systems can potentially interact in some context.
- The transformation of systems is constrained by the scope of systems, and systems may have partial membership within the scope of a system.
- Computation is transformation.

In systemic computation, everything is a system, and computations arise from interactions between systems. Two systems can interact in the context of a third system. All systems can potentially act as contexts to determine the effect of interacting systems. A system is divided into three parts: two schemata and one kernel. These three parts can be used to hold anything (data, typing, etc.) in binary as shown in Figure 1(a). The kernel defines the result of two systems interacting in its context (and may also optionally hold data if it is interacting with another system). The two schemata define which subject systems may interact in this context as shown in Figures 1(b) and 1(c). A system can also contain or be contained by other systems. This enables the notion of scope. Interactions can only occur between systems within the same scope. An SC program therefore comprises systems that are instantiated and positioned within a hierarchy (some inside each other). It thus defines an initial state from which the systems can then randomly interact, transforming each other through those interactions and following an emergent process rather than a deterministic algorithm. For full details see [1] and [2].

4   ANN Model

Modelling a neural network keeping all its natural characteristics should involve the same entities that form a real one: neurons, their inner mechanism and their communication mechanism. These mechanisms could be modelled a priori at several levels. One model could represent the interaction of neurons using synapses to make the link between axon and dendrites. Another one could involve presynapse, post-synapse, protein exchange, protein transfer, etc. We chose to study and create our model at the neuron level of abstraction and not explicitly represent protein interactions. A neuron receives inputs from its dendrites that are processed in the soma; the resulting signal is then sent through the axon [4].

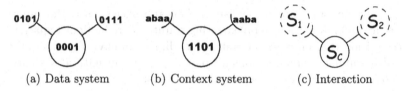

(a) Data system   (b) Context system   (c) Interaction

Fig. 1. (a): A system used primarily for data storage. The kernel (in the circle) and the two schemata (at the end of the two arms) hold data. (b): A system acting as a context. Its kernel defines the result of the interaction while its schemata define allowable interacting systems. (c): An interacting context. The contextual system S_c matches two appropriate systems S_1 and S_2 with its schemata and specifies the transformation resulting from their interaction as defined in its kernel.

Axon signals are weighted and transmitted to further neurons through synapses which communicate with their dendrites. The signal will thus be a value transmitted across the network rather than many molecular and electrical entities.

4.1 Systemic Analysis

Using SC implies a systemic analysis of the problem to define the interacting systems and how they interact [1]. The synapse which transfers signals from axon to dendrites can be chosen as a context of interaction between neurons. However, neurons interaction do not provide information regarding the signal flow direction. This flow is by definition directional from axons to dendrites. Therefore the model should have the more precise notions of axons and dendrites to precise the signal direction. Dendrites can be modelled as one system representing the dendritic tree rather than one system per dendrite which would add unnecessary complexity to the model. A synapse connecting an axon with a dendrites system, each systems triplet belongs to the scope of a connection (Figure 2(a)).

Two types of synapses could be considered here: excitatory and inhibitory synapses [4]; not to mention that synapses can be electrical or chemical [4], which we do not explicitly model here. For modelling simplicity and not to introduce inconsistencies we chose to allow both excitatory and inhibitory excitations within one synapse. This is modelled by a weight taken within [-1; 1]. A positive weight simulates an excitatory synapse and a negative weight an inhibitory one.

To model the signal processing between dendrites and axon inside a neuron, we can consider the ionic transmissions in the membrane and the membrane as a whole and define the membrane as context of interaction between dendrites and axon, as shown in Figure 2(b). A membrane also owns a threshold of signal activation, real value also taken within [-1; 1].

To keep neuronal integrity, scopes are used to group what is part of a neuron, of the outside or of both. All the inherent neuron interactions happen within its soma. A neuron is therefore represented as dendrites, a soma, a membrane and an axon. However, dendrites and axons also belong to the outside (they are exposed to the outside of the soma) as their role is to receive and transmit signals from or to other neurons. Therefore, neurons can be modelled as shown in Figure 2(b).

Neurons belong to a NN, therefore it is sensible for integrity to encompass them in a "network" system itself contained in the systemic "universe". The universe is here a system which encloses everything within the program. It is also used as the interface between the program and the user (Figure 2(c)). However, the network inputs and outputs as well as the data transfer between them and the universe are still to be defined. A real brain receives axons from neurons located outside, like visual inputs, and sends signals also outside, like to muscles. Thus, axons can naturally also play the role of network inputs and outputs. Then "InputTransfer" (IT) and "OutputTransfer" (OT) context systems transfer data between the universe and the input and output axons. Figure 3 shows a single neuron systemic neural network.

So far, this model can organise interactions disregarding the physical location of the neurons. Nonetheless, the notion of neuron neighbourhood can be easily handled using scopes. An "area" system can encompass neurons and neurons can belong to several areas. This partition and sharing of neurons would thus create neighbourhoods in the network. Note that the physical neighbourhood is defined by relationships between systems rather than by physical coordinates. Figure 4 shows a more complex network with areas and recurrent connections.

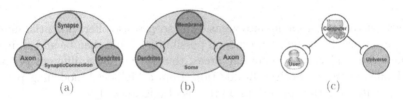

(a)   (b)   (c)

Fig. 2. (a): Axon-dendrites interaction in the context of a synapse. (b): Systemic model of a neuron showing the dendrites-axon interaction in the context of a membrane, and within a soma. (c): User-program interaction in the context of the computer.

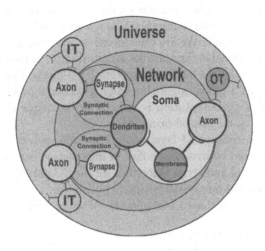

Fig. 3. Systemic NN with 2 inputs and 1 neuron

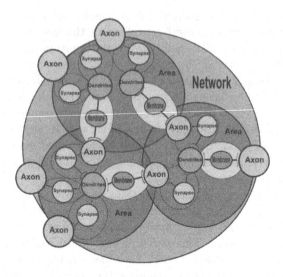

Fig. 4. Network with four inputs, one output and three areas sharing neurons. Each area defines a neighbourhood for the neurons inside.

This network partitioning into areas using scopes also offers potential interest for future work. Some more interaction possibilities could then be added, injecting new context systems in specific areas, thus giving one a different potential and behaviour from another. In addition, from a biological modelling point of view, partitioning the network into areas is of relevance [4].

4.2 Rules

The organisation of neurons is based on observations taken from biological studies [4]. However, knowing the organisation does not explain the inner behaviour of the entities involved. Unfortunately, this is not well understood yet how everything happens at this stage. We are thus forced to use methods that may or may not be biologically plausible, and use an adaptation for asynchronous and local computation of the gradient back propagation (BP) method [3] for learning. BP is often described as a global algorithm relying on some precise network structure [3]. The aim of our adaptation is to keep the principle of this method but adapt it to be a local-rule based principle.

BP relies on the concept of layers to group independent neurons together, which provides an easy control of the flow of information from layer to layer and therefore suits a global and serial algorithm. In the SC paradigm, we can use the very same principle without any structure hypothesis by defining the information flow process locally. Equations 1 to 3 give the BP rules with a momentum factor:

(1) $x_i = g(h_i) = g(\sum_k w_{ik}.x_k)$

(2) $\Delta w_{ij}(t) = \lambda.e_i.x_j + \alpha.\Delta.w_{ij}(t-1)$

(3) $e_i = g'(h_i).\sum_j w_{ji}e_j = \sum_j(g'(h_i).w_{ji}e_j)$

with x_i, h_i and e_i the signal output, the weighted input sum and the backprop-agated error value of neuron i, w_{ij} the weight from neuron j to neuron i, λ the learning rate, α the momentum term, g the transfer function and g' its gradient.

The mathematical principles of the rules can be kept. However their imple-mentation needs to be local. Equation (3) shows that the error can be written as a sum. It can therefore be performed by a sequence of independent computa-tions as long as their common term $g'(h_i)$ remains constant during computations. Figure 5 shows a flowchart of the error backpropagation and delta weight update.

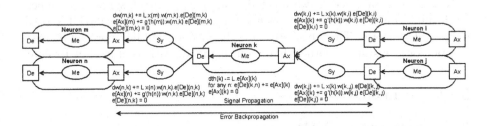

Fig. 5. Neuron k receives error values from ahead neurons i and j and backpropagates error values to neurons m and n. Error is transmitted between dendrites (De) and axons (Ax) by the context systems membrane (Me) and synapse (Sy). A synapse updates its delta weight (dw), a membrane its delta threshold (dth), L is the learning rate and e is the error. The momentum term is not shown for simplicity and readability.

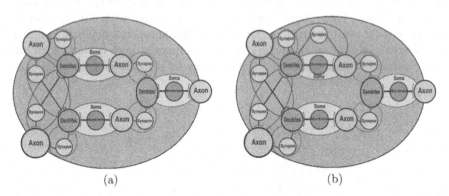

(a)   (b)

Fig. 6. (a): A feed forward network. (b): Same network with a recursive synapse. The program is initially the same but then topped up with one more synapse. (Synaptic Connection systems are made discreet for readability but the synapses schemata clearly indicate the interacting systems).

Each neuron keeps a current error value where further neurons can add their backpropagated error contribution. To avoid reusing twice any information, a neuron resets to zero its error value as soon as it is backpropagated. To assert the constancy of the terms $g'(h_i)$, the weights are updated only at the end of the computation (like in a classical BP) when a new sample is presented.

Neurons and synapses are therefore autonomous and responsible for their own local data. These local rules imply that no global algorithm is defined and therefore no constraint is imposed on the network structure. This model can be used to design feed-forward networks as well as recurrent NN as shown in 6(a) and 6(b). The biological plausibility comes in this work from the autonomy and organisation of the systems, caused by the natural characteristics of asynchrony and local knowledge built into SC, leading to an emerging global behaviour, like the global learning. Also, the model could use any other kind of learning within the neuron and synapse systems, still keeping the very same organisation.

Note that a stabilised network could easily have its weak synapses trimmed by the injection of a new context system, programmed for instance to kill settled redundant synapses. This illustrates how the model could be improved by easy addition of new systems rather than requiring modifications of code at its core.

5   Experiments

5.1   Experiment 1 – X-Or

The X-Or problem is a common example of non-linearly separable problems, problems simple perceptrons cannot solve. Usually, BP feed-forward multi-layer perceptrons are used [3] and a common solution involves 2 hidden neurons and 1 output neuron (Figure 7(a)) [9]. However, the X-Or problem becomes a linearly separable problem when adding a third input, doing for instance the AND of the 2 others [9]. A 2 neurons network is thus enough to solve the X-Or problem [9] (Figure 7(b)). These structures can be simply created with our SC model by just assembling neurons together (i.e., adding the appropriate dendrite, soma and axon systems into the environment). In the experiments, both network structures were created and their performance was evaluated with the new, local BP rules.

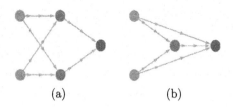

(a)   (b)

Fig. 7. (a) and (b): 2 networks for the X-Or problem

We compare these results to the network 7(a) using the Matlab ANN toolbox. We instantiate a network using a hyperbolic tangent sigmoid transfer function ($sig(x) = \frac{2}{1+e^{-2.x}} - 1$) on the hidden layers and a linear transfer function on the output node. The rest of the setup is the toolbox's default (Matlab 7.1, NN Toolbox 4.0.6). There is no Matlab implementation of the network 7(b) as classical BP only deals with layered networks. The SC networks use the same transfer function as in the Matlab network for each node including the output one. However, it sets the error on the output node using the gradient of the identity function (i.e. $g'(h) = 1$). The gradient of a sigmoid function on the last node provides poor error estimation as a sum around the worst value (i.e. 1 instead of -1) is little penalised ($g'(h) \approx 0$) compared to a neutral value ($g'(h) >> 0$). The learning rate is set to 0.5 with no momentum. The networks are allowed 100 epochs for learning. Each test is run 25 times. Table 2 summarises the results. The binary input values are -1 for false and 1 for true. The results show that both SC networks outperform the Matlab implementation by a wide margin.

Table 2. X-Or experiments results giving for each network implementation (7(a) and 7(b)) the percentage of success (perfect truth table) over 25 runs in solving the problem

Matlab 7(a)	S.C. 7(a)	S.C. 7(b)
47%	84%	100%

5.2 Experiment 2 – Iris Data

The second experiment uses the well-known Iris plant data set [10]. The data set contains three classes of fifty instances each, where each class refers to a type of iris plant (Setosa, Versicolour and Virginica). One class is linearly separable from the other two; the latter are not linearly separable from each other.

The network we use in both the Matlab and SC implementations has 4 inputs, 2 hidden neurons and 3 output neurons, as shown in Figure 8(a). The learning and momentum rates are respectively taken at 0.1 and 0.75. The maximum number of epochs was set to 50.

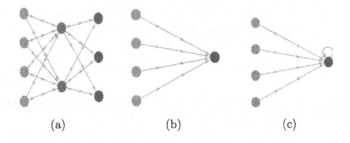

(a)   (b)   (c)

Fig. 8. (a):Feed forward 4-2-3 network for Iris plant data classification. (b): Perceptron, (c): Amplified perceptron.

Table 3 shows the classification results over 10 runs taking half of the samples (75) for learning and the other half (75) for testing. The simulation in Matlab used the same setup and default settings. The Matlab implementation, learning in batch mode, required many more epochs to classify correctly; we set the limit at 1000. Then, the final error level is fairly similar. The results clearly show that our SC model can perform at least as well as conventional networks implementation in such classification task.

Table 3. Averaged percentage of success over 10 runs of the 3 Iris data sets and total percentage of success (L and T respectively stand for the learning and the testing sets)

	Setosa		Versicolour		Virginica		Total		
	L	T	L	T	L	T	L	T	L&T
Matlab	100	100	96.4	94	98	95.6	98.13	96.53	97.33
S.C.	100	100	93.2	94	99.2	97.6	97.47	97.2	97.33

5.3   Experiment 3 – Recursive ANNs

Another advantage of the SC model is that it can also handle recursive connections. One example of such a network is a simple signal amplifier (i.e. where the signal of a neuron is reinforced by itself). In this third experiment, we made the two networks shown in Figures 8(b) and 8(c) learn a small amount of two sets to classify (Setosa and Versicolour, linearly separable). Each set consists of 50 samples and we give 5 of them for each set to the networks to learn within 3 epochs. We then test the networks with the rest of the sets samples. The learning rate is 0.25 and no momentum factor is used. Table 4 provides the results.

Table 4. Average classification value for the Setosa and Versicolour (repectively taught at 1 and -1) sets over 10 runs with a simple perceptron and an amplified perceptron. "Average" gives the network response: the closer to the taught value, the stronger the belief in the classification. "Std.Dev." gives the standard deviation over the samples of each set. L and T respectively refer to the learning and testing sets.

		Perceptron		Amplified Perceptron	
		Average	Std. Dev.	Average	Std. Dev.
L	Setosa	0.8982	0.0148	0.9370	0.0119
	Versicolour	-0.8076	0.1314	-0.8645	0.0838
T	Setosa	0.8769	0.0435	0.9264	0.0260
	Versicolour	-0.6092	0.2578	-0.6982	0.2258

Learning has been performed on very few epochs and samples; the network should thus be insensitive to noise. The signal reinforcement allows a strong response in a short learning time without requiring a steeper sigmoid function.

6   Conclusion

In this paper we continued our exploration of systemic computation, a novel paradigm designed to improve our ability to model and implement biological processes. We showed how its intrinsic (non-simulated) properties of local knowledge and asynchrony naturally provide more flexibility for artificial neural network structures. The example implementation contrasts significantly with classical approaches where data and algorithm are interdependent separate parts making network implementations more rigid and less biologically plausible. Our implementation gave full autonomy to neurons, and is compatible with any neuron model (first, second, third generation [7]). It thus highlights the potential of SC for the modelling of such natural processes. Future work will explore other features of SC such as fault tolerance and self-repair.

References

1. Bentley, P.J.: Systemic computation: A Model of Interacting Systems with Natural Characteristics. Int.J. Parallel, Emergent and Distributed Systems 22, 103–121 (2007)
2. Le Martelot, E., Bentley, P.J., Lotto, R.B.: A Systemic Computation Platform for the Modelling and Analysis of Processes with Natural Characteristics. In: Proc. of Genetic and Evolutionary Computation Conference, pp. 2809–2816 (2007)
3. Tang, H., Tan, K.C., Yi, Z.: Neural Networks: Computational Models and Applications. Springer, Heidelberg (2007)
4. Kandel, E.R., Schwartz, J.H., Jessel, T.M.: Principles of Neural Science, 3rd edn., ch. 1,3. Elsevier, Amsterdam (1991)
5. Peterson, C., Anderson, J.R.: A Mean Field Theory Learning Algorithm for Neural Networks. Complex Systems 1, 995–1019 (1987)
6. Hinton, G.E.: Deterministic Boltzmann Learning Performs Steepest Descent in Weight-space. Neural computation 1, 143–150 (1990)
7. Maass, W.: Networks of spiking neurons: the third generation of neural network models. Neural Networks 10, 1659 (1997)
8. O'Reilley, R.C.: Biologically Plausible Error-driven Learning using Local Activation Differences: The Generalized Recirculation Algorithm. Neural computation 8, 895–938 (1996)
9. Yanling, Z., Bimin, D., Zhanrong, W.: Analysis and Study of Perceptron to Solve XOR Problem. In: Proc. of the 2nd Int. Workshop on Autonomous Decentralized System (2002)
10. Fisher, R.A., Marshall, M.: Iris Plants Database, UCI Machine Learning Repository (1988), http://www.ics.uci.edu/~mlearn/MLRepository.html

Molecular Communication: Simulation of Microtubule Topology

Michael J. Moore[1], Akihiro Enomoto[1], Tadashi Nakano[1], Atsushi Kayasuga[2], Hiroaki Kojima[2], Hitoshi Sakakibara[2], Kazuhiro Oiwa[2], and Tatsuya Suda[1]

[1] Information and Computer Science, University of California, Irvine, USA
{mikemo,enomoto,tnakano,suda}@ics.uci.edu
[2] National Institute of Information and Communications Technology(NICT), Japan
{kayasuga,kojima,sakaki,oiwa}@nict.go.jp

Abstract. Molecular communication is one method for communication among biological nanomachines. Nanomachines are artificial or biological nano-scale devices that perform simple computation, sensing, or actuation. Future applications using nanomachines may require various communication mechanisms. For example, broadcast is one primitive communication for transmission from one sender to many receivers. In this paper, we discuss preliminary work on designing a molecular communication system that is adapted from the molecular motor transport mechanism existing in biological cells. In the proposed molecular motor mechanism, a sender releases information molecules, and molecular motors transport the information molecules along microtubule filaments to receiver nanomachines up to hundreds of micrometers away. This paper describes some possible arrangements for microtubule filaments and simulations to evaluate sending of one information molecule to many receivers. The simulation results indicate that the proposed molecular motor system transports simulated information molecules (100nm radius spheres) more quickly than a diffusion-only communication and that placement of receivers at the plus-end of microtubules results in lower propagation delay.

Keywords: Bionanotechnology, nanomachine communication, molecular motor, self-organization, microtubule topology.

1 Introduction

Molecular communication [1][2] is a possible solution for nano-scale communication between nanomachines. A nanomachine uses molecular communication to send information molecules over a short-range to a nanomachine capable of receiving the information molecule.

Nanomachines, both those found in biological systems and artificially created, have limited size and limited complexity, and thus nanomachines are capable of performing only very simple computation, sensing, or actuation (e.g., detection of molecules, generation of motion, or performing chemical reactions). Some examples of nanomachines in biological systems include molecular motors [3] that produce motion or protein receptors [4][5] that react to specific

Y. Suzuki et al. (Eds.): IWNC 2007, PICT 1, pp. 134–144, 2009.

molecules. Examples of artificial nanomachines include nanomachines synthesized using NEMS (Nanoelectro- mechanical Systems) technology from organic and/or artificial components at the submicron dimension [6][7][8].

If multiple nanomachines communicate, they may cooperate and perform complex tasks such as nano-scale computing. Researchers are currently attempting to create nano-scale logic gates (e.g., an inverter and a NAND gate) [9][10] and memory [11] using existing components from biological systems. If nanomachines implementing logic gates and memory communicate, by for instance, using signal molecules (e.g., ions, proteins, DNA) in an aqueous environment, they can perform more complex computing functionality (e.g., a full adder).

In this paper, we describe one proposed molecular communication system based on observations of existing biological cells which use molecular motors to transport molecules along protein filaments. In the near future, it may become relatively easier to adapt existing molecular communication components from biological systems using techniques developed from current research in synthetic biology [10][12][13][14][15] and in bio-nanotechnologies [16][17] (e.g., receptors, nano-scale reactions, communication molecules).

We evaluate several variations of networks to identify what topology is potentially suitable for broadcast. Broadcast of information to multiple receivers without communication relay (e.g. multiple computers connected to the same LAN) is a primitive of communication in communication networks. Topologies in this study include individual protein filaments randomly bound to a surface and protein filament aster topologies (multiple star-topologies).

2   Biological Systems Using Molecular Motors

Inside a single biological cell, molecular motors (e.g. kinesin, dynein, and myosin) bind to filaments (e.g. microtubules and actin filaments) and can then walk along the filaments by consuming chemical energy, such as ATP (Figure 1). If cargo (e.g. an information molecule) is loaded onto the molecular motor, the motor transports the cargo towards the end of the microtubule (e.g. kinesin carries cargo and moves it toward the plus-end of the microtubule). A single protein motor stochastically detaches from a protein filament as it walks, thus a single protein motor walks only a short distance along the protein filament. Multiple molecular motors may be bound to the cargo to increase the distance walked before detaching or for larger cargo [18].

Protein filaments dynamically change their length, which is known as dynamic instability [19]. The dynamic instability of microtubules is well-characterized. In this instability, the process depends upon the concentration of tubulin (the structural unit of microtubules) and upon the presence of microtubule associated protein (MAP) activity. For example, during cell division in a eukaryotic cell, the cell forms asters and rearranges microtubules into a spindle (a star-like arrangement with microtubules radiating from a single center), which separates chromosomes into two daughter cells. Structures such as asters, vortices, and random mesh can be formed in vitro using characterized protein components,

such as protein motors and microtubules. The reconstitution of these structures are well characterized in computational simulations [20][21][22]. Addition
of MAPs into the reconstitution system allows control over the shape of the
structures and microfabrication techniques also modify the shape and dynamics
of the microtubule structures [23][24].

In cells microtubules are dynamically organized for different activities such as
transport of vesicles, placement of organelles, and cell replication. For molecular
communication, the random mesh may provide a mechanism for evenly distributing molecules by facilitating diffusion across the mesh. An aster topology may
provide a mechanism for distributing molecules away from a single point to
far-away points (e.g. broadcasting molecules from a single source) or to gather
molecules to a location within the cell (e.g. gathering molecules for analysis by
a nanomachine).

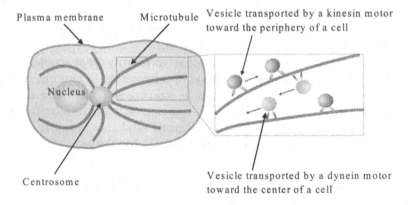

Fig. 1. Vesicle transport by molecular motors along filaments inside a single biological
cell

3   Proposed System Using Molecular Motors

The system of molecular motors and protein filaments described in section 2 can
be applied to develop a molecular communication system (Figure 2). High dura-
bility and availability of kinesin and dynamic instability of microtubules allow
us to focus on the kinesin-microtubule system as a molecular communication
system.

3.1   System Components

The system components of molecular motor system include sender and receiver
nanomachines, information molecules, kinesin motors, and the microtubules on
which the kinesin walks. Microtubules form connections between nanomachines,
and kinesin motors transport vesicles containing information molecules toward
the plus-end of microtubules. This paper focuses on communication properties
of transmission, therefore the sender and receiver are unspecified but must be

capable of sending and receiving information molecules (e.g. a cell releases hormones and reacts to received information molecules). Information molecules (or a vesicle containing information molecules) must also be capable of being loaded onto and released from a molecular motor which transports the information molecules. The energy source of kinesin motility, ATP, is supplied from environmental solutions.

3.2 Molecular Communication Using Molecular Motors

The proposed system using molecular motors consists of the following five processes:

Encoding. Sender nanomachines encode information on information molecules (e.g., DNA, proteins, peptides). For example, nanomachines encode information on sequences of peptides and inject the peptides into vesicles [4]. The information molecules should not react while in the vesicle, and thus a variety of encoded molecules can be sent.

Sending. Sender nanomachines then emit the information molecules (or vesicle) to molecular motors that walk along protein filaments. Information molecules (or vesicles) are then loaded on molecular motors.

Propagation. Propagation is performed through molecular motors that walk along protein filaments from sender nanomachines to receiver nanomachines in a directed manner. For example, microtubules grow in Figure 2 to form a topology in which senders and receivers are dynamically connected with microtubules. However, in the proposed system, microtubules are not necessarily confined to cells and may form structures with dimensions much larger than those in biological cells.

Receiving. The receiver can be specified by a protein tag that binds to specific receptors on receiver nanomachines. If the information molecule is inside a vesicle, the vesicle must first fuse to the receiver nanomachine.

Decoding. Receiver nanomachines invoke reactions in response to information molecules. For example, peptides (e.g. neurotransmitters) transported through molecular motors in a neuron cause receiver neurons to generate an action potential.

The form of the microtubule topology determines in what direction molecular motors will propagate. In biological systems, the microtubule topology occurs within the confined volume of a biological cell and often exists in random mesh and aster forms.

3.3 Self-organization of Microtubule Topology

A random mesh topology is a distribution of microtubules that covers a surface (or fills a volume). A random mesh starts initially as microtubule seeds (i.e. short microtubule segments) that grow through polymerization of microtubules (Figure 3). The microtubules also undergo dynamic instability which

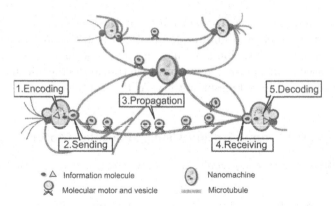

Fig. 2. Proposed system applying molecular motors

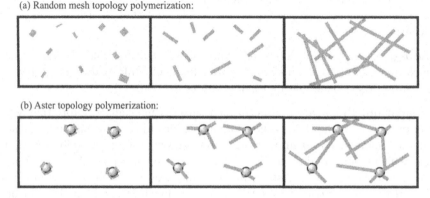

Fig. 3. Self organization of random mesh (a) and aster topologies (b). Microtubules are initially microtubule seeds (left). Microtubules polymerize (lengthen through dynamic instability) to form some structure (right).

involves stochastic switching between growing and shrinking of microtubules. In the proposed system, a nanomachine grows microtubules that stabilize when contacting other nanomachines (e.g. through binding a protein that caps the end of the microtubule).

Eukaryotic cells can be formed artificially by, for example, having many microtubule seeds chemically conjugated to a silica bead (Figure 3), and then the microtubule are polymerized from the seeds and are extended using an appropriate tubulin concentration. In the proposed system in Figure 2, receivers at the center of each aster self-organize connections to other receivers without knowledge of the location of other receivers.

4   Simulation of Proposed System

We have been conducting wet-lab experiments and simulations to improve the design of the proposed molecular motor system. Measuring the communication properties of various microtubule topologies (e.g. random mesh, star-like aster) may help identify the desirable features of a microtubule topology. In computer networks, important physical layer communication measurements include delay for propagation, channel capacity, or coverage. In this paper, we focus on improving the design of the proposed molecular motor system by conducting simulations to measure delay characteristics.

4.1   Simulation Model of the Proposed System

In the proposed system, molecular communication occurs over hundreds of micrometers and is on the order of minutes. The simulator for the proposed system makes geometry and statistical simplifications to execute in a reasonable amount of time similar to simulators for the self-organization of microtubules [20] [25] [26]. The sender, receiver, and information molecules are modeled as spheres, and the microtubules are modeled as cylinders. Chemical reactions occur when the spheres/cylinders touch. The time step of the simulator is a millisecond. The environment is modeled as a planar container containing a aqueous solution (viscosity 0.02 Pa·s representing water with many proteins) with dimensions $100\mu m \times 100\mu m$ and a height of $10\mu m$. Thus the scale of communication in the simulation is on the order of 10's of micrometers.

Sending and receiving information molecules. There exist several models of a communication processes using molecules. The simulation of the proposed system is similar to [27] in which the sender generates information molecules, and a receiver reacts to single information molecules. In these simulations, the sender is assumed to release one information molecule with the molecular motors already attached. The receiver is assumed to start decoding when the information molecule is received. This is unlike [28][29] in which the receiver detects information as the concentration of many information molecules.

Information molecule propagation. A single molecular motor cannot reliably transport information molecules over a long range [18], and thus multiple motors transport the information molecule. A large information molecule (100 nm radius in these simulations) is necessary to allow binding of multiple molecular motors which are around ~50 nm long. In this simulation, when the molecular motors of an information molecule are bound to a microtubule, the motor walks towards the plus-end of the microtubule at 800 nm/sec. When the molecular motors on the information molecule binds two crossing microtubules, the information molecule switches with some probability similar to the microtubule switching in [26]. When the information molecule is not bound to any microtubules by molecular motors, the information molecule diffuses according to the diffusion coefficient for a sphere of radius 150 nm (100 nm silica bead and 50 nm motor) and may collide with surfaces.

Topology. The environment contains microtubules, senders, and receivers in a variety of arrangements that may be reasonable to experimentally produce. The microtubules, senders, and receivers are all directly bound to a single surface. A single sender is located at the center on the $100\mu m \times 100\mu m$ surface. The microtubules form one of three arrangements (Figure 4): a mesh of microtubules on the surface (M), multiple asters distributed across the surface with either the plus-end of the microtubule at the center of the aster (M+), or with the minus-end at the center (M-). Each aster has 4 microtubules radiating from the center. For these simulations, the topology is statically formed at the start of the simulation and does not change over the duration of the simulation. The same number of microtubules (400 10μm-microtubules) is used in each arrangement (M, M+, M-). We also simulate no microtubules (O) to compare with a purely diffusion-based propagation. 400 receivers are in one of three arrangements (Figure 4): randomly (uniform) on the 100μm × 100μm surface (R), at the plus-end of each microtubule (R+), or at the minus-end of each microtubule (R-).

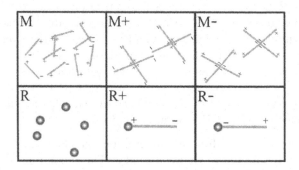

Fig. 4. Microtubule configurations (M, M+, M-). Receiver configurations (R, R+, R-). For R+, R-, the receiver is placed at the end of each microtubule available.

4.2   Measurement: Delay for Information Molecule Propagation

One goal of a broadcast is to quickly spread information to receivers. Propagation delay measures the time necessary for an information molecule to propagate from the sender to a receiver. Once the information molecule reaches a receiver, the information molecule no longer propagates. Simulation data is gathered from the propagation of 2400 information molecules on one of 240 randomly generated topologies for each of the ten arrangements.

Figure 5a shows data for the probability that an information molecule is received by any of the 400 receivers. As time progresses, an information molecule has more time to propagate and thus becomes more likely to reach a receiver. Figure 5b also shows data for the probability that an information molecule is received, but only shows a snapshot of the probability at 480 seconds. The ten arrangements correspond to combinations of the topology section in 4.1. Each arrangement is defined by two parameters: an arrangement of microtubules (M, M+, M-, O) and how the where the receivers located on the microtubules (R, R+, R-).

4.3   Discussion

From the data in Figure 5a, molecular motor propagation along microtubules (M) is beneficial for reducing the propagation delay compared to diffusion only (O).

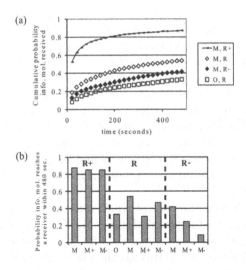

Fig. 5. (a) Time at which a single information molecule contacts any receiver for random mesh microtubule topologies (M) and diffusion only (O). Receivers are randomly on the surface (R), at the plus-end of microtubules (R+) or at the minus-end of microtubules (R-). (b) Other configurations include asters with microtubule minus-ends at the center (M-) and plus-ends at the center (M+).

This is likely the case since walking along microtubules more quickly displaces a somewhat large information molecule (100 nm radius) through the environment compared to diffusion alone. From the design perspective, developing arrangements of microtubules may be worthwhile for improving molecular communications.

Also from the data in Figure 5a, positioning receivers at the plus-end of a microtubule appears to be the most significant factor for random mesh microtubules (M). Since the molecular motors propagate from the minus-end of a microtubule to the plus-end of a microtubule, an information molecule that binds to any part of the microtubule is likely to reach the plus-end of the microtubule. Thus, the effective probability of reaching the receiver in the plus-end case (R+) is the probability of the information molecule binding any microtubule. On the other hand, having the receiver at the minus-end reduces the probability of contacting the receiver. This is most apparent with the receiver at the center of a minus-end aster (M-, R-) (Figure 5b). In this case, when the molecule motor binds a microtubule, the molecular motor walks the information molecule away from the center of the aster where the receiver is. Thus, the information molecule must avoid binding all of an aster's microtubules to contact the receiver in the aster. On the other hand, this may be beneficial for molecular communication since it is possible to design a system in which certain receivers placed at the center of a minus-end aster avoid reacting to kinesin-associated information molecules. Also, a sender may be appropriately placed at the center of the minus-end aster (M-, R-) to disperse information molecules away from the sender and to keep information molecules concentrated around receivers.

Based on the results of Figure 5a, it would be experimentally beneficial to focus on identifying mechanisms to place the receiver at the plus-end of a microtubule. One possibility is to add receivers into the environment and then grow the minus-end of the microtubule away from the receiver[23]. Another possibility is to localize receivers to the plus-end by stabilizing microtubules with MAP's and binding the receiver to the MAP. In the proposed system in Figure 2, the sender is an M-, R- aster (microtubules grow out from senders) and receivers are an M+, R+ aster (the plus-end of the microtubules are stabilized at receivers). The proposed system in Figure 2 (not simulated since not characterized experimentally) directly links senders to receivers and thus is expected to do better since information molecules do not require diffusion to reach a microtubule for walking to a receiver.

Another factor affecting the time at which information molecules reach a receiver is the arrangement of microtubules (i.e. M, M-, M+). Asters (M-, M+) do not appear to be beneficial for reducing the time. Since the sender is located independent of microtubules on the surface, the information molecule first diffuses to a microtubule before propagating along the microtubule. Arranging the microtubules into an aster produces a patchy distribution of microtubules (given the same number and length of microtubules as the random mesh), and thus increases the average time an information molecule spends diffusing before it reaches a microtubule. However, other aster-related configurations are possible (e.g. higher microtubule density or the target system described in Figure 2) and may be beneficial for reducing delay. Also, asters may still be beneficial towards other communication properties such as coverage or channel capacity.

5   Conclusion and Future Work

For some applications of molecular communication, it may be necessary to quickly broadcast specific information molecules to nearby receivers. In this paper, several simple microtubule arrangements were compared to identify the arrangement most beneficial for broadcast communication. The proposed molecular motor system was able to reduce the delay for the information molecules to reach receivers depending on the orientation of microtubules and receivers. However, these conclusions are for a very specific configuration (e.g. one possible density of microtubules, senders and receivers) and only for the measurement of propagation delay (i.e. other microtubule arrangements may be better for other communication measures). Studying other measures (e.g. coverage, channel capacity) and other arrangements of microtubules (e.g. the vortices in [22] or top-down constructed through photolithographic techniques [16]) may lead to other conclusions about selecting a configuration.

For some applications of molecular communication other communications functionality may be more important such as point-to-point communication, high channel capacity, or robustness to environment conditions. Molecular communication may become more applicable with the ability to achieve different types of communication objectives (e.g. broadcast, point-to-point, or multi-cast communication). Comparison of molecular communication under various environment conditions will help identify which molecular communication system is appropriate for which application. However, it also remains an open issue to identify applications that require molecular communication.

Acknowledgments. This research is supported by the NICT (the National Institute of Communication Technology, Japan), by the NSF through grants ANI-0083074, ANI-9903427 and ANI-0508506, by DARPA through grant MDA972-99-1-0007, by AFOSR through grant MURI F49620-00-1-0330, and by grants from the California MICRO and CoRe programs, Hitachi, Hitachi America, Hitachi CRL, Hitachi SDL, DENSO IT Laboratory, DENSO International America LA Laboratories, NTT Docomo and Novell.

References

1. Moritani, Y., Hiyama, S., Suda, T.: Molecular Communication for Health Care Applications. In: Fourth Annual IEEE Conference on Pervasive Computing and Communications and Workshops (2006)
2. Suda, T., Moore, M., Nakano, T., Egashira, R., Enomoto, A.: Exploratory Research on Molecular Communication between Nanomachines. In: Proc. of the Genetic and Evolutionary Computation Conference (GECCO) (2005)
3. Kinosita, K., Adachi, K., Itoh, H.: Rotation of F1-ATPASE: How an ATP-Driven Molecular Machine May Work. Annual Review of Biophysics and Biomolecular Structure 33, 245–268 (2004)
4. Alberts, B., Johnson, A., Lewis, J., Raff, M., Roberts, K., Walter, P.: Molecular Biology of the Cell. Garland Science, 4th Bk & Cdr edn. (2002)
5. Pawson, T., Nash, P.: Protein-protein Interactions Define Specificity in Signal Transduction 14(9), 1027–1047 (2000)
6. Holliger, P., Hoogenboom, H.R.: Artificial Antibodies and Enzymes: Mimicking Nature and Beyond. Trends Biotechnol. 13(1), 7–9 (1995)
7. Pelesko, J.A., Bernstein, D.H.: Modeling MEMS and NEMS. CRC Press, Boca Raton (2002)
8. Roukes, M.L.: Nanoelectromechanical Systems. In: Tech. Digest of the 2000 Solid State Sensor and Actuator Workshop (2000)
9. Dueber, J.E., Yeh, B.J., Bhattacharyya, R.P., Lim, W.A.: Rewiring cell signaling: the logic and plasticity of eukaryotic protein circuitry. Current Opinion in Structural Biology 14, 690–699 (2004)
10. Weiss, R., Basu, S., Hooshangi, S., Kalmbach, A., Karig, D., Mehreja, R., Netravali, I.: Genetic Circuit Building Blocks for Cellular Computation, Communications, and Signal Processing. Natural Computing 2, 47–84 (2003)
11. Head, T., Yamamura, M., Gal, S.: Aqueous Computing: Writing on Molecules. In: Proc. the Congress on Evolutionary Computation (1999)
12. Elowttz, M.B., Leibler, S.: A synthetic oscillatory network of transcriptional regulators. Nature 403, 335–338 (2000)
13. Endy, D., Brent, R.: Modeling cellular behavior. Nature 409, 391–395 (2001)
14. Kobayashi, H., Karn, M., Araki, M., Chung, K., Gardner, T.S., Cantor, C.R., Collins, J.J.: Programmable cells: Interfacing natural and engineered gene networks. PNAS 101(22), 8414–8419 (2004)

15. You, L., Cox III, R.S., Weiss, R., Arnold, F.H.: Programmed population control by cell-cell communication and regulated killing. Nature 428, 868–871 (2004)
16. Hess, H., Matzke, C., Doot, R., Clemmens, J., Bachand, G., Bunker, B., Vogel, V.: Molecular shuttles operating undercover: A new photolithographic approach for the fabrication of structured surfaces supporting directed motility. Nano Letters 3, 1651–1655 (2003)
17. Hiratsuka, Y., Tada, T., Oiwa, K., Kanayama, T., Uyeda, T.Q.: Controlling the direction of kinesin-driven microtubule movements along microlithographic tracks. Biophysics Journal 81, 1555–1561 (2001)
18. Klumpp, S., Lipowsky, R.: Cooperative cargo transport by several molecular motors. PNAS 102(48), 17284–17289 (2005)
19. Hotani, H., Horio, T.: Dynamics of Microscopy: Microtubules Visualized by Dark-field Treadmilling and Dynamic Instability. Cell Motility and the Cytoskeleton 10, 229–236 (1988)
20. Chakravarty, A., Howard, L., Compto, D.A.: A mechanistic Model for the Organization of Microtubule Asters by Motor and Non-Motor Proteins in a Mammalian Mitotic Extract. MBC (2004)
21. Malikov, V., Cytrynbaum, E.N., Kashina, A., Mogilner, A., Rodionov, V.: Centering of a radial microtubule array by translocation along microtubules spontaneously nucleated in the cytoplasm. Nature, Cell biology (2005)
22. Nedelec, F.J., Surrey, T., Maggs, A.C., Leibler, S.: Self-organization of microtubules and motors. Nature 389, 305–308 (1997)
23. Mitchison, T.J.: Localization of an Exchangeable GTP binding site at the plus end of microtubules. Science 261, 1044 (1993)
24. Doot, R.K., Hess, H., Vogel, V.: Engineered networks of oriented microtubule filaments for directed cargo transport. Soft Matter (2006)
25. Nedelec, F.: Computer Simulations Reveal Motor Properties Generating Stable Anti-Parallel Microtubule Interactions. Journal of Cell Biology 158(6), 1005–1015 (2002)
26. Snider, J., Lin, F., Zahedi, N., Rodionov, V., Clare, Y.C., Gross, S. P.: Intracellular actin-based transport: How far you go depends on how often you switch. PNAS (2004)
27. Eckford, A.W.: Nanoscale Communication with Brownian Motion. arXiv.org., Computer Science Information Theory, arXiv:cs/0703034v1 (2007)
28. Prank, K., Gabbiani, F., Brabant, G.: Coding efficiency and information rates in transmembrane signaling. BioSystems 55, 15–22 (2000)
29. Thomas, P.J., Spencer, D.J., Hampton, S.K., Park, P., Zurkus, J.P.: The Diffusion Mediated Biochemical Signal Relay Channel. In: Advances in Neural Information Processing Systems 16. MIT Press, Cambridge (2004)

Monte Carlo Simulation in Lattice Ecosystem: Top-Predator Conservation and Population Uncertainty

Hiroyasu Nagata[1], Kei-ichi Tainaka[2], Nariyuki Nakagiri[3], and Jin Yoshimura[4]

[1] Graduate School of Science and Technology, Shizuoka University,
Hamamatsu 432-8561, Japan
`f5645024@ipc.shizuoka.ac.jp`
[2] Graduate School of Science and Technology, Shizuoka University,
Hamamatsu 432-8561, Japan
`tainaka@sys.eng.shizuoka.ac.jp`
[3] School of Human Science and Environment, University of Hyogo,
Himeji 670-0092, Japan
`nakagiri@shse.u-hyogo.ac.jp`
[4] Graduate School of Science and Technology, Shizuoka University,
Hamamatsu 432-8561, Japan
`jin@sys.eng.shizuoka.ac.jp`

Abstract. The conservation of biodiversity is one of the most important problems in this century. Under human management, ecosystems suffer perturbations or disturbances. The investigation of perturbation experiments is essential to conserve species and habitat. We carry out Monte-Carlo simulations on finite-size lattices composed of species ($n \leq 4$). The value of mortality rate m of top predator is altered to a higher or lower level and a fluctuation enhancement (FE) is explored. Here FE means an uncertainty in population dynamics. It is found for that FE is observed when m is decreased. Namely, when we protect the top predator, its population dynamics becomes very difficult to predict.

Keywords: Monte Carlo simulation, population uncertainty, finite size lattice.

1 Introduction

In the field of ecology, time dependence of species abundance (population dynamics) is studied by spatial and non-spatial models. The former approach mainly uses either lattice models or partial differential equations. Lattice models are listed in the left column of Table 1. The lattice Lotka-Volterra model (LLVM), first introduced by one of the present authors (KT) [1, 2], is usually applied in ecology. Sometime LLVM can be regarded as one of stochastic cellular automata. A distinct property of LLVM is that it has a firm mathematical basis (mean-field theory). Simulation on the lattice is usually carried out by two different methods: global and local interactions. The mean-field theory (global interaction) of LLVM is just equivalent to Lotka-Volterra equation.

Y. Suzuki et al. (Eds.): IWNC 2007, PICT 1, pp. 145–154, 2009.

In recent years, many biospecies go extinct. Almost all extinctions are caused by human perturbations (disturbances). Hence, study of perturbation experiments is important for biological conservation and control [1-7]. The aim of the present paper is to report the uncertainty in the prediction of dynamical process. The uncertainty is called fluctuation enhancement (FE) [8, 9]. Here FE is originated in stochastic properties due to the finite size of lattice, and it associates with a critical behavior near extinction.

Recently, coworkers in our laboratory studied the population uncertainty caused by perturbations [10, 11]. They altered the value of mortality rate m of a target species to a higher or lower level. So far opposite results for FE have been reported between one- and two-species systems. In a one-species case, FE was observed, only when the value of m is increased. In contrast, Itoh and Tainaka [11] applied the same perturbation to a two-species (prey-predator) system, and obtained just the opposite result: FE occurred, only when m is decreased. In the present paper, we deal with more general systems composed of n species ( ) to know universal properties for FE. We find for that FE is observed when m is decreased. Namely, when we protect the top predator, its population dynamics becomes very difficult to predict.

Table 1. Lattice model (left-) and its mean-field theory (right-column)

# of species	lattice models	non-spatial model
one-species system	contact process (Harris 1974)	logistic equation (Verhulst 1838)
more than one species	lattice Lotka-Volterra model (Tainaka 1988[1])	Lotka-Volterra model (Lotka, Volterra 1926)

2   Model and Method

We deal with square lattice systems composed of n species [12]. The size of lattice is finite (L), and the total number of lattice sites is given by $L \times L$. Each lattice site is labeled by either vacant site (X_0) or the occupied site X_j by species j ($j = 1, ..., n$). Interactions are defined by

$$X_j + X_{j-1} \longrightarrow 2X_j \quad \text{(rate } r_j), \tag{1a}$$

$$X_j \longrightarrow X_O \quad \text{(rate } m_j). \tag{1b}$$

The reaction (1a) means the predation (reproduction) of species j, and the parameter r_j is the reproduction rate of the species. On the other hand, the reaction (1b) and parameter m_j denote the death process and the mortality rate of species j, respectively. In the present paper, we assume that $r_j = 1$ for every species and that the mortality rates m_k takes the same value besides the top predator ($m_1 = m_2 = ... = m_{n-1}$). Our system (1) corresponds to the contact process [13] for $n = 1$ and to the prey-predator model [14, 15, 16] for $n = 2$. Provided that interaction occurs globally, the mean-field theory is applicable as explained in the section 3: then, the system (1) is called the logistic model for $n = 1$, and Lotka-Volterra model [17, 18] for $n \geq 2$. In Fig. 1, the present model (1) is schematically shown for $n = 4$.

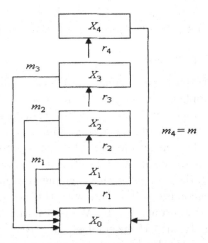

Fig. 1. The chart of the species relation for four-species system ($n = 4$). The species X_j eats X_{j-1} ($j = 1, ..., 4$), and X_0 means the empty site (resource). The top predator is thus represented by X_4.

2.1 Simulation Method

The reactions (1a) and (1b) are carried out in two different ways: local and global interactions. We first describe the simulation method for local interaction:

1) Initially, we distribute individuals X_j of species j on the square lattice, where $j = 1, ..., n$. The initial distribution is not so important, since the system evolves into a stationary state.
2) Spatial pattern is updated in the following two steps:
    (i) we perform two-body reaction (1a): Choose one lattice site randomly, and then randomly specify one of eight neighboring sites (Moore neighborhood). If the pair of chosen sites are (X_j, X_{j-1}), then, the latter site is changed into X_j. For any other pairs, we skip to the next step. Note that the pair (X_{j-1}, X_j) is also skipped.
    (ii) we perform one-body reaction (1b). Choose one lattice point randomly; if the site is occupied by X_j, the site will become the vacant site (X_0) by the rate m_j.
3) Repeat step 2) $L \times L = 10^4$) times, where, is the total number of lattice points. This is the Monte Carlo step [1].
4) Repeat step 3) until the system reaches a stationary state. Here we have employed periodic boundary conditions (replacing any index that exceeds the boundary, L, by using the modulo operator on the index; $L+1$ is replaced by 1).

Next, we describe the method for the global interaction (mean-field simulation: MFS) in which long-ranged interactions are allowed. The simulation method for MFS is very similar to that of local interaction, but step (i) in 2) for local interaction is replaced with the following:

(i)' Choose one lattice site randomly. Choose the next site randomly. If these sites are (X_j, X_{j-1}) in order, then the latter site is changed into X_j.

2.2 Perturbation Experiment

Next we explain the perturbation experiment and fluctuation enhancement (FE). The perturbations are applied. The mortality rate of a target species are altered and held at higher or lower levels. To get a universal property, we focus on the top predator as the target species, and we put $m_n = m$. Our experiment is performed as follows: The initial mortality rate of top predator is set as m1, where all species are assumed to survive. Once this initial population has reached a steady state ($t = 100$), the mortality rate is changed from m_1 to a new value m_2, and is held at this value thereafter. Following this perturbation, the species eventually goes to a new stationary state. We repeat this experiment with M kinds of initial spatial patterns (M ensembles), and record the density $x_i(t)$ of a target species ($i = 1, ..., M$). Each simulation proceeds with $m = m_1$; each of them has a distinct initial density $x_i(0)$, but these initial conditions do not effect the results. Because the system evolves into a stationary state, the value of $x_i(t)$ becomes very close to the steady-state density at $m = m_1$. At a certain time, we apply a perturbation from $m = m_1$ to $m = m_2$. After the perturbation, we hold at $m = m_2$. From the density $x_i(t)$, we obtain the time dependences of the ensemble average $A(t)$ and the variance $V(t)$ which are defined by [10]

$$A(t) = \frac{1}{M} \sum_{i=1}^{M} x_i(t), \tag{2}$$

$$V(t) = \frac{1}{M} \sum_{i=1}^{M} [x_i(t) - A(t)]^2. \tag{3}$$

It should be emphasize that the quantities $A(t)$ and $V(t)$ are averaged over M kinds of ensembles. To confirm the indeterminacy, we explore the fluctuation enhancement (FE), which constitutes an extreme increase in the value of $V(t)$. When FE occurs, or when the variance rapidly increases, there are a variety of dynamic processes.

3 Mean-Field Theory

If the size L of lattice system is infinitely large ($L \rightarrow \infty$), then the population dynamics for mean-field simulation (MFS) is given by the mean-field theory. Note that the variance $V(t)$ is zero for the mean-field theory, while MFS has a nonzero value of $V(t)$. For the top predator (the species n), we have

$$\dot{x_n} = r_n x_n x_{n-1} - m_n x_n. \tag{4a}$$

Except for the top predator ($1 \leq k \leq n - 1$), we have

$$\dot{x}_k = r_{k-1}x_kx_{k-1} - r_kx_kx_{k+1} - m_kx_k. \tag{4b}$$

Here the dots represent the time derivative, and x_k is the density of species k. The time is measured by the Monte Carlo step [1]. The right hand side of (4b) represents the following meanings: the first and second terms denote the predations by species k and $k + 1$, respectively. The last term means the death process. Note that the total density is unity, so that the density of empty site is given by

$$x_0 = 1 - \sum_{j=1}^{n} x_j. \tag{5}$$

When the system contains only one species ($n = 1$), equations (4b) and (5) lead to the logistic equation (6):

$$\dot{x}_1 = r_1r_x(1 - x_1) - m_1x_1. \tag{6}$$

The steady-state solution (equilibrium) in mean-field limit can be obtained by setting the time derivative to be zero. It follows that (7):

$$x_1 = 1 - m_1/r_1. \tag{7}$$

This density is known to be globally stable, if it is positive. When $n = 2$, equation (4) becomes the Lotka-Volterra model with density effect. The equilibrium is also globally stable [17, 18], if the equilibrium densities of both species are positive (coexistence). For $3 \leq n \leq 5$, Takeuchi shows the following result

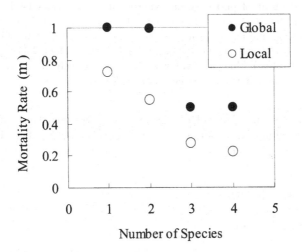

Fig. 2. Coexistence region is summarized for both local and global interactions. The critical (maximum) value of m for the coexistence is depicted against n.

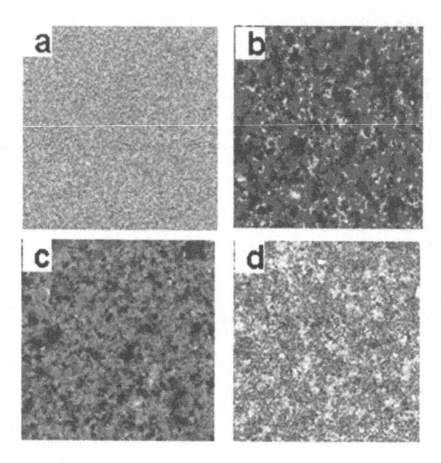

Fig. 3. A typical result of perturbation experiment for 4 species lattice model. (a) $t=0$, (b) $t=380$, (c) $t=420$, (d) $t=600$. The perturbation from $m=0.2$ to 0.01 is applied at $t=400$. (a) initial random pattern, (b) stationary state, (c) transient state after perturbation, (d) spatial pattern near new stationary state. The colors represent grey (X_4), green (X_3), red (X_2), blue (X_1) and white (X_0) respectively. In (c), the population size of top predator (X_4) increases, while its prey (X_3) is decreased.

(private communication [19]): In the case of $n = 3$, the coexisting equilibrium is locally stable, in which all densities are positive. In contrast, there is no stable equilibrium of coexistence for $n \geq 4$.

4   Simulation Results

4.1   Steady-State Density

Computer simulations are carried out for both global (MFS) and local interactions. We first describe the results of global interaction. The dynamics is well predicted by mean-field theory. When , the system evolves into a stationary state,

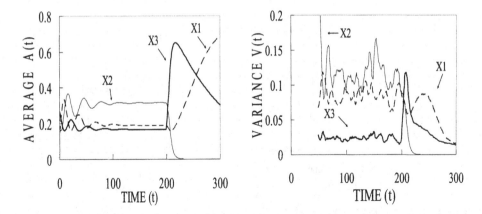

Fig. 4. A typical result of perturbation experiment for local interaction in three-species system ($n = 3$). The time dependencies of average (left) and variance (right; $\times 10^3$) for each species are depicted. At time $t = 200$, the value of mortality rate m is suddenly decreased from $m_1 = 0.2$ to $m_2 = 0.01$. We repeat the same experiment 100 times ($M = 100$) with different initial patterns.

so long as m takes a value below a critical value. The condition for coexistence is given by

$$0 < m < m_c, \tag{8}$$

where m_c is the maximum value of coexistence region. We have $m_c = 1$ for $n = 1$. Similarly, the above relation (8) holds for $n \geq 2$, where m_c takes $m_c = 1 - m_k, (1 - 2m_k)/2$, and $(1 - 2m_k)/2$ for n=2,3 and 4, respectively ($k \neq n$) [18, 19].

On the other hand, in the case of local interaction, the system evolves into stable stationary state for every value of n (even for $n = 4$). Figure 2 summarizes surviving region, where the critical (maximum) value of mortality rate m in coexisting phase is depicted against the number of species n. From Fig. 2, we find the following results:

i) The surviving region for global interaction is wider than that for local interaction.

ii) For both interactions, the surviving region becomes narrow, when n is increased.

According to recent studies of lattice models, space or local interaction never promoted the coexistence of multiple species. In fact, the result i) reveals such a trend. However, the opposite result is found for $n = 4$: in local interaction, space or local interaction promotes the coexistence of multiple species.

4.2   Results of Perturbation Experiment

We explore the uncertainty in population dynamics. We first report the case of local interaction. A typical example of perturbation experiment is shown in

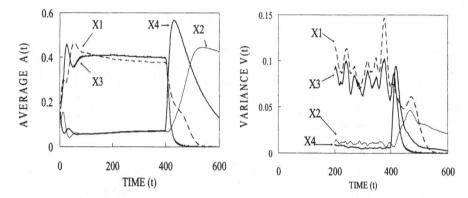

Fig. 5. Same as Fig. 4 (local interaction), but for four-species system ($n = 4$). The perturbation of $m_1 = 0.2$ and $m_2 = 0.01$ is applied at $t = 400$.

Fig. 3. We universally find for $n \geq 2$ that the fluctuation enhancement (FE) can be observed, when the value of death rate m is decreased. Examples of FE are displayed in Figs. 4 and 5. In Fig. 4 (three-species system: $n = 3$), the value of mortality rate is largely decreased from $m_1 = 0.2$ to $m_2 = 0.01$ at $t = 200$. Just after this perturbation, the variance $V(t)$ of top predator is rapidly increased (FE). The ecological meaning of this result is important. Namely, when we conserve a top predator, it becomes very hard to predict the time dependence of the target species. The similar result can be obtained for $n = 4$ (Fig. 5). In contrast, when m is increased, clear FE is not usually observed. In few cases, however, FE occurs: the variance of the prey of top predator (the species $n - 1$) significantly increases. This is because the density of prey is increased due to the increase of m.

Next, we report the results of global interaction. Since there is no stable equilibrium for $n = 4$, we report only the result for $n = 3$. When m is decreased, the variance of top predator significantly increased. Hence, the fluctuation enhancement (FE) can be universally observed, when the value of death rate m is decreased. When m is increased, we obtain the similar results as the local interaction.

5 Discussions

So far, coworkers in our laboratory dealt with one- and two-species systems, and reported opposite results. In a single-species case [10], the fluctuation enhancement (FE) was observed, only when the value of m is increased. In contrast, in a two-species (prey-predator) system [11], FE occurred, only when m is decreased.

In the present paper, we newly study the three- and four-species systems. By the use of Monte Carlo simulations, perturbation experiments are carried out on a finite size of square lattice. The mortality rate m of top predator is suddenly increased or decreased from m1 to m_2, where all species can survive at $m = m_1$ (coexisting phase). We find a common property for $n \geq 2$: the fluctuation enhancement (FE) is observed, when m is decreased. Especially when m_2 takes a value near the extinction point of the species $n - 1$ (the prey of top predator), then the enhancement of variation (fluctuation) in dynamic processes clearly takes place (Figs. 4 and 5). When the mortality rate of top predator is decreased, there are a variety of paths in its population dynamics. In particular, FE becomes clear for the local interaction, compared to the global (mean-field) simulation. Note that FE arises for finite sizes of lattice, but we assume that the size is significantly large.

Our results indicate that the uncertainty comes from the conservation of top predator. Since the population size of top predator is generally small, several conservation policies for top predator have been performed [20, 21]. In most cases, however, the time dependence of top predator is not so simple, after a perturbation (conservation policy) takes place. An example is the conservation of deer [22, 23]. Since the deer feeds on grasses, the conservation of deer leads to the reduction of grasses. Owing to both the overabundance of deer and the over reduction of grasses, complicated population dynamics are brought about, such as chaos and abrupt decrease (clash) of top predator. The previous works usually account for such a complexity from deterministic aspects [20, 21]. In the present article, however, the uncertainty can be explained from a stochastic aspect (FE). There is unavoidable uncertainty in the conservation of top predator. Here FE is associated with a critical behavior near extinction. When we protect the top predator, its population size increases. By the direct effect, its prey may become endangered. The critical behavior of prey indirectly leads to the uncertainty via food chain. For these reason, the population dynamics of top predator becomes very difficult to predict.

We discuss the parameter sensitivity. Our results have the robustness for various values of parameters; namely, the size L of lattice, reproduction rates r_j and mortality rate m_j. For example, we carry out simulations for $L=100$, 200 and 500. The value of $V_j(t)$ is slightly decreased with the increase of L. Nevertheless, the variance $V_j(t)$ exhibits the same profiles for the different values of L. We assume the mortality rate m_k besides the top predator ($k \neq n$) takes very small values. This is because the coexisting region becomes narrow, as m_k increases. We also set $m_k \neq 0$, since the four-species system ($n = 4$) has no stable equilibrium for $m_k = 0$.

References

1. Tainaka, K.: Lattice model for the Lotka-Volterra system. J. Phys. Soc. Jpn. 57, 2588–2590 (1988)
2. Tainaka, K.: Stationary pattern of vortices or strings in biological systems, lattice version of the Lotka-Volterra model. Phys. Rev. Lett. 63, 2688–2691 (1989)
3. Paine, R.T.: Food web complexity and species diversity. The American Naturalist. 100, 65–75 (1966)
4. Tilman, D., Downing, J.A.: Biodiversity and stability in grassland. Nature 367, 363–365 (1994)

5. Caswell, H., Cohen, J.E.: Red, white and blue, environmental variance spectra and coexistence in metapopulations. J. Theor. Biol. 176, 301–316 (1995)
6. Yodzis, P.: The indeterminacy of ecological interactions as perceived through perturbation experiments. Ecology 69, 508–515 (1988)
7. Tainaka, K.: Intrinsic uncertainty in ecological catastrophe. J. Theor. Biol. 166, 91–99 (1994)
8. Kubo, R., Matsuo, K., Kitahara, K.: Fluctuations and relaxation of macrovariables. J. Stat. Phys. 9, 51–96 (1973)
9. Tsuchiya, Y., Horie, S.: Evolution process of the Williams domain in a nematic liquid crystal. J. Phys. Soc. Jpn. 54, 1–4 (1985)
10. Tainaka, K., Hosiyama, M., Takeuchi, Y.: Dynamic process and variation in the contact process. Phys. Lett. A 272, 416–420 (2000)
11. Itoh, Y., Tainaka, K.: Spatial Enhancement of Population Uncertainty in model ecosystems. J. Phys. Soc. Jpn. 73(2004), 53–59 (1994)
12. Kobayashi, K., Tainaka, K.: Critical phenomena in cyclic ecosystems, parity law and self-structuring extinction pattern. J. Phys. Soc. Jpn. 66, 38–41 (1997)
13. Harris, T.E.: Contact interaction on a lattice. Ann.Prob. 2, 969–988 (1974)
14. Tainaka, K., Fukazawa, S.: Spatial pattern in a chemical reaction system, prey and predator in the position-fixed limit. J. Phys. Soc. Jpn. 61, 1891–1894 (1992)
15. Satulovsky, J.E., Tome, T.: Stochastic lattice gas model for a predator -prey system. Phys. Rev. E 49, 5073–5079 (1994)
16. Sutherland, B.R., Jacobs, A.E.: Self-organization and scaling in a lattice prey-predator model. Complex Systems 8, 385–405 (1994)
17. Hofbauer, J., Sigmund, K.: The theory of evolution and dynamical systems. Cambridge Univ. Press, Cambridge (1988)
18. Takeuchi, Y.: Gloval dynamical properties of Lotka-Volterra systems. World Scientific, Singapore (1996)
19. Takeuchi, Y.: Private communication (2006)
20. May, R.M.: Thresholds and breakpoints in ecosystems with a multiplicity of stable states. Nature 269, 471–477 (1977)
21. Krivan, V.: Optimal Foraging and Predator-Prey Dynamics. Theoretical Population Biology 49, 265–290 (1996)
22. McShea, W.J., Underwood, H.B., Rappole, J.H. (eds.): The science of overabundance deer ecology and population management. Smithsonian Institution Press, Washington (1997)
23. Cote, S.D., Thomas Rooney, P., Tremblay, J.P., Dussault, C., Walleret, D.M.: Ecological impacts of deer overabundance. Annual Review of Ecology, Evolution, and Systematics 35, 113–147 (2004)

Toward Biologically Inspired Constructive Computation

Hideyuki Nakashima

Future University, Hakodate

Abstract. We focused on the interaction between a system and the environment, or the situatedness of the system of biological systems, and tried to realize it in our Organic programming language called Gaea. When we tried to design a system that allows rich interaction with the environment while taking advantage of being embedded in it, the interaction became a complex system. The view of the interaction of system with its environment led us to become aware of constructive methodology.

1 Introduction

Biological systems, in contrast to artificially manufactured systems, have many desirable characteristics. This is the reason why some researchers try to learn from biological systems. We are not the exceptions.

In particular, we focused on the interaction between a system and the environment, or the situatedness of the system[1]. There are two aspects for this kind of interactions that we want to draw attention of the readers. One is how to design a system that allows rich interaction with the environment while taking advantage of being embedded in it. One of the key concepts to approach complex interaction is *situation thickness* (section 2). A system is called situation-thick if it can adapt to wide variety of situations. We introduce our design of a situation-thick organic programming language Gaea in Sec. 3.

The other is that the interaction forms a complex system. Traditional understanding of a system cannot be applied here. The view of the interaction of system with its environment led us to become aware of constructive methodology, which we will explore in detail in Sec. 4. The interaction between a system and its environment plays an important role in the methodology. Since the interaction is a complex system, we have no way to directly control the interaction or its outcome. Evolutional process is the only effective procedure here. We discuss how we can cope with complex systems in our constructive methodology in Sec. 5.

2 Situation-Thickness

Havel[2] proposed a measure of the complexity of systems, namely, distribution over "scale dimensions". We can imagine scales in both directions, downward to small scales, and upward to large scales. For each point on the axis, there is defined the "significance" of the scale, which indicates the meaningfulness of

Y. Suzuki et al. (Eds.): IWNC 2007, PICT 1, pp. 155–166, 2009.

Scale-thickness

A scale-thick system
(example: living things)

A scale-thin system
(example: tools, furniture)

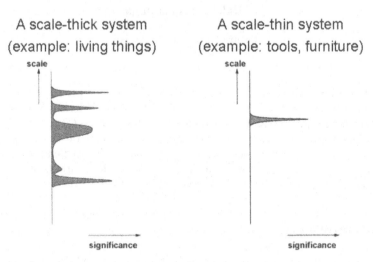

Fig. 1. Scale Thickness

the scale to a certain object. Somewhere in the middle of the scale axis is our habitat, the scale-local world of human magnitudes.

He claims that complex objects have non-local significance on the scale (Fig. 1 left). For example, a living organism such as a tree is meaningful on many scales: the angstrom scale for its DNA structure, millimeter scale for its cell structure, meter scale for its overall shape, and so on. On the other hand, a simple object such as a clothespin is significant only on a narrow range of scales (Fig. 1 right). So called *scale-thickness* can be used as a measure of complexity.

Now we can also imagine a scale along the hierarchical structure of an object. If the object has meaning on many levels, it is also scale-thick. A subsumption architecture[3] is used to implement such a scale-thick system. Each layer of the architecture corresponds to a level in the hierarchy.

Scale-thickness is a prerequisite for a complex system. We need one more measure for the flexibility of a system. We call this the *situation-thickness* of the system. This is a measure of the thickness of the system against (unexpected) changes in situation. While scale-thickness is a static measure, situation-thickness is a dynamic measure of environmental change.

3   Organic Programming

3.1   Design of Gaea

Organic Programming is a concept pursued in "Cooperative Architecture Project" [4]. The goal of the project was to find a new software methodology for building large, complicated systems out of simple units.

An agent

Other agents

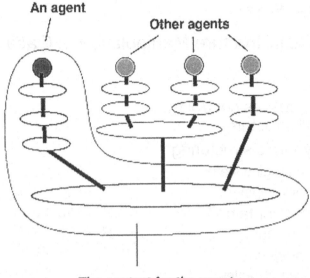

The context for the agent

Fig. 2. Environments for agents

Webster's Third New International Dictionary defines "organic" as follows:

organic: 5 b (1): constituting a whole whose parts are mutually dependent or intrinsically related: having a systematic coordination (2): forming a complex entity in which the whole is more than the sum of the individual parts and the parts have a life and character deriving from their participation in the whole: having the character of an organism.

In particular, we tried to realize the following characteristics (ability) of living entities in programming languages:

- Situated behavior: Although all cells have the same program (genetic information coded in genes), they behave differently according to their environment (surrounding cells). Some cells become a stem, some become a leaf, and some others become a petal.

    The shape of a tree, layout of branches and leaves, is determined by two factors: individual development and genetic characteristics of the species. Or, it should be said that interaction between genetic programs encoded in genes and the environmental situation determine how each branches grow and where leaves are placed during individual development. Each tree grows their own branch formations in accordance with the environment. Each leaf readjusts its position to get maximum sun light. If the stem cannot get enough light, it grows faster to reach brighter area.
- Situated representation: Genes do not have complete information. Information that genes lack, such as the gravitational constant and temperature range are provided by the environment.

Cell Structure Manipulation in Gaea

- **Processes control the cell structure**
- **Dynamic structuring**
  - changing status
  - development
- **Cells contain information**
  - programs
  - cell variables

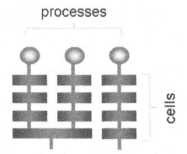

9

Fig. 3. Processes and Cells

A beautiful example of situated representation can be seen in *imprinting*[5] of new born birds. A baby bird remembers the first seen moving object as its mother. This system takes advantage that it is almost always the mother that the baby first see (otherwise, the baby do not have a good chance for survival anyway). It minimizes the need to represent details of how mother look like, or how to find her.

The above all characteristics should be understood within the environmental situation in which living entities are placed. Our Organic Programming System Gaea[6,7] use cells to represent fragments of a situation. Each cell should contain specialized programs that correspond to a specific fragment of the situation.

A running Gaea program consists of multiple processes, and each process has an associated list of cells, which we call the *environment* for the process. An environment for a process consists of a linear list of cells. The total environment with multi-processes may look like Fig. 2. The environment determines the set of clauses accessible from the process. Those clauses are ordered in the same way that clauses in a cell are ordered. Prolog-like selection of a clause using unification with backtracking is used. When there are multiple clauses that can be unified with a call, then a clause in the cell earlier in the list has higher priority. This property of giving precedence to clauses in earlier cells (located higher in the figures) is important in implementing dynamic subsumption architecture (Section 3.2). If the execution of its guard fails, then backtracking occurs to try other clauses in cells deeper in the list.

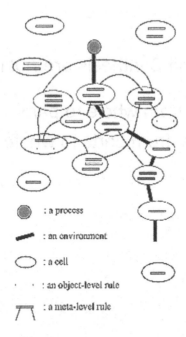

: a process

: an environment

: a cell

: an object-level rule

: a meta-level rule

Fig. 4. Organic Programming Viewed as a Holistic System

Organic systems develop over time. Development is a sequence of changes with a larger time constant whereas adaptation is a change with a small time constant. There are three ways for a system to develop:

- By programming. One of the design goals of organic programming is to add higher layers without changing the lower layers at all.

  Subsumptive programming allows programming by functional layers. We can first debug low-level functions. Once they are satisfactory, we can then develop higher-level function layers on top.[1]
- By learning. Learning is a kind of automatic programming. It involves generalization and/or specialization of existing programs.

  Cell structure in organic programming provides us with a good structural unit. Generalization, for example, can simply be achieved by enlarging the application conditions of a cell without changing the program in the cell.
- By growth. The programmer or the designer may not have to consider all situations a program might encounter during its execution. The system develops a cell structure that corresponds to its environment, by assimilating new cells which are prepared by the programmer beforehand, and/or by spawning new processes. The detailed mechanism will be explained in Sec. 3.2.

Gaea system provides the following primitives to observe and to manipulate the environment:

---

[1] Note that this process includes programmer in the loop. The philosophy behind it is described in Sec. 4.

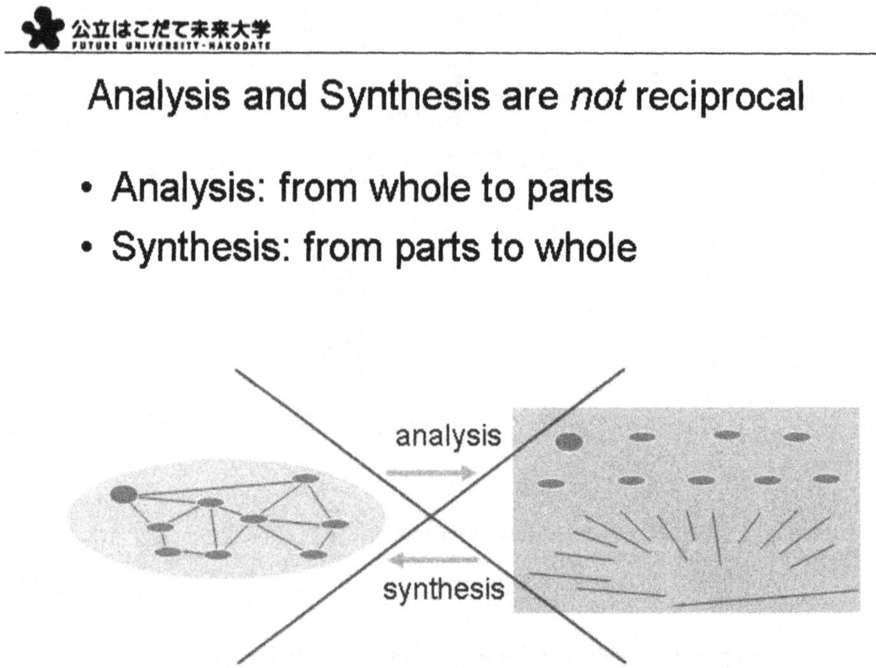

Fig. 5. Analysis and Synthesis (wrong view)

- push a cell into the environment;
- pop a cell from the environment;
- swap cells;
- get a list of cells of the environment; and
- set the environment as described by a list of cells.

3.2 Dynamic Subsumption Architecture

Gaea allows bottom-up programming of behavior. It is similar to subsumption architecture[3], but more flexible. We call it *dynamic subsumption architecture*[8] because any function layer is dynamically replaceable with another function, or a new function is dynamically added, using context reflection. These are explained below.

- Introducing a new layer of programs
  The new layer of the program can (1) use existing programs as sub-routines (2) with possible modifications of their behavior.
  If the newly added layer is not adequate for handling a particular situation, then programs in older layers are used. Therefore, by providing general purpose behavior in basic layers, the system can remain robust.
- Replacing a portion of a program
  When the situation changes, it is simpler to change the corresponding program accordingly than to have a decision tree like structure to select only proper programs for the situation.

Synthetic Science vs. Analytic Science

- Synthesis
  - Agents' view
  - Insects' view

- Analysis
  - Theorists' view
  - God's eyes' view

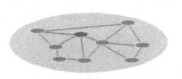

- *Autopoiesis*
- *quantum physics*

Fig. 6. Different View Points for Different Sciences

The above two operations are intended to be used during run-time. The first operation is also applicable during programming or system design. In particular, it is handy when a part of the specification is changed after a program is complete.

3.3 Context Reflection and Autopoiesis

The concept of *autopoiesis*[9] (self=$\alpha \upsilon \tau o$ production=$\pi o \iota \eta \sigma \iota \varsigma$) is formed as a definition of "life". It refers to a system that continuously reproduces itself. This continuity is important and thus autopoiesis differs from mere self-organizing systems in that it continuously changes its architecture. An autopoietic system is a reflective self-organizing system, which determines its own method of self-organization. Gaea with its reflective capability has the potential to be an autopoietic system, *if* a programmer knows how to program the initial state of such a system.

In general system theory[10], organic systems are given the opposite position to mechanical systems and are characterized as being open, holistic, hierarchical, and active. Programs, on the other hand, are mechanical and deterministic. Our aim is to make programs organic, which seems contradictory at first glance. This may be the case for a simple program with a single layer, in other words, a scale-thin program. However, when a program is scale-thick, and moreover, situation-thick, it can hardly be said to be mechanical. In particular, in organic

162   H. Nakashima

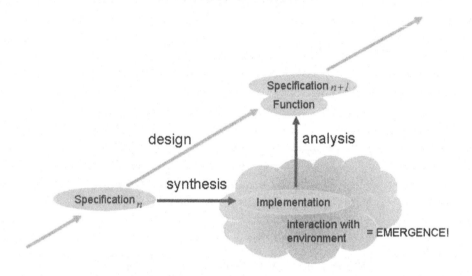

Fig. 7. F-Diagram of Synthesis

programming, by its context reflection[11], the whole determines the behavior of the parts, and the parts determine the whole.

One of the important aspects of life is that its components are not fixed: it is an open system. At the moment, Gaea has only a fixed number of cells, which are preprogrammed. We have to give the system abilities to learn and reprogram to make it into a fully autopoietic system.

In context reflection, higher-level information on the relationships among cells as well as lower-level information on objects is stored in cells. Therefore the whole system is closed under the description in the sense that all information is stored in a set of cells. It forms an autopoietic system because this descriptively closed system changes over time by its own action. Figure 4 is a conceptual diagram of organic programming viewed in such a way. The configuration as a whole determines the behavior of the system. The sum of components accessible with some link from a process determines the "self" of the process, but other processes may interfere with this configuration by pushing other cells from outside.

4   Emergent Computation and Constructive Methodology

Havel[2] claimed it impossible to design a scale-thick system and we have to rely on "emergence" instead. Emergence here can be defined as a presence of an

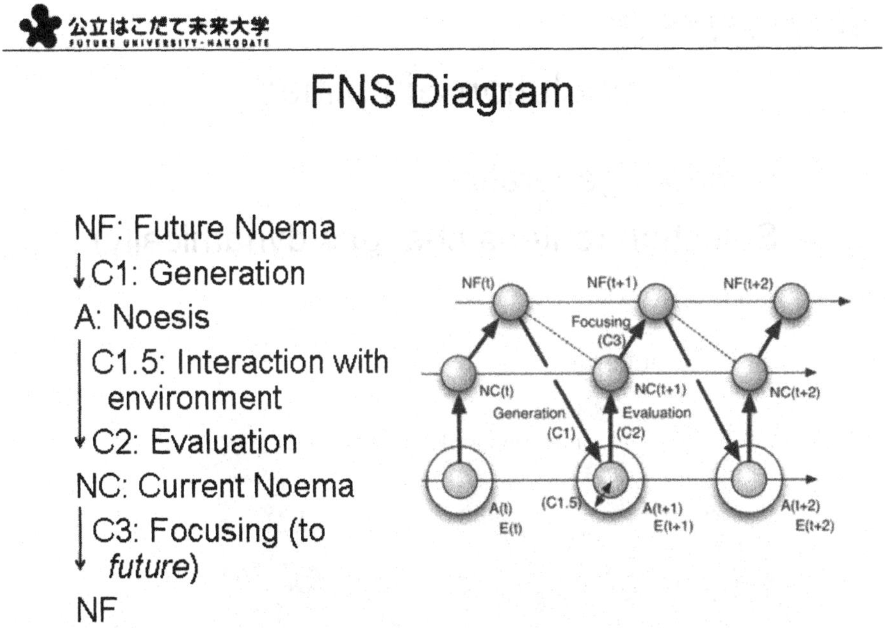

FNS Diagram

NF: Future Noema

↓C1: Generation

A: Noesis

C1.5: Interaction with
environment

↓C2: Evaluation

NC: Current Noema

C3: Focusing (to
future)

NF

Fig. 8. FNS-Diagram of Synthetic Sciences

unpredicted or unplanned property on a higher layer out of designed mechanism of lower layers. Innovation on artificial products is realized through emergence. We claim that the essence of an innovation process, including natural evolution, is a loop of trial and error[12].

The concept of autopoiesis tells us that the boundary of a system is not fixed. It is determined while in operation. Organic programming includes the researcher or the programmer as an integrated part of the system. A program seldom shows perfect behavior even under some restricted designed domains. It is thus important to fix the program to overcome some behavioral shortcomings in certain conditions. The programmer is the integrated part of the program development.

Artificial Intelligence, a research methodology to construct a program that behaves intelligently, needs analysis by synthesis: construct a program, observe its behavior, and then fix any shortcomings, run it, observe its behavior - This loop is repeated infinitely.

It is generally understood that analysis is from the whole to the parts and synthesis is from the parts to the whole (Fig. 5). When we try to understand a complex system, we usually try to divide them into less complex systems. It is not a simple task when those sub-systems interfere each other. Simon called it nearly decomposable systems.[13] Synthesis is usually understood as the reciprocal process of analysis.

However, we found it differently. First of all, those two processes presuppose different view points of systems (Fig. 6). Analytic science typically requires that

Evolution Simplified

- ## Random generation
- ## Selection (criteria changes dynamically)

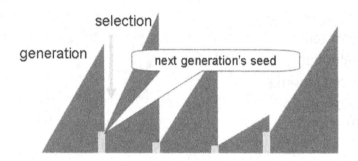

Fig. 9. Simplified Evolution Process

observation do not interfere with the system in question. Synthetic science, on the other hand, cannot have a separate observer since the agent is constructing the system in question.

Secondly, in our formalization, analysis is part of synthesis (Fig. 7).[14] Let us take an architect as an example. When a designer is given specification of a building to build, he cannot directly design the perfect one on a paper for the first time. Trial and error loop is unavoidable. He first *synthesizes* a model. The model here should be understood in a very broad sense. It may be a small scaled model but may also be the real one (a real building). Anything but the final version falls into this category of models, and it even covers real buildings with people actually living or working in it.[2] He then analyses the properties of the built model. If the result of the analysis satisfies the original specification, the design is complete. However, this rarely is the case. There are some differences from the original specification. Then the whole cycle recurs by changing the model to meet the specification. Sometimes, the original specification may be updated reflecting some findings from the model.

F-diagram shown in Fig. 7 is the formalization of the above process. Note that the analytic loop is a part of F-diagram that represents a synthetic loop. Thus we can say that analysis is a part of synthesis. Even when we take synthesis narrower to only mean the horizontal synthetic arrow, it is orthogonal to analysis and not reciprocal to it.

---

[2] A field test may be the close concept of a model here.

Note also that F-diagram also applies to theory forming, by mapping model synthesis to experiments and a specification to a theory.

We are trying to formalize a synthetic (or, constructive) methodology of situation-thick systems by extending the F-diagram. To understand the concept of multi-layered system consisting of more than one significant layers, we found the concepts of *noema* and *noesis*[15] are useful. Suppose one is playing a piano. He first plans to produce music. It is in a conceptual level, called *noema*. Since the concept is not realized yet, we call it "future noema". He then begins to realize the music by playing keys of the piano. This activity is called *noesis*. His activity interacts with the environment, including the room and audience, and actual music is produced. The player then listens to the music produced, called "current noema". The player must readjust his plan (music to be produced) according to the generated music.

In the above process, only two levels – music level and play level – are involved. If the system consists of more layers, we will see a hierarchy of nemesis's and corresponding noema's.

The following is a synthesis loop explained as noema and noesis:

(C1) Generation of noesis $A(t+1)$ from future noema $NF(t)$.

(C1.5) Generated noesis $A(t+1)$ interacts with the environment $E(t+1)$ and may produce some phenomena.

(C2) Generated phenomena (larger than $A(t+1)$) is then analyzed to produce the current noema $NC(t+1)$.

(C3) Since generated noema $NC(t+1)$ is different from planned noema $NF(t)$, future noema $NF(t+1)$ must be readjusted. This is the most difficult and creative process.

5 Harnessing Complex Systems

The FNS-diagram tells us the following:

> We have to repeat a synthetic loop to approach our goal (future Noema).
> However, the goal itself may change during the process.

The process itself forms a complex and holistic system.

In other words, we cannot directly control complex interactions. We have to harness[16] the system, as we do when we ride horses. Then the next question is how we can learn to harness a system. I believe that the answer lies in the evolution process. Evolution process simplified to its bone consists of the following two phases taking place one after another (Fig. 9):

1. Random generation.
2. Selection (criteria changes dynamically).

The constructive process to harness a system includes the researcher in the process. It is a loop from C1 to C3 of our FNS-diagram (Fig. 8). Each sub-allows (C1, C2 and C3) consists of the above try and error loop, and the whole diagram is also the try and error loop. In case of scale-thick systems, the diagram becomes multi-layered. In this case, C1.5 is further decomposed into lower-level FNS diagram, thus forming a fractal system.

Acknowledgment

The work to formalize synthetic methodology is a joint work with Masaki Suwa and Haruhiko Fujii. F-diagram is named after Fujii, and FNS-diagram is named after Fujii, Nakashima and Suwa.

References

1. Nakashima, H.: AI as complex information processing. Minds and Machines 9(1), 57–80 (1999)
2. Havel, I.M.: Artificial thought and emergent mind. In: Proc. of International Joint Conference on Artificial Intelligence, vol. 93, pp. 758–766 (1993)
3. Brooks, R.A.: Intelligence without representation. Artificial Intelligence 47, 139–160 (1991)
4. Nakashima, H.: Organic programming for situation-thick ai systems. In: Proc. of IMSA 1997 International Symposium on Biologically Inspired Computation, pp. 156–163 (1997)
5. Lorenz, K.Z.: King Solomon's Ring. Methuen & Co., Ltd. (1952)
6. Nakashima, H., Itsuki Noda, K.H.: Organic programming for complex systems. In: Proc. of Poster Session of Fifteenth International Joint Conference on Artificial Intelligence, IJCAI, p. 76 (August 1997)
7. Nakashima, H., Noda, I., Handa, K.: Organic programming language Gaea for multi-agents. In: Proc. of International Conf. on Multi-Agent Systems 1996, pp. 236–243. AAAI Press, Menlo Park (1996)
8. Nakashima, H., Noda, I.: Dynamic subsumption architecture for programming intelligent agents. In: Proc. of International Conf. on Multi-Agent Systems 1998, pp. 190–197. AAAI Press, Menlo Park (1998)
9. Maturana, H.R., Varela, F.J.: Autopoiesis and Cognition: The Realization of the Living. D. Reidel Publishing Co., Dordrecht (1980)
10. Bertalanffy, L.: General System Theory. George Braziller, New York (1968)
11. Nakashima, H.: Context reflection. In: Proc. of IMSA 1992 International Workshop on Reflection and Meta-Level Architecture, pp. 172–177 (1992)
12. Nakashima, H., Suwa, M., Fujii, H.: Innovaton in the framework of methodology for constructive informatics. IPSJ Journal 49 (in Japanese)
13. Simon, H.A.: The Sciences of the Artificial, 3rd edn. MIT Press, Cambridge (1996)
14. Nakashima, H., Suwa, M., Fujii, H.: Endo-system view as a method for constructive science. In: Proc. 5th International Conference of the Cognitive Science (ICCS 2006), pp. 63–71 (2006)
15. Kimura, B.: Aida (in-between). Kobun-do (1988)
16. Allen, P.: Harnessing complexity. Emergence: Complexity and Organization (2000), http://www.complexity-society.com/journal.html

A Classification of Triplet Local Rules with Inverse Image Sequences

Tatsuro Sato, Kazumasa Honda, Hyen Yeal Lee, and Yasuo Kawahara

Oita National College of Technology, Oita, 870-0152, Japan
School of Electrical and Computer Engineering, Pusan National University,
Busan 609-735, Korea
Department of Informatics, Kyushu University, Fukuoka 819-0395, Japan

Abstract. In a general transition system the number of inverse images of a configuration by its global transition is often related with some characteristic behaviors (for example, the reversibility) of the system. This paper studies sequences of such numbers of inverse images, and gives a necessary and sufficient condition for the global transitions to be reversible, and finally we show how to determine the recursive formulas of inverse image sequences defined for triplet local rules by using de Bruijn subautomata.

1 Introduction

Natural phenomena were traditionally represented by differential equations. However, exceptional phenomena such as fractals and chaos have been found. Thus it is getting more improtant to understand nature from a view point of computing. Cellular automata are theoretical models introduced by von Neumann to simulate self-reproduction mechanism of cells. In 1980's Wolfram studied one-dimensional cellualr auotmata as theoretical models for complex systems in physics. Recently the reversibility of cellular automata and the computational universality of CA-110 are remarked.

Global transitions of many cellular automata are constructed by triplet local rules. Although a cellular automaton has a simple structure consisting of small uniform automata, it globally involves very complicated behaviors. It is trivial that cellular automata with symmetric or complementary local rules are isomorphic to original ones as dynamical systems. Shingai [3] proved that one-dimensional cellular automata with threshold local rules have no limit cycle of period greater than 4. It is well-known that Wolfram [4] classified broadly the local rules according to global behaviors of infinite cellular automata into four classes. Thus it is a fundamental job to classify local rules related with global behaviors of cellular automata. On the other hand Inokuchi et al. [1] showed that all reversible automata have four inverse images of any partial configuration. The result was applied to completely determine the reversibility of one-dimensional finite cellular automata [1]. Thus the number of inverse images of a partial configuration is often related with some characteristic behaviors of cellular automata.

Y. Suzuki et al. (Eds.): IWNC 2007, PICT 1, pp. 167–178, 2009.

This paper studies sequences consisting of the numbers of inverse images, and gives a necessary and sufficient condition for the global transitions to be reversible, and finally we show how to determine the recursive formulas of inverse image sequences defined for triplet local rules by using de Bruijn subautomata.

2   Transition Systems on Graphs

In this section we will review transition systems on graphs defined by local rules, and give a general necessary and sufficient condition for the reversibility (bijectivity) of global transitions. The condition is a simple extension of the sufficient condition [1] to determine the reversibility for one-dimensional cellular automata with triplet local rules.

A (simple directed) graph $G = (V, E)$ is a pair of a finite set V of vertices and a (reflexive) relation $E \subseteq V \times V$. For every subset T of V the nearest neighbor $E(T)$ of T is the subset of V defined by

$$w \in E(T) \leftrightarrow \exists v \in T. \, (v, w) \in E.$$

As E is reflexive, $T \subseteq E(T)$ is always true. For a vertex $v \in V$ the nearest neighbor $E(\{v\})$ will be denoted by $E(v)$, for short. Let S be a finite set of states. An S-configuration q on T is a function $q : T \to S$ assigning a state $q(v) \in S$ to each vertex $v \in T$. The set of all S-configurations on T will be denoted by S^T. For an S-configuration $q \in S^V$ on V its restriction onto T will be denoted by $q|T$. It is trivial that $q|T \in Q^T$.

Definition 1. A *transition system* $\mathcal{A}$ on a graph $G = (V, E)$ consists of a finite state set S and a family of local rules (functions) $f_v : S^{E(v)} \to S$ for all $v \in V$. □

Let $\mathcal{A}$ be a transition system on a graph G. For a subset T of V a function $\delta_T : S^{E(T)} \to S^T$ on T is defined by $\delta_T(q)(v) = f_v(q|E(v))$ for $q \in S^T$ and $v \in T$. We define the global transition $\delta : S^V \to S^V$ of $\mathcal{A}$ by $\delta = \delta_V$. It is trivial that $\delta_T = \delta|S^T$ and $\delta_v = f_v$. For a subset Q of S^T the inverse images $\delta_T^{-1}(Q)$ is a subset of $S^{E(T)}$ defined by $\delta_T^{-1}(Q) = \{p \in S^T \mid \delta_T(p) \in Q\}$.

Proposition 1. *Let $\mathcal{A}$ be a transition system on a graph $G = (V, E)$ and T a subset of V. Then the identity $|\delta_T^{-1}(S^T)| = |S|^{|E(T)|}$ holds.*

Proof. The identity is trivial, since $\delta_T : S^{E(T)} \to S^T$ is a totally defined function. □

It is clear that the identity obtained in the last proposition is equivalent to the following identity

$$\sum_{p \in S^T} \frac{|\delta_T^{-1}(p)|}{|S^T|} = |S|^{|E(T)| - |T|},$$

which means the average of $|\delta_T^{-1}(p)|$ for all S-configurations $p \in S^T$. The following theorem gives an important property of reversible transition systems.

Theorem 1. *Let $\mathcal{A}$ be a transition system on a graph $G = (V, E)$. Then the global transition $\delta : S^V \to S^V$ of $\mathcal{A}$ is bijective if and only if the identity*

$$|\delta_T^{-1}(p)| = |S|^{|E(T)|-|T|}$$

holds for all subsets T of V and all S-configurations $p \in S^T$.

Proof. First assume that δ is bijective. Define two subsets X and Y of S^V by

$$X = \{q \in S^V \mid q|E(T) \in \delta_T^{-1}(p)\} \quad \text{and} \quad Y = \{q \in S^V \mid q|T = p\}.$$

Then it is easy to see $|X| = |\delta_T^{-1}(p)| \times |S|^{|V|-|E(T)|}$ and $|Y| = |S|^{|V|-|T|}$, where $|X|$ denotes the cardinality of X. On the other hand we readily verify $\delta_V(X) = Y$ and so $|X| = |Y|$ by the assumption that $\delta = \delta_V$ is a bijection. The converse statement immediately follows from a fact that $\delta_V = \delta$ and $E(V) = V$ (since E is reflexive). This completes the proof.   □

Corollary 1. *Let $\mathcal{A}$ be a transition system on a graph $G = (V, E)$. If the global transition $\delta : S^V \to S^V$ of $\mathcal{A}$ is bijective, then $|f_v^{-1}(s)| = |S|^{|E(v)|-1}$ holds for all vertices $v \in V$.*   □

3   Cellular Automata CA-R(n)

In this section we recall some basic notions such as triplet local rules, Wolfram numbers, global transition functions related with one-dimensional finite cellular automata CA-$R(n)$, which are original examples of transition systems on graphs.

A (triplet local) rule f over the state set $B = \{0, 1\}$ is a function assigning just one state in B to each triple $abc \in B^3$ of states. Formally the rule f is merely a function $f : B^3 \to B$ illustrated by the following table

Rule	111	110	101	100	011	010	001	000
f	r_7	r_6	r_5	r_4	r_3	r_2	r_1	r_0

where $r_{4a+2b+c} = f(abc)$. The Wolfram number R $(0 \le R \le 225)$ of the rule f is the natural number defined by

$$R = \sum_{k=0}^{7} r_k 2^k = \sum_{abc \in B^3} f(abc) 2^{4a+2b+c}.$$

The rule f with Wolfram number R will be often denoted by f_R. A *linear array* of length $n \ge 1$ is a graph consisting of a set $V = \{1, 2, \cdots, n\}$ of vertices (cells) and a set $E = \{(v, u) \in V \times V \mid v - 1 \le u \le v + 1\}$ of edges. A *cellular automaton* CA-$R(n)$ is a transition system on a linear array of length n. The local rule $f_v : B^{E(v)} \to B$ of CA-$R(n)$ is usually defined by $f_v(x_{v-1}x_vx_{v+1}) = f_R(x_{v-1}x_vx_{v+1})$ if $2 \leq v \leq n-1$. However this definition does not work for two boundary (rightmost and leftmost) cells 1 and n. To perfectly decide a transition system we need the special rule for boundary cells, called the boundary condition. We just state three kinds of boundary conditions. (i) Fixed boundary a-b: $f_1(x_1x_2) = f_R(ax_1x_2)$ and $f_n(x_{n-1}x_n) = f_R(x_{n-1}x_nb)$, where $a, b \in B$. (ii) Free boundary $*$-$*$: $f_1(x_1x_2) = f_R(x_1x_1x_2)$ and $f_n(x_{n-1}x_n) = f_R(x_{n-1}x_nx_n)$. (iii) Cyclic boundary $*$: $f_1(x_1x_2) = f_R(x_nx_1x_2)$ and $f_n(x_{n-1}x_n) = f_R(x_{n-1}x_nx_1)$. Thus we obtain a cellular automaton CA-$R_\bullet(n)$ according to the boundary conditions $\bullet = a$-b (fixed boundary), $*$-$*$ (free boundary), or $*$ (cyclic boundary).

Consider a cellular automaton CA-$R(N)$ and let $T = \{k+1, k+2, \ldots, k+n\}$ be a subset of $V = \{1, 2, \ldots, N\}$ with $1 \leq k \leq N - n - 1$, and $p \in B^n (= B^T)$ a B-configuration. Then it is easy to see that $E(T) = \{k, k+1, k+2, \ldots, k+n, k+n+1\}$ and the inverse images $\delta_T^{-1}(p)$ is independent of N and k.

Proposition 2. *The inequality $\sum_{p \in B^n} \left\{|\delta_T^{-1}(p)| - 4\right\}^2 \leq 2^{2n+4} - 2^{n+4}$ holds. The equality holds only for $R = 0$ and $R = 255$.*

Proof. Set $c(p) = |\delta_T^{-1}(p)|$. First note that $\sum_{p \in B^n} |\delta_T^{-1}(p)| = 2^{n+2}$. Hence we have

$$
\begin{aligned}
&\sum_{p \in B^n} \left\{c(p) - 4\right\}^2 \\
&= \sum_{p \in B^n} \left\{c(p)^2 - 8c(p) + 16\right\} \\
&= \sum_{p \in B^n} \left\{c(p)\right\}^2 - 2^{n+4} \qquad &\left\{ \textstyle\sum_{p \in B^n} c(p) = 2^{n+2} \right\} \\
&\leq \left\{\textstyle\sum_{p \in B^n} c(p)\right\}^2 - 2^{n+4} \qquad &\left\{ c(p) \geq 0 \right\} \\
&= 2^{2n+4} - 2^{n+4}. &\left\{ \textstyle\sum_{p \in B^n} c(p) = 2^{n+2} \right\} \qquad \square
\end{aligned}
$$

The next corollary is a discrete version of the result in [2].

Corollary 2. *Set $A_n = \dfrac{1}{n} \sum_{x_1x_2\ldots x_n \in B^n} \dfrac{|\delta_T^{-1}(x_1x_2\ldots x_n)|}{2^{n+2}}(x_1 + x_2 + \cdots + x_n)$. If the global transition δ of CA-$R(N)$ is bijective, then $A_n = \dfrac{1}{2}$.*

By computer experiments we may observe the statistical behavior of the set $\{|\delta_T^{-1}(p)| \mid p \in B^T\}$ of natural numbers and reach a classification of triplet local rules f_R. Two functions $\delta : X \to Y$ and $\gamma : X \to Y$ are called to be *conjugate* if there are bijections $\phi : X \to X$ and $\psi : Y \to Y$ such that $\gamma(\phi(x)) = \psi(\delta(x))$ for all $x \in X$. Then the following is trivial.

Proposition 3. *If two functions $\delta : X \to Y$ and $\gamma : X \to Y$ are conjugate, then $\sum_{y \in Y} |\delta^{-1}(y)|^n = \sum_{y \in Y} |\gamma^{-1}(y)|^n$ for all natural numbers n.* $\qquad \square$

4   Inverse Image Sequences

To simplify the problem we will reformulate the definition of inverse images $\delta_T^{-1}(p)$ with $T = \{k+1, k+2, \ldots, k+n\}$. Let R be a Wolfram number. Define a function $\delta_R : B^{n+2} \to B^n$ for $n \geq 1$ by

$$\delta_R(x_0 x_1 \ldots x_{n+1}) = f_R(x_0 x_1 x_2) f_R(x_1 x_2 x_3) \ldots f_R(x_{n-1} x_n x_{n+1})$$

for all $x_0 x_1 \ldots x_{n+1} \in B^{n+2}$.

In the rest of the paper we investigate about the inverse images $\delta_R^{-1}(1^n)$ and the cardinality $|\delta_R^{-1}(1^n)|$, where 1^n denotes the string $11 \cdots 1$ of length $n \, (\geq 1)$.

A table of the inverse image sequences for Wolfram numbers $0 \leq R \leq 255$ and $n = 1, 2, \ldots, 10$ will given in the Appendix A at the end of the paper.

Set $X = \cup_{n=1}^{\infty} \delta_R^{-1}(1^n)$ (disjoint union) and let X_{abc} be the set of all strings in X prefixed with $abc \in B^3$. Then we have the following proposition.

Proposition 4. *Let* $abc, a'b'c' \in B^3$.

(a) *If* $f(abc) = 0$, *then* $X_{abc} = \emptyset$,
(b) $X_{abc} = abc + aX_{bc0} + aX_{bc1}$,
(c) *If* $abc \neq a'b'c'$ *then* $X_{abc} \cap X_{a'b'c'} = \emptyset$,
(d) $X \cap B^{n+2} = \delta_R^{-1}(1^n)$ *and* $X = \cup_{abc \in B^3} X_{abc}$,
(e) $|\delta_R^{-1}(1^n)| = \sum_{abc \in B^3} |X_{abc} \cap B^{n+2}|$.   □

An inverse image sequence $c_n = c_n(R) \, (n = 1, 2, 3, \ldots)$ with Wolfram number R is defined by $c_n = |\delta_R^{-1}(1^n)|$. The above proposition indicates that the inverse images $\delta_R^{-1}(1^n)$ is a regular language over the alphabet $B = \{0, 1\}$ and how to calculate its regular expression.

5   de Bruijn Subautomata

The de Bruijn graph $\mathcal{A}$ has 8 vertices $abc \in B^3$ and 16 labeled edges (abc, d, bcd) from abc to bcd for all $a, b, c, d \in B$.

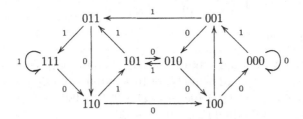

Fig. 1. de Bruijn graph $\mathcal{A}$

For each rule $f_R : B^3 \to B$ we define de Bruijn subgraph $\mathcal{A}_R$ consists of all vertices $abc \in B^3$ satisfying $f_R(abc) = 1$. Note that $\mathcal{A}_{255} = \mathcal{A}$. de Bruijn subgraphs can be easily regarded as automata, so in what follows we call $\mathcal{A}_R$ de Bruijn subautomaton with Wolfram number R.

A string $x_0 x_1 \ldots x_{n+1} \in B^{n+2} \, (n \geq 1)$ is *accepted* by $\mathcal{A}_R$ if $x_i x_{i+1} x_{i+2} \in \mathcal{A}_R$ for all $i = 0, 1, 2, \ldots, n-1$. (Remark that all the states in $\mathcal{A}_R$ are both of initial and final states.) Thus the following theorem is immediate.

Theorem 2. $\mathcal{A}_R$ *recognizes the language* $X = \cup_{n=0}^{\infty} \delta_R^{-1}(1^n)$.

Now we give some examples of calculation of the regular expressions of $X = \cup_{n=0}^{\infty} \delta_R^{-1}(1^n)$.

Example 1. For a Wolfram number $R = 46 = 2^1 + 2^2 + 2^3 + 2^5$ we have the following equations by Proposition 4 (a) and (b):

$$\begin{cases} X_{000} = X_{100} = X_{110} = X_{111} = \emptyset \\ X_{001} = 001 + 0X_{010} + 0011 \\ X_{010} = 010 + 0X_{101} \\ X_{011} = 011 \\ X_{101} = 101 + 1X_{010} + 1011 \end{cases}$$

The equations yield

$$\begin{aligned} X_{010} &= 010 + 0101 + 01011 + 01X_{010} \\ &= (01)^*(010 + 0101 + 01011) \\ &= (01)^+(0 + 01 + 011). \end{aligned}$$

Hence $\delta_R^{-1}(1^n) = [001 + 011 + 101 + 0011 + 1011 + (\varepsilon + 0 + 1)(01)^+(0 + 01 + 011)] \cap B^{n+2}$. $\square$

Example 2. For a Wolfram number $R = 30 = 2^1 + 2^2 + 2^3 + 2^4$ we have the following equations:

$$\begin{cases} X_{000} = X_{101} = X_{110} = X_{111} = \emptyset \\ X_{001} = 001 + 0X_{010} + 0011 \\ X_{010} = 010 + 0X_{100} \\ X_{011} = 011 \\ X_{100} = 100 + 1X_{001} \end{cases}$$

The equations yield

$$\begin{aligned} X_{001} &= 001 + 0011 + 0(010 + 0(100 + 1X_{001})) \\ &= 001 + 0011 + 0010 + 00100 + 001X_{001} \\ &= (001)^*(001 + 0011 + 0010 + 00100) \\ &= (001)^+(\varepsilon + 0 + 1 + 00). \end{aligned}$$

Hence $\delta_R^{-1}(1^n) = [010 + 011 + 100 + 0100 + (\varepsilon + 1 + 01)(001)^+(\varepsilon + 0 + 1 + 00)] \cap B^{n+2}$. $\square$

To calculate inverse image sequences we give the following lemma.

Lemma 1. *Set* $X(abc, n) = |X_{abc} \cap B^{n+2}|$. *Then*

(a) $X(abc, 1) = f(abc)$,
(b) $X(abc, n + 1) = f(abc)X(bc0, n) + f(abc)X(bc1, n)$,
(c) $c_n = |\delta_R^{-1}(1^n)| = \sum_{abc \in B^3} X(abc, n)$. $\square$

Remark that $X(abc, n) = X(a^- bc, n)$ if $f(abc) = f(a^- bc)$.

Proposition 5. *If a Wolfram number R satisfies $r_0 = r_6 = r_7 = r_2 r_5 = r_1 r_2 r_4 = 0$, then $c_n = 0$ for $n \geq 4$.*

Proof. Since $r_0 = r_6 = r_7 = 0$, we have $X(000, n) = X(110, n) = X(111, n) = 0$ (for all $n \geq 1$), and $X(001, 1) = r_1$, $X(010, 1) = r_2$, $X(011, 1) = r_3$, $X(100, 1) = r_4$ and $X(101, 1) = r_5$. First note that $X(011, n+1) = X(110, n) + X(111, n) = 0$. For $n = 2$

$$\begin{cases} X(001, 2) = r_1 X(010, 1) + r_1 X(011, 1) = r_1(r_2 + r_3) \\ X(010, 2) = r_2 X(100, 1) + r_2 X(101, 1) = r_2(r_4 + r_5) \\ X(100, 2) = r_4 X(000, 1) + r_4 X(001, 1) = r_4 r_1 \\ X(101, 2) = r_5 X(010, 1) + r_5 X(011, 1) = r_5(r_2 + r_3). \end{cases}$$

For $n = 3$

$$\begin{cases} X(001, 3) = r_1 X(010, 2) + r_1 X(011, 2) = r_1 r_2(r_4 + r_5) \\ X(010, 3) = r_2 X(100, 2) + r_2 X(101, 2) = r_1 r_2 r_4 + r_2 r_5(1 + r_3) \\ X(100, 3) = r_4 X(000, 2) + r_4 X(001, 2) = r_1 r_4(r_2 + r_3) \\ X(101, 3) = r_5 X(010, 2) + r_5 X(011, 2) = r_2 r_5(r_4 + 1). \end{cases}$$

For $n = 4$

$$\begin{cases} X(001, 4) = r_1 X(010, 3) + r_1 X(011, 3) = r_1 r_2 r_4 + r_1 r_2 r_5(1 + r_3) \\ X(010, 4) = r_2 X(100, 3) + r_2 X(101, 3) = r_1 r_2 r_4(1 + r_3) + r_2 r_5(1 + r_4) \\ X(100, 4) = r_4 X(000, 3) + r_4 X(001, 3) = r_1 r_2 r_4(1 + r_5) \\ X(101, 4) = r_5 X(010, 3) + r_5 X(011, 3) = r_2 r_5(1 + r_3 + r_1 r_4). \end{cases}$$

This yields $X(abc, n) = 0$ and $c_n = 0$ for all $abc \in B^3$ and $n \geq 4$.   □

Wolfram numbers $0, 2, 4, 6, 10, 12, 14, 18, 24, 26, 28, 50$ and 58 satisfies the condition $r_0 = r_6 = r_7 = r_2 r_5 = r_1 r_2 r_4 = 0$.

Example 3. For a Wolfram number $R = 36 = 2^2 + 2^5$ it holds that

$$\begin{cases} X(abc, n) = 0 \quad (abc \neq 010 \text{ and } abc \neq 101) \\ X(010, n + 1) = X(101, n) \\ X(101, n + 1) = X(010, n), \end{cases}$$

from which we have

$$\begin{aligned} c_{n+1} &= X(010, n + 1) + X(101, n + 1) \\ &= X(101, n) + X(010, n) \\ &= c_n. \end{aligned}$$

Therefore $c_n = 2$ since $c_1 = 2$.   □

Example 4. For a Wolfram number $R = 30 = 2^1 + 2^2 + 2^3 + 2^4$ it holds that

$$\begin{cases} X(000, n) = X(101, n) = X(110, n) = X(111, n) = 0 \\ X(001, n+1) = X(010, n) + X(011, n) \\ X(010, n+1) = X(100, n) \\ X(011, n+1) = 0 \\ X(100, n+1) = X(001, n), \end{cases}$$

from which we have

$$\begin{aligned} c_{n+1} &= X(001, n+1) + X(010, n+1) + X(011, n+1) + X(100, n+1) \\ &= X(010, n) + X(011, n) + X(100, n) + X(001, n) \\ &= c_n. \end{aligned}$$

Therefore $c_n = 4$ since $c_1 = 4$.   □

Example 5. For a Wolfram number $R = 46 = 2^1 + 2^2 + 2^3 + 2^5$ it holds that

$$\begin{cases} X(000, n) = X(100, n) = X(110, n) = X(111, n) = 0 \\ X(001, n+1) = X(101, n+1) = X(010, n) + X(011, n) \\ X(010, n+1) = X(101, n) \\ X(011, n+1) = 0, \end{cases}$$

from which we have $X(001, n) = X(101, n)$ and so

$$\begin{aligned} c_{n+2} &= 2X(010, n+1) + X(101, n+1) \\ &= 2X(101, n) + X(010, n) + X(011, n) \\ &= X(001, n) + X(010, n) + X(011, n) + X(101, n) \\ &= c_n. \end{aligned}$$

Therefore $c_{2n+1} = 4$ and $c_{2n} = 5$ because $c_1 = 4$ and $c_2 = 5$.   □

Example 6. For a Wolfram number $R = 39 = 2^0 + 2^1 + 2^2 + 2^5$ it holds that

$$\begin{cases} X(011, n) = X(100, n) = X(110, n) = X(111, n) = 0 \\ X(000, n+1) = X(000, n) + X(001, n) \\ X(001, n+1) = X(101, n+1) = X(010, n) \\ X(010, n+1) = X(101, n), \end{cases}$$

from which we have $X(001, n) = X(010, n) = 1$ since $X(001, 1) = X(010, 1) = 1$, $X(001, n+1) = X(010, n)$ and $X(010, n+1) = X(001, n)$. Hence

$$\begin{aligned} c_{n+1} &= X(000, n) + X(001, n) + 2X(010, n) + X(101, n) \\ &= X(000, n) + X(001, n) + X(010, n) + X(101, n) + 1 \\ &= c_n + 1. \end{aligned}$$

Therefore $c_n = n + 3$ because $c_1 = 4$.   □

Example 7. For a Wolfram number $R = 23 = 2^0 + 2^1 + 2^2 + 2^4$ it holds that

$$
\begin{cases}
X(011, n) = X(101, n) = X(110, n) = X(111, n) = 0 \\
X(000, n+1) = X(100, n+1) = X(000, n) + X(001, n) \\
X(001, n+1) = X(010, n) \\
X(010, n+1) = X(100, n),
\end{cases}
$$

from which we have

$$
\begin{aligned}
c_{n+3} &= c_{n+2} + X(000, n+3) \\
&= c_{n+2} + X(000, n+2) + X(001, n+2) \\
&= c_{n+2} + X(000, n+1) + X(001, n+1) + X(010, n+1) \\
&= c_{n+2} + X(000, n) + X(001, n) + X(010, n) + X(100, n) \\
&= c_{n+2} + c_n.
\end{aligned}
$$

Remark that the inverse image sequence c_n for $R = 151$ is calculated by adding one to each c_n for $R = 23$. This is illustrated in state-transition diagrams of de Bruijn automata in Appendix B at the end of the paper.   □

Example 8. For a Wolfram number $R = 55 = 2^5 + 2^4 + 2^2 + 2^1 + 2^0$ it holds that

$$
\begin{cases}
X(011, n) = X(110, n) = X(111, n) = 0 \\
X(000, n+1) = X(100, n+1) = X(000, n) + X(001, n) \\
X(001, n+1) = X(101, n+1) = X(010, n) \\
X(010, n+1) = X(100, n) + X(101, n),
\end{cases}
$$

from which we have

$$
\begin{aligned}
c_{n+2} &= c_{n+1} + X(000, n+2) + X(001, n+2) \\
&= c_{n+1} + X(000, n+1) + X(001, n+1) + X(010, n+1) \\
&= c_{n+1} + X(000, n) + X(001, n) + X(010, n) + X(100, n) + X(101, n) \\
&= c_{n+1} + c_n.
\end{aligned}
$$

The inverse image sequence c_n for $R = 183$ is calculated by adding one to each c_n for $R = 55$. (Cf. Appendix B.)   □

6   Conclusion

In this paper we gave a sufficient and necessary condition for global transitions of transition systems on graphs to be bijective and classified triplet local rules (Wolfram numbers) by using the inverse image sequences. Also the paper presented how to verify the recursive formulae satisfied by the inverse image sequences and how to calculate the regular expressions of inverse images of 1^n. There are some similarities between inverse image sequences of different Wolfram numbers, related to the notion of conjugate functions. To analyze the essence for the phenomena is one of future works.

References

1. Inokuchi, S., et al.: On reversible cellular automata with finite cell array. In: Calude, C.S., Dinneen, M.J., Păun, G., Jesús Pérez-Jímenez, M., Rozenberg, G. (eds.) UC 2005. LNCS, vol. 3699, pp. 130–141. Springer, Heidelberg (2005)
2. Inui, N., et al.: Statistical properties of a quantum cellular automaton. Physical Review A 72, 032323
3. Shingai, R.: The maximum period realized in 1-D uniform neural networks. Trans. IECE, Japan E61, 804–808 (1978)
4. Wolfram, S.: Universality and complexity in cellular automata. Physica 10D, 1–35 (1984)

Appendix A. Table of Inverse Image Sequences

R	c_1	c_2	c_3	c_4	c_5	c_6	c_7	c_8	c_9	c_{10}
0	0	0	0	0	0	0	0	0	0	0
$2, 4, 8, 16, 32, 64$	1	0	0	0	0	0	0	0	0	0
$12, 24, 34, 48, 66, 68$	2	0	0	0	0	0	0	0	0	0
$6, 10, 18, 20, 40, 72, 80, 96$	2	1	0	0	0	0	0	0	0	0
$28, 50, 56, 70, 76, 98$	3	1	0	0	0	0	0	0	0	0
$14, 42, 84, 112$	3	2	0	0	0	0	0	0	0	0
$26, 74, 82, 88$	3	2	1	0	0	0	0	0	0	0
$58, 78, 92, 114$	4	3	1	0	0	0	0	0	0	0
$1, 128$	1	1	1	1	1	1	1	1	1	1
$5, 9, 33, 65, 130, 132, 144, 160$	2	1	1	1	1	1	1	1	1	1
$13, 69, 162, 176$	3	1	1	1	1	1	1	1	1	1
$41, 73, 97, 134, 146, 148$	3	2	1	1	1	1	1	1	1	1
$77, 178$	4	2	1	1	1	1	1	1	1	1
$3, 17, 36, 129, 136, 192$	2	2	2	2	2	2	2	2	2	2
$25, 35, 49, 67, 133, 140, 152, 161, 194, 196$	3	2	2	2	2	2	2	2	2	2
$57, 99, 156, 198$	4	3	2	2	2	2	2	2	2	2
$7, 11, 21, 22, 37, 38, 44, 52, 81, 100, 104,$ $131, 137, 138, 145, 164, 168, 193, 208, 224$	3	3	3	3	3	3	3	3	3	3
$29, 71, 141, 163, 177, 184, 197, 226$	4	3	3	3	3	3	3	3	3	3
$43, 113, 142, 212$	4	4	3	3	3	3	3	3	3	3

R	c_1	c_2	c_3	c_4	c_5	c_6	c_7	c_8	c_9	c_{10}
$19, 200$	3	4	4	4	4	4	4	4	4	4
$15, 30, 45, 51, 60, 75, 85, 86, 89, 90, 101, 102,$ $105, 106, 120, 135, 149, 150, 153, 154, 165,$ $166, 169, 170, 180, 195, 204, 210, 225, 240$	4	4	4	4	4	4	4	4	4	4
$147, 201$	4	5	5	5	5	5	5	5	5	5
$79, 93, 157, 179, 185, 186, 199, 205, 227, 242$	5	5	5	5	5	5	5	5	5	5
$27, 83, 202, 216$	4	5	6	6	6	6	6	6	6	6
$59, 115, 206, 220$	5	6	6	6	6	6	6	6	6	6
$46, 116$	4	5	4	5	4	5	4	5	4	5
$39, 53, 139, 172, 209, 228$	4	5	6	7	8	9	10	11	12	13
$61, 103, 107, 121, 143, 158, 167, 171,$ $173, 181, 188, 213, 214, 229, 230, 241$	5	6	7	8	9	10	11	12	13	14
$47, 117, 174, 244$	5	7	8	10	11	13	14	16	17	19
$155, 203, 211, 217$	5	7	9	11	13	15	17	19	21	23
$187, 189, 207, 221, 231, 243$	6	8	10	12	14	16	18	20	22	24
$55, 236$	5	8	13	21	34	55	89	144	233	377
$63, 119, 126, 219, 238, 252$	6	10	16	26	42	68	110	178	288	466
$23, 232$	4	6	9	13	19	28	41	60	88	129
$31, 87, 234, 248$	5	7	11	16	23	34	50	73	107	157
$123, 222$	6	9	13	19	28	41	60	88	129	189
$91, 218$	5	7	10	14	19	26	36	50	60	95
$54, 108$	4	5	7	9	12	16	21	28	37	49
$62, 110, 118, 124$	5	7	9	12	16	21	28	37	49	65
$94, 122$	5	6	7	9	11	13	16	20	24	29
$95, 250$	6	9	15	25	40	64	104	169	273	441
$175, 245$	6	9	12	16	20	25	30	36	42	49
$183, 237$	6	9	14	22	35	56	90	145	234	378
$191, 239, 247, 253$	7	12	20	33	54	88	143	232	376	609
$151, 233$	5	7	10	14	20	29	42	61	89	130
$159, 215, 235, 249$	6	9	14	21	31	46	68	100	147	216
$109, 182$	5	6	8	10	13	17	22	29	38	50
$111, 125, 190, 246$	6	9	13	18	25	34	46	62	83	111
$127, 254$	7	13	24	44	81	149	274	504	927	1705
$223, 251$	7	12	21	37	65	114	200	351	616	1081
255	8	16	32	64	128	256	512	1024	2048	4096

Appendix B. Examples of de Brujin Automata

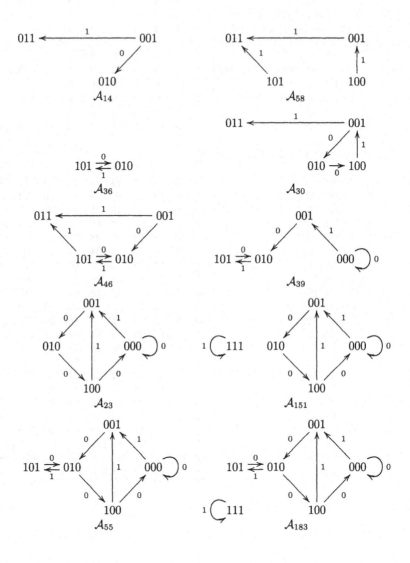

An Efficient Multiple Alignment Method for RNA Secondary Structures Including Pseudoknots

Shinnosuke Seki[1] and Satoshi Kobayashi[2]

[1] Department of Computer Science, University of Western Ontario,
London, Ontario, Canada, N6A 5B7
sseki@csd.uwo.ca
[2] Department of Computer Science, The University of Electro-Communications,
1-5-1 Chofugaoka, Chofu, Tokyo, Japan, 182-8585
satoshi@cs.uec.ac.jp

Abstract. Pseudoknots, one of the key components of RNA secondary structures, have been almost systematically intractable because of the difficulty in modeling them. Tree adjoining grammars have proved to be promising for this problem but the question of how to make TAG-based applications practical enough to analyze RNAs of thousands nucleotides remains open. This paper addresses this problem. It makes use of biological properties of pseudoknots, the *scarcity* and *short-bp property*. Experiments showed that our algorithm can align RNAs of the length up to about 2400 nucleotides with biologically meaningful outputs extremely fast on the standard workstation environment. An executable version of our implementation is available at http://www.csd.uwo.ca/~sseki/

1 Introduction

Genetic computation *in vivo* makes use of 2 or 3 dimensional structures (called *secondary* and tertiary structure) of nucleic acids with chemical reactions among them as its computational unit. For example, the well-known *cloverleaf structure* of transfer RNAs (tRNAs) consists of 3 stem-loops like hairpins. It in turn folds into itself so as to form the L-shaped 3D structure. Another example is the transfer-messenger RNA (tmRNA), in which crossing-dependent secondary structures, generally-called *pseudoknots*, play an important role in the conformational change during their transition from the tRNA phase to the mRNA phase [1]. More and more pseudoknots have proved crucial for determining biological functions of RNAs.

The use of RNA structures as computational units in artificial biological computing demands that we should know which structures achieve which functions. Since similar structures are very likely to be responsible for similar functions, the *alignment* of RNA structures offers promise. For given RNA structures, the alignment extracts common or similar substructures (components) based on a measure of similarity such as *edit distance*. By aligning with known relationships

Y. Suzuki et al. (Eds.): IWNC 2007, PICT 1, pp. 179–188, 2009.

between its components and functions, we may infer the function of an unknown RNA. The latest result based on this line is an algorithm to align a query RNA with a target RNA whose structure is unknown [2].

Formal language theory makes it possible to model RNA structures for various algorithms of importance. In particular, context-free grammars (CFGs) have brought about substantial results in bioinformatics [3], [4], [5], [6]. The *tree adjoining grammar* (TAG) was proposed in [7] as a stronger grammar than CFGs in terms of the Chomsky hierarchy. It was employed to model pseudoknots in an RNA structure prediction method [8], and since then TAG-based studies have proposed prediction or alignment algorithms for pseudoknotted RNA structures [9], [10]. One of the difficulties in using a formal grammar is its *ambiguity*. In other words, a number of derivations by the grammar result in the same word. The ambiguity is inherent in CFGs; we cannot free some CFGs from ambiguity, and the problem to decide whether a given CFG is ambiguous is undecidable [11]. Since TAGs are more descriptive than CFGs, the ambiguity gets more serious. Even from the viewpoint of TAG's applications, however, the ambiguity is essential because it is not until all possible derivations are considered that we can use their outputs as a reliable model for further application. Most of TAG's applications ignored this fact for the efficiency of their algorithms. In contrast, our previous work [10] investigated how to solve the ambiguity of TAGs completely for the pairwise alignment of RNA structures each including at most one pseudoknot, and studied the resulting increase in its time complexity.

This paper investigates the problems of how to improve the time complexity of our algorithm and how to align RNAs including *multiple* pseudoknots while considering the ambiguity as much as possible. The intractable complexity derives from the fact that it models a whole RNA structure by one TAG. Since the TAG is used to model pseudoknots in the RNA, we need not to model its non-pseudoknotted components by TAGs. Thus we take a strategy that (1) decomposes an RNA structure into pseudoknots and non-pseudoknotted components, (2) models each component by an appropriate grammar (e.g., pseudoknots by SLTAGs and others by CFGs or regular grammars) and (3) aligns the models using an algorithm for alignment of SLTAG models [10] with slight modification. The scarcity of pseudoknots guarantees that almost all component alignments are practical. Alignments of pseudoknots are less efficient but not unfeasible because the length of pseudoknots tends to be by far shorter than that of an RNA including them. It is, therefore, very likely that the complexity of the entire algorithm is feasible.

2   Preliminaries

A single-stranded RNA is numbered from its 5'-end to 3'-end. A bonded pair between the i-th and j-th bases is denoted as (i, j) with $i < j$. A base bonded to no base is called *single*. An RNA structure is defined as (s, P), where $s \in \{\text{A}, \text{C}, \text{G}, \text{U}\}^*$ and $P = \{(i, j) \mid i\text{-th and } j\text{-th bases of } s \text{ form a base-pair}\}$.

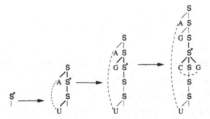

Fig. 1. A derived tree of a TAG and the corresponding secondary structure, where replaceable nodes are denoted with an asterisk. The part of each tree which was created by the preceding adjoining operation is accentuated by bold lines.

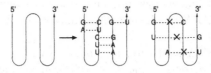

Fig. 2. SLTAG's generative capacity. The rightmost figure shows unacceptable lines.

Tree Adjoining Grammars. A *tree adjoining grammar* (TAG) grows a set of trees by replacing a "replaceable" node of a derived tree with a tree called the adjunct tree (see Fig. 1). This operation is called *adjoining*. We interpret a derived tree as a structure whose sequence is obtained through its postorder traversal of leaves, and whose bonded pairs are a pair of leaves generated simultaneously. For example, the rightmost tree in Fig. 1 is regarded as a structure 5'-AGCUG-3' with $\{(1,4),(3,5)\}$. For the formal definition of TAGs, readers are referred to [7]. Two subclasses of TAGs are known to have useful applications in bioinfomatics. A TAG is said to be *simple linear* (written as SLTAG) if a tree derived from it has an unique replaceable node [8]. SLTAGs are well-suited to represent RNA structures that contain a sole pseudoknot.

We consider SLTAGs promising enough for our algorithm. The prefix "simple" does not mean that they can model only biologically trivial pseudoknots. In fact, SLTAGs can model any pseudoknots drawn in the following 3 steps as two-dimensional figures (see Fig. 2): (1) describe a $5' \to 3'$ directed W-shaped curve; (2) draw horizontal line segments (slanted lines disallowed) between two adjacent vertical lines; (3) label each segment with A-U, C-G, G-U, U-A, G-C, or U-G. In this way, SLTAGs can model not only $xy\tilde{x}\tilde{y}$-type but $xy\tilde{x}z\tilde{y}\tilde{z}$-type pseudoknots, where $\tilde{x}$ is the Watson-Crick complementarity of x. Although $xy\tilde{x}z\tilde{y}w\tilde{z}\tilde{w}$-type is beyond SLTAG's generating power, the first two types are known to be prevailing enough to ignore the others. Indeed, the recent re-implementation of pknotsRG [13], a web server for pseudoknotted RNA secondary structure prediction, takes only the first type into consideration.

ARNAS Classification and Construction of ARNAS Models. Toward the pairwise alignment problem of RNA structures, we take a bigradient strategy that firstly converts structures into a tree-like model called the *abstract RNA* *structure (ARNAS) model*, and then aligns them based on the tree alignment algorithm proposed in [12]. An ARNAS model is a tree whose nodes are substructures of the modelled structure. In this respect it is similar to the RNA secondary structure tree [14]. The two models differ substantially, however, in what substructures their nodes are. Nodes of RNA secondary structure trees are biological entities such as hairpin, bulge, internal, and multiple loops. On the other hand, we decompose a targeted structure into *strings*, *tandems*, and *pseudoknots*, depending on how difficult it is to model in terms of Chomsky hierarchy, a hierarchy of four classes of formal languages, i.e., regular (also-called Type-3), context-free (-2), context-sensitive (-1), and recursively enumerable (-0). An RNA structure is divided in such a manner that Type-3, -2, and -1 grammars are necessary and sufficient for modeling strings, tandems, and pseudoknots, respectively. We call this process the *ARNAS classification*, and resulting components *ARNAS components*.

Let (s, P) be an RNA structure, and $p_1 = (i_1, j_1), p_2 = (i_2, j_2) \in P$. Let $p_1 \succ p_2$ if $i_1 \leq i_2 \leq j_1$ or $i_1 \leq j_2 \leq j_1$. The reflexive and transitive closure of $\succ$ is denoted by $\succ^*$. We define $p_1 \equiv_p p_2$ if both $p_1 \succ^* p_2$ and $p_2 \succ^* p_1$. A *pseudoknot* can be defined as an equivalence class in $P/\equiv_p$ whose size is larger than one, which is known to correspond with biological pseudoknots. To extract pseudoknots from (s, P), we construct a directed graph (V, E), where $V = P$ and $E = \{(p_1, p_2) \mid p_1, p_2 \in P, p_1 \succ^* p_2\}$. Due to the definition of E, the equivalence class in $P/\equiv_p$ is a strongly-connected component on this graph. Using an existing algorithm for finding strongly-connected components of a given graph, whose time complexity is linear on the number of its nodes, we can obtain all pseudoknots in $O(|s|)$ time. Let P_t be a subset of P whose elements do not belong to any pseudoknots. A *tandem* is defined as a maximal set $\{p_1, \ldots, p_k \mid p_i \in P_t, p_{i+1} \succ p_i\}$. A *string* is defined to be a single base chain of maximal length. This definition guarantees that any RNA structure including only pseudoknots that can be modelled by SLTAGs to be uniquely converted into the set of ARNAS components.

In order to make ARNAS components cluster together so as to form a tree, it is necessary to introduce parent-child and sibling relationships between them. An ARNAS component is the parent of another if there are a base-pair (i_1, j_1) in the former and a base k in the latter such that the pair *directly* encompass the base; that is, there exists no base-pair (i_2, j_2) satisfying $i_1 < i_2 < k < j_2 < j_1$. The 5'-3' directionality of RNA imposes the order among sibling entities. These relationships transform a set of ARNAS components into a tree called the *ARNAS model*, whose nodes are labeled with *S(tring)*, *T(andem)*, or *P(seudoknot)*.

ARNAS Alignment Algorithms. Figure 4 shows an outline of the alignment of ARNAS models A_1 and A_2: the alignment A is a tree whose nodes are labeled with a pair of labels of nodes of ARNAS models representing substitution or a pair of node with gap character "_" representing insertion or deletion. It is highly likely that there exist a number of candidates for an alignment of ARNAS models. The algorithm evaluates which candidate is optimal according to the score assigned to the candidates based on the edit distance. A score of an alignment

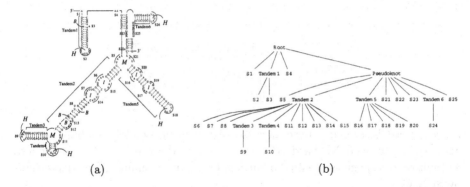

(a)   (b)

Fig. 3. Illustration of how an RNA secondary structure is reduced to an ARNAS model. (a) represents a part of the secondary structure of the *Tetrahymena thermophila* nuclear LSU rRNA [15]. Strings and tandems are indexed in order of increasing base number, respectively. Hairpin, bulge, internal, and multibranch loops are also labeled with respective initial characters in *italics*. (b) represents the ARNAS model converted.

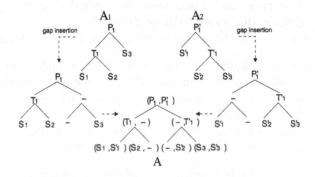

Fig. 4. An alignment A of ARNAS models A_1 and A_2

of trees is defined to be the sum of the score assigned to each pair of labels on the nodes of the alignment, which are available through a precalculated matrix. In the case of ARNAS models, however, it is necessary to calculate the matrix after the ARNAS model construction using a pairwise alignment algorithm for ARNAS components. This is because each node represents an ARNAS component rather than a mere symbol, and thus, a score of a pair of labels of nodes of ARNAS models is equivalent to the score of an optimal alignment between components to which the nodes correspond.

Our algorithm proposed in [10] was for the pairwise alignment of SLTAG models, which was defined there as the optimal alignment of derivations for the models by the SLTAG. The score of an alignment is measured by the edit distance between derivations by an SLTAG. It runs an SLTAG-parser on the input models each, resulting in a set of derivations for it. Then based on the dynamic programming, it calculates the derivations of alignments in all possible combinations. The algorithm is designed to align pseudoknot components of

Table 1. The time complexities of the generalized algorithm for each pair of modeling grammars, where s_1 and s_2 are the lengths of components C_1 and C_2, respectively

		A model grammar for C_2		
		Type-3	Type-2	SLTAG
A model grammar for C_1	Type-3	$O(s_1 s_2)$	$O(s_1 s_2^2)$	$O(s_1 s_2^4)$
	Type-2	$O(s_1^2 s_2)$	$O(s_1^2 s_2^2)$	$O(s_1^2 s_2^4)$
	SLTAG	$O(s_1^4 s_2)$	$O(s_1^4 s_2^2)$	$O(s_1^4 s_2^4)$

ARNAS models. In general the pairwise alignment of pseudoknots based on the distance has proven NP-hard [16], we overcame the difficulty by taking into account only sequences of edit operations that can be simulated as derivations by SLTAGs.

We extend this algorithm so that it can align any ARNAS components by choosing appropriate grammars (parsers) according to the kinds of components being aligned. The theoretical time complexity of the generalized algorithm varies among component types as shown in Table 1. It is essential that in cases where at least one of the components being aligned is a string or a tandem, the new algorithm runs much faster than the original algorithm (whose time complexity is given in the bottom-right of Table 1.)

We summarize the ARNAS pairwise alignment algorithm as follows:

1. Construct ARNAS models out of given two RNA secondary structures.
2. Calculate an alignment between two ARNAS components of the respective ARNAS models, and the score of that alignment in all possible combinations using the extended algorithm.
3. Align the ARNAS models using the tree alignment algorithm based on the scores of component alignments obtained in the preceding step.

The time complexity of this algorithm is analyzed as follows: Let n_1 and n_2 be lengths of input RNAs. Step 1 constructs the ARNAS models in $O(n_1+n_2)$ time. Step 3 employs the tree alignment algorithm, whose complexity is $O(n_1 n_2)$. Although the complexity of Step 2 varies depending on components, very probably it is fast enough for practical use by virtue of the scarcity and *short-bp property* of pseudoknots. The short-bp property means that a pseudoknot in an RNA tends to be much shorter than the RNA itself. The scarcity, along with Table 1, implies that almost all alignments of ARNAS components take at most $O(s_1^2 s_2^2)$ time, where s_1 and s_2 are the sizes of the largest pseudoknots in the RNAs. For the few alignments of pseudoknots, the short-bp property alleviates their complexity to the maximum extent possible. The sum of the processing times of these cases is dominated by s_1 and s_2, and $s_1 \ll n_1$ and $s_2 \ll n_2$ due to the short-bp property. Consequently, the time complexity $s_1^i s_2^j$ is much smaller than $n_1^i n_2^j$ for any $1 \leq i, j \leq 4$.

We conclude this section by extending the algorithm to handle multiple alignments. The algorithm follows the progressive alignment approach [17], with modifications to make it capable of dealing with ARNAS models. An overview of the algorithm follows:

1. Construct a set of ARNAS models $\{A_1, \ldots, A_n\}$ from input structures.
2. Find the two models A_i and A_j with the highest similarity, and align them using the pairwise alignment algorithm mentioned above. The alignment turns into an ARNAS model A_{ij}.
3. Remove A_i and A_j from the set of ARNAS models, and add A_{ij}.
4. Iterate Steps 2 and 3 until only a single ARNAS model $A_{1\ldots n}$ is left.

A similar approach was taken in [18] for the multiple alignment of pseudoknot-free RNA structures. Like our approach it converts RNA structures into trees, but nodes of the trees are a base-pair or single base rather than components.

3   Discussion and Conclusion

We have made experiments on the precision, efficiency, and biological significance of the outputs of the ARNAS approach. RNA data with structural information were taken from the databases [15] and [19]. Our implementation of the ARNAS progressive alignment approach was written in C++ and run under Intel(R) Xeon processors 2.8GHz × 2 with a 2GB memory. Note that in this environment it takes about 600 seconds for our original algorithm without ARNAS modification to align pseudoknots of length around 80 nucleotides. Space being limited, we do not mention the precision.

First off, we show the experimental time complexity of ARNAS algorithm. 675 RNA structures available in [15] were examined for their length and the size of largest pseudoknots included (see Fig. 5 (Left)). The symbol '+' represents data which can be converted into ARNAS models, and thus is processible in our system. Test results show that 561 of 675 (83.1%) are processible, and so are all but one of the RNAs of length up to about 2400. The least-square method fits the set of the processible data to the following theoretical curve:

$$P(\ell) = 5.400005\ell^{0.191187}. \tag{1}$$

The exponent implies that the size of largest pseudoknots in an RNA is proportional to the length of the RNA raised to a power much less than 1, though it depends on the data.

This experimental evidence of short-bp property leads us to the validation of the computational efficiency of ARNAS alignment. The measurement of the runtime of the ARNAS pairwise alignment employed 150 pairs of processible secondary structures. This dataset does not include any structures located around $(1200, 80)$ of the graph in Fig. 5 (Left) because they deviate from the theoretical approximation function $P(\ell)$ substantially. Runtimes of our algorithm on the data shown in Fig. 5 (Right) is fit by:

$$T(\ell) = 0.000036\ell^{1.69092}. \tag{2}$$

It is essential that the exponent 1.69092 is small enough to keep ARNAS alignment within computational reach. Fairness demands runtimes of our algorithm

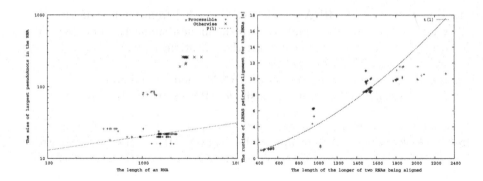

Fig. 5. (Left) the correlation of the size of largest pseudoknots with the length of RNA secondary structures. $P(l)$ is the approximate function for the processible data. (Right) the runtimes of ARNAS alignment for 150 pairs of processible data, which consist of 25 pairs each randomly derived from the following 6 sections of Gutell: *Archaea 16S Nucleus, Bacteria 16S Nucleus, Eukaryota 16S Mitochondrion, Eukaryota 16S Nucleus, Eukaryota 16S Chloroplast,* and *Eukaryota Group I introns.*

on data around $(1200, 80)$. It took 640.45 [sec] on average for the 9 RNAs (only 1.33% of the data tested) whose largest pseudoknots are of length around 80. This is because the time complexity of pseudoknot alignments dominates the runtime of ARNAS algorithm as pseudoknots elongate.

The validity of $T(\ell)$ as the approximation of runtime is supported by the following experiment on the multiple alignment algorithm. 10 structures were chosen as inputs from the tmRNA family in [19], and the output is shown in Fig. 6[1]. We did the same experiment three times and the processing time averaged 183.19 [sec]. The system calculated 165 pairwise alignments for the 10 data. The largest RNA was of length 411. Thus, it was to take $T(411) \times 165 = 156.17$ [sec], theoretically. Considering the dispersion of data shown in Fig. 5, it would appear that the observed runtime is well-fit by the approximation.

The preceding experimental result also shows that the ARNAS approach precisely captures the common substructures of tmRNAs: the 4 pseudoknots, the tag reading frame, and the tRNA-like domain. This is attributed to the process by which we extract component-based models from RNA secondary structures. Needless to say, the fact that ARNAS approach can handle pseudoknots contributes to the accuracy of pseudoknots matching among the family members. More noteworthy is the component-oriented aspect of ARNAS models that enables the algorithm to precisely align substructures that are not shared by every member of a family, or that are common but differ widely in their lengths or nucleotides. This, in turn, allows the ARNAS algorithm to align families including

---

[1] Space being limited, Fig. 6 contains only parts of the multiple alignment that play an important role for the following discussion. A complete alignment result is available at http://www.csd.uwo.ca/~sseki/files/IWNC/figures.pdf. This file also contains all figures in this paper of original size.

Fig. 6. A part of the multiple alingment of 10 tmRNAs derived from Rfam [19] by ARNAS progressive method. We borrow the notations of substructures P1, P2, ..., P12 shown in **structur** row from the database. Capital letters indicate paired bases specified in the Rfam database, and small letters do single ones or additional paired ones not included in it; our system treats them equally from the viewpoint of scoring. Underlines show resume and stop codons of the tag reading frame. A complete alignment result is available at http://www.csd.uwo.ca/~sseki/files/IWNC/figures.pdf. It also contains the names of species shown as abbreviations like D90888 here.

more distantly related RNAs with high accuracy. Tandem P1 and the tag reading frame in Fig. 6 provide examples for these cases. The tmRNAs AF440330, U68077, and U68080 do not include P1. The tag reading frame of U39713 or S67602 is twice as long as that of *E. coli* (D90888).

Pre- and post-processes are necessary for the ARNAS alignment algorithm to overcome its drawbacks. As a preprocess, the pseudoknotted structure prediction algorithm [8] is promising because it is rather practical to take sequential information of RNAs only as input rather than with structural one. With this, the time complexity of alignment algorithm gets higher much because the prediction of pseudoknotted structures is computationally costly; indeed, the prediction algorithm has the time complexity of $O(n^4)$ for an input RNA sequence of length n. On the other hand, a postprocess may enable us to improve the alignment accuracy. The multiple alignment in Fig. 6 is less dense than that of Rfam. This is because, unlike existing biological methods, the ARNAS progressive approach cannot align both single and paired ones into one column, and because it is not the case that two parts of an RNA structures which belong to different ARNAS components are aligned to an ARNAS component of another. It is an undeniable fact, however, that the restriction makes a large contribution towards the feasibility of the system by reducing the search domain of alignments. A post-process which applies sequence-based alignment methods to low-density regions is a promising approach to solve this problem. Another disadvantage is a problem which all progressive alignment algorithms share: the subalignments are "frozen". Iterative refinement algorithms [20] make it possible to circumvent this. Alignment scores, which are given only empirically in the current system, should be modified so as to capture highly-conserved sequential characterisitics like RESUME and STOP codons in Fig. 6.

References

1. Felden, B., et al.: Probing the structure of the *Escherichia coli* 10Sa RNA (tm-RNA). RNA 3, 89–103 (1997)
2. Dost, B., et al.: Structural alignment of Pseudoknotted RNA. In: Apostolico, A., Guerra, C., Istrail, S., Pevzner, P.A., Waterman, M. (eds.) RECOMB 2006. LNCS (LNBI), vol. 3909, pp. 143–158. Springer, Heidelberg (2006)
3. Dowell, R.D., Eddy, S.R.: Efficient pairwise RNA structure prediction and alignment using sequence alignment constraints. BMC Bioinformatics 7, 400 (2006)
4. Holmes, I., Rubin, G.M.: Pairwise RNA structure comparison with stochastic context-free grammars. Pacif. Symp. Biocomput. 7, 163–174 (2002)
5. Rivas, E., Eddy, S.R.: The language of RNA: a formal grammar that includes pseudoknots. Bioinformatics 16, 334–340 (1999)
6. Sakakibara, Y.: Pair hidden Markov models on tree structures. Bioinformatics 19 (suppl.1), i232–i240 (2003)
7. Joshi, A.K., Levy, L.S., Takahashi, M.: Tree adjunct grammars. J. Comput. Syst. Sci. 10, 136–163 (1975)
8. Uemura, Y., et al.: Tree adjoining grammars for RNA structure prediction. Theor. Comput. Sci. 210, 277–303 (1999)
9. Matsui, H., Sato, K., Sakakibara, Y.: Pair stochastic tree adjoining grammars for aligning and predicting pseudoknot RNA structures. In: Proc. 2004 IEEE Comput. Syst. Bioinf. Conf. (CSB 2004), pp. 1–11 (2004)
10. Seki, S., Kobayashi, S.: A grammatical approach to the alignment of structure-annotated strings. IEICE Trans. Inf. & Syst. E88-D 12, 2727–2737 (2003)
11. Hopcroft, J.E., Motwani, R., Ullman, J.D.: Introduction to Automata Theory, Languages, and Computation. Addison-Wesley, Reading (2001)
12. Jiang, T., Wang, L., Zhang, K.: Alignment of trees - an alternative to tree edit. Theor. Comput. Sci. 143, 137–148 (1995)
13. Reeder, J., Steffen, P., Giegerich, R.: PknotsRG: RNA pseudoknot folding including near-optimal structures and sliding windows. Nucleic Acids Res. 324, W320–W324 (2007)
14. Shapiro, B.: An algorithm for comparing multiple RNA secondary structures. Comput. Applic. Biosci. 4(3), 387–393 (1988)
15. Cannone, J.J., et al.: The comparative RNA Web (CRW) Site: An online database of comparative sequence and structure information for ribosomal, intron, and other RNAs. BioMed. Cent. Bioinf. 3(15) (2002), http://www.rna.icmb.utexas.edu
16. Jiang, T., Wang, L., Zhang, K.: A general edit distance between RNA structures. In: Proc. 5th a. Int. Conf. Comput. Molec. Biol. (RECOMB 2001), pp. 211–220 (2001)
17. Feng, D.-F., Doolittle, R.F.: Progressive sequence alignment as a prerequisite to correct phylogenetic trees. J. Molec. Evolution 25, 351–360 (1987)
18. Höchsmann, M., Voss, B., Giegrich, R.: Pure multiple RNA secondary structure alignments: a progressive profile approach. IEEE/ACM Trans. Comput. Biol. Bioinform. 1, 53–62 (2004)
19. Griffiths-Jones, S., et al.: Rfam: annotating non-coding RNAs in complete genomes. Nucl. Acids Res. 33, D121–D124 (2005)
20. Barton, G.J., Sternberg, M.J.E.: A strategy for the rapid multiple alignment of protein sequences. J. Molec. Biol. 198, 327–337 (1987)

Asymmetric Interaction in Non-equilibrium Dissipative System towards Dynamics for Biological System

Yuki Sugiyama

Department of Complex Systems Science, Nagoya University, Nagoya 464-8601, Japan

Abstract. What is a physical system for describing dynamics of biological systems? A candidate is a non-equilibrium dissipative system with asymmetric interaction. A minimal model formulated with Newtonian equation of particles in such a system is presented and analyzed mathematically and numerically. Through the investigations of models, we show general properties in such systems.

1 Physical Properties for Biological Systems

From the physical viewpoint a biological system is a non-equilibrium dissipative system, where many "particles" such as organisms, cells, or bio-molecules move dynamically with some interactions. The energy flows through the system and is not conserved. In such a many-particle system, a non-trivial macroscopic phenomenon appears on the non-equilibrium balance due to the effect of collective motions of particles. General characteristic properties of behaviors in such systems are, i) dynamical phase transition (bifurcation) to a non-trivial state, ii) emergence of macroscopic spatial scale (pattern formation), iii) emergence of macroscopic temporal scale (rhythm), iv) power law behavior of fluctuations, etc. We should search a physical system of many particles which provide these aspects for macroscopic phenomena.

2 Mathematical Model of Asymmetric Interaction in Dissipative System

The physical aspects for biological systems fully appear in a mathematical model, so called the Optimal Velocity Model [1995][1996]. The OV model is a simple Newtonian system of particles in nonlinear asymmetric interaction with dissipative (viscous) term, which has been first introduced as a model for traffic flow. We call such a system in general as simply "Asymmetric Dissipative System (ADS)".

For the purpose of clarifying general properties for ADS, we investigate a simple model of 1-dimensional interacting particles with dissipative term formulated as

$$m\frac{d^2 x_n}{dt^2} = V(\Delta x_n) - W(\Delta x_{n-1}) - \epsilon\frac{dx_n}{dt}, \qquad (1)$$

Y. Suzuki et al. (Eds.): IWNC 2007, PICT 1, pp. 189–200, 2009.

where x_n is the position of the nth particle, and $\Delta x_n = x_{n+1} - x_n$ is the headway distance. m is a control parameter for inertia, such as mass, typical relaxation time, or sensitivity. $V(\Delta x_n)$, so called OV-function, determines the interaction with a particle ahead. $W(\Delta x_{n-1})$ is the interaction with a particle behind. Here, we remark that they are not the same function in general. If $W = V$, the system consists of ordinal nonlinear-interacting particles, where the action-reaction principle is satisfied and the total momentum is conserved. If $W \neq V$, we break the "symmetry" in interactions, hence the action-reaction principle and the total momentum-conservation are no more satisfied. We call it "asymmetric interaction". The freedom from the restriction of energy-momentum conservation open the new world in non-equilibrium dynamics. This type of interaction can not be permitted in the material systems in traditional physics, but can be seen in dynamics of self-driven particles in social, chemical, and biological systems[1]. In the case that $W = V$ and switching off the dissipation $\epsilon = 0$, the model is reduced to the system satisfying both momentum and energy conservation, such as an ordinal nonlinear-interacting oscillator systems, (e.g. Toda Lattice).

3 Basic Properties of Dynamics in Asymmetric Dissipative System (ADS)

3.1 Linear Stability of a Trivial State and Dispersion Relation

We investigate the stability of a trivial solution of the model (1); particles are distributed uniformly with the same distance b (or the average density of particles), and they are stationary or moving with the same velocity. For this purpose we derive the dispersion relation for the linear equation of motion for a small deviation $y_n = \exp(ink + zt)$, where $z(k) = ikz_1 + (ik)^2 z_2 + o(k)^3$ by long wave-length (small k) expansion, beyond the trivial solution. The result is

$$z(k) = ik\frac{\{V'(b) - W'(b)\}}{\epsilon}$$
$$+ k^2 \left\{ \frac{2m\{V'(b) - W'(b)\}^2}{\{V'(b) + W'(b)\}\epsilon^2} - 1 \right\} \frac{\{V'(b) + W'(b)\}}{2\epsilon} + o(k^3), \quad (2)$$

where V', W' are the derivatives of V, W and supposed to be positive. Whether the coefficient of k^2-term is positive or negative determines that the trivial solution is unstable or stable, which is controlled by m and b. In general the stability increases for $W \neq 0$ [2001] in comparison with the original OV model ($W = 0$). For the symmetric interaction with dissipation ($W = V, \epsilon \neq 0$), it is absolutely stable for arbitrary b. Inversely say, the asymmetry of interaction induces the instability controlled by b. If we switch off the dissipation keeping the asymmetry ($W \neq V, \epsilon = 0$), the behavior becomes singular, meaning that the asymmetric

---

[1] The model of this type was introduced as the forward-backward looking OV model for traffic flow [2001]. In the case that $W = 0$ and $\epsilon = 1$, the model is reduced to the original OV model (the extremely asymmetric model).

interaction has a significance as long as coexisting with dissipation. The coexistence can lead to a non-trivial dynamical behavior for a dissipative system. If we tune the limit of $W \to V$ and $\epsilon \to 0$ with the ratio fixed as Eq.(3), the k^2-term vanishes and the dispersion of harmonic-oscillator chain is reproduced.

$$z(k) = \pm ik\sqrt{V'(b)/m} + o(k^3) \tag{3}$$

3.2 Dynamical Phase Transition Controlled by Particle-Density

Here we investigate the original OV model for the purpose of studying general properties of ADS, where we choose the OV-function as

$$V(\Delta x) = \tanh(\Delta x - d) + \tanh d, \ (d > 0). \tag{4}$$

The model has the homogeneous flow solution, in which particles are moving uniformly distributed with the same velocity $V(b)$, where $b = L/N$ is the average distance, or 1/particle-density. (N is the number of particles and L is the length of 1-dimesional periodic space). The homogeneous flow is linearly unstable under the condition [1995][1996]

$$2mV'(b) > 1, \tag{5}$$

which is derived from Eq.(2) with $W = 0, \epsilon = 1$. In this case, the homogeneous flow solution can not be maintained any more. Instead, a cluster as a non-trivial solution as shown in Fig.1 (Left), is spontaneously formed. The change in the stability of the two solutions controlled by the particle-density is caused by the effect of collective motions of particles in the asymmetric interaction.

3.3 Emergence of a Moving Cluster

In a cluster flow solution, a particle leaving the front of the cluster and another particle joining the back, makes the cluster itself travel backwards like a solitary wave as Fig.1 (Left).

Profile of Cluster Flow Solution as a "Limit Cycle". We recognize the profile of a cluster flow solution by the trajectory of particles in the phase space of headway and velocity $(\Delta x_n, v_n)$ in Fig.1 (Right). In the cluster flow solution all particles are moving along the specific loop, which is a kind of limit cycle [1995][1996]. The limit cycle shows the non-equilibrium balance of in-and-out flow of particles through a cluster.

Induced Characteristic Time. Particles move in the same way with the time-delay τ, which is a characteristic temporal scale induced by the effect of collective dynamics. It determines any characteristic behavior of a moving cluster. As the result, a macroscopic object (cluster) is formed and moves with its own velocity, $v_c = -\Delta x_c/\tau$, where Δx_c is the particle-distance in a cluster as Fig.1 (Right).

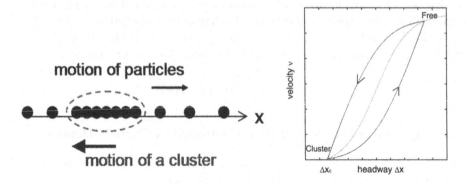

Fig. 1. An emerged cluster and its motion, (Left). The profile of cluster flow solution. 'Free' and 'Cluster' denote free moving region and a cluster, respectively. All particles move along the closed loop in the direction of arrow. Thus, all clusters move backward with the same velocity. A dotted curve represents the OV-function, (Right).

3.4   Properties of Dynamical Phase Transition

Phase Diagram and Hopf Bifurcation. Figure 2 (Left) is the phase diagram of the OV model in the parameter space of b (1/density) and $1/m$ (1/mass). The space is divided into three phases corresponding to three states: (i) The homogeneous flow solution is stable. (iii) Only the cluster flow solution is stable. (ii) Both solutions are stable, (meta-stable phase). Figure 2 (Right) shows that the transition has the property of Hoph bifurcation controlled by the parameter m. For $m < m_c = 0.5$, a limit cycle disappears and only the trivial solution exists. The existence of phase-(ii) indicates sub-critical Hopf bifurcation.

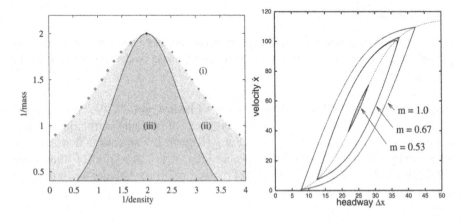

Fig. 2. The phase diagram of the OV model. The bold curve is derived from the analysis of the linear stability of the trivial solution, (Left). The variation for m-dependency of limit cycles. $m_c = 0.5$ is in the case of $d = 2$ in the OV-function (4), (Right).

Asymmetric Interaction and Hopf Bifurcation. A Hopf bifurcation in ADS originates from asymmetric interaction. Let $z \equiv \sigma - i\omega$, where σ and ω are real and imaginary parts of the eigen value of the linearized equation for Eq.(1). They satisfy the following relations as

$$\begin{cases} m(\sigma^2 - \omega^2) = (V'(b) + W'(b)) \cos \theta - \sigma, \\ -2m\sigma\omega = (V'(b) - W'(b)) \sin \theta + \omega. \end{cases} \tag{6}$$

If the interaction is symmetric $V = W$, $\omega = 0$ is the only solution, thus no imaginary eigen value. In contrast, the interaction is asymmetric $V \neq W$, Eq.(6) is reduced to the equation for ω^2, which always has the positive solution. Thus, the eigen values are the pure imaginary conjugate solutions at the bifurcation point $\sigma = 0$. This means Hopf bifurcation. In general, ADS always shows Hopf bifurcation at the transition point. The inverse statement is a very interesting question. If Hopf bifurcation appears in a macroscopic phenomenon, there exists some dynamics of asymmetric interaction in the underlying microscopic system?

3.5 Power Law Behavior

Probability Distribution of Cluster-Size. Clusters emerged in the OV model have various sizes. Figure 3 shows the probability distribution of cluster-size, which is defined by the number of particles in a cluster. $P(x)$ denotes the probability for the existence of cluster size larger than x. In the results of simulations, we observe the power-law behavior as $P(x) \propto x^{-\gamma}$, where $\gamma \sim 1$, (Zipf's law).

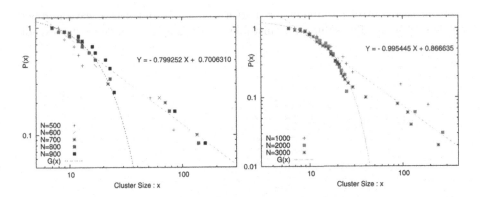

Fig. 3. Distribution of cluster-size. The vertical axis is $P(x)$, and the horizontal axis is the size of cluster. A Straight line denotes a power-low, comparing with the reference curve of Gaussian distribution. $N = 500 \sim 900$ (Left), $N = 1000 \sim 3000$ (Right).

Spectrum of the Fluctuations in Density. The temporal spectra of the fluctuations in the density of particles also obey the power law. $I(k)$ denotes the amplitude of spectrum k, where k is the wave-number of particle-density. We observe the power-law behavior as $I(k) \propto k^{-\beta}$, where $\beta \sim 1.4$ as in Fig.4.

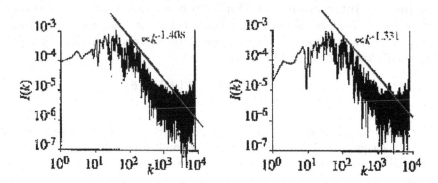

Fig. 4. The temporal spectra in the density. The vertical axis is $I(k)$, and the horizontal axis is the wave-number. A straight line denotes a power-low. $\beta = 1.408$ for noise level 0.3 (Left), $\beta = 1.331$ for noise level 0.06 (Right).

4   Other Specific Properties of Dynamics in ADS

4.1   Dependence of Particle-Number N in ADS

Instability Emerges in $N \geq 3$. The instability of the trivial solution is analyzed for each mode of density-wave. The condition for unstable mode is

$$a < 2V'(b) \cos^2 \frac{k}{2}, \quad k = \frac{2\pi}{N} n, \ (n = 0, 1, 2, \cdots, N-1), \qquad (7)$$

where a is a control parameter for inertia $a = m^{-1}$, and k is a wave number for density-wave. The solution is unstable even if only one mode exists (except

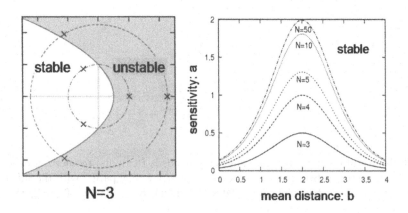

Fig. 5. Each mode k is presented in the polar coordinates $(r, \theta) = (1/a, k)$ for two different values of a in $N = 3$, for example. The critical curve is $1/r = 2V'(b) \cos^2 \theta$, (Left). Phase diagram of the linear stability for the trivial solution for give N. Critical curve is derived from the condition for the existence of unstable mode, (Right).

zero-mode, $k = 0$) in the unstable region (the shaded region) in Fig.5 (Left). For $N = 2$, it is impossible for any mode satisfying the condition. In contrast, if $N \geq 3$, such a mode can exist for taking a small enough value of sensitivity parameter a (large radius). The instability can occur in the system that consists of only three particles, $N = 3$. The unstable region in control-parameter space (a, b) extends as N increases. The smaller-N system is more stable in the trivial state (the homogeneous flow solution) as shown in Fig.5 (Right).

Emergence of a Cluster in $N = 3$. When the homogeneous flow solution is unstable, the state of cluster flow becomes stable even for $N = 3$ as in Fig.6. The profile of the solution is clearly shown as a limit cycle, and qualitatively the same as the cluster flow for the system of large-N particles in Fig.1.

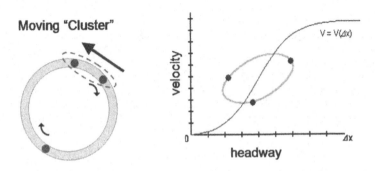

Fig. 6. A snapshot of a two-particle cluster moving backward opposed to the direction of particles moving in a circular track, (Left). The limit cycle profile of the cluster flow solution in $N = 3$, drawn together with the OV-function, (Right).

Small-N Is Large Enough as Many-Particle System. First, we remind that the difference in phase diagram for N shrinks rapidly as in Fig.5 (Right) (Compare the cases for $N = 3, \cdots, 10, 50$, and $N \to \infty$ as Fig.2 (Left).)

The solution of the emerged moving cluster is exactly obtained in $N = 2, 3, 4, \cdots$, for the model of choosing the Heviside step-function as the OV-function, such that $V(\Delta x) = 0$ for $\Delta x < d$ and $V(\Delta x) = v_{max}$ for $\Delta x \geq d$, [2007]. The velocity of a cluster v_c is obtained by using the value of τ for given a as

$$v_c = -\frac{d - \frac{1}{2}v_{max}\tau}{\tau}. \tag{8}$$

The characteristic time τ in arbitrary N is obtained as the solution of $a\tau$ (dimensionless value) for the following equation,

$$a\tau(1 + e^{-\frac{N}{2}a\tau}) = 2(1 - e^{-a\tau}). \tag{9}$$

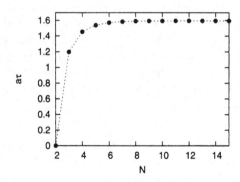

Fig. 7. N-dependence of the solution $a\tau$ of Eq.(9)

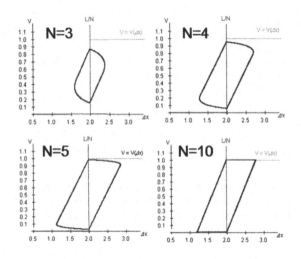

Fig. 8. The dependence of the number of particles N for limit cycle in the case for fixed $b = d$ and fixed a. Heviside step-function as OV-function is drawn together.

The solution $a\tau$ of Eq.(9) depends on N as in Fig.7. For $N = 10$ the value $a\tau$ is almost the same as for $N = \infty$. [2] Thus, $N = 10$ is large enough number for the system to quantitatively have the same behavior as that of $N = \infty$.

Figure 8 shows limit cycles for given N. We remark that the shape of limit cycle depends on the number of particles N and the density b in general, even for a fixed a. The difference among limit cycles shrinks rapidly as N increases. Actually the limit cycle for $N = 10$ is not different from that for $N = \infty$, which is obtained in the previous work [1997]. For large enough N the limit cycle is

---

[2] If we put the limit $N \to \infty$, the equation (9) is reduced to the result of the previous work, which solution is $a\tau = 1.59..$ [1997].

unique for given a, not depends on b. [3] We recognize that $N = 10$ is already large enough in the OV model by Fig.8 as well as by Fig.7. We can naturally guess that the dynamical behaviors in ADS for "small number" of particles, are essentially the same as a many-body system for "large number" of particles.

4.2   Properties of Emerged Objects and Patterns

Similarity Between Temporal and Spatial Structures. Similarity between the temporal structure in the process of emerging patterns and the spatial structure of stable patterns is observed in nature, such as biological development, growth of plants, morphogenesis, etc. Such a kind of the phenomenon can be observed in ADS. The simulation of the OV model shows the temporal process of forming a cluster in periodic boundary with homogeneous condition, Fig.9 (Left) [1995], and the stable structure of flow emerged in an open system with the "bottleneck" (the suppression of flow), Fig.9 (Right) [2000][2003]. After the relaxation time three distinct spatial patterns of flow are formed upstream of a bottleneck; a uniform flow, an "oscillatory wave flow", and a cluster flow. Comparing the results of two simulations, the similarity is clearly observed. Can we explain that this similarity is observed as a general property in dissipative non-equilibrium systems and originated in asymmetric interactions ? [2007]

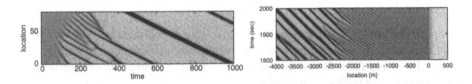

Fig. 9. Space-time plot of cluster formation. The vertical axis is location on the circuit. The horizontal axis is time evolution, (Left). The stable spatial patterns of particle flow on the upstream of a bottleneck after the relaxation time. The bottleneck is placed at 0-point, and the length is 100. Particles move from left to right, (Right).

Variety of Patterns for Emerged Objects. In the 2-dimensional OV model, a big variety of patterns can be created in group formations, such as collective bio-motions, by changing only two control-parameters and the number of particles. We show several typical pattern formations in Fig.10. In general, the homogeneous flow is not stable in 2-dimensional space even for a system of a small number of particles (low density), even if a tiny attractive interaction exists. The system transits to the state of the emergence of localized patterns in the result of the stability caused by the effect of collective motions. The following behavior by the attractive force and the exclusion behavior by the repulsive

---

[3] The qualitative difference exists depending on $b < d$, $b = d$, $b > d$ for a fixed N. However, any difference vanishes for large enough N. Note that the stability of a limit cycle depends on b.

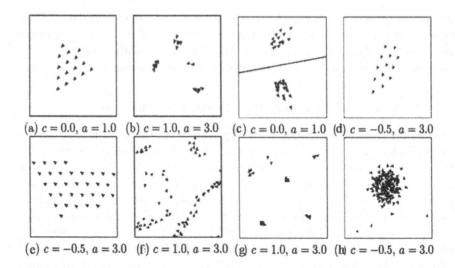

(a) $c = 0.0, a = 1.0$ (b) $c = 1.0, a = 3.0$ (c) $c = 0.0, a = 1.0$ (d) $c = -0.5, a = 3.0$

(e) $c = -0.5, a = 3.0$ (f) $c = 1.0, a = 3.0$ (g) $c = 1.0, a = 3.0$ (h) $c = -0.5, a = 3.0$

Fig. 10. The typical patterns of emerged objects in the 2-dim. OV model. Each triangle represents a particle and its direction of movement. Two types of model; the interaction with all particles within the area, (c)(d)(g)(h), and the nearest-neighbor interaction, (a)(b)(e)(f). The upper group-patterns are emerged in the system with the total particle number $N = 15$, and the lower patterns are for $N = 100$, in the fixed size of space.

force are naturally separated only by extending the dimensionality of space. The parameter c is introduced for controlling the distance dominated by the attractive or repulsive forces, in addition to $a = m^{-1}$ (sensitivity or inertia) and the number of particles N or density.

Random Motion of Deterministic System and Rapid Response. An emerged object in Fig.10 (b)(c)(f)(g), moves randomly in the optimized state after the relaxation time, though the system is a deterministic process with no noise. Groups easily decay by the collision with each other, but they exchange particles through the collision and easily rearrange the member of particles and reform new groups. These behaviors are caused by the high degeneracy of states, those have the same energy, corresponding to the continuum degree of freedom in the deformation of a macroscopic object. The degeneracy also leads to the rapid response of an object to a stimulus. Actually, a group as Fig.10(e) changes the direction of motion very rapidly according to a tiny external flow, and move collectively in the direction of the external flow.

High Degeneracy of Emerged Patterns and Hidden Symmetry. These specific behaviors of emerged objects in non-equilibrium dissipative system are representations of high degeneracy of states in ADS. This high degeneracy may indicate an underlying hidden local symmetry, "gauge symmetry".

4.3   Natural Computing Simulated by ADS

If the particles have high sensitivity (large a) and attractive interactions in ADS, the collective motion of such particles shows the string-like patterns wandering randomly as in Fig.11 (Left). These units can form several patterns with a large variation according to given conditions. Fig.11 (Right) looks like a pattern of a trail of ants, or a network formed by true slime moulds. They can choose the most adaptive shape of pattern as solving the variational problem of geometry in mathematics. This indicates a very interesting possibility that such natural computations can be simulated by the motions in many-particle system of ADS.

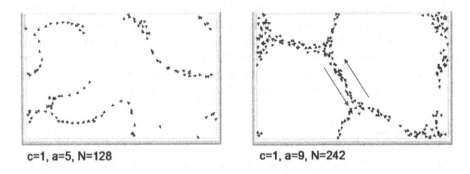

| c=1, a=5, N=128 | c=1, a=9, N=242 |

Fig. 11. The patterns emerged in collective motions for high-sensitivity particles with the attractive interaction in the 2-dim. OV model, (Left). The OV-particles occasionally form a pattern in quasi-stable state. The red arrows mean that a counter flow of particles is formed. The pattern looks like a solution of "Steiner problem", (Right).

5   Summary and Discussion

Summarizing the results of investigations, especially for OV model as the simplest model, we can guess and provide characteristic properties for ADS (a non-equilibrium dissipative system with asymmetric interaction) in general. They are sharply contrasted with properties of equilibrium systems with symmetric interactions, energy-momentum conserved systems.

In ADS, there exists the inseparable connection between the asymmetry of interaction and dissipation. If the dissipation is switched off and only the asymmetry of interaction exists, the system is singular. While, the dissipation with symmetric interaction leads the system to a stationary state, which is no interesting for non-equilibrium dynamics. If and only if both the asymmetry and dissipation coexist, the system shows a non-trivial dynamics in non-equilibrium physics. In this system, a particle-density or a number of particles is a control parameter for the instability of a trivial state and the dynamical phase transition to a non-trivial state. The transition emerges even in a small-N particle system (e.g. $N \geq 3$ in OV model). In contrast, a phase transition never controlled by a density or a number of particles in energy-momentum conserved systems.

Strictly say, the transition appears in the infinite degree of freedom ($N = \infty$) in such equilibrium systems. In ADS, the system of a "small number" of particles can be regarded as the system of a "large number" in the meaning that it shows the same behavior as that of infinite number of particles both qualitatively and quantitatively.

Moreover, there are several interesting properties in emerged macroscopic phenomena in ADS. The similarity between temporal and spatial structures exists in emerged patterns. The big variety of emerged macroscopic objects is observed, which is controlled by a few parameters. Random motion in the deterministic process and rapid response of emerged object are remarkable properties in ADS. They are caused by the degeneracy of states in the continuum degree of freedom for the deformation of a macroscopic object. Such a kind of high degeneracy is usually connected to a local symmetry. In equilibrium systems with energy-momentum conservation, the phase transition is originated in a global symmetry using the rigid infinite number of particles. Comparing with the conventional physical systems, a lot of new physical aspects appeared in ADS indicate that ADS is a good candidate for dynamics of biological systems.

References

[1995]   Bando, M., Hasebe, K., Nakayama, A., Shibata, A., Sugiyama, Y.: Dynamical Model of Traffic Congestion and Numerical Simulation. Phys. Rev. E 51, 1035–1042 (1995); Japan J. of Ind. and Appl. Math. 11, 203–223 (1994)

[1996]   Sugiyama, Y.: Dynamical Model for Congestion of Freeway Traffic and its Structural Stability. In: Wolf, D.E., Schreckenberg, M., Bachem, A. (eds.) Proceedings of International Workshop of Traffic and Granular Flow in Juelich, pp. 137–149. World Scientific, Singapore (1996)

[2001]   Nakayama, A., Sugiyama, Y., Hasebe, K.: Effect of looking at the car that follows in an optimal velocity model of traffic flow. Phys. Rev. E 65, 016112 (2001)

[1997]   Sugiyama, Y., Yamada, H.: Simple and Exactly Solvable Model for Queue Dynamics. Physical Review E 55, 7749–7752 (1997)

[2007]   Sugiyama, Y., Masuoka, K., Ishida, T.: in preparation

[2000]   Mitarai, N., Nakanishi, H.: Spatiotemporal Structure of Traffic Flow in a System with an Open Boundary. Phys. Rev. Lett. 85, 1766–1769 (2000)

[2003]   Sugiyama, Y., Nakayama, A.: Modeling, simulation and observations for freeway traffic and pedestrians. In: Emmerich, H., Nestler, B., Schreckenberg, M. (eds.) Computational Physics of Transport and Interface Dynamics, pp. 406–421. Springer, Heidelberg (2003)

[2007]   Akiyama, R., Watanabe, H., Sugiyama, Y.: in preparation

Design and Numerical Analysis of RNA Oscillator

Masahiro Takinoue[1], Daisuke Kiga[2], Koh-ichiroh Shohda[1], and Akira Suyama[1]

[1] Department of Life Sciences and Institute of Physics, The University of Tokyo,
3-8-1 Komaba, Meguro-ku, Tokyo 153-8902, Japan
`takinoue@genta.c.u-tokyo.ac.jp`, `takinoue@chem.scphys.kyoto-u.ac.jp`
[2] Department of Computational Intelligence and System Science, Tokyo Institute of
Technology, 4259 Nagatsuta-cho, Midori-ku, Yokohama, Kanagawa 226-8503, Japan
`suyama@dna.c.u-tokyo.ac.jp`

Abstract. In recent years, various types of DNA nanomachines driven
by DNA hybridizations have been developed as one of remarkable applications of DNA computer for nanotechnology. Here, we propose an
oscillator as a nanosystem to control the nanomachines. It was modeled after a circadian rhythm in life systems and utilized DNA/RNA
and their molecular reactions. The molecular reactions were composed
of nucleic-acid hybridization, RNA transcription, DNA extension, RNA
degradation, and uracil-containing DNA degradation. Results of numerical analyses of rate equations for the reactions demonstrated that oscillatory condition of the system was decided by balance between RNA influx
into the system and RNA degradation out of the system. The analytical
results will provide much important information when the oscillator is
constructed in *in vitro* experiments.

1 Introduction

A DNA computer is a bio-inspired computing machine that can process information using DNA molecular reactions. DNA has a unique property, that is,
it hybridizes with its complementary strand through a highly specific hydrogen
bond, which allows an accurate replication of genetic information. In 1994, Adleman demonstrated that the property can be also used for parallel computation
to solve combinatorial problems [1]. At the beginning, the DNA computer attracted attention as a parallel computer that might exceed electric computers,
but much attention is currently focused on its direct interface with biological
molecules. Therefore the DNA computer has been applied for biotechnology and
nanotechnology in recent years [2,3,4,5].

Various types of DNA nanomachines have been developed as one of the applications of DNA computer for nanotechnology [6,7,8,9,10,11,12,13,14]. The
nanomachines are constructed with DNA molecules and exploit a DNA hybridization as a trigger of their movement. The trigger DNA molecule is called a
DNA fuel. Most of the nanomachines require step-by-step injections of microliter
solution including DNA fuels, so that they are non-autonomous nanomachines.

Y. Suzuki et al. (Eds.): IWNC 2007, PICT 1, pp. 201–212, 2009.

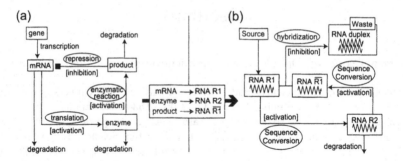

Fig. 1. Design of RNA oscillator. (a) Reaction model of circadian rhythm. The feedback circuit generates oscillation. (b) Outline of RNA oscillator. mRNA, enzyme, and product in (a) are changed into RNA R1, R2, and $\overline{\text{R1}}$, respectively.

External nanosystems to control nanomachines are required to run autonomously the non-autonomous nanomachines though autonomously-moving nanomachines [12,13,14] or DNA fuels for free-running nanomachines [15,16] have also been developed. From this point of view, we are developing an autonomously oscillating system available for actuating the non-autonomous nanomachines periodically. Here, we report the design and analysis of the oscillating system.

2   Design of RNA Oscillator

Many biochemical oscillatory systems have been studied up to the present. One of the best-studied oscillatory reactions is a circadian rhythm in a living cell. A reaction model of the circadian rhythm is shown in Fig. 1a. First, an mRNA is transcribed from a gene. Second, an enzyme is translated from the mRNA. Third, a product is created with the enzyme. Finally, the product represses the mRNA transcription from the gene. That is to say, increase of mRNA activates increase of enzyme, and the increase of enzyme activates increase of product, but the increase of product inhibits the increase of mRNA. The feedback circuit including two activation reactions and one inhibition reaction can generate oscillation of the biomolecules [17].

An outline of oscillatory reaction proposed here is shown in Fig. 1b. It was modeled after the circadian rhythm, so that it includes two activation reactions and one inhibition reaction in a similar way. RNA R1, RNA R2, and RNA $\overline{\text{R1}}$ correspond to the mRNA, enzyme, and product in Fig. 1a, respectively. This reaction system has potential to oscillate the three RNA molecules. First, R1 is generated from a source. Second, R2 is created from R1 by an RNA-sequence conversion reaction. Third, $\overline{\text{R1}}$ is created from R2 by an RNA-sequence conversion reaction likewise. Finally, $\overline{\text{R1}}$ inhibits increase of R1 by hybridization with each other because $\overline{\text{R1}}$ has a complementary sequence of R1. In addition, degradation of R2 is introduced in order to prevent divergence of R2 amount.

The detail of RNA-sequence conversion reaction is shown in Fig. 2. R1 is an RNA before conversion and R2 is an RNA after conversion. R2 is produced from

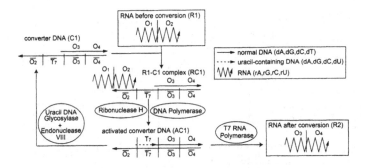

Fig. 2. RNA-sequence conversion reaction. RNA R1 is converted to RNA R2 through a series of molecular reactions.

R1 through a series of molecular reactions. At the beginning, R1 hybridizes with a converter DNA C1 and they form an R1-C1 complex RC1. R1 is a concatemer of sequences O_1 and O_2, and C1 has $\overline{O_2}$ sequence complementary to O_1, so that they can hybridize with each other. RC1 is turned into an activated converter DNA AC1 with two enzymes, a DNA polymerase and an ribonuclease H. The DNA polymerase can synthesize a complementary DNA strand using its opposite strand as template. Here, the DNA polymerase synthesizes T_7 sequence complementary to $\overline{T_7}$. The ribonuclease H has an activity to degrade an RNA strand of DNA/RNA hybrid selectively. Here, RNA strand O_2 of RC1 is degraded. The reactions with the two enzymes proceed at the same instant. R2 is transcribed from AC1 with T7 RNA polymerase. This enzyme can synthesize an RNA strand using a double-stranded DNA as template. The synthesis starts only when the T7 RNA polymerase recognizes a double-stranded T7 promoter sequence T_7. Here, the T7 RNA polymerase can recognize only AC1 but cannot recognize C1 and RC1 because T7 promoters of C1 and RC1 are single-stranded sequences.

AC1 returns to C1 with two enzymes, a uracil DNA glycosylase and an endonuclease VIII. In cooperation with the endonuclease VIII, the uracil DNA glycosylase can degrade a uracil-containing DNA, which is a DNA molecule containing uracil bases in spite of thymine bases. Here, the two enzymes degrade only the sequence T_7 of AC1 because only T_7 includes uracil bases but the other part of AC1 uses thymine bases not uracil bases. The uracil bases are introduced into T_7 of AC1 when the DNA polymerase synthesizes T_7 at the step from RC1 to AC1 because the synthesis proceeds in a reaction solution with uracil bases without thymine bases.

The production of R2 depends on the initial amount of R1. If R1 is present, C1 turns into AC1 through a DNA/RNA hybridization and enzymatic reactions with a DNA polymerase and a ribonuclease H. AC1 produces R2 with a T7 RNA polymerase. This reaction continues while R1 exists. However, the creation of AC1 stop after R1 is exhausted through the reactions themselves. As a result, R2 cannot be generated because AC1 disappears by returning to C1 with a uracil DNA glycosylase and an endonuclease VIII. Therefore, R2 is produced depending on the initial amount of R1.

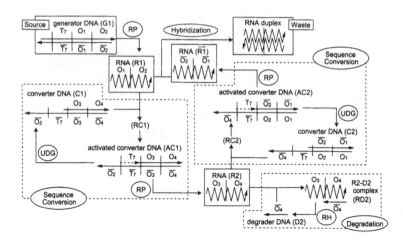

Fig. 3. Whole reaction of RNA oscillator. This feedback circuit can generate oscillation.

Figure 3 shows a whole reaction of an RNA oscillator. The whole reaction model is obtained by applying the detailed reaction of Fig. 2 to the outline of Fig. 1b. R1 is always generated from a generator DNA G1 by RNA transcription with a T7 RNA polymerase. R2 is produced from R1 by the sequence conversion reaction. RC1 is omitted in the sequence conversion reaction of Fig. 3. Since a creation rate of AC1 from RC1 is very high in the case that a DNA polymerase is present enough, it is unnecessary to consider RC1. $\overline{R1}$ is produced from R2 by the sequence conversion reaction likewise. In this sequence conversion reaction, R2 hybridizes with a converter DNA C2, and they form R2-C2 complex RC2, and then RC2 turn into AC2 that can transcribe $\overline{R1}$. RC2 is also omitted because of the same reason as RC1. $\overline{R1}$ reduces the amount of R1 by hybridization because $\overline{R1}$ has a complementary sequence of R1. Moreover, R2 is gradually degraded by a degrader DNA D2. R2 hybridizes with D2 and they turn into a DNA/RNA hybrid RD2. RNA strand O_4 in RD2 is degraded with a ribonuclease H. The degradation is necessary to prevent too much increase of R2.

3   Simulation Model

The reaction model in Fig. 3 can be described by rate equations for DNA/RNA molecules as follows. R1 is generated from G1 with a T7 RNA polymerase, and it is reduced by hybridization with C1 and $\overline{R1}$. The enzymatic reaction with T7 RNA polymerase is represented using an assumption of the Michaelis-Menten model:

$$E_{RP} + G1 \underset{k_{2RP}}{\overset{k_{1RP}}{\rightleftharpoons}} E_{RP}G1 \xrightarrow{k_{3RP}} E_{RP} + G1 + R1, \tag{1}$$

where E_{RP} indicates the T7 RNA polymerase, and k_{1RP}, k_{2RP}, and k_{3RP} mean its rate constants. The rate equation for the enzymatic reaction is described as

$$\frac{d[R1]}{dt} = \frac{k_{catRP}[E_{RP}]_T[G1]}{K_{mRP} + [G1]}, \tag{2}$$

where $[\mathrm{E_{RP}}]_T$ is a total concentration of T7 RNA polymerase. k_{catRP} and K_{mRP} are Michaelis-Menten parameters for T7 RNA polymerase, which are defined as

$$k_{\mathrm{catRP}} \equiv k_{\mathrm{3RP}}, \quad K_{\mathrm{mRP}} \equiv \frac{k_{\mathrm{2RP}} + k_{\mathrm{3RP}}}{k_{\mathrm{1RP}}}. \tag{3}$$

R1 produced from G1 hybridizes with C1. If the two-state model is assumed for nucleic-acid hybridizations, the hybridization between R1 and C1 is represented as

$$\mathrm{R1 + C1} \xrightarrow{k} \mathrm{RC1}, \tag{4}$$

where k is a hybridization rate. Since it is assumed that oscillation reaction is carried out under the condition that the double strand RC1 is stable, the back reaction from RC1 to R1 + C1 is not considered here. In addition, RC1 can be omitted in the case that a DNA polymerase is present enough as explained already. Therefore, the hybridization between R1 and C1 can be rewritten as

$$\mathrm{R1 + C1} \xrightarrow{k} \mathrm{AC1}. \tag{5}$$

Rate equations for the hybridization are given by

$$\frac{d[\mathrm{R1}]}{dt} = -k[\mathrm{R1}][\mathrm{C1}], \tag{6}$$

$$\frac{d[\mathrm{C1}]}{dt} = -k[\mathrm{R1}][\mathrm{C1}], \tag{7}$$

$$\frac{d[\mathrm{AC1}]}{dt} = k[\mathrm{R1}][\mathrm{C1}]. \tag{8}$$

In a similar way, rate equations for hybridization between R1 and $\overline{\mathrm{R1}}$ are described as

$$\frac{d[\mathrm{R1}]}{dt} = -k[\mathrm{R1}][\overline{\mathrm{R1}}], \tag{9}$$

$$\frac{d[\overline{\mathrm{R1}}]}{dt} = -k[\mathrm{R1}][\overline{\mathrm{R1}}]. \tag{10}$$

The whole rate equation for R1 is obtained by combining Eqs. (2), (6), and (9). Therefore, a normalized rate equation for R1 is given by

$$\frac{du_{\mathrm{R1}}}{d\tau} = \frac{\nu_{\mathrm{RP}} c_{\mathrm{G1}}}{\kappa_{\mathrm{RP}} + c_{\mathrm{G1}}} - u_{\mathrm{R1}} u_{\mathrm{C1}} - u_{\mathrm{R1}} u_{\overline{\mathrm{R1}}}, \tag{11}$$

where the first, second, and third terms are contributions from Eqs. (2), (6), and (9), respectively. The nucleic acids concentrations, time, and enzymatic parameters in Eq. (11) are normalized as

$$u_{\mathrm{R1}} \equiv \frac{[\mathrm{R1}]}{[\mathrm{C1}]_T}, \quad u_{\overline{\mathrm{R1}}} \equiv \frac{[\overline{\mathrm{R1}}]}{[\mathrm{C1}]_T}, \quad c_{\mathrm{G1}} \equiv \frac{[\mathrm{G1}]}{[\mathrm{C1}]_T}, \quad \tau \equiv \frac{t}{(k[\mathrm{C1}]_T)^{-1}}, \tag{12}$$

$$\nu_{RP} \equiv \frac{k_{catRP}[E_{RP}]_T}{k[C1]_T{}^2}, \quad \kappa_{RP} \equiv \frac{K_{mRP}}{[C1]_T}, \tag{13}$$

where $[C1]_T$ is a total concentration of C1, namely, $[C1]_T \equiv [C1]+[AC1]$. $[RC1]$ is ignored. The other nucleic acids concentrations and enzymatic parameters in the oscillatory reaction are also normalized in a similar way. In addition, normalized equation for the $[C1]_T$ definition is written as

$$u_{C1} + u_{AC1} = 1, \tag{14}$$

where u_{AC1} is a normalized concentration of AC1. Eq. (14) means a conservation low for C1.

C1 is reduced by hybridization between R1 and C1, and it increases as a result of AC1 degradation with a uracil DNA glycosylase and an endonuclease VIII. A rate equation for the hybridization is represented as Eq. (7). C1 creation by the degradation of AC1 is represented using an assumption of the Michaelis-Menten model likewise:

$$E_{DG} + AC1 \underset{k_{2DG}}{\overset{k_{1DG}}{\rightleftharpoons}} E_{DG}AC1 \xrightarrow{k_{3DG}} E_{DG} + C1, \tag{15}$$

where E_{DG} indicates the uracil DNA glycosylase and k_{1DG}, k_{2DG}, and k_{3DG} mean its rate constants. It is assumed that the enzymatic reaction rate is determined by only the uracil DNA glycosylase because the endonuclease VIII only supports the degradation. A normalized rate equation for C1 creation is given by

$$\frac{du_{C1}}{dt} = \frac{\nu_{DG}u_{AC1}}{\kappa_{DG} + u_{AC1}}, \tag{16}$$

where κ_{DG} and ν_{DG} are normalized Michaelis-Menten parameters for the uracil DNA glycosylase. They are defined in the similar way to Eqs. (3) and (13). From Eqs. (7) and (16), a normalized rate equation for C1 is obtained as

$$\frac{du_{C1}}{d\tau} = -u_{R1}u_{C1} + \frac{\nu_{DG}u_{AC1}}{\kappa_{DG} + u_{AC1}}, \tag{17}$$

where the first term is a contribution from Eq. (7) and the second term is a contribution from Eq. (16). Although AC1 is also involved in the reaction, AC1 kinetics is automatically decided by Eqs. (14) and (17), so that a rate equation for AC1 is not needed.

R2 is produced from AC1 with a T7 RNA polymerase, and it decreased through hybridization with C2 and D2. In a similar way, a normalized rate equation for R2 is described as

$$\frac{du_{R2}}{d\tau} = \frac{\nu_{RP}u_{AC1}}{\kappa_{RP} + u_{AC1}} - u_{R2}u_{C2} - u_{R2}u_{D2}, \tag{18}$$

where the first term means R2 production with the T7 RNA polymerase, and the second and third terms indicate decrease by the hybridization with C2 and D2, respectively.

D2 decreases by the hybridization with R2, while it increases as a result of RD2 degradation with a ribonuclease H. Therefore, a normalized rate equation for D2 is given by

$$\frac{du_{D2}}{d\tau} = -u_{R2}u_{D2} + \frac{\nu_{RH}u_{RD2}}{\kappa_{RH} + u_{RD2}}, \tag{19}$$

where the first term means the hybridization and the second indicates the D2 increase by RD2 degradation with the ribonuclease H. κ_{RH} and ν_{RH} are normalized Michaelis-Menten parameters for the ribonuclease H. They are also defined in the similar way to Eqs. (3) and (13). A total concentration of D2 must be conserved. The conservation low for D2 is given by a normalized equation as

$$u_{D2} + u_{RD2} = c_{D2}, \tag{20}$$

where c_{D2} is a normalized total concentration of D2.

C2 is reduced by the hybridization with R2, while it increases by AC2 degradation with a uracil DNA glycosylase and an endonuclease VIII. Therefore, a normalized rate equation for C2 is described as

$$\frac{du_{C2}}{d\tau} = -u_{R2}u_{C2} + \frac{\nu_{DG}u_{AC2}}{\kappa_{DG} + u_{AC2}}, \tag{21}$$

where the first term is the hybridization and the second means the C2 increase by AC2 degradation. C2 also has a conservation low, which are represented by a normalized equation as

$$u_{C2} + u_{AC2} = 1. \tag{22}$$

A rate equation for AC2 is not needed because AC2 kinetics is also automatically decided by Eqs. (21) and (22).

$\overline{R1}$ is transcribed from AC2 with T7 RNA polymerase and it decreases by the hybridization with R1. A normalized rate equation for $\overline{R1}$ is given by

$$\frac{du_{\overline{R1}}}{d\tau} = \frac{\nu_{RP}u_{AC2}}{\kappa_{RP} + u_{AC2}} - u_{R1}u_{\overline{R1}}, \tag{23}$$

where the first term is the transcription and the second is the hybridization with R1.

The RNA oscillator is described by Eqs. (11), (17), (18), (19), (21), (23) (differential equations) and Eqs. (14), (20), (22) (conservation equations). The differential equations were analyzed using the linear stability analysis, which is a method to investigate a stability of solution of nonlinear differential equations by linearization of the equations around their steady state. If a steady state is stable, a solution of the differential equations converges to the steady state as $\tau \to \infty$. On the other hand, if the steady state is unstable, a solution of the differential equations diverges as $\tau \to \infty$ or oscillates forever in a finite space. When the differential equations of the RNA oscillator are rewritten as

$$\frac{du_i}{d\tau} = f_i(\boldsymbol{u}), \quad i = R1, C1, R2, D2, C2, \overline{R1},$$
$$\boldsymbol{u} \equiv (u_{R1}, u_{C1}, u_{R2}, u_{D2}, u_{C2}, u_{\overline{R1}}), \tag{24}$$

the steady state $\boldsymbol{u}^\circ$ of the differential equations is given by

$$f_i(\boldsymbol{u}^\circ) = 0, \quad i = \text{R1, C1, R2, D2, C2}, \overline{\text{R1}},$$
$$\boldsymbol{u}^\circ \equiv \left(u_{\text{R1}}^\circ, u_{\text{C1}}^\circ, u_{\text{R2}}^\circ, u_{\text{D2}}^\circ, u_{\text{C2}}^\circ, u_{\overline{\text{R1}}}^\circ\right). \tag{25}$$

Eq. (24) is linearized around the steady state as

$$\frac{\mathrm{d}\Delta u_i}{\mathrm{d}\tau} = \sum_j P_{ij}\Delta u_j, \quad P_{ij} \equiv \left.\frac{\partial f_i}{\partial u_j}\right|_{\boldsymbol{u}=\boldsymbol{u}^\circ},$$
$$\Delta u_i \equiv u_i - u_i^\circ, \quad i, j = \text{R1, C1, R2, D2, C2}, \overline{\text{R1}}, \tag{26}$$

where Δu_i is a small perturbation around the steady state and P is called a stability matrix of the differential equations. The stability around the steady state is determined by the eigenvalues λ of P given by

$$|P - \lambda I| = 0 \quad (I : \text{identity matrix}). \tag{27}$$

If $\text{Re}(\lambda) < 0$ for all of the eigen values, the steady state is stable. Thus, a solution of the differential equations converges to the steady state. If the condition is not satisfied, the steady state is unstable. Then a solution of the differential equations diverges or oscillates. The divergence or oscillation of solution cannot be determined by stability of the steady state, so that a long time trajectory of solution of the differential equations must be estimated.

The differential equations were numerically analyzed because they cannot be analytically solved. The steady state $\boldsymbol{u}^\circ$ of the differential equations was calculated using the bisection method. The eigenvalues λ were calculated using LAPACK (Linear Algebra PACKage), which is the most famous library for solving linear algebra problems. To analyze a long time trajectory of solution, bifurcation diagrams and kinetic simulations were used. The bifurcation diagrams were calculated using a software XPPAUT [18] and kinetic simulations were carried out using the fourth order Runge-Kutta method. In all the analyses, an initial condition was set to be $(u_{\text{R1}}, u_{\text{C1}}, u_{\text{R2}}, u_{\text{D2}}, u_{\text{C2}}, u_{\overline{\text{R1}}}) = (0, 1, 0, c_{\text{D2}}, 1, 0)$. c_{D2} varied according to simulation conditions.

The Michaelis-Menten parameters reported in the previous works [19,20,21] were used in the simulation: T7 RNA polymerase ($K_{\text{mRP}} = 0.026~\mu\text{M}$, $k_{\text{catRP}}^* = 54~\text{min}^{-1}$) [19], *Thermus thermophilus* ribonuclease H ($K_{\text{mRH}}^* = 7.8~\mu\text{M}$, $k_{\text{catRH}}^* = 4.9~\text{min}^{-1}$) [20], and uracil DNA glycosylase ($K_{\text{mDG}}^* = 0.129~\mu\text{M}$, $k_{\text{catDG}}^* = 461~\text{min}^{-1}$) [21]. k_{catRP}^* was reported as a rate constant to synthesize one base of RNA, so that k_{cat} per RNA strand was calculated as $k_{\text{catRP}} = 1.1~\text{min}^{-1}$ by assuming that the RNA strand has 50 bases. K_{mRH}^* was reported as a value per base pair, so that K_{m} per DNA/RNA hybrid was calculated as $K_{\text{mRH}} = 0.34~\mu\text{M}$ by assuming that the hybrid has 23 base pairs. k_{catRH}^* was reported as a value per cleavage reaction, so that k_{cat} per DNA/RNA hybrid was calculated as $k_{\text{catRH}} = 0.98~\text{min}^{-1}$ by assuming that 5 cleavage reactions are required for RNA degradation of the hybrid. K_{mDG}^* was reported as a value per dU, so that K_{m} per DNA was calculated as $K_{\text{mDG}} = 6.5 \times 10^{-3}~\mu\text{M}$ by assuming that the uracil-containing DNA includes 20 dUs. k_{catDG}^* was reported as a value per cleavage reaction, so that k_{cat} per uracil-containing DNA strand was calculated as $k_{catDG} = 9.2 \times 10^1$ min^{-1} by assuming that 5 cleavage reactions are required for DNA degradation. In addition, all hybridization rates were assumed to be 1.0 μM^{-1}s^{-1}.

4   Simulation Results

The result of linear stability analysis for the RNA oscillator is shown in Fig. 4a. It represents dependence of steady-state stability on total concentrations of G1 and D2 (c_{G1} and c_{D2}). Enzyme concentrations were fixed. As a result of analyses, steady states were stable in black area and unstable in white area. In the condition of gray area, physically significant steady states were not obtained. This results suggests that steady-state stability is determined by balance of c_{G1} and c_{D2}. G1 is an RNA source of the system and D2 is involved in RNA degradation rate. Thus, steady-state stability of this system is decided by balance of RNA supply and RNA degradation.

Figure 4b-e show bifurcation diagrams for Fig. 4a. Behaviors of long time trajectories of the system can be estimated by the diagram. The diagrams have two areas, namely area of a single solid line and area of double solid lines with a single broken line. A long time trajectory at the black area of Fig. 4a converged

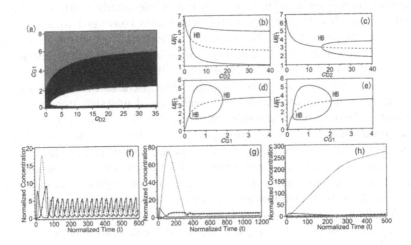

Fig. 4. Analytical results of RNA oscillator. (a) Stability diagram by linear stability analysis on the condition of $[E_{RP}]_T = 1.5$ μM, $[E_{DG}]_T = 3.5 \times 10^{-6}$ μM, $[E_{RH}]_T = 0.61$ μM. Steady states are stable in black area and unstable in white area. Physically significant steady states are not obtained in gray area. (b)-(e) Bifurcation diagrams of (a). Solid and broken lines represent stable and unstable solutions of $u_{\overline{RI}}$ after long time kinetic simulations. Single solid lines indicate convergence to stable steady states. Double solid lines with a broken line represent maximum and minimum values of stable limit cycle solutions. "HB" is a Hopf bifurcation point. (b) $c_{G1}=1$. (c) $c_{G1}=2$. (d) $c_{D2}=10$. (e) $c_{D2}=20$. (f)-(h) Kinetic simulations under the condition of (a). Solid line, broken line, and solid line with solid circle indicate R1, R2 and $\overline{R1}$, respectively. (f) $c_{G1}=1.0$, $c_{D2}=10.0$. (g) $c_{G1}=3.0$, $c_{D2}=10.0$. (h) $c_{G1}=6.0$, $c_{D2}=10.0$.

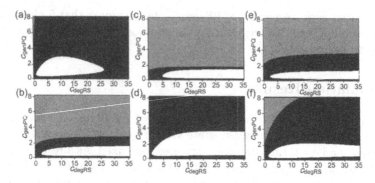

Fig. 5. Dependence of stability diagram on enzyme concentrations. Steady states are stable in black area and unstable in white area. Physically significant steady states are not obtained in gray area. (a) $[E_{RP}]_T=1.1$, $[E_{DG}]_T=3.5 \times 10^{-6}$, $[E_{RH}]_T=0.61$. (b) $[E_{RP}]_T=1.9$, $[E_{DG}]_T=3.5 \times 10^{-6}$, $[E_{RH}]_T=0.61$. (c) $[E_{RP}]_T=1.5$, $[E_{DG}]_T=1.7 \times 10^{-6}$, $[E_{RH}]_T=0.61$. (d) $[E_{RP}]_T=1.5$, $[E_{DG}]_T=5.2 \times 10^{-6}$, $[E_{RH}]_T=0.61$. (e) $[E_{RP}]_T=1.5$, $[E_{DG}]_T=3.5 \times 10^{-6}$, $[E_{RH}]_T=0.31$. (f) $[E_{RP}]_T=1.5$, $[E_{DG}]_T=3.5 \times 10^{-6}$, $[E_{RH}]_T=0.92$. (concentration unit: μM).

to its stable steady state. The value of the single solid line of the bifurcation diagrams represents a value of $u_{\overline{RI}}$ in the stable steady state. On the other hand, a long time trajectories at the white area converged to a stable limit cycle. The values of the double solid lines above and below the single broken line represent maximum and minimum values of the limit cycle solution of $u_{\overline{RI}}$, respectively. The value of the single broken line represents a value of $u_{\overline{RI}}$ in the unstable steady state. The diagrams demonstrates that the system does not diverge but oscillates under the conditions of unstable steady state. The bifurcation from steady state solution to limit cycle solution occurs at a Hopf bifurcation point "HB", which corresponds to the border between the black and white area. Kinetic simulations for Fig. 4a are shown in Fig. 4f-h. Figure 4f demonstrates a limit cycle oscillation under the condition of unstable steady state. Figure 4g represents a dumped oscillation converging to its stable steady state. In the case that physically significant steady states does not exist, the solution diverged as $\tau \to \infty$, which are shown in Fig. 4h.

Dependence of stability diagram on enzyme concentration is shown in Fig. 5, which demonstrates that linear stability of the oscillatory reaction system varied depending on concentrations of three enzymes, RNA polymerase, uracil DNA glycosylase, and ribonuclease H. As a result of bifurcation analyses and kinetic simulations for all the stability diagrams, solutions in black area converged to their stable steady states, those in white area were limit cycle oscillations, and those in gray area diverged. When concentration of RNA polymerase increased from Fig. 5a to Fig. 5b, divergent solution area enlarged. RNA synthesis increased by the RNA polymerase increase, so that RNA consumption in the sequence conversion reactions and RNA degradation by D2 could not prevent too much increase of RNA. In contrast, when concentration of uracil DNA glycosylase increased from Fig. 5c to Fig. 5d, divergent solution area shrank. The increase of uracil DNA glycosylase strengthened degradation of activated converter DNA AC1 and AC2, so that RNA synthesis from AC1 and AC2 decreased. Thus RNA consumption and degradation could prevent too much increase of RNA. When concentration of ribonuclease H increased from Fig. 5e to Fig. 5f, divergent solution area shrank likewise. The increase of ribonuclease H strengthened R2 degradation, so that too much increase of RNA could be prevented.

5 Discussion

The RNA oscillator was designed as a feedback circuit composed of two activation reactions and one inhibition reaction. The activation reaction was an RNA-sequence conversion reaction based on enzymatic reactions and a nucleic-acid hybridization. The inhibition reaction was an RNA hybridization. The whole reaction of RNA oscillator was described using simultaneous nonlinear differential equations, which were analyzed using the linear stability analysis, the bifurcation analysis and kinetic simulations. The analyses revealed that oscillatory condition of the reaction system was decided on balance of RNA supply into the system and RNA degradation out of the system. That is to say, considering that the RNA supply is an energy influx into the system and the RNA degradation is an energy efflux out of the system, the RNA oscillator forms a temporal dissipative structure using RNA molecule as energy.

Recently, the utilization of gene regulatory mechanism to control DNA nanomachines has been proposed [22,23]. This system can open/close a DNA nanomechanical device "DNA tweezers" [7]. However, it can only either open or close the DNA tweezers and cannot continuously actuate it. To achieve continuous actuations, more complex systems such as oscillators are required. Oscillatory systems have a potential to fluctuate periodically concentrations of fuel molecules for continuous actuations. Artificial biological oscillators have also been studied [24,25,26], which attract attention because of being developed using artificial genetic circuits in *Escherichia coli*. However, the biological oscillators based on gene regulatory networks have less versatility because only limited types of gene regulatory networks can be exploited to construct them. On the other hand, the oscillator we have proposed will become a useful method to control DNA nanomechanical devices because of continuously periodic reactions and the versatility caused by sequence programmability. In the next work, we will carry out *in vitro* experiments of the RNA oscillator. The numerical simulations represented here will help set up the *in vitro* experiments and save a lot of work before the experiments.

Acknowledgment

We thank Dr. M. Takano and Dr. H. Yoshida for helpful discussions. This work was supported by grants-in-aid from the Ministry of Education, Culture, Sports, Science, and Technology of Japan, and by Research Fellowship of the Japan Society for the Promotion of Science for Young Scientists to M. Takinoue.

References

1. Adleman, L.M.: Science 266, 1021–1024 (1994)
2. Seeman, N.C.: Nature 421, 427–431 (2003)
3. Seeman, N.C., Lukeman, P.S.: Rep. Prog. Phys. 68, 237–270 (2005)
4. Bath, J., Turberfield, A.J.: Nat. Nanotechnol. 2, 275–284 (2007)
5. Simmel, F.C., Dittmer, W.U.: Small 1, 284–299 (2005)
6. Mao, C., Sun, W., Shen, Z., Seeman, N.C.: Nature 397, 144–146 (1999)
7. Yurke, B., Turberfield, A.J., Mills Jr., A.P., Simmel, F.C., Neumann, J.L.: Nature 406, 605–608 (2000)
8. Yan, H., Zhang, X., Shen, Z., Seeman, N.C.: Nature 415, 62–65 (2002)
9. Shin, J.S., Pierce, N.A.: J. Am. Chem. Soc. 126, 10834–10835 (2004)
10. Tian, Y., Mao, C.: J. Am. Chem. Soc. 126, 11410–11411 (2004)
11. Sherman, W.B., Seeman, N.C.: Nano Lett. 4, 1203–1207 (2004)
12. Chen, Y., Mao, C.: J. Am. Chem. Soc. 126, 8626–8627 (2004)
13. Yin, P., Yan, H., Daniell, X.G., Turberfield, A.J., Reif, J.H.: Angew. Chem. Int. Ed. 43, 4906–4911 (2004)
14. Tian, Y., He, Y., Chen, Y., Yin, P., Mao, C.: Angew. Chem. Int. Ed. 44, 2–5 (2005)
15. Turberfield, A.J., Mitchell, J.C., Yurke, B., Mills Jr., A.P., Blakey, M.I., Simmel, F.C.: Phys. Rev. Lett. 90, 118102 (2003)
16. Seelig, G., Yurke, B., Winfree, E.: J. Am. Chem. Soc. 128, 12211–12220 (2006)
17. Murray, J.D.: Springer, New York (2002)
18. Fall, C.P., Marland, E.S., Wagner, J.M., Tyson, J.J.: Springer, New York (2002)
19. Martint, C.T., Coleman, J.E.: Biochemistry 26, 2690–2696 (1987)
20. Hirano, N., Haruki, M., Morikawa, M., Kanaya, S.: Biochemistry 39, 13285–13294 (2000)
21. Varshney, U., van de Sande, J.H.: Biochemistry 30, 4055–4061 (1991)
22. Dittmer, W.U., Simmel, F.C.: Nano Lett. 4, 689–691 (2004)
23. Dittmer, W.U., Kempter, S., Radler, J.O., Simmel, F.C.: Small 1, 709–712 (2005)
24. Elowitz, M.B., Leibler, S.: Nature 403, 335–338 (2000)
25. Fung, E., Wong, W.W., Suen, J.K., Bulter, T., Lee, S.G., Liao, J.C.: Nature 435, 118–122 (2005)
26. Atkinson, M.R., Savageau, M.A., Myers, J.T., Ninfa, A.J.: Cell 113, 597–607 (2003)

Protoplasmic Computing to Memorize and Recall Periodic Environmental Events

Atsushi Tero[1,2], Tetsu Saigusa[1,3], and Toshiyuki Nakagaki[1]

[1] Research Institute For Electronic Science,
Hokkaido University, N12 W6, Sapporo 060-0812, Japan
[2] PRESTO, Japan Science and Technology Agency,
4-1-8 Honcho Kawaguchi, Saitama, Japan
[3] Graduate School of Engineering,
Hokkaido University, N13 W8, Sapporo 060-8628, Japan

Abstract. Single-celled organisms might be more intelligent than previously envisaged[1]-[5]. The acts of anticipating and recalling events are higher functions performed by the brains of higher animals; their evolutionary origins and the way they self-organize, however, remain open questions. Here we show that an amoeboid organism can anticipate the timing of periodic events. The plasmodium of the true slime mold *Physarum polycephalum* moves rapidly under favorable conditions, but stops moving when transferred to less-favorable conditions. For example, plasmodia exposed to low temperature and low humidity, presented in three consecutive pulses at constant intervals, reduced their locomotive speed in response to each episode. When favorable conditions were subsequently reintroduced, the plasmodia spontaneously reduced their locomotive speed at the point in time when the next unfavorable episode would have occurred. This implies that the plasmodia are able to anticipate impending environmental change. After this anticipatory response had been evoked several times, the locomotion of the plasmodia returned to normal speed; however, the slowing down could subsequently be induced by a single unfavorable pulse, implying recall of the periodicity that had been memorized. We have explored the mechanisms underlying this behavior from a dynamical systems perspective. Our results suggest that this primitive intelligence is of cellular origin and that simple dynamics might be sufficient to explain its emergence. *abstract* environment.

Keywords: *Physarum*, cell memory, subcellular computing, primitive intelligence.

1   Introduction

Information processing is an interesting feature of biological systems. Although the brain has evolved specifically to perform this function in higher organisms, a degree of information processing is also possible in the absence of a brain, and even organisms as simple as amoebae are much more intelligent than generally considered. For example, the true slime mold *Physarum polycephalum* can

Y. Suzuki et al. (Eds.): IWNC 2007, PICT 1, pp. 213–221, 2009.

find the shortest path through a maze and solve certain geometrical puzzles in order to fulfill its requirements for the efficient absorption of nutrients and for intracellular communication [1-4].

Intelligent behavior is often associated with an optimization for survival task, regarding which two questions arise: how well does the behavioral process work and how is it computed? In order to address these questions, it is necessary to extract a computational algorithm for optimization of the relevant process. Biological algorithms often involve parallel processing because the computation is implemented by an autonomous, decentralized system, which consists of a collection of many similar elements.

For instance, the brain is composed of an intricate network of neurons, while cells are composed of a distribution of chemicals that are coupled through complex networks of biochemical reactions. Such biochemical reactions include the assembly and disassembly of cytoskeletal proteins and contractile proteins as well as signal transduction, metabolism and anabolism. Although the appearance of the brain is completely different to that of single-celled organisms, it is possible to find similarities in terms of system dynamics and computational algorithms. This implies that there may be common principles running through a wide range of organisms. Thus, it is reasonable to focus our attention on computational algorithms in an elementary organism such as *Physarum*. From an evolutionary perspective, information processing by unicellular organisms might represent a simple precursor of brain-dependent higher functions.

Physarum polycephalum is a useful model organism for studying behavioral intelligence [5]. Its plasmodium consists of a large aggregate of protoplasm, which possesses an intricate network of tubular structures and crawls across agar plates at a speed of approximately 1 cm/h at room temperature. In order to investigate primitive forms of brain function such as learning, memory, anticipation and recall, we have previously examined the rhythmicity of cell behaviour [6,7] and the adaptability of cells to periodic environmental changes [8,9]. In the present study we exposed the organism to periodic changes in the ambient conditions and observed the behavioral responses. We propose a mathematical model to describe our experimental observations and we extract a core mechanism for the observed behavior from the nonlinear dynamics point of view.

2   Physiological Experiments on Anticipatory Behavior in *Physarum*

A large plasmodium was cultured using oat flakes in a trough (25 cm × 35 cm) on an agar plate under dim light. The tip region of an extended front of the plasmodium (approximate wet weight of 15 mg) was removed and placed in a narrow lane of dimensions 0.5 cm × 28 cm, as shown in Fig. 1a, at 26°C and 90% humidity (hereafter referred to as standard conditions). All experiments were conducted under standard conditions unless otherwise specified. As the organism migrated along the lane, the position of its tip was measured every 10 min. After migration had been permitted for a few hours, the ambient conditions were changed to cooler (23°C) and drier (60%) (hereafter referred to as 'dry stimulation') conditions for 10 min, as shown in Fig. 2a. This dry stimulation was repeated three times at intervals of τ; the values of τ tested were 30, 40, 50, 60, 70, 80, and 90 min. These experiments were performed in an incubator (Type KCL-10000, Eyela Co), in which the temperature and humidity could be controlled. The organism moving along the lane was illuminated from below by a matrix of infra-red light sources and was viewed using a charge-coupled device (CCD) camera. The window of the incubator was covered with a cut-off filter in order to transmit only infra-red light; the experimental setup was thus kept in the dark.

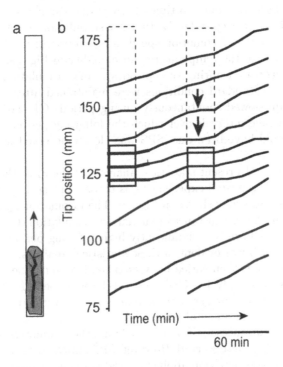

Fig. 1. Tip position of the plasmodium as a function of time, subjected to periodic changes in ambient temperature and humidity. (a) Schematic illustration of experimental setup. A piece of the organism (wet weight of approximately 15 mg) was placed at one end of a narrow lane and began to migrate towards the other end. The position of the tip of the plasmodium was monitored. (b) Plot of tip position as a function of time in the form of a so-called double-plot raster: the right-hand half of each line is the same as that of the left-hand half of the line above. Pulses of dry stimulation were applied periodically during the time intervals indicated by solid boxes. The subsequent virtual pulses of dry stimulation, at which dry stimulation was due but over which standard conditions were actually maintained, are indicated by dashed lines. The first two virtual pulses of dry stimulation coincide with a spontaneous slowdown of migration, indicated by arrows.

Figure 1 shows typical plots of the time-dependence of the tip position of the organism. Under favorable conditions, the tip position migrated at a rate of approximately 0.3 mm/min. However, the locomotion slowed down during the pulses of dry stimulation (indicated by the solid boxes in Fig. 1b). Although the ambient conditions were kept favorable after three episodes of periodic dry stimulation had been applied, the organism sometimes stopped migrating or slowed down during the time intervals indicated by the arrows. The timing of the spontaneous slowing down corresponded to the time intervals during which dry stimulation would have been applied if the periodic sequence of stimulation pulses had been maintained (indicated by the dashed boxes). We refer to this slowing of locomotion as spontaneous in-phase slowdown (SPS). SPS occurred at the first and second points in time at which dry stimulation pulses were due after the third and last episode of actual dry stimulation had been applied.

Figure 2b shows the locomotion speed as a function of time calculated from Fig. 1, together with the temperature and humidity in Fig. 2a. The locomotion speed clearly decreased during the episodes of dry stimulation S1, S2 and S3, for $\tau = 60$ min. Standard conditions were maintained after S3; however, the movement again slowed spontaneously during periods C1 and C2, which coincided with the time intervals over which the following periodic episodes of dry stimulation would have been due. SPS was clearly observed in the locomotion velocity.

Figures 2c and 2d present statistical analyses of the SPS; the average speed, calculated over 30 repeated experiments, is plotted in Fig. 2c and the statistical occurrence of slowdown is shown in Fig. 2d. The locomotion speed dropped significantly during the first instance of virtual dry stimulation (C1). The statistical occurrence of slowdown was significantly higher during period C1 than that of the basal level. SPS was evident in these statistical analyses.

The value of τ was then varied between 30 and 90 min. The overall frequency of SPS was approximately $40-50\%$. Intervals between periods of dry stimulation shorter than 30 min or longer than 90 min were not tested due to the technical limitations of our experimental setup.

After a few occurrences of SPS at $\tau = 60$ min, the locomotion speed fluctuated and no further SPS was observed. However, SPS appeared again in response to a single pulse of dry stimulation applied several hours after the last episode of periodic stimulation. We refer to this phenomenon as SPS after one disappearance (SPSD). SPSD was examined using a statistical analysis of the average speed and the occurrence of slowdown. SPSD was clearly observed for $\tau = 60$ min but was absent for $\tau = 40$ min and $\tau = 80$ min. The SPSD response was thus limited to a specific periodic interval of dry stimulation.

3   Mathematical Modeling to Describe How the Organism Anticipates and Recalls Periodic Events

We have developed a dynamical systems model that reproduces the experimentally observed phenomena. Poly-rhythmic amoeboid movement in *Physarum* has

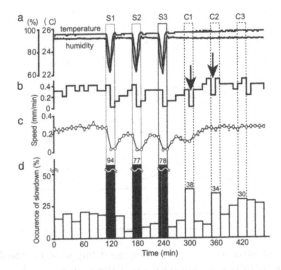

Fig. 2. SPS response: typical time course of locomotion for an organism (wet weight = 15 mg) before and after three periodic applications of dry stimulation. (a) Temperature (upper line) and humidity (lower line) as a function of time. (b) Locomotion speed calculated over successive 10 min intervals from the data in Fig. 1b. (c) Statistical analysis of the SPS response in terms of mean speed, together with standard errors. (d) Statistical occurrence of spontaneous slowdown. The mean speed was calculated from 121 repeated experiments (5 - 30 mg wet weight). The numbers on the tops of the columns in (d) show the percentage of experiments in which spontaneous slowdown occurred. S1, S2 and S3 indicate the time intervals over which dry stimulation was applied, and C1, C2 and C3 indicate the time intervals corresponding to the virtual stimulations.

previously been reported by two independent research groups[6,7]. Oscillations were observed with a series of different periods (600, 240, 30, 10, 2, 0.5, and 0.05 minutes), and the overall activity showed a 1/f-type power spectrum in the Fourier analysis. These results imply that there are oscillations with a series of frequencies and that the frequency distribution is wide and continuous. This is the most fundamental assumption used in the mathematical modeling. Figure 3 shows a schematic illustration of this idea of modeling. Because the multi-rhythmicity can appear in a tiny portion (0.3×0.3×0.1 mm) of the organism, we assume that there are multiple oscillators, as shown in each bar of Fig. 3a. The different shades of grey indicate oscillators with different biochemical identities. Because biochemically identical oscillators show fluctuations in their natural frequency from place to place, there are deviations in the frequency distribution, as shown in Fig. 3b. The overall frequency distribution for all biochemical identities may take the kind of shape shown in Fig. 3c. For the purposes of our model, we assume that the shape of the overall frequency distribution is flat (continuous and homogeneous), as shown in Fig. 3d. We consider the locomotion activity as the collective motion of different oscillators, but we neglect the amplitudes of oscillation.

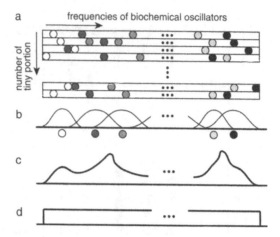

Fig. 3. Schematic illustration of mathematical modeling idea. (a) Oscillators with different biochemical identities in tiny portions of the protoplasm. The different shades of grey indicate biochemically different oscillators. Each bar indicates a portion of the protoplasm. Oscillators with the same biochemical identity show fluctuations of their natural frequency from portion to portion, which are spatially distributed. (b) Distribution of natural frequency for each biochemical identity. (c) Overall frequency distribution summed over all biochemical identities. (d) Simplified distribution of frequency assumed in our mathematical model. The shape of the distribution is flat.

Based on the above assumptions, we have proposed a mathematical model for the dynamics in a previous paper[11]. Here we provide an overview of the equations used in the model. Our first assumption is that there are biochemical phase oscillators with a series of frequencies ω_α in a small portion of the protoplasm. Our second assumption is that there are many oscillators (a total of i) with the same frequency because the organism used in the experiments consists of a large aggregate of protoplasm. The dynamics of phase $\theta_{\alpha,i}$ ($0 \leq \theta \leq 1$) is then expressed as

$$\frac{d\theta_{\alpha,i}}{dt} = \omega_\alpha + \beta H(t) \sin 2\pi\theta_{\alpha,i} + \xi_{\alpha,i}, \tag{1}$$

where ω_α is the natural frequency and $\xi_{\alpha,i}$ represents a low level of random noise. The second term on the right-hand side of Eq. (1) represents the periodic stimulation. $H(t)$ expresses the periodicity of the stimulation and takes the form of a step-wise function: $H(t)$ is equal to one whenever the stimulation is applied, and zero otherwise.

The locomotion velocity S is given by a kind of order parameter as follows:

$$S = \sum_j \tanh(2 \sum_i^N \frac{\cos 2\pi\theta_{i,j}}{N} + 3). \tag{2}$$

This summation is divided into two steps: the summation over the oscillators with the same biochemical identity is carried out first and the summation over

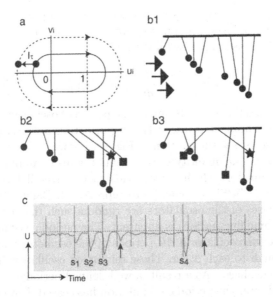

Fig. 4. Simple dynamics model and simulation of SPS and SPSD responses. (a,b) Schematic illustration of the model behavior, assuming a series of pendulums with simple dynamics. (a) Trajectory of the dynamics in state space. The functions f_i and g_i in the governing equations are: $f_i = 1/(0.4T_i)$, $g_i = 0$ for $\{(u,v)|0 < u_i < 1, 0 < v_i\}$, $f_i = \pi v_i/(0.5T_i)$, $g_i = -5\pi(u_i - 1)/(0.1T_i)$ for $\{(u,v)|1 < u_i\}$, $f_i = -1/(0.4T_i)$, $g_i = 0$ for $\{(u,v)|0 < u_i < 1, v_i < 0\}$, $f_i = \pi v_i/(0.5T_i)$, $g_i = -5\pi u_i/(0.1T_i)$ for $\{(u,v)|u_i < 0\}$, for $i = 0, 1, 2, \cdots, 119$, $T_i = 0.5i + 30$, and for the mean amplitude, $U = \tanh\{5(\sum_i v_i) + 3\}/120$. Under the initial conditions, each pendulum swings with a small amplitude (b1). No coherent motion is observed, so the mean amplitude U is close to zero with small fluctuations. After periodic perturbations are applied to all the pendulums, some oscillators with similar periods to those of the perturbations have large amplitudes and similar phases (b2). At this point, U shows well-defined periodic variations with the same period as the external perturbations; this state is maintained until the coherent oscillators with large amplitudes become desynchronized in phase due to differences in their intrinsic periods (b3). We note that although U does not show any well-defined periodic behavior, its amplitude still remains large. When the perturbation is applied again, the oscillators with large amplitudes are likely to become synchronized in phase, such that U once again shows periodic behavior. (c) Simulation of the variation of locomotion speed, U, with time.

the different biochemical identities is performed second. The function tanh is introduced in order to incorporate saturation of the locomotion velocity, because it has been reported that the locomotion velocity becomes saturated for high concentrations of a key chemical[10]. The model equations (1) and (2) reproduce the observed behavior of anticipation and recall.

In this paper, we simplify the previously reported model to obtain a toy model that is able to reproduce the anticipatory and recall behavior. The toy model helps us to understand the core mechanism that underlies the observed behavior. It is possible to grasp an intuitive picture of this mechanism. Let us assume that several pendulum-like oscillators with a series of periods are responsible for the multi-rhythmicity of locomotion in *Physarum*, as shown in Figs.4a and b. These might be described as simple oscillators, where

$$\frac{du_i}{dt} = f(u_i, v_i; T_i) + I_\tau, \frac{dv_i}{dt} = g(u_i, v_i; T_i), U = F(\sum u_i). \tag{3}$$

Here, T_i is a parameter that determines the period of oscillation and I_τ is a pulse of dry stimulation applied at intervals of τ (for details of the equations that govern these oscillators, see the caption of Fig. 4). Figure 4c shows a simulation for a given value of τ. The quantity U represents the mean amplitude of oscillation as an order parameter, which corresponds to the overall locomotion activity. Both the SPS and SPSD responses are reproduced. Before dry stimulation is applied, the phases of the oscillators are random such that no well-defined periodicity (but some fluctuation) is apparent. The periodic stimulation reinforces the amplitude of an oscillator if the periods of the oscillator and the stimulation are similar enough to each other. These reinforced oscillators have large amplitudes and similar phases. As a result, a well-defined periodicity in U is observed and maintained after the periodic stimulation has ceased. However, within a few periods of oscillation, the amplified oscillators become desynchronized and the well-defined periodicity of U disappears. Nevertheless, periodicity reappears in response to a single episode of dry stimulation, because it causes the phases of the oscillators once again to resemble one another. SPS and SPSD can thus be accounted for by these simple dynamics.

It should be noted that our model does not take into account interactions between the oscillators. Furthermore, the oscillators are not limit-cycle oscillators, but rather resemble simple pendulums with amplitudes that never return to their original states, remaining shifted after the removal of an external perturbation. The behavior of the model described above is still reproduced if interactions occur between the oscillators, provided that they are sufficiently weak, or, if the oscillators are limit-cycle oscillators, that their amplitudes relax sufficiently slowly after a perturbation has occurred.

The overall locomotion activity does not show any oscillatory variations just before the single trigger stimulation is applied, because it looks similar to the state that exists before the onset of the periodic stimulations. However, the internal state of the collective pendulums is different because some of the pendulums still have reinforced amplitudes, as shown in Fig 4b3. Even though the appearance of the total activity is similar, it is possible to form a different internal state in the system.

As above, the core mechanism can be explained by using a simplified toy model of collective pendulums.

4   Discussion

The toy model proposed in this report is able to reproduce the failure of anticipation, as observed experimentally with an occurrence of 50 %, even though the previous model did not succeed in reproducing it. Another deficiency in the previous model is that the locomotion velocity decreased after the periodic stimulation had been applied; the velocity remains similar before and after the stimulation in a real organism. Thus, the toy model is more accurate in this respect.

The toy model has one disadvantage: the amplitude of a pendulum with a frequency of twice the external forcing frequency is also magnified. This is not the case in the previous model. Thus, further improvement of the toy model is needed.

We have ascertained that the core mechanism underlying the anticipatory behavior in *Physarum* is simple. Because the 1/f-type power spectrum has been found in many biological systems, similar anticipatory behavior may exist in other organisms; we will look for further examples in the future.

Acknowledgements

This work was supported by MEXT KAKENHI, JST PRESTO and a HFSP Research Grant.

References

1. Nakagaki, T., Yamada, H., Tóth, Á.: Maze-solving by an amoeboid organism. Nature 407, 470 (2000)
2. Nakagaki, T., Yamada, H., Tóth, Á.: Path finding by tube morphogenesis in an amoeboid organism. Biophys. Chem. 92, 47–52 (2001)
3. Nakagaki, T., Kobayashi, R., Ueda, T., Nishiura, Y., Nishiura, Y.: Obtaining multiple separate food sources: behavioral intelligence in the *Physarum plasmodium*. Proc. R. Soc. Lond. B 271, 2305–2310 (2004)
4. Nakagaki, T., Yamada, H., Hara, M.: Smart network solutions in an amoeboid organism. Biophys. Chem. 107, 1–5 (2004)
5. Nakagaki, T.: Smart behavior of true slime mold in labyrinth. Res. Microbiol. 152, 767–770 (2001)
6. Coggin, S.J., Pazun, J.L.: Dynamic complexity in *Physarum polycephalum* shuttle streaming. Protoplasma 194, 243–249 (1996)
7. Kakiuchi, Y., Ueda, T.: Multiple oscillations in changing cell shape by the plasmodium of *Physarum polycephalum*: general formula governing oscillatory phenomena by the *Physarum plasmodium*. Biol. Rhythms Res. 37, 137–146 (2005)
8. Winfree, A.: The Geometry of Biological Time, 2nd edn. Springer, New York (2001)
9. Kuramoto, Y.: Chemical Oscillations, Waves, and Turbulence. Springer, Heidelberg (1984)
10. Ueda, T., Nakagaki, T., Kobatake, Y.: Patterns in intracellular ATP distribution and rhythmic contraction in relation to amoeboid locomotion in the plasmodium of *Physarum polycephalum*. Protoplasma (suppl. 1), 51–56 (1988)
11. Saigusa, T., Tero, A., Nakagaki, T., Kuramoto, Y.: Amoebae anticipate periodic events. Phys. Rev. Lett. 100, 018101 (2008)

A Synchronization Problem in Two-Dimensional Cellular Automata

Hiroshi Umeo

Univ. of Osaka Electro-Communication,
Neyagawa-shi, Hatsu-cho, 18-8, Osaka, 572-8530, Japan
umeo@cyt.osakac.ac.jp

Abstract. The firing squad synchronization problem on cellular automata has been studied extensively for more than forty years, and a rich variety of synchronization algorithms have been proposed so far. In the present paper, we give a survey on recent developments in firing squad synchronization algorithms for large-scale two-dimensional cellular automata. Several state-efficient implementations of the two-dimensional synchronization algorithms are given.

1 Introduction

We study a synchronization problem that gives a finite-state protocol for synchronizing large-scale cellular automata. The synchronization in cellular automata has been known as firing squad synchronization problem since its development, in which it was originally proposed by J. Myhill in Moore [1964] to synchronize all parts of self-reproducing cellular automata. The problem has been studied extensively for more than 40 years [1-24]. In this paper, we give a survey on recent developments in designing optimum- and non-optimum-time synchronization algorithms and their implementations for two-dimensional cellular arrays. Several simple, state-efficient mapping schemes are proposed for embedding one-dimensional firing squad synchronization algorithms onto two-dimensional arrays. Throughout this paper we focus our attention to the algorithms for synchronizing two-dimensional rectangular arrays with the general at one corner of the array. In section 2, we introduce three types of firing squad synchronization algorithms for one-dimensional arrays: an optimum-time firing squad synchronization algorithm with a general at one end of the array, its generalized version where the general can be positioned at an arbitrary cell of the array, and a delayed version which can delay the synchronization time for Δt (described later) steps. In section 3 it can be seen that these three algorithms for one-dimensional arrays will be efficiently employed, together with several mapping schemes, for designing optimum- and non-optimum-time synchronization algorithms for two-dimensional arrays.

Y. Suzuki et al. (Eds.): IWNC 2007, PICT 1, pp. 222–237, 2009.
© Springer 2009

2 Firing Squad Synchronization Problem

2.1 FSSP on One-Dimensional Cellular Arrays

The firing squad synchronization problem is formalized in terms of the model of cellular automata. A finite one-dimensional (1-D) cellular array consists of n cells, denoted by C_i, where $1 \leq i \leq n$. All cells (except the end cells) are identical finite state automata. The array operates in lock-step mode such that the next state of each cell (except the end cells) is determined by both its own present state and the present states of its right and left neighbors. All cells (*soldiers*), except the left end cell, are initially in the *quiescent* state at time $t = 0$ and have the property whereby the next state of a quiescent cell having quiescent neighbors is the quiescent state. At time $t = 0$ the left end cell (*general*) is in the *fire-when-ready* state, which is an initiation signal to the array.

The firing squad synchronization problem (FSSP) is stated as follows: Given an array of n identical cellular automata, including a *general* on the left end which is activated at time $t = 0$, we want to give the description (state set and next-state transition function) of the automata so that, *at some future time*, all of the cells will *simultaneously* and, *for the first time*, enter a special *firing* state. The set of states and the next-state transition function must be independent of n. Without loss of generality, we assume $n \geq 2$. The tricky part of the problem is that the same kind of soldier having a fixed number of states must be synchronized, regardless of the length n of the array.

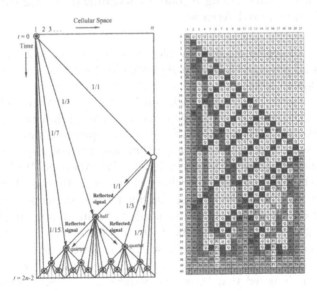

Fig. 1. Time-space diagram for optimum-time firing squad synchronization algorithm (left) and snapshots of the Waksman's 16-state optimum-time synchronization algorithm on 21 cells (right)

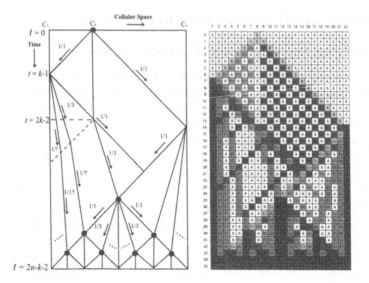

Fig. 2. Time-space diagram for generalized optimum-time firing squad synchronization algorithm (left) and snapshots of the three Russians' 10-state generalized optimum-time synchronization algorithm on 22 cells (right)

2.2 Optimum-Time Firing Squad Synchronization Algorithms on One-Dimensional Arrays

The firing squad synchronization problem was first solved by J. McCarthy and M. Minsky who presented a $3n$-step algorithm. In 1962, the first optimum-time, i.e. $(2n - 2)$-step, synchronization algorithm for 1-D arrays of length n was presented by Goto [1962], with each cell having several thousands of states. Waksman [1966] presented a 16-state optimum-time synchronization algorithm. Afterward, Balzer [1967] and Gerken [1987] developed an eight-state algorithm and a seven-state synchronization algorithm, respectively, thus decreasing the number of states required for the synchronization. Mazoyer [1987] developed a six-state synchronization algorithm which, at present, is the algorithm having the fewest states. Figure 1 is a time-space diagram for the optimum-step firing squad synchronization algorithm (left) and snapshots for its 16-state implementation (right). The general at left end emits at time $t = 0$ an infinite number of signals which propagate at $1/(2^{k+1} - 1)$ speed, where k is positive integer. These signals meet with a reflected signal at half point, quarter points, ..., etc., denoted by $\odot$ in Fig. 1. It is noted that these cells indicated by $\odot$ are synchronized. By increasing the number of synchronized cells exponentially, eventually all of the cells are synchronized.

[Theorem 1][Goto [1962], Waksman [1966]]: There exists a cellular automaton that can synchronize any one-dimensional array of length n in optimum $2n - 2$ steps, where the general is located at a left or right end.

Now we consider a *generalized* firing squad synchronization problem which allows the general to be located anywhere on the array. It has been shown impossible to synchronize any array of length n less than $n - 2 + \max(k, n - k + 1)$ steps, where the general is located on C_k. Moore and Langdon [1968], Szwerinski [1982] and Varshavsky, Marakhovsky and Peschansky [1970] developed a generalized optimum-time synchronization algorithm with 17, 10 and 10 internal states, respectively, that can synchronize any array of length n at exactly $n - 2 + \max(k, n - k + 1)$ steps. Recently, Settle and Simon [2002] and Umeo, Hisaoka, Michisaka, Nishioka and Maeda [2002] have proposed a 9-state generalized synchronization algorithm operating in optimum-step. In Fig. 2 we show a time-space diagram for the generalized optimum-time synchronization algorithms (left) and snapshots for synchronization configurations based on the rule set of Varshavsky, Marakhovsky and Peschansky [1970] (right).

[Theorem 2][Moore and Langdon 1968]: There exists a cellular automaton that can synchronize any one-dimensional array of length n in optimum $n - 2 + max(k, n - k + 1)$ steps, where the general is located on the kth cell from left end.

2.3   Delayed Synchronization Scheme for One-Dimensional Array

We introduce a *freezing-thawing* technique that yields a delayed synchronization algorithm for one-dimensional array.

[Theorem 3][Umeo 2004]: Let t_0, t_1, t_2 and Δt be any integer such that $t_0 \geq 0$, $t_0 \leq t_1 \leq t_0 + n - 1$, $t_1 \leq t_2$ and $\Delta t = t_2 - t_1$. We assume that a usual synchronization operation is started at time $t = t_0$ by generating a special signal at the left end of one-dimensional array and the right end cell of the array receives another special signals from outside at time $t = t_1$ and t_2, respectively. Then, there exists a one-dimensional cellular automaton that can synchronize the array of length n at time $t = t_0 + 2n - 2 + \Delta t$.

The array operates as follows:

1. Start an optimum-time firing squad synchronization algorithm in Section 2.2 at time $t = t_0$ at the left end of the array. A 1/1 speed, 1 cell per 1 step, signal is propagated towards the right direction to wake-up cells in quiescent state. We refer the signal as *wake-up signal*. A *freezing* signal is given from outside at time $t = t_1$ at the right end of the array. The signal is propagated in the left direction at its maximum speed, that is, 1 cell per 1 step, and freezes the configuration progressively. Any cell that receives the freezing signal from its right neighbor has to stop its state-change and transmits the freezing signal to its left neighbor. The frozen cell keeps its state as long as no thawing signal will arrive.

2. A special signal supplied with outside at time $t = t_2$ is used as a *thawing* signal that thaws the frozen configuration progressively. The thawing signal forces the frozen cell to resume its state-change procedures immediately. The signal is also transmitted toward the left end at speed 1/1.

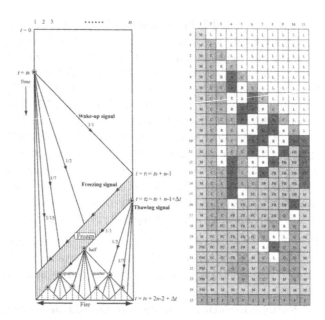

Fig. 3. Time-space diagram for delayed firing squad synchronization scheme based on the *freezing-thawing* technique (left) and a delayed (for $\Delta t = 5$ steps) configuration in Balzer's optimum-time firing squad synchronization algorithm on $n = 11$ cells (right)

The readers can see how those three special signals work. We can freeze the entire configuration during Δt steps and delay the synchronization on the array for Δt steps. It is easily seen that the freezing signal can be replaced by the reflected signal of the wake-up signal, that is generated at the right end cell at time $t = t_0 + n - 1$. See Fig. 3. Note that the freezing signal must be given at latest at time $t = t_0 + n - 1$, otherwise some cells of the array will fire before freezing operations. We refer the scheme as *freezing-thawing* technique. In the next section, the freezing-thawing technique will be employed efficiently in the design of optimum-time synchronization algorithms for two-dimensional cellular arrays. A similar technique was used by Romani [1977] in the tree synchronization and by Umeo [2004] for designing fault-tolerant firing squad synchronization algorithms for one-dimensional arrays.

2.4 FSSP on Two-Dimensional Cellular Arrays

Figure 4 shows a finite two-dimensional (2-D) cellular array consisting of $m \times n$ cells. Each cell is an identical (except the border cells) finite-state automaton. The array operates in lock-step mode in such a way that the next state of each cell (except border cells) is determined by both its own present state and the present states of its north, south, east and west neighbors. All cells (*soldiers*), except the north-west corner cell (*general*), are initially in the quiescent state at time $t = 0$ with the property that the next state of a quiescent cell with quiescent

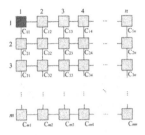

Fig. 4. A two-dimensional cellular automaton

neighbors is the quiescent state again. At time $t = 0$, the north-west corner cell $C_{1,1}$ is in the *fire-when-ready* state, which is the initiation signal for the array. The firing squad synchronization problem is to determine a description (state set and next-state function) for cells that ensures all cells enter the *fire* state at exactly the same time and for the first time. The same kind of soldier having a fixed number of states must be synchronized, regardless of the size $m \times n$ of the array. The set of states and transition rules must be independent of m and n. Several synchronization algorithms on 2-D arrays have been proposed by Beyer [1969], Grasselli [1975], Shinahr [1974], Szwerinski [1982] and Umeo, Maeda, Hisaoka and Teraoka [2006]. As for the time optimality of the two-dimensional firing squad synchronization algorithms, the following theorems have been shown.

[Theorem 4][Beyer [1969], Shinahr [1974]]: There exists no cellular automaton that can synchronize any two-dimensional array of size $m \times n$ in less than $m + n + max(m, n) - 3$ steps, where the general is located at one corner of the array.

[Theorem 5][Beyer [1969], Shinahr [1974]]: There exists an cellular automaton that can synchronize any two-dimensional array of size $m \times n$ at exactly $m + n + max(m, n) - 3$ steps, where the general is located at one corner of the array.

3   Orthogonal Mapping: A Simple Non-optimum-Time Algorithm $\mathcal{A}_1$

In this section, we give a very simple synchronization algorithm for 2-D arrays. The overview of the algorithm is as follows:

1. First, *synchronize* the first column cells using a usual optimum-time 1-D algorithm with a general at one end, thus requiring $2m - 2$ steps.
2. Then, *start the row synchronization operation* on each row simultaneously. Additional $2n - 2$ steps are required for the row synchronization. Totally, its time complexity is $2(m + n) - 4$ steps.

We refer the implementation as *orthogonal mapping*. It is shown that $s + 2$ states are enough for the implementation of the algorithm above, where s is the number of internal states of the 1-D base algorithm.

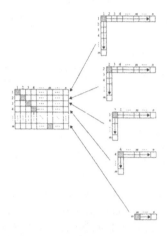

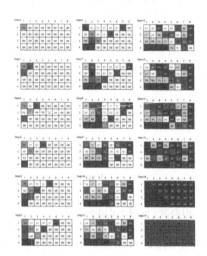

Fig. 5. An optimum-time synchronization scheme for rectangular arrays

Fig. 6. Snapshots of the synchronization process on 4×8 array

[Theorem 6]: There exists an $(s+2)$-state protocol for synchronizing any $m \times n$ rectangular arrays in non-optimum $2(m+n)-4$ steps, where s is the number of states of any optimum-time one-dimensional synchronization protocol with the general at one end.

4   Rotated L-Shaped Mapping

4.1   Optimum-Time Algorithm $\mathcal{A}_2$

The first optimum-time synchronization algorithm was developed independently by Beyer [1969] and Shinar [1974] based on the rotated L-shaped mapping. The rectangular array of size $m \times n$ is regarded as $\min(m,n)$ rotated L-shaped 1-D arrays, where they are synchronized independently using the generalized firing squad synchronization algorithm. The configuration of the generalized synchronization on 1-D array can be mapped on 2-D array. See Fig. 5. Thus, an $m \times n$ array synchronization problem is reduced to independent $\min(m,n)$ 1-D generalized synchronization problems such that $\mathcal{P}(m, m+n-1)$, $\mathcal{P}(m-1, m+n-3)$, ..., $\mathcal{P}(1, n-m+1)$ in the case $m \leq n$ and $\mathcal{P}(m, m+n-1)$, $\mathcal{P}(m-1, m+n-3)$, ..., $\mathcal{P}(m-n+1, m-n+1)$ in the case $m > n$, where $\mathcal{P}(k, \ell)$ means the 1-D generalized synchronization problem for ℓ cells with a general on the kth cell from left end. Beyer [1969] and Shinahr [1974] presented an optimum-time synchronization scheme in order to synchronize any $m \times n$ arrays in $m + n + max(m,n) - 3$ steps. Shinahr [1974] has given a 28-state implementation. Figure 6 illustrates snapshots of the configurations on an array of size 4×8 based on our new 28-state 12849-rule implementation.

[Theorem 7]: There exists an optimum-time $(2s \pm O(1))$-state protocol for synchronizing any $m \times n$ rectangular arrays in $m + n + max(m,n) - 3$ steps,

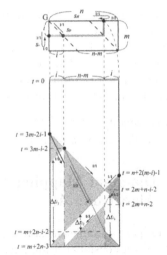

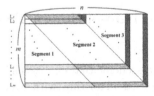

Fig. 7. A two-dimensional array of size $m \times n$ ($m \leq n$) is regarded as consisting of m rotated (90° in counterclockwise direction) L-shaped 1-D array

Fig. 8. Time-space diagram for synchronizing L_i

where s is number of states of any generalized optimum-time one-dimensional synchronization protocol.

[Theorem 8][Shinahr [1974]]: There exists an optimum-time 28-state protocol for synchronizing any $m \times n$ rectangular arrays in $m + n + max(m, n) - 3$ steps.

4.2   Time-Optimum Algorithm $\mathcal{A}_3$

In this subsection we present a new synchronization algorithm $\mathcal{A}_3$ based on a rotated L-shaped mapping. The synchronization scheme is quite different from previous designs. The scheme uses a freezing-thawing technique presented in Section 2.3. Without loss of generality we assume that $m \leq n$. We regard a rectangular array of size $m \times n$ as m *rotated* (90° in counterclockwise direction) *L-shaped* 1-D arrays. Each L-shaped array is denoted by $L_i, 1 \leq i \leq m$. See Fig. 7. Each L_i consists of three segments of length i, $n - m$, and i, respectively. Each segment can be synchronized by the freezing-thawing technique presented in [Theorem 3]. Synchronization operations for $L_i, 1 \leq i \leq m$ are as follows: Figure 8 shows a time-space diagram for synchronizing L_i. The wake-up signals for the three segments of L_i are generated at time $t = 3m - 2i - 1, 3m - i - 2$, and $n + 2(m - i) - 1$, respectively. Synchronization operations on each segments are delayed for $\Delta t_{i_j}, 1 \leq j \leq 3$ such that:

$$\Delta t_{i_j} = \begin{cases} 2(n - m) & j = 1 \\ i & j = 2 \\ n - m & j = 3 \end{cases} \tag{1}$$

The synchronization for the first segment of L_i is started at time $t = 3m - 2i - 1$ and its operations are delayed for $\Delta t = \Delta t_{i_1} = 2(n - m)$ steps. Now letting $t_0 = 3m - 2i - 1, \Delta t = \Delta t_{i_1} = 2(n - m)$ in [Theorem 3], the first segment of L_i can be synchronized at time $t = t_0 + 2i - 2 + \Delta t = m + 2n - 3$. In a similar way, the second and the third segments can be synchronized at time $t = m + 2n - 3$. Thus, L_i can be synchronized at time $t = m + 2n - 3$.

[**Theorem 9**]$^{\text{Umeo and Uchino [2007]}}$: The algorithm $\mathcal{A}_3$ can synchronize any $m \times n$ rectangular array in optimum $m + n + max(m, n) - 3$ steps.

5   Diagonal Mapping I: Six-State Non-optimum-Time Algorithm $\mathcal{A}_4$

We propose a simple and state-efficient mapping scheme that enables us to embed any one-dimensional firing squad synchronization algorithm with a general at one end onto two-dimensional arrays without introducing additional states. We consider a 2-D array of size $m \times n$, where $m, n \geq 2$. We divide mn cells on the array into $m + n - 1$ groups g_k, $1 \leq k \leq m + n - 1$, defined as follows.

$$g_k = \{C_{i,j} | (i - 1) + (j - 1) = k - 1\}, \text{ i.e.,}$$

$g_1 = \{C_{1,1}\}, g_2 = \{C_{1,2}, C_{2,1}\}, g_3 = \{C_{1,3}, C_{2,2}, C_{3,1}\}, \ldots, g_{m+n-1} = \{C_{m,n}\}$.
Figure 9 shows the division of the two-dimensional array of size $m \times n$ into $m + n - 1$ groups. For convenience, we define $g_0 = \{C_{0,0}\}$ and $g_{m+n} = \{C_{m+1,n+1}\}$.
Let $M = (Q, \delta_1, w)$ be any one-dimensional CA that synchronizes ℓ cells in $T(\ell)$ steps, where Q is the finite state set of M, $\delta_1 : Q^3 \to Q$ is the transition function, and $w \in Q$ is the state of the right and left ends. We assume that M

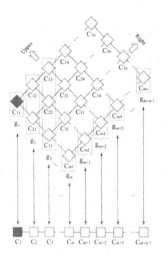

Fig. 9. A correspondence between 1-D and 2-D arrays

has $m + n - 1$ cells, denoted by C_i, where $1 \leq i \leq m + n - 1$. For convenience, we assume that M has a left and right end cells, denoted by C_0 and C_{m+n}, respectively. Both end cells C_0 and C_{m+n} always take the end state $w(\in Q)$. We consider the one-to-one correspondence between the ith group g_i and the ith cell C_i on M such that $g_i \leftrightarrow C_i$, where $1 \leq i \leq m + n - 1$ (see Fig. 9). We can construct a 2-D CA $N = (Q, \delta_2, w)$ such that all cells in g_i simulate the ith cell C_i in real-time and N can synchronize any $m \times n$ arrays at time $t = T(m + n - 1)$ if and only if M synchronizes 1-D arrays of length $m + n - 1$ at time $t = T(m + n - 1)$, where $\delta_2 : Q^5 \to Q$ is the transition function, and $w \in Q$ is the border state of the array. Note that the set of internal states of N is the same as M. For the details of the construction of the transition rule set, see Umeo, Maeda, Hisaoka and Teraoka [2006].

Now let M have $m + n - 1$ cells. Here we show that the construction of 2-D CA N can generate the configuration of M in real-time. Specifically, for any i, $1 \leq i \leq m + n - 1$, the state of any cell in g_i at any step is the same and is identical to the state of C_i at the corresponding step. Let S_i^t, $S_{i,j}^t$ and $S_{g_i}^t$ denote the state of C_i, $C_{i,j}$ at step t and the set of states of the cells in g_i at step t, respectively. Then, we can get the following lemma.

[**Lemma 10**]$^{\text{Umeo et al. [2006]}}$: Let i and t be any integers such that $1 \leq i \leq m + n - 1$, $0 \leq t \leq T(m + n - 1)$. Then, $S_{g_i}^t = \{S_i^t\}$.
Base on [Lemma 10] we can establish the following theorem.

[**Theorem 11**]$^{\text{Umeo et al. [2006]}}$: Let A be any s-state firing synchronization algorithm operating in $T(\ell)$ steps on 1-D ℓ cells. Then, there exists a 2-D s-state cellular automaton that can synchronize any $m \times n$ rectangular array in $T(m + n - 1)$ steps.

Thus, an $m \times n$ 2-D array synchronization problem is reduced to one 1-D synchronization problem with the general at left end. Umeo, Maeda, Hisaoka and Teraoka [2006] presented a 6-state two-dimensional synchronization algorithm

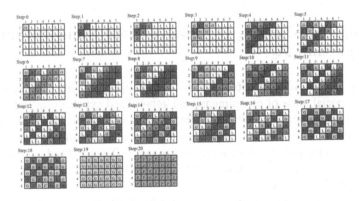

Fig. 10. Snapshots of the proposed 6-state linear-time firing squad synchronization algorithm on rectangular arrays

that synchronizes any $m \times n$ arrays in $2(m + n) - 4$ steps. See Fig. 10. The algorithm is slightly slower than the optimum-time ones, but the number of internal states is considerably smaller.

[**Theorem 12**]$^{\text{Umeo et al. [2006]}}$: There exists a 6-state 2-D CA that can synchronize any $m \times n$ rectangular array in $2(m + n) - 4$ steps.

The mapping scheme can be applied to more generalized synchronization problems.

[**Theorem 13**]$^{\text{Umeo et al. [2006]}}$: There exists a 6-state 2-D CA that can synchronize any $m \times n$ rectangular array containing isolated rectangular holes in $2(m + n) - 4$ steps.

[**Theorem 14**]$^{\text{Umeo et al. [2006]}}$: There exists a 6-state firing squad synchronization algorithm that can synchronize any 3-D $m \times n \times \ell$ solid arrays in $2(m + n + \ell) - 6$ steps.

[**Theorem 15**]$^{\text{Umeo et al. [2006]}}$: There exists a 14-state 2-D CA that can synchronize any $m \times n$ rectangular array in $m + n + \max(r + s, m + n - r - s + 2) - 4$ steps with the general at an arbitrary initial position (r, s).

Szwerinski [1982] also proposed an optimum-time generalized 2-D synchronization algorithm with 25,600 internal states that can synchronize any $m \times n$ array in $m + n + \max(m, n) - \min(r, m - r + 1) - \min(s, n - s + 1) - 1$ steps, where (r, s) is the general's initial position. Our 2-D generalized synchronization algorithm is $\max(r + s, m + n - r - s + 2) - \max(m, n) + \min(r, m - r + 1) + \min(s, n - s + 1) - 3$ steps larger than the optimum algorithm proposed by Szwerinski [1982]. However, the number of internal states required to yield the synchronizing condition is the smallest known at present. Note that [Theorem 15] includes an optimum-time synchronization algorithm in case where the general is north-east or south-west corner of the array.

6   Diagonal Mapping II: Twelve-State Time-Optimum Algorithm $\mathcal{A}_5$

The second proposal is a simple and efficient mapping scheme that enables us to embed a special class of one-dimensional generalized synchronization algorithm onto two-dimensional arrays without introducing additional states. Without loss of generality we can assume that $m \leq n$. In the diagonal mapping II an $m \times n$ 2-D array synchronization problem is reduced to one 1-D generalized synchronization problem: $\mathcal{P}(m, m + n - 1)$ that synchronizes $m + n - 1$ cells with a general on the mth cell from left end.

We divide mn cells into $m + n - 1$ groups g_k defined as follows, where k is any integer such that $-(m - 1) \leq k \leq n - 1$,

$$g_k = \{C_{i,j} | j - i = k\}, \quad -(m - 1) \leq k \leq n - 1.$$

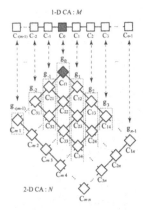

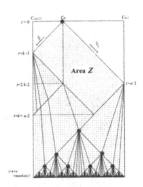

Fig. 11. Correspondence between 1-D and 2-D cellular arrays

Fig. 12. Area $\mathcal{Z}$ in time-space diagram for generalized optimum-step firing squad synchronization algorithm

Figure 11 shows the correspondence between 1-D and 2-D arrays. It has been shown in Umeo et al. [2005] that any one-dimensional generalized firing squad synchronization algorithm with the property $\mathcal{Z}$ (below) can be easily embedded onto two-dimensional arrays without introducing additional states. Figure 12 shows the area $\mathcal{Z}$ in the time-space diagram for generalized optimum-step firing squad synchronization algorithm.

Property $\mathcal{Z}$: Let S_i^t denote the state of C_i at step t. We say that a generalized firing algorithm has *property $\mathcal{Z}$*, where any state S_i^t appearing *in the area $\mathcal{Z}$* can be computed from its left and right neighbor states S_{i-1}^{t-1} and S_{i+1}^{t-1} but it never depends on its own previous state S_i^{t-1}.

[Lemma 16][Umeo et al. [2005]]: Let M be any s-state generalized synchronization algorithm with the property $\mathcal{Z}$ operating in $T(k,\ell)$ steps on 1-D ℓ cells with a general on the k-th cell from the left end. Then, based on M, we can construct a 2-D s-state cellular automaton that can synchronize any $m \times n$ rectangular array in $T(m, m+n-1)$ steps.

The next theorem is a 12-state implementation of the generalized optimum-time synchronization algorithms having the property $\mathcal{Z}$.

[Lemma 17][Umeo et al. [2005]]: There exists a 12-state 1-D cellular automaton with the property $\mathcal{Z}$ that can synchronize ℓ cells with a general on the k-th cell from the left end in optimum $\ell - 2 + max(k, \ell - k + 1)$ steps.

Based on [Lemmas 16, 17] we can get a 12-state optimum-time synchronization algorithm for rectangular arrays. Figure 13 shows snapshots of the proposed 12-state optimum-time firing squad synchronization algorithm operating on a 7×9 array.

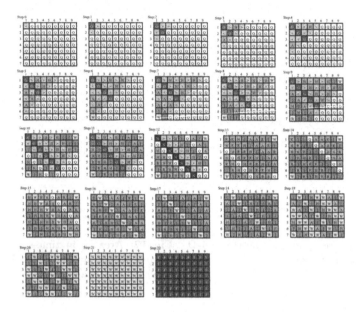

Fig. 13. Snapshots of the proposed 12-state optimum-time firing squad synchronization algorithm on rectangular arrays

[**Theorem 18**]$^{\text{Umeo et al. [2005]}}$: There exists a 12-state firing squad synchronization algorithm that can synchronize any $m \times n$ rectangular array in optimum $m + n + max(m, n) - 3$ steps.

7   Frame Mapping: Time-Optimum Algorithm $\mathcal{A}_6$

In this section, we present an optimum-time 2-D synchronization algorithm based on a new mapping scheme: *frame mapping*. Without loss of generality we assume that $m \leq n$. We regard a rectangular array of size $m \times n$ as consisting of rectangle-shaped *frames* of width 1. See Fig. 14. Each frame $L_i, 1 \leq i \leq \lceil m/2 \rceil - 1$, is divided into six segments and these six segments are synchronized using the freezing-thawing technique presented in [Theorem 3]. The length of each segment of L_i is $m - 2i$, $m - 2i$, $n - m$, $m - 2i$, $m - 2i$, and $n - m$, respectively. In Fig. 15 we show a time-space diagram of the synchronization operations for the outermost frame L_1. Synchronization operations on jth segment of L_1 are delayed for Δt_{1_j} steps, $1 \leq j \leq 6$ such that:

$$\Delta t_{1_j} = \begin{cases} 2(n - m) & j = 1 \\ 2(n - m) & j = 2 \\ m & j = 3 \\ n - m & j = 4 \\ n - m & j = 5 \\ m & j = 6 \end{cases} \qquad (2)$$

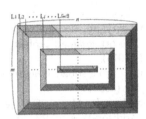

Fig. 14. A two-dimensional array of size $m \times n$ is regarded as consisting of $\lceil m/2 \rceil$ frames

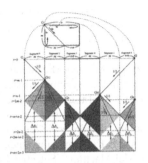

Fig. 15. Time-space diagram for synchronizing L_1

Based on [Theorem 3], L_1 can be synchronized at time $t = m + 2n - 3$. Let $|L_i|$ be number of cells on L_i. For any i such that $1 \leq i \leq \lceil m/2 \rceil - 2$, we have:

$$|L_i| - |L_{i+1}| = 4.$$

We employ an optimum-time synchronization algorithm for each frame, that is, $2\ell - 2$ steps are needed for synchronizing an array of length ℓ. Therefore, we delay each starting time for synchronizing each frame for $6(= 2 \times 4 - 2)$ steps so that synchronization operations in each frame can be finished simultaneously. For this purpose an activating signal for starting the synchronization is given to the north-west corner cell of each L_i at time $t = 6i$. The activating signal is transmitted along the diagonal line at $1/6$ speed. In this way all of the frames can be synchronized.

[Theorem 19][Umeo et al. [2007]]: The algorithm $\mathcal{A}_6$ can synchronize any $m \times n$ rectangular array in $m + n + max(m, n) - 3$ optimum steps.

8 Conclusions

We have given a survey on recent developments of optimum-time algorithms that can synchronize any $m \times n$ two-dimensional rectangular arrays in $m + n + max(m, n) - 3$ steps. Those algorithms are based on efficient mapping schemes for embedding some one-dimensional optimum-time firing squad synchronization algorithms onto 2-D rectangular arrays.

References

1. Balzer, R.: An 8-state minimal time solution to the firing squad synchronization problem. Information and Control 10, 22–42 (1967)
2. Beyer, W.T.: Recognition of topological invariants by iterative arrays. Ph.D. Thesis, MIT, p. 144 (1969)

3. Hans-D., Gerken.: Über Synchronisations - Probleme bei Zellularautomaten. Diplomarbeit, Institut für Theoretische Informatik, Technische Universität Braunschweig, p. 50 (1987)
4. Goto, E.: A minimal time solution of the firing squad problem. Dittoed course notes for Applied Mathematics 298. Harvard University, pp. 52–59 (1962)
5. Grasselli, A.: Synchronization of cellular arrays: The firing squad problem in two dimensions. Information and Control 28, 113–124 (1975)
6. Mazoyer, J.: A six-state minimal time solution to the firing squad synchronization problem. Theoretical Computer Science 50, 183–238 (1987)
7. Moore, E.F.: The firing squad synchronization problem. In: Moore, E.F. (ed.) Sequential Machines, Selected Papers, pp. 213–214. Addison-Wesley, Reading (1964)
8. Moore, F.R., Langdon, G.G.: A generalized firing squad problem. Information and Control 12, 212–220 (1968)
9. Nguyen, H.B., Hamacher, V.C.: Pattern synchronization in two-dimensional cellular space. Information and Control 26, 12–23 (1974)
10. Romani, F.: On the fast synchronization of tree connected networks. Information Sciences 12, 229–244 (1977)
11. Schmid, H.: Synchronisationsprobleme für zelluläre Automaten mit mehreren Generälen. Diplomarbeit, Universität Karsruhe (2003)
12. Settle, A., Simon, J.: Smaller solutions for the firing squad. Theoretical Computer Science 276, 83–109 (2002)
13. Shinahr, I.: Two- and three-dimensional firing squad synchronization problems. Information and Control 24, 163–180 (1974)
14. Szwerinski, H.: Time-optimum solution of the firing-squad-synchronization-problem for n-dimensional rectangles with the general at an arbitrary position. Theoretical Computer Science 19, 305–320 (1982)
15. Umeo, H.: A simple design of time-efficient firing squad synchronization algorithms with fault-tolerance. IEICE Trans. on Information and Systems E87-D(3), 733–739 (2004)
16. Umeo, H., Hisaoka, M., Akiguchi, S.: Twelve-state optimum-time synchronization algorithm for two-dimensional rectangular cellular arrays. In: UC 2005. LNCS, vol. 3699, pp. 214–223. Springer, Heidelberg (2005)
17. Umeo, H., Hisaoka, M., Michisaka, K., Nishioka, K., Maeda, M.: Some new generalized synchronization algorithms and their implementations for large scale cellular automata. In: Calude, C.S., Dinneen, M.J., Peper, F. (eds.) UMC 2002, vol. 2509, pp. 276–286. Springer, Heidelberg (2002)
18. Umeo, H., Hisaoka, M., Sogabe, T.: A survey on optimum-time firing squad synchronization algorithms for one-dimensional cellular automata. Intern. J. of Unconventional Computing 1, 403–426 (2005)
19. Umeo, H., Hisaoka, M., Teraoka, M., Maeda, M.: Several new generalized linear- and optimum-time synchronization algorithms for two-dimensional rectangular arrays. In: Margenstern, M. (ed.) MCU 2004, vol. 3354, pp. 223–232. Springer, Heidelberg (2005)
20. Umeo, H., Maeda, M., Hisaoka, M., Teraoka, M.: A state-efficient mapping scheme for designing two-dimensional firing squad synchronization algorithms. Fundamenta Informaticae 74(4), 603–623 (2006)
21. Umeo, H., Uchino, H.: A new time-optimum synchronization algorithm for two-dimensional cellular arrays. In: Moreno Díaz, R., Pichler, F., Quesada Arencibia, A. (eds.) EUROCAST 2007. LNCS, vol. 4739, pp. 604–611. Springer, Heidelberg (2007)

22. Umeo, H., Yamawaki, T., Shimizu, N., Uchino, H.: Modeling and simulation of global synchronization processes for large-scale-of two-dimensional cellular arrays. In: Proc. of Intern. Conf. on Modeling and Simulation, AMS 2007, pp. 139–144 (2007)
23. Varshavsky, V.I., Marakhovsky, V.B., Peschansky, V.A.: Synchronization of Interacting Automata. Mathematical Systems Theory 4(3), 212–230 (1970)
24. Waksman, A.: An optimum solution to the firing squad synchronization problem. Information and Control 9, 66–78 (1966)

Information Exchange between Moving Particles and Defects

Takashi Teramoto[1], Kei-Ichi Ueda[2], Xiaohui Yuan[3], and Yasumasa Nishiura[3]

[1] Chitose Institute of Science and Technology, Chitose 066-8655
[2] Research Institute for Mathematical Sciences, Kyoto University, Kyoto 606-8502
[3] Research Institute for Electronic Science, Hokkaido University, Sapporo 060-0812
teramoto@photon.chitose.ac.jp, ueda@kurims.kyoto-u.ac.jp,
yuan@nsc.es.hokudai.ac.jp, nishiura@nsc.es.hokudai.ac.jp

Abstract. Pulse wave is one of the main careers of information and the effect of heterogeneity of the media in which it propagates is of great importance for the understanding of signaling processes in biological and chemical systems. A typical one dimensional heterogeneity is a spatially localized bump or dent, which creates associated defects in the media. To know the behaviors of pulse in such media is equivalent to study the collision process between the pulse and the defect. A variety of outputs are observed depending on the height and width of the bump such as rebound, pinning, oscillatory motion as well as penetration. A remarkable thing is that PDE dynamics can be reduced to finite dimensional one near a drift bifurcation and the defects become equilibrium points of the reduced ODEs. The basin of each equilibrium point and the switching among those basins explain all the outputs after collision with the defects. We employ a three-component reaction-diffusion system of one-activator-two-inhibitor type to illustrate these issues.

Keywords: Reaction-diffusion system, heterogeneous media, bifurcation analysis.

1 Introduction

Spatially localized moving patterns that display a variety of dynamics are fundamental objects arising in many dissipative systems [2,3,7,15,17]. Recently, considerable interest has been attracted to computational ability of pulse waves in chemical logic and switching devices [1,6]. In such reaction-diffusion processors, data are represented by concentration profiles of chemical substances and computation is performed by propagating and interaction of localized moving patterns. One particularly exciting perspective comes from the dramatic increase in research on unconventional computing architectures by using traveling chemical waves in a sensible and programmable way.

The effect of heterogeneity on information exchange as conveyed by pulse propagation is also of great importance for the understanding of signaling processes in chemical and biological tissues [8,14,18]. We focus on how the heterogeneity influences the propagating manner of spatially localized traveling waves, especially

Y. Suzuki et al. (Eds.): IWNC 2007, PICT 1, pp. 238–249, 2009.

when they encounter the heterogeneities of bump or dent type[13]. Qualitative dynamic transitions, including pinning, rebound, and penetration, may occur via interaction through collision with the defect induced by heterogeneity or intrinsic instabilities, which eventually leads to drastic change of outputs as parameters vary[9,13,19]. In order to understand the whole dynamics of such complex patterns, a computer-aided geometric approach is quite useful and it has been illustrated with the global behaviors of bifurcation branches and precise numerical spectral analysis as was shown in Refs.[10,11,12,16]. Our approach to head-on collision between moving particles in those references was to find the origin of the sorting mechanism, in which the output can be predictable by using information on the local dynamics near scattors which form a special class of unstable solutions linking input to output at collision point.

In this paper, we employ a three-component reaction-diffusion system of one-activator-two-inhibitor type and study the dynamics when traveling pulses encounter heterogeneities. Suppose that the associated parameter values are located close to the drift bifurcation point. A reduction from partial differential equation (PDE) system to finite dimensional ordinary differential equations (ODEs) is possible as shown in the previous paper [13], and the resulting system inherits most of the essential dynamics from the original PDE. It turns out that there are various types of heterogeneity-induced localized patterns smoothing the bump heterogeneity, associated with the equilibrium points of reduced ODEs. They play a pivotal role to understand the transitions among different responses, in fact various bifurcations such as Hopf, homoclinic and heteroclinic ones of localized patterns cause the onset of those transitions.

The paper is organized as follows. In Sec. 2, we introduce our model system and the precise form of bump heterogeneity. A reduction method to ODEs and comparison of phase diagrams between PDE and ODE dynamics are presented. In Sec. 3, a detailed study of reduced ODEs clarifies how dynamic transitions occur depending on the width and height of the bump. The most important difference from the moderate bump case studied in [13] lies in the fact that the oscillatory behaviors (OSC2 and OSC3) disappear as the steepness of the slope is sharpened. Instead, the stationary behaviors (STA2 and STA3) are observed for the present sharp case. In view of the global bifurcation structure, the offset of such OSC2 and OSC3 behaviors is related to the appearance of unstable periodic orbits, depending on the positional relation of Hopf and homoclinic bifurcation points.

2   Model and Theory

In order to investigate the dynamics of traveling pulses in heterogeneous media, we employ the following three-component reaction-diffusion system, which was proposed as a qualitative model of gas discharge phenomena[3,15]:

$$u_t = D_u \triangle u + k_2 u - u^3 - k_3 v - k_4 w + k_1,$$
$$\tau v_t = D_v \triangle v + u - v, \tag{1}$$
$$w_t = D_w \triangle w + u - w,$$

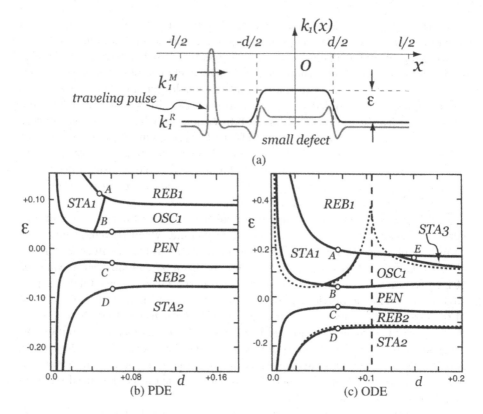

Fig. 1. (a) Schematic picture of initial condition for heterogeneous case. Solid line shows how $k_1(x)$ changes in spatial direction, and gray line displays a manner how a traveling pulse hits a small stable defect created by the heterogeneity. The (d, ϵ)-phase diagrams of PDE and ODE dynamics for the heterogeneous media of bump type are depicted in (b) and (c), respectively. We employ the following parameter values $k_1 = -6.5$, $k_2 = 2.0$, $k_3 = 1.0$, $k_4 = 8.5$, $(D_u, D_v, D_w) = (0.9 \times 10^{-4}, 1.0 \times 10^{-3}, 1.0 \times 10^{-2})$ and $\tau = 40.0$. There are six qualitatively different regimes: Penetration(PEN), Stationary (STA1, STA2), Rebound (REB1, REB2) and Oscillatory (OSC1), those phase boundaries are indicated by solid lines. The dotted lines in (c) correspond to the Hopf bifurcation lines for the equilibrium points. The details of the pattern dynamics around the points from A to D marked by white circles are described in Fig. 2. We set $\gamma = 1000$ for PDE and 100 for ODEs.

where $\triangle$ is the laplacian, $u = u(t, x), v = v(t, x)$ and $w = w(t, x)$ depend on time t and $x \in \mathbb{R}^1$, k_1, k_2, k_3 and k_4 are kinetic parameters, τ and the diffusion coefficients D_u, D_v, D_w are positive constants. The second inhibitor w is indispensable for the coexistence of multiple number of stable traveling spots in higher dimensional spaces. The system (1) is a simple and a prototypical model for the study of interaction among moving particle patterns in dissipative systems. It was studied in [19] under the parameter setting used here that (1) becomes an excitable system with unique stable equilibrium point and has a stable traveling pulse. The velocity of the pulse is an increasing function of k_1.

In this study, we consider the pulse dynamics in bump-shaped inhomogeneous media as shown in Fig. 1(a), especially how these dynamics depend on the height ϵ and width d of bump. For definiteness, we introduce spatial heterogeneity to parameter k_1 as $k_1(x) = k_1^R + \epsilon\chi(x, d)$ where

$$\chi(x, d) = \frac{1}{1 + e^{-\gamma(x+d/2)}} + \frac{1}{1 + e^{+\gamma(x-d/2)}} - 1 \tag{2}$$

and $\epsilon \equiv k_1^M - k_1^R$. Numerically, we can set $k_1(-l/2) = k_1(l/2) = k_1^R$ and $k_1(0) = k_1^M$ for an appropriate system size. The parameter γ controls the slope of bump edge. After we introduced spatial heterogeneity to the kinetic coefficient, the uniform state is no more a background state for the resulting system, several inhomogeneous steady states were observed for each (d, ϵ). In this paper, we employ the smallest defect in amplitude as the background state for the heterogeneous system. When a stable traveling pulse approaching the bump-shaped regime, it collides with small defects, so our problem can be looked as the collision problem between the pulse and defect as schematically shown in Fig. 1(a).

2.1 Reduction to ODEs

The pulse dynamics in heterogeneous media can be reduced to a finite-dimensional one when the associated parameter values are close to the drift bifurcation of $k_1 = k_1^c$, namely the pulse velocity is slow[4,5,9,13]. Considering (1) in a neighborhood of $k_1 = k_1^c$, with small parameter η as $k_1 = k_1^c + \eta$,

$$u_t = \mathcal{A}(u; k_1^c) + (\eta + \epsilon\chi(x, d))g(u), \tag{3}$$

where g is N-dimensional vector-valued functions. For our system (1), $g = {}^t(1, 0, 0)$. Let $X := \{L^2(\mathbb{R})\}^N$, $u = u(t, x) = (u_1, \cdots, u_N)^T \in X$ be an N-dimensional vector, $\chi(x, d)$ be a C^1-function. We assume that there exists a $k_1 = k_1^c$ such that the non-trivial standing pulse solution $S(x; k)$ of (1) exists, i.e., $\mathcal{A}(S; k_1^c) = 0$.

Let L be the linearized operator of $\mathcal{A}$ with respect to u at $u = S(x, k_1^c)$. L has a singularity at $k_1 = k_1^c$ consisting of drift bifurcation in addition to the translation free zero eigenvalue. That is, there exist two eigenfunctions $\phi(x)$ and $\psi(x)$ such that

$$L\phi = 0, \quad L\psi = -\phi,$$

where $\phi = \partial S/\partial x$. Note that $\phi(x)$ and $\psi(x)$ are odd functions. $\psi(x)$ represents the deformation vector with Jordan form for the drift bifurcation. Similar properties also hold for L^*. That is, there exist ϕ^* and ψ^* such that $L^*\phi^* = 0$ and $L^*\psi^* = -\phi^*$, where $\phi^*(x)$ and $\psi^*(x)$ are odd functions.

Let $E := span\{\phi, \psi\}$ and set a function

$$u = S(x - p) + q\psi(x - p) + q^2\zeta_1(x - p) + q\eta\zeta_2(x - p) + w, \tag{4}$$

where p and q are scalar functions of time t; p denotes the location of pulse, q for its velocity. The remaining three terms ζ_1, ζ_2 and w belong to $E^\perp$.

Substituting (4) into (3), we obtain the principal part by the following system.

$$\begin{cases} \dot{p} = q - \epsilon\Gamma_0(p), \\ \dot{q} = M_1 q^3 + M_2 q\eta + \epsilon\Gamma_1(p), \end{cases} \qquad (5)$$

where

$$\Gamma_0(p) = \int_{-\infty}^{\infty} \chi(x,d)\boldsymbol{g}(S(x-p)) \cdot \psi^*(x-p)dx,$$

$$\Gamma_1(p) = \int_{-\infty}^{\infty} \chi(x,d)\boldsymbol{g}(S(x-p)) \cdot \phi^*(x-p)dx. \qquad (6)$$

Here p stands for the location of the pulse, q for its velocity, and the effect of heterogeneity becomes acceleration (resp. deceleration) when $\epsilon\Gamma_1 >$ (resp. $<$) 0. The coefficients M_1, M_2 and heterogeneous term $\Gamma_i(p)$ depend on the model system and influence a lot over the dynamics. A more complete treatment were shown in [13]. For our system (1) with $k_1^c \approx -6.79$, they are computed as $M_1 \approx -11451 < 0$ and $M_2 \approx 0.031 > 0$ and profiles of Γ_i are obtained numerically as in Fig. 3(a).

2.2   Comparison between PDE and ODE

The pulse behaviors in PDE dynamics are classified as in the phase diagram of Fig. 1(b), depending on the width d and the height ϵ. The sign of ϵ indicates the velocity variation of traveling pulses. $\epsilon > 0$ means the velocity is larger inside the bump than the outside and vice versa, $\epsilon = 0$ represents the homogeneous case. There are six different outputs: penetration (PEN), rebound (REB1, REB2), stationary (STA1, STA2) and oscillatory (OSC1) states depending on (d, ϵ). As in Fig. 1(c), the reduced ODEs reflects the original PDE dynamics quite well. The typical spatio-temporal patterns and their orbit flows in (p,q)-space are shown in Fig. 2. The only difference is that the STA3 behavior (to be described in the next section) is observed in ODE phase diagram for large d region.

It is natural that pulses can penetrate the bump regime when $|\epsilon|$ is suffi-cient small. When d is relatively small, the pulse dynamics depends both on the amplitude and sign of ϵ. For small amplitude $|\epsilon|$, the pulse is trapped by the standing pulse at the center of the bump for positive ϵ or the pulse rebounds for negative ϵ. Intuitively, we can understand these transitions from the profiles of Γ_i ($i = 0, 1$). Γ_1 indicates the variation of pulse velocity, positive Γ_1 value means acceleration and negative value means deceleration. Let us image a right-going pulse, its speed will vary according to the Γ_1 function, when ϵ is enough small, it moves at an almost constant speed, so pulses will penetrate the heterogeneous region; when $|\epsilon|$ becomes slightly larger, for positive ϵ, the pulse feels like: small deceleration $\rightarrow$ large acceleration $\rightarrow$ large deceleration $\rightarrow$ small acceleration and vice versa with opposite effect for negative ϵ. Therefore what is expected after the penetration, as ϵ is increased, is that some sort of trapping between large acceleration and large deceleration regions. On the other hand, for negative ϵ,

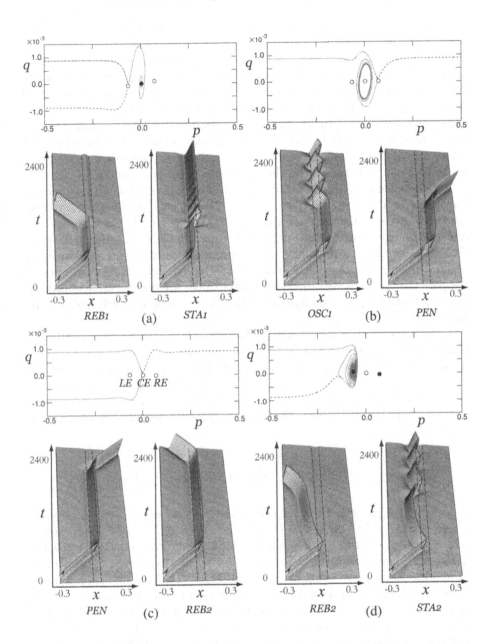

Fig. 2. The spatio-temporal patterns of PDE dynamics and the orbit flows in (p, q)-space of ODE dynamics are depicted in (a) for transition from REB1 to STA1 near point A in the phase diagrams of Figs.1(b)(c). We set $d = 0.06$ for PDE and 0.07 for ODEs. (b) for transition from OSC1 to PEN near point B, (c) for transition from PEN to REB2 near point C and (d) for transition from REB2 to STA2 near point D. The solid and open circles in orbit flows indicate the stable and unstable equilibrium points, respectively.

the second large deceleration region dominates the dynamics, and hence rebound occurs instead.

For larger $|\epsilon|$, rebound occurs for positive case and trapping to stationary state is observed for negative case. The typical spatio-temporal patterns are shown in Fig. 2. For larger d, oscillatory pulses were observed with small positive ϵ instead of stationary pulse. If we look carefully at the behaviors of the pulse near the transition points from A to D in the phase diagram, we observe a common feature for all transitions except D that the solution takes a quasi-static form before it makes a final decision where to go. Numerically, these quasi-static states turn out to be scattors which control the transitions between dynamics.

More detailed analysis of ODE dynamics allows us to explain all the dynamic transitions in a precise way. The profile of Γ_1 also contains information about the width of the bump. As shown in Figs. 3(a) and 4(a), it has three and five zero points depending on the width d. These unstable equilibrium points and their stable or unstable manifolds play a crucial role for the dynamic transitions, which correspond to the role of scattors in PDE dynamics. Note that when we compare the two dynamics, their parameter values are not the same in order to have qualitatively the same dynamics. We set $\gamma = 1000$ for PDE and $\gamma = 100$ for ODEs.

As we have already mentioned in the previous subsection, the locations of equilibrium points of reduced ODEs are determined by Γ_1 via implicit function theorem. It is confirmed numerically that Γ_1 has three zeros (LE, CE, RE) for small d and five zeros for large d (LE, LCE, CE, RCE, RE). Here LCE is an abbreviation of left-center-equilibrium and similarly for other equilibrium points. Local stability of each equilibrium of $(p, q) = (\overline{p}, \overline{q})$ is determined by the following linearized system.

$$\begin{pmatrix} \dot{p} \\ \dot{q} \end{pmatrix} = \begin{pmatrix} -\epsilon\partial_p\Gamma_0 & 1 \\ \epsilon\partial_p\Gamma_1 & 3M_1\epsilon^2\Gamma_0^2 + M_2\eta \end{pmatrix}\Bigg|_{(\overline{p},\overline{q})} \begin{pmatrix} p \\ q \end{pmatrix}. \qquad (7)$$

The eigenvalue problem $L\Psi = \lambda\Psi$ can be solved easily as $\lambda = \frac{1}{2}(\tau \pm \sqrt{\tau^2 - 4\Delta})$, where $\tau = 3M_1\epsilon^2\Gamma_0^2 + M_2\eta - \epsilon\partial_p\Gamma_0$ and $\Delta = -\epsilon\partial_p\Gamma_0(3M_1\epsilon^2\Gamma_0^2 + M_2\eta) - \epsilon\partial_p\Gamma_1$. The associated eigenvectors Ψ are obtained in the directions of $(2, \tau + 2\epsilon\partial_p\Gamma_0 \pm \sqrt{\tau^2 - 4\Delta})$. For small η and ϵ, the dominant terms of the trace τ, determinant Δ and discriminant $\tau^2 - 4\Delta$ are given by $M_2\eta - \epsilon\partial_p\Gamma_0$, $-\epsilon\partial_p\Gamma_1$, and $4\epsilon\partial_p\Gamma_1$, respectively. The bifurcation diagram with respect to ϵ are depicted in Fig. 3(b), in which the equilibrium points change their stability property depending on the sign of ϵ. Next, we will discuss the details in the sequel and clarify how these behaviors are relevant to the dynamic transitions shown in Figs. 1 and 2.

3   Results and Discussions

Firstly, we focus on the dynamics near four transition points A, B, C, and D in Fig. 1(c). The associated orbit flows are depicted in Fig. 2. Let us look at the bifurcation diagram of Fig. 3(b), in which ϵ is varied with fixed $d(= 0.07)$.

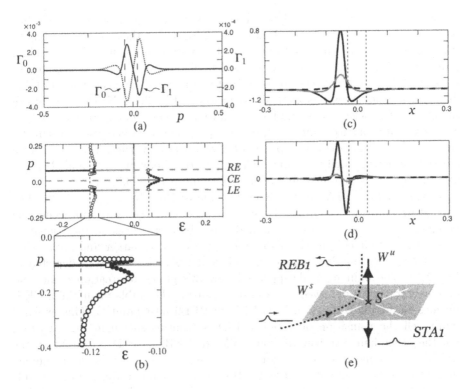

Fig. 3. (a) The profiles of the heterogeneity functions Γ_i for the narrow bump of $d = 0.07$. The dotted and solid lines correspond to Γ_0 and Γ_1, respectively. (b) Bifurcation diagram of ODE dynamics with respect to the bump height ϵ for the three zero case of $d = 0.07$. The positions of equilibrium points almost do not depend on the ϵ value. The black and gray solid lines indicate the stable and unstable spirals, respectively. The gray broken and dotted lines indicate the unstable saddle and node, respectively. The white squares indicate the Hopf bifurcation points. The vertical gray line at $\epsilon = 0$ indicates the translation free zero solution. The black and white disks correspond to the stable and unstable limit cycles, respectively. The vertical broken lines indicate the global bifurcations for the limit cycles. Global behavior of periodic branch around LE point is magnified as shown in the inset bottom. The profiles of scattor and the associated eigenfunction between REB1 and STA1 of Fig. 2(a) are depicted in (c) and (d), which has only one (real) unstable eigenvalue of $\lambda \approx 0.0337$. The solid, gray, and broken lines represent the u-, v-, and w-components, respectively. (e) A schematic picture of the dynamics near scattor S.

The CE point is a spiral for positive ϵ and becomes a saddle for negative ϵ. A supercritical Hopf bifurcation occurs at this equilibrium around $\epsilon \approx +0.08$, and the cycle exists up to the global bifurcation point. The details of which is described below.

Around point A, the transition from REB1 to STA1 occurs at $\epsilon \approx 0.194$ and the (left-upper) stable manifold of the LE point plays a role as scattor. The associated PDE dynamics are shown in Fig. 2(a), in which the solution takes a quasi-steady state for certain time before reaching the bump region, then either rebounds or settles down to the standing pulse located at the center of the bump. It is numerically confirmed that the quasi-steady state turns out to be a standing pulse of codim 1 located slightly to the left of the jump point as depicted in Figs. 3(c)(d). The orbit flows are sorted out according to which side of the stable manifold it belongs as schematically depicted in Fig. 3(e). This is exactly the same type of structure we found for the collision process among traveling pulses. This may not be a surprising thing, because propagation in heterogeneous media can be regarded as a collision process between the traveling pulse and defects created by heterogeneity. Around point C, scattor between PEN and REB2 is also the (upper) stable manifold of the CE point at $\epsilon \approx -0.041$.

Transition from STA1 to OSC1 occurs due to Hopf bifurcation of CE. The emanating limit cycle from the Hopf point becomes larger and approaches the heteroclinic cycle connecting LE and RE as ϵ becomes closer to the transition point B at $\epsilon \approx 0.047$, in which the amplitude becomes larger and approaches a double heteroclinic loop connecting LE and RE at $\epsilon \approx 0.040$ as depicted in Fig. 3(b). The limit cycle disappears below this global bifurcation point, and only penetration is observed. By still decreasing ϵ, the stable manifold of CE is responsible for the transition from PEN to REB2 near point C. This explains quite well the transition observed in PDE setting as shown in Figs. 1(b)(c). On the other hand, transition from STA2 to REB2 near D is caused by the unfolding of homoclinic bifurcation at $\epsilon \approx -0.125$. As shown in the magnified figure of Fig. 3(b), actually, there is a Hopf bifurcation and the resulting stable oscillatory branch. However we are interested in a special type of initial data, namely traveling pulse starting at $p = -\infty$. The unstable oscillatory branch blocks the entering of the orbit starting from such an initial data, therefore it must rebound. The details are the same as discussed in Ref.[13].

For the wide bump case of $d = 0.15$, the profiles of Γ_i have five zero points as shown in Fig. 4(a). Due to the pitchfork bifurcation at $|d| \approx 0.10$, as d is increased, the number of equilibrium points changes from 3 to 5 as clearly seen from Fig. 4(b). According to Fig. 4(c) of the bifurcation diagram with respect to ϵ, the CE point becomes a saddle for all positive ϵ and changes to unstable node and spiral for negative ϵ. On the other hand, the resulting two equilibrium points of LCE and RCE branching from CE are spirals for positive ϵ and become saddles for negative ϵ. Two supercritical Hopf bifurcations occur simultaneously at these two equilibrium points around $\epsilon \approx +0.131$, and those cycles coexist up to the global bifurcation point, the details of which are described below.

Around point E in Fig. 1(c), there are two transitions: REB1 to STA3 and STA3 to OSC1. The transition from REB1 to STA3 near E ($\epsilon \approx 0.167$) is controlled by the (upper) stable manifold of LE, namely which is the scattor for this transition. As depicted in Figs. 4(d)(e), a pair of small limit cycle is emanated from Hopf bifurcations for LCE and RCE, as ϵ is decreased. The amplitudes become larger and the two cycles deform into one large limit cycle of peanut shape enclosing the three equilibrium points of LCE, CE and RCE via a figure-of-eight-bifurcation at $\epsilon \approx 0.142$. The transition from STA3 to OSC1 is caused

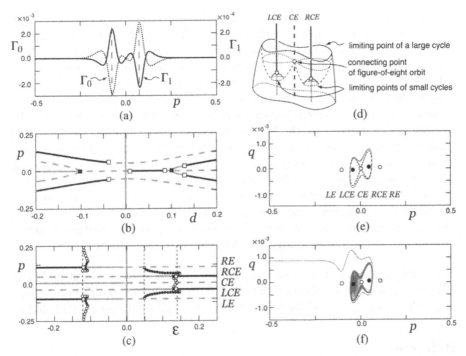

Fig. 4. (a) The profiles of the heterogeneity functions Γ_i for the wide bump of $d = 0.15$. (b) Bifurcation diagram of ODE dynamics with respect to the bump width d for $\epsilon = 0.15$. By increasing the bump width d, the number of equilibrium points changes from 3 to 5 through the pitchfork bifurcation at $|d| \approx 0.10$. The black and white squares indicate the pitchfork and Hopf bifurcation points, respectively. The black and gray solid lines indicate the stable and unstable spirals, respectively. The gray broken and dotted lines indicate the saddle and unstable node, respectively. The gray vertical line indicates the translation free zero solution. (c) Bifurcation diagram of defects with respect to ϵ for ODE dynamics for the five zeros case. The positions of equilibrium points almost do not depend on the ϵ value. The black and white disks correspond to the stable and unstable limit cycles, respectively. The vertical broken lines indicate the global bifurcation points for the limit cycles. (d) The whole structure of the limit cycles for positive ϵ forms a surface similar to trousers. Small limit cycles around LCE and RCE are emanated from the supercritical Hopf bifurcations at $\epsilon \approx 1.32$. These two cycles merge into one large cycle via a figure-of-eight bifurcation at $\epsilon \approx 0.142$. The connected limit cycle disappears by the heteroclinic bifurcations at $\epsilon \approx 0.040$. All three cycles change the stability via saddle-node bifurcations at $\epsilon \approx 0.145$ and 0.131, respectively. (e) Phase portrait in (p, q)-space at the figure-of-eight point near point E in Fig. 1(c). The solid and dotted lines show the stable large cycle and the figure-of-eight orbit, respectively. The solid and open circles indicate the stable and unstable equilibrium points, respectively. (f) Orbital behavior of STA3 at $\epsilon \approx 0.145$ which is close to a saddle-node bifurcation for the large limit cycle.

by a saddle-node bifurcation for the resulting large cycle at $\epsilon \approx 0.145$. As shown in Fig. 4(f), the orbital behavior of STA3 just above transition displays an aftereffect of the limiting point, in which there remains a temporary large oscillatory motion and the orbit will converge to the stable focus of LCE. As ϵ is decreased, the large cycle grows and approaches a double heteroclinic loop connecting LE and RE at $\epsilon \approx 0.040$, which is responsible for the transition from OSC1 to PEN. It disappears after the global bifurcation, and only penetration is observed.

In this paper, pulse propagation as modified by the presence of localized heterogeneities is studied using the three-component model in dissipative systems. A variety of outputs emerge through the collision between the traveling pulse and the defect induced by the heterogeneity, including pinning, rebound, and penetration. One of the origins of such rich behaviors is that the pulse has potential instabilities that display a variety of dynamics such as drift, saddle-node and Hopf bifurcations. It should be remarked that all the characteristic features of pulse dynamics in heterogeneous media can be found in the reduced finite dimensional system, which actually not only clarifies the existence and stabilities of scattors, but also shows us the underlying global bifurcation structure controlling the transitions among the different dynamic regimes.

Acknowledgments. This work was partially supported by the Grant-in-Aid for Scientific Research (A)16204008 and the Ministry of Education, Science, Sports and Culture, Grant-in-Aid for Young Scientists (B)18740050 and (B)18740238.

References

1. Adamatzky, A., Costello, B.D.L., Asai, T.: Reaction-Diffusion Computers. Elsevier Science, Amsterdam (2005)
2. Bär, M., Eiswirth, M., Rotermund, H.-H., Ertl, G.: Solitary-wave phenomena in an excitable surface reaction. Phys. Rev. Lett. 69, 945–948 (1992)
3. Bode, M., Liehr, A.W., Shenk, C.P., Purwins, H.-G.: Interaction of dissipative solitons: particle-like behavior of localized structures in a three-component reaction-diffusion system. Physica D 161, 45–66 (2002)
4. Ei, S.-I.: The motion of weakly interacting pulses in reaction diffusion systems. J. Dyn. Diff. Eqns 14, 85–137 (2002)
5. Ei, S.-I., Mimura, M., Nagayama, M.: Pulse-pulse interaction in reaction-diffusion systems. Physica D 165, 176–198 (2002)
6. Gorecki, J., Gorecka, J.N., Yoshikawa, K., Igarashi, Y., Nagahara, H.: Sensing the distance to a source of periodic oscillations in a nonlinear chemical medium with the output information coded in frequency of excitation pulses. Phys. Rev. E 72, 046201 (2005)
7. Hayase, Y., Ohta, T.: Self-replicating pulses and Sierpinski gaskets in excitable media. Phys. Rev. E 62, 5998–6003 (2000)
8. Miyazaki, J., Kinoshita, S.: Stopping and initiation of a chemical pulse at the interface of excitable media with different diffusivity. Phys. Rev. E 76, 066201 (2007)
9. Nishiura, Y., Oyama, Y., Ueda, K.-I.: Dynamics of traveling pulses in heterogeneous media of jump type. Hokkaido Math. J. 36, 207 (2007)
10. Nishiura, Y., Teramoto, T., Ueda, K.-I.: Scattering and separators in dissipative systems. Phys. Rev. E 67, 056210 (2003)
11. Nishiura, Y., Teramoto, T., Ueda, K.-I.: Dynamic transitions through scattors in dissipative systems. Chaos 13, 962–972 (2003)

12. Nishiura, Y., Teramoto, T., Ueda, K.-I.: Scattering of traveling spots in dissipative systems. Chaos 15, 047509 (2005)
13. Nishiura, Y., Teramoto, T., Yuan, X., Ueda, K.-I.: Dynamics of traveling pulses in heterogeneous media. Chaos 17, 037104 (2007)
14. Prat, A., Li, Y.-X., Bressloff, P.: Inhomogeneity-induced bifurcation of stationary and oscillatory pulses. Physica D 202, 177–199 (2005)
15. Schenk, C.P., Or-Guil, M., Bode, M., Purwins, H.-G.: Interacting pulses in three-component reaction-diffusion systems on two-dimensional domains. Phys. Rev. Lett. 78, 3781–3784 (1997)
16. Teramoto, T., Ueda, K.-I., Nishiura, Y.: Phase-dependent output of scattering process for traveling breathers. Phys. Rev. E 69, 056224 (2004)
17. Vanag, V.K., Epstein, I.R.: Localized patterns in reaction-diffusion systems. Chaos 17, 037110 (2007)
18. Xin, J.: Front Propagation in Heterogeneous Media. SIAM Rev. 42, 161–230 (2000)
19. Yuan, X., Teramoto, T., Nishiura, Y.: Heterogeneity-induced defect bifurcation and pulse dynamics for a three-component reaction-diffusion system. Phys. Rev. E 75, 036220 (2007)

Author Index